Visual C++ User's Guide

Microsoft® Visual C++™

**Development System for Windows™ and Windows NT™
Version 2.0**

Microsoft Corporation

PUBLISHED BY
Microsoft Press
A Division of Microsoft Corporation
One Microsoft Way
Redmond, Washington 98052-6399

Library of Congress Cataloging-in-Publication Data
Microsoft Visual C++ user's guide / Microsoft Corporation.
    p.   cm.
   Includes index.
   ISBN 1-55615-800-9
   1. Object-oriented programming (Computer science) 2. Microsoft
Visual C++. I. Microsoft Corporation.
QA76.64.M53   1994
005.265--dc20   94-26957
                                        CIP

Printed and bound in the United States of America.

2 3 4 5 6 7 8 9 MLML 9 8 7 6 5

Distributed to the book trade in Canada by Macmillan of Canada, a division of Canada Publishing Corporation.

A CIP catalogue record for this book is available from the British Library.

Microsoft Press books are available through booksellers and distributors worldwide. For further information about international editions, contact your local Microsoft Corporation office. Or contact Microsoft Press International directly at fax (206) 936-7329.

U.S. Patent No. 4955066

Document No. DB57171-0694

Contents

Part 2   Visual C++ Reference

Part 3   Appendixes

Figures and Tables

Tables

Introduction

The Microsoft® Visual C++™ 2.0 Development System for Windows™ and Windows NT™ is an integrated development environment for C and C++ applications, with support for multiplatform and cross-platform development. It includes a C++ application framework, the Microsoft Foundation Class Library, Version 3 (MFC), which facilitates the development of applications for Windows as well as the porting of applications to multiple platforms. You can easily develop an application for Windows on one platform using Visual C++ and MFC, and then use the same code to build applications for other platforms.

Visual Development Environment

The Visual C++ development environment consists of an integrated set of tools that all run under Windows. This gives you the tools to complete, test, and refine your application all in one place. Visual C++ includes a text editor, resource editors, project build facilities, an optimizing compiler, an incremental linker, a source code browse window and an integrated debugger. You can control the operation of all the tools from a single application. Because these tools run under Windows, they use a variety of familiar methods in their operation. For example, you can select a variable name in an editor window while debugging, drag that name into the Watch window and drop it there. The debugger then evaluates the variable and displays the result in the Watch window. Or you can select and drop a control from the toolbar in the dialog box editor onto a dialog box under creation. You can then size and position the control as required for your application. The development environment also includes toolbars so you can quickly invoke commands by clicking a button. To help you choose the correct button, each one displays a descriptive label if the mouse pointer rests on it. If the default toolbars are not to your liking, you can customize them or create your own toolbars and populate them with the toolbar buttons of your choice.

Powerful Wizards

Visual C++ provides two powerful tools that work in conjunction with the MFC application framework:

- AppWizard. AppWizard generates a complete suite of source files and resource files based on classes from the MFC library. By selecting options in AppWizard, you can customize starter files with different kinds of functionality. Once you have completed your selections in AppWizard, Visual C++ builds a functional skeleton application for Windows from those starter files, without any further work on your part.

- ClassWizard. ClassWizard automates the creation and editing of classes, and creates additional classes based on MFC. It creates the source code for new classes, and creates member functions and message maps in those classes as well as making it easy to bind Windows messages to code. It also maps dialog-box data to member variables and validates that data.

When you build an application for Windows with Visual C++, you run AppWizard to create the skeleton of your application. You then run ClassWizard to flesh out the application's classes, message handling and data handling. Finally, in your classes, you add the functionality required for your application.

Visual C++ Projects

Visual C++ organizes development into projects. A project consists of the source files required for your application, along with the specifications for building the project. Each project can specify multiple targets to build from its source files. A target specifies such things as the type of application to build, the platform on which it is to run, and the tool settings to use when building. The inclusion of multiple targets allows you to extend the scope of a project but still maintain a consistent source code base from which to work. The development environment includes a project window, which displays the files contained in the project as a graph, and lets you examine visually the relationships among the files in your project. Within a project, you can create groups of files which reflect closer relationships among certain files. The Project Settings dialog box allows you to specify tool settings for the entire project, for certain targets or for certain files. For instance, you can specify certain kinds of compiler optimizations for your project in general, but turn them off for certain targets or certain files.

Once you have specified the files in your project, the targets that your project is to build and the tool settings for those targets, you can build the project with the commands on the Project menu. If you are creating an application for a platform other than the one on which you are running Visual C++, the development environment can automatically transfer the application to the remote machine after it is built.

Build Error Correction

If your build has errors, Visual C++ also helps you fix them more quickly. The Output window displays a list of errors generated during a build. If you press F4, Visual C++ displays an editor window with the source file and marks the line of code associated with the first error in the Output window so you can immediately correct the code. Menu commands and keyboard shortcuts then will move you quickly to the next or the previous error.

Integrated Debugger

After you have corrected all the build errors, you can use the integrated debugger to correct logic errors. The debugger allows you to monitor your program as it runs and to stop it at locations or situations of your choosing. You can set a breakpoint on a particular line of code, for instance, and have your application execute until the application reaches that line. You can have your application suspend execution when it receives a specified Windows message or when a specific exception occurs. If you are interested in the values assigned to a variable, you can have the debugger break whenever your application changes the variable's value.

With the integrated debugger, you can debug both client and server applications that use Object Linking and Embedding (OLE). The debugger can execute a client OLE application line by line, and when the client calls the server OLE application, another instance of Visual C++ starts with its debugger executing the server application. This allows you to determine if both the client and server sides of your OLE application are functioning properly.

Visual C++ can also start its integrated debugger for any program that fails while it is running, whether the program has debug information or not, and whether Visual C++ was running beforehand or not. The debugger starts up while the program is still alive, and this "Just-In-Time" debugging allows you to analyze the living program rather than conduct a postmortem examination after it dies. With Just-In-Time debugging, it is possible to find and fix the problem in the program and let it continue running.

The debugger also supports multiplatform and cross-platform development by allowing you to debug an application running on a remote machine.

Source Code Browse Window

As you are developing and debugging your application, you need to see the classes and other symbols that you are using in a variety of contexts. When you build your application, Visual C++ automatically creates a browse information file with information about the symbols in your program. The browse window displays this information, and allows you to move readily among instances of the symbols in your source code. In the browse window, you can view graphs of inheritance relationships among classes or calling relationships among functions. You can easily view all the symbols contained in a given file, display the definition of any symbol in the file and all its references in your project, and then open the file containing a particular reference by double-clicking the entry in the window. The ease with which you can examine these relationships and move among the files containing them facilitates maintenance, revision, and debugging of your code.

User Preferences

Visual C++ also allows you to customize its operation to suit your preferences. In text editor windows, the development environment allows you to display language elements, such as comments or keywords, in the color of your choice, or to display the text in one window in a specific font. When you establish a layout for the windows associated with a particular project, Visual C++ retains that layout of open files and window positions the next time you start the project. When you are debugging an application, you can choose which windows and toolbars to display, and Visual C++ will retain that selection for all subsequent debugging sessions. If you have some preferences for shortcut keys other than the defaults, you can change any of the shortcut keys to your liking, add shortcut keys, set multiple shortcut keys for a command, and specify the windows in which any shortcut is active. In a text editor window, you can record keystrokes and then play them back to recreate that sequence of commands.

Extensive Information

Visual C++ provides several methods to get information about the development environment or the supporting software. *Introducing Visual C++* contains a series of tutorials to familiarize you with the development environment, with the methods and processes you need to use within the development environment, and with the development of applications using the Microsoft Foundation Class Library. From your source code in an editor window, you can readily get information about a class from the Microsoft Foundation Class Library, a function name from the C Runtime Library, or a language element. If you select a name, and press F1 or CTRL+F1, Visual C++ displays reference information for that name. The Books Online command on the Help menu displays the table of contents for the entire Visual C++ book set. You can browse through the table of contents and select topics to view. From any topic, you can search through all the text of the online books for the occurrence of a selected word or combination of words with the Search Plus command. If you need information about an open dialog box, you can click the Help button to provide you with descriptions of its controls, and methods to access further information, if necessary.

Visual C++ User's Guide

In the *Visual C++ User's Guide*, you will find procedures that show you how to undertake various development tasks with the visual development environment. It also includes reference information on underlying command-line tools.

Document Conventions

This book uses the following typographic conventions:

Example	Description
STDIO.H	Uppercase letters indicate filenames, registers, and terms used at the operating-system command level.
char, **_alloca**	Bold type indicates C and C++ keywords, operators, language-specific characters, and library routines. Within discussions of syntax, bold type indicates that the text must be entered exactly as shown.
	Many constants, functions, and keywords begin with either a single or double underscore. These are part of the name and are mandatory. For example, to have the **__cplusplus** manifest constant be recognized by the compiler, you must type the leading double underscore.
expression	Words in italics indicate placeholders for information you must supply, such as a filename. Italic type is also used occasionally for emphasis in the text.
[[*option*]]	Items inside double square brackets are optional.
#pragma pack {1 | 2}	Braces and a vertical bar indicate a choice among two or more items. You must choose one of these items unless double square brackets ([[ ]]) surround the braces.
`#include <io.h>`	This font is used for examples, user input, program output, and error messages in text.
CL [[*option...*]] *file...*	Three dots (an ellipsis) following an item indicate that more items having the same form may appear.

`while()`
`{`
`    .`
`    .`
`    .`
`}`
	A column or row of three dots tells you that part of an example program has been intentionally omitted.

Example	Description
CTRL+ENTER	Small capital letters are used to indicate the names of keys on the keyboard. When you see a plus sign (+) between two key names, you should hold down the first key while pressing the second.
	The carriage-return key, sometimes marked as a bent arrow on the keyboard, is called ENTER.
"argument"	Quotation marks enclose a new term the first time it is defined in text.
"C string"	Some C constructs, such as strings, require quotation marks. Quotation marks required by the language are bold and have the form " " and ' ' rather than " " and ' '.
Dynamic-Link Library (DLL)	The first time an acronym is used, it is usually spelled out.
x86 Specific → . . . **END x86 Specific**	Information presented in this book may not apply to all target platforms. Therefore, information that applies only to x86 targets is labeled as such.

PART 1

Using Visual C++

C H A P T E R   1

Creating a New Application Using AppWizard

AppWizard displays a series of dialog boxes used to generate a set of starter files for a Visual C++ application that uses the Microsoft Foundation Class Library (MFC). AppWizard must be used first in the development process, primarily so that you have starter files, but also so that your files are compatible with ClassWizard.

AppWizard lets you specify a number of application- and project-specific options. You specify an application with either a single-document, multiple-document, or dialog-based interface. You can choose object linking and embedding (OLE) support and database (ODBC) support. And you can get immediate built-in functionality such as handling of the Open, Save As, and Print commands on the File menu. You also choose whether to create an external or internal makefile.

When you are finished defining application and project options, the starter files will include all the files required to build a Windows-based application: source files, header files, resource files, a project file, and so on. The Visual C++ source files have skeletal versions of the classes that make up your application. The code that implements these classes is supplied by AppWizard, based on the options you have chosen in the AppWizard dialog boxes. Building the resulting project produces a skeleton application with a wealth of built-in functionality.

Creating an AppWizard Project

AppWizard displays a series of dialog boxes showing options for the features of your application. The series is a forking path depending on your application's architecture, so some of the option dialog boxes may not be displayed. You select options by cycling through the dialog boxes, forwards or backwards. You can change the options at any time before you create an AppWizard application.

▶ **To create a new project**

1. Start Visual C++.

2. From the File menu, choose New (CTRL+N).

   The New dialog box appears.

3. In the New box, select Project.

   The New box allows selection of various resource types—Code/Text, Project, Resource Script, Binary File, Bitmap File, Icon File, or Cursor File.

4. Choose OK. The New Project dialog box appears.

5. In the Project Type list, select MFC AppWizard (exe).

   The Project Type list allows selection of various project types—MFC AppWizard (exe), MFC AppWizard (dll), Application, Dynamic-Link Library, Console Application, and Static Library.

6. Type a name in the Project Name box.

   Visual C++ automatically enters the name you type as a directory name in the New Subdirectory box. It is also entered in the project file path above the Directory box. AppWizard uses the name that you specify in the Project Name box to derive default names for most of its files and classes.

Tip If a non-AppWizard project type is selected (such as Application or Static Library), the New Subdirectory field remains blank, since it is assumed that there is an existing directory of source files for this project. You can still directly type a name in the New Subdirectory box or type the entire path in the Project Name box. When you create a non-AppWizard project type, AppWizard displays the Project Files dialog box so that you can add existing files to your new project.

---

7. Specify the Target platforms for this project.

   Use the list box provided to select any of the available target platforms.

Note Win32 is the default target platform. To select other target platforms, the associated cross-development edition of Visual C++ must be installed.

---

8. In the Directory box, specify the path for this project.

   Use the list box to navigate through the directories on the selected drive.

9. Optionally, change the project's New Subdirectory name.

   The New Subdirectory will contain the project's files. AppWizard automatically enters the project name as the New Subdirectory name.

10. Choose Create. The AppWizard architecture options are displayed (Figure 1.1).

You choose application options here.

Selected features are modeled here by AppWizard.

Figure 1.1   AppWizard's architecture options

▶ **To select an architecture type and resource language**

1. Select one of the three architecture types:

   Single document A single document interface (SDI) architecture allows a user to work with just one document at a time. Windows Notepad is an example of an SDI application.

   Multiple documents A multiple document interface (MDI) architecture allows a user to open multiple documents, each with its own window. Windows File Manager is an example of an MDI application.

   Dialog-based A dialog-based architecture displays a simple dialog box for user input. MFC Trace Options is an example of a dialog-based application.

   Note As you make AppWizard feature selections, the left-side of AppWizard's dialog box displays a representation of the selected features. For example, selecting multiple-document architecture displays two documents in the "application's" window on the left side of the AppWizard dialog box.

   ---

2. Select a language for the resource text:

- English
- French
- German
- Japanese

Note English is the default language for resource text. To select other languages, the *LANGUAGE*.DLL file must already be installed on your system.

---

3. Choose Next to display the next AppWizard dialog box.

If your application is for single or multiple documents, the AppWizard database support options are displayed.

Choosing Database and OLE Options

The next two dialog boxes in the process of planning your project allow you to choose whether and to what degree you want your project to support open database connectivity (ODBC) and OLE.

▶ **To select a database support option**

1. Select one of the database support options:

None This option excludes the libraries that support open database connectivity. If the application does not use a database, choosing this option builds a smaller application.

Only include header files This option provides the minimal level of database support by including all the database header files and link libraries. With this option, AppWizard does not create any database-specific classes; you must do it yourself.

A database view, without file support This option also includes all the database header files and link libraries. In addition, AppWizard creates a record view and recordset for you. With this option, the application has document support with no serialization support.

Both a database view and file support This option also includes all the database header files and link libraries. In addition, AppWizard creates a record view and recordset. With this option, the application has document support and also has serialization support.

For additional information about MFC database support, see Chapter 6 in *Programming with the Microsoft Foundation Class Library*.

2. If your application includes a database view, you must define a data source and select a table.

   - Choose Data Source to display the SQL Data Sources dialog box. Select the name of a data source already registered on your machine through ODBC Administrator.

   - In the Select a Table dialog box, double-click the name of a table in the data source whose columns you want to bind to your recordset.

   - Close both the Select A Table and Data Source dialog boxes.

3. Choose Next to display the next AppWizard dialog box.

   If your application is for single or multiple documents (not dialog-based), the AppWizard OLE options are displayed.

▶ **To select OLE options**

AppWizard generates application support code for a variety of object linking and embedding (OLE) application types. Selecting any of the OLE options enables the standard OLE resources and adds extra OLE commands to the application's menu bar.

1. Select the type of OLE compound document support:

   None By default, AppWizard does not create an application with OLE support.

   Container Enables your application to contain linked and embedded objects.

   Mini-Server A mini-server application allows only creation of embedded objects.

   Full-Server Enables your application to run stand alone and support both linked and embedded items in addition to creating objects to be contained in compound documents.

   Both Container and Server Enables your application to be both a container and a server.

   For additional information about MFC OLE support, see Chapter 5 in *Programming with the Microsoft Foundation Class Library*.

2. Select whether to have OLE automation support:

   Yes Enables OLE Automation in MFC to allow creation of objects that support OLE methods and properties. If you choose this option, your document class is available as a programmable object that any automation client can use. By default, AppWizard does not create an application with OLE support.

   No Disables OLE Automation in MFC, and AppWizard creates an application without OLE Automation support.

3. Choose Next to display the next AppWizard dialog box.

   The AppWizard application options are displayed.

Choosing Application and Project Options

Depending on the application's architecture, you can select from among various options.

▶ **To select application options**

1. Specify the basic features you want your application to have by selecting from the options described below.

   Dockable Toolbar AppWizard generates code for a toolbar. The toolbar contains buttons for creating a new document, opening and saving document files, cutting, copying, pasting, printing, displaying the About Box, and entering Shift-F1 Help mode. Enabling this option also adds menu commands to display or hide the toolbar.

   Initial Status Bar AppWizard generates code for a status bar. The status bar contains automatic indicators for the keyboard's CAPS LOCK, NUM LOCK, and SCROLL LOCK keys and a message line that displays help strings for menu commands and toolbar buttons. Enabling this option also adds menu commands to display or hide the status bar.

   Printing and Print Preview AppWizard generates the code to handle print, print setup, and print preview commands by calling member functions in the **CView** class from MFC. It also adds commands for these functions to the application's File menu.

   About Box AppWizard creates a dialog box that shows the software version and copyright notice. The About box is typically edited to also contain brief product- and author-specific information. Selecting this option in a dialog-based application creates an About command on the main dialog box's control menu. For SDI and MDI applications, the About box is automatically included.

   Context Sensitive Help AppWizard generates a set of files that are used to provide context-sensitive help. The Help compiler is provided with Visual C++.

   Use 3D Controls AppWizard creates the visual interface using three-dimensional shading.

   MRU List Files Sets the number of files to be remembered on the "most recently used" list.

   Dialog Title For dialog-based applications, type the name for the dialog's title bar.

2. If your application is SDI or MDI architecture and requires adjustment of other advanced options, choose Advanced to display the Advanced Options dialog box:

   ▪ Select the Document Template Strings tab and modify the strings as required.

   ▪ If your application is SDI architecture, select the Main Frame tab and modify the Caption and the Main Frame Styles. Optionally, select Use Splitter Window.

   ▪ If your application is MDI architecture, select the Main Frame tab and modify the Caption and Main Frame Styles. Also select the MDI Child Frame tab and modify the MDI Child Frame Styles. Optionally, select Use Splitter Window. (For more information on this feature, see "Adding Splitter Windows" in Chapter 13 of *Introducing Visual C++*.)

   ▪ Choose Close.

3. Choose Next to display the next AppWizard dialog box.

   The AppWizard project options are displayed.

▶ **To select project options**

1. You can select settings for these project options:

   Generate Source File Comments   AppWizard generates and inserts comments in the source files that guide you in writing your program. This includes indicators where you need to add your own code and README.TXT describing each of the files produced. This option is recommended.

   Type of Makefile   By default, AppWizard generates a Visual C++ makefile that is compatible with Visual C++ and NMAKE. Select External Makefile if you want AppWizard to generate an NMAKE makefile that can be directly edited but must be used as an external project from within Visual C++.

   MFC Library Linkage   The Microsoft Foundation classes can be linked from a static library or a dynamic-link library.

2. Choose Next to display the next AppWizard dialog box.

   The AppWizard class summary options are displayed.

Completing the AppWizard Process

AppWizard displays the names it will create for the classes, headers, and implementation files. Some classes allow more name modification than others. You cannot change information in a text box that is dimmed.

▶ **To change the names of class information**

- Select a class name in the list box at the top of the Classes dialog box. The information in the other four boxes lists the related class names and implementation files. You can change the names of class information as required by your application. For an MDI/SDI application, you can also change your view's base class.

▶ **To create your application**

1. Choose Finish to display AppWizard's New Project Information summary.
2. Choose OK when you are satisfied that the options are correct. AppWizard will generate the new application's source files according to the options you have selected. If you want to modify any of these options, choose Cancel to close the New Project Information dialog box. This action gives you access to the other dialog boxes you have used in this procedure.

AppWizard-Created Files

AppWizard always creates a basic list of files, regardless of which options you choose. AppWizard uses the name that you specify in the Project Name box to derive names for most of its files and classes. For some filenames, the project name is truncated to five characters.

You'll undoubtedly want to examine the source code files you create. To orient you, AppWizard creates a text file, README.TXT, in your new application directory. This file explains the contents and uses of the other new files created by AppWizard.

For additional information about the files that AppWizard creates, see the article "AppWizard: Files Created" in *Programming with the Microsoft Foundation Class Library*.

C H A P T E R   2

Working with Projects

A project stores information about a particular program or library that you want to build. It contains three kinds of information:

- The names and locations of the source files that are used to build your program.
- The settings for the tools required to build the program, such as compiler and linker options.
- The look and organization of the Visual C++ workspace on your display.

There are essentially two ways to create new projects:

- Choosing the AppWizard project type for C++ projects using the Microsoft Foundation Class Library (MFC). AppWizard automatically creates certain files with the appropriate classes and adds them to the project. See Chapter 1, "Creating a New Application Using AppWizard," for more details.
- Choosing another project type. In this case, you must create all the files and select the files to add to the project.

The project window displays a graph showing the relationships among the source files used to build your project, as shown in Figure 2.1. The relationships in the window are logical relationships, not physical relationships, and do not reflect the organization of files on your hard disk, for instance. The window is titled *project*.MAK. You can access information about components of the project from the project window.

Figure 2.1   Project Window

Tip   While using the project window, in many instances you can click the right mouse button to display a shortcut menu of frequently used commands. The commands available depend on what the pointer is pointing at. For example, if you click while pointing at a source file, the shortcut menu shows the Properties command and several commands also available on the Project menu, such as Build and Compile.

Project Types

Each project has a type, which you choose when you create the project. The project type specifies the kind of target to generate and determines the various options that Visual C++ sets by default for the project.

You can select the following six project types in Visual C++ 2.0:

MFC AppWizard (exe)
>   Applications with a full graphical interface, developed with MFC. Visual C++ automatically creates skeleton files with the appropriate classes and adds the files to the project. The file extension is .EXE.

MFC AppWizard (dll)
>   Function libraries developed with MFC. Visual C++ automatically creates skeleton files with the appropriate classes and adds the files to the project. The file extension is .DLL.

Application
>   Applications with a full graphical interface, developed with Windows NT Win32® API functions or with MFC. The file extension is .EXE.

Dynamic-Link Library
Function libraries developed with Windows NT Win32 API functions, called dynamically at run time by 32-bit Windows-based programs. The file extension is .DLL.

Console Application
Applications developed with the Console APIs, which provide character-mode support in console windows. The Visual C++ run-time libraries also provide output and input from console windows with standard I/O functions, such as **printf**() and **scanf**(). The file extension is .EXE.

Static Library
Standard libraries created directly by the build, using the object files and other library files belonging to the project. The generated library is composed of all the object files in the project, all the object files generated by the project, and all the libraries in the project. The file extension is .LIB.

Using Projects

Within a project, you can add and remove files, update dependencies when a changes are made, and add or delete targets.

Creating a Project

When you create a project, you create the following two files:

- Makefile. The makefile has the extension .MAK. It contains all commands, macro definitions, options, and so forth to specify how to build the target of the project.

- Project configuration file. This file has the extension .VCP. It contains environment settings for Visual C++, such as window sizes and positions, insertion point locations, state of project breakpoints, contents of the Watch window, and so on.

You cannot modify these files directly.

▶ **To create a project**

1. From the File menu, choose New.

   The New dialog box appears.

2. Select Project from the list.

3. Choose OK.

   The New Project dialog box appears.

4. Type the name for the project in the Project Name text box.

   The same name also appears in the New Subdirectory text box. You can change this subdirectory name if you want. Visual C++ automatically creates this new subdirectory for your project files.

5. From the Project Type drop-down list, select the type of application that you want to create.

6. If necessary, select the drive and directory in which to create the subdirectory.

7. After you have completed making your selections, choose Create.

   If you did not choose an MFC AppWizard type for your project, the Project Files dialog box appears.

   If you chose an MFC AppWizard type, see "Creating an AppWizard Project" on page 3 in Chapter 1 for further details.

8. Add the files that make up your application to the project. See "Adding and Removing Files" on page 15 for more information.

9. Choose Close.

When you close the Project Files dialog box, Visual C++ scans the project files in order to update dependencies and then displays the project window with all the project files and their dependencies, as shown in Figure 2.1.

Visual C++ automatically scans the added project files recursively for **#include** directives, both bracketed (*<incl.h>*) and quoted (*"incl.h"*). It scans both source files (.C, .CPP, or .CXX) and resource files (.RC), and adds all the included files that it finds to a Dependencies subgroup. You cannot directly add or delete the files included in this subgroup. The files in this group can have extensions of .H, .HXX, .INC, .FON, .CUR, .BMP, .ICO, or .DLG.

Visual C++ also refers to the following two exclusion files:

SYSINCL.DAT
    This file, which contains a default list of system include files, is installed by the setup program on your system in the directory in which you install Visual C++ (MSVC.EXE).

MSVCINCL.DAT
    This is a text file which you can create and put in your Windows directory. You can list in it additional files which you want to exclude. You should use this file for additions, because SYSINCL.DAT may be overwritten if you reinstall Visual C++, if you modify your installation with Setup, or if you update your installation. If you use the Visual C++ text editor to create this file, you must exit Visual C++ and then restart it for the file to become effective.

These lists should contain only files that are not likely to change often. Whenever Visual C++ updates dependencies, it excludes the files in these lists from dependency scanning and does not display them in the Dependencies subgroup. If you change only files in either of these lists, you must choose Rebuild All on the Project menu in order to build your selected target. If you merely choose Build, the dependency subgroup has no changes in it, and Visual C++ reports that your target is up to date.

Using the Shortcut Menu

The project window has a shortcut menu that lists commands appropriate for the current selection in the window. This is a quick method to display commands that are also available from the main menu bar.

▶ **To display the shortcut menu**

- Move the mouse pointer into the project window and click the right mouse button.

You can now select project commands that are appropriate for your current selection in the project window.

Adding and Removing Files

You can use menu commands to add and remove files from your project. You can also use the mouse to add files by dragging them into the project window.

▶ **To add files to a project**

1. From the Project menu, choose Files.

   The Project Files dialog box appears.

2. If you have more than one group in your project, select the group in the Add Files To This Group drop-down list.

3. Select the file type to display from the List Files Of Type drop-down list box. The files of this type appear in the File Name list box.

4. If necessary, select the drive and directory to view.

5. Add files with the following methods:

   - Single file: Select the file in the File Name list and choose Add.
   - Single file: Double-click the file in the File Name list.
   - All files in the File Name list: Choose the Add All button.

Repeat the steps for all types of files that you want to add. When you close the Project Files dialog box, Visual C++ automatically scans the files for dependencies. It adds all the included files that it finds to the Dependencies subgroup for each group to which you added files. You cannot directly modify the files included in this subgroup.

You can also add files by dragging their graphical representations into your project. You can use this method to add files from the File Manager to a project, for instance.

Note This method only alters the lists of files in your project; it does not physically change the locations of files on your system. In particular, dragging files from the File Manager to your project simply adds the filenames to the project list; it does not add files to your project directory.

▶ **To remove files from a project**

1. From the Project menu, choose Files.

   The Project Files dialog box appears.

2. If you have more than one group in your project, select the desired group in the Add Files To This Group drop-down list.

3. If necessary, select the drive and directory to view.

4. Select the file in the Files In Group list and choose Remove.

Repeat the steps for all types of files that you want to remove. When you close the Project Files dialog box, Visual C++ automatically scans the files for dependencies. It automatically removes all the included files in the removed files from the Dependencies subgroup for each group if no other remaining file depends on them. You cannot directly remove the files included in this subgroup.

▶ **To quickly remove files from a project**

- Select the file in the project window, and from the Edit menu, choose Delete (DEL).

You can hold down the CTRL or SHIFT keys to select multiple files in the project window.

Saving a Project

You must always select the project window when using the Save or Save As commands to save a project, because those commands on the File menu affect only the window that currently has the focus.

▶ **To save a project**

1. Select the project window.

2. From the File menu, choose Save (CTRL+S).

   Toolbar: 🖫

   Visual C++ saves the project without any further action on your part.

▶ **To save an existing project under a new name**

1. Select the project window.

2. From the File menu, choose Save As (F12).

   The Save As dialog box appears.

3. In the Save As dialog box, type a new filename, and select the desired drive, directory, and file type.

4. Choose OK.

▶ **To save all files in a project**

• From the File menu, choose Save All.

   Visual C++ saves all files that you have modified in Visual C++—whether or not they are included in a project—without any further action on your part.

Opening an Existing Project

Opening an existing project restores all the environment settings to their state when you last saved the project. It also opens the browse information file for the project.

▶ **To open an existing project**

1. From the File menu, choose Open (CTRL+O).

   The Open dialog box appears. The default selection in the List Files Of Type drop-down list is Main Files, which includes project .MAK files. If you want to see .MAK files only, select Projects from the drop-down list.

2. Select the drive and directory containing the project that you want to open.

3. Select the .MAK file for the project from the File Name list and choose OK, or double-click the filename in the list.

A project window titled *project*.MAK appears, as shown in Figure 2.1, and displays a graphical representation of the files in the project.

If you open a project from any previous version of Visual C++, it asks if you want to convert the project's makefile to a makefile compatible with the current version. If you choose to convert the file, Visual C++ displays the Save As dialog box so that you can save it under a new name. The default name is the current makefile name from the previous version; if you don't change that name, Visual C++

overwrites the existing file. You should set the directories for intermediate and output files as well, so that Visual C++ does not overwrite the files created by the previous version. See "Selecting the Directories for Output Files" on page 23 for more information.

Closing a Project

▶ **To close an open project**

- Move the focus to the project window, and choose Close from the File menu.

  –Or–

- Open another project.

  –Or–

- Create a new project.

Updating Dependencies in a Project

After editing one or more source files to add **#include** directives, you need to update the project dependencies to add included files to the appropriate dependency groups.

▶ **To update dependencies in all the files in the project**

- From the Project menu, choose Update All Dependencies.

▶ **To update dependencies in a single file in the project**

1. In the project window, select the file for which you want to update dependencies.

   –Or–

   Open the file.

2. From the Project menu, choose Update Dependencies.

Visual C++ scans the project files recursively for **#include** directives, both bracketed (*<incl.h>*) and quoted (*"incl.h"*). It also refers to the following two exclusion files:

SYSINCL.DAT
  This file, which contains a default list of system include files, is installed by the setup program on your system in the directory in which you install Visual C++ (MSVC.EXE).

MSVCINCL.DAT

> This is a text file which you can create and put in your Windows directory. You can list in it additional files which you want to exclude. You should use this file for additions, because SYSINCL.DAT may be overwritten if you reinstall Visual C++, modify your installation with Setup, or update your installation. If you use the Visual C++ text editor to create this file, you must exit Visual C++ and then restart it for the file to become effective.

These lists should contain only files that are not likely to change often. Whenever Visual C++ updates dependencies, it excludes the files in these lists from dependency scanning and does not display them in the Dependencies subgroup. If you change only files in either of these lists, you must choose Rebuild All on the Project menu in order to build your selected target. If you merely choose Build, the dependency subgroup has no changes in it, and Visual C++ reports that your target is up to date.

Using Targets

A build target is a final binary output file that you can create from a project. To generate a target, Visual C++ uses the source files that you have specified for input and translates them according to your project specifications. Visual C++ creates a target from the following combination of specifications:

- The platform for which you are building
- The type of binary output file (application, static library, dynamic-link library, and so on)
- The settings for the compiler, linker, and so on
- The specified source files

You choose the particular target to build at any given time from the drop-down list in the project window.

You can define new build targets which use different sets of options to build multiple versions of your project. When you define a new target from the Project Target dialog box, you can set build options specifically for that target, using the Project Settings dialog box. You could choose a different set of optimizations, for instance.

▶ **To define a new target**

1. From the Project menu, choose Targets.

   The Targets dialog box appears.

2. Choose New.

   The New Target dialog box appears.

3. Type a descriptive name for the new target in the Target Name text box.

4. If you want to use the defined defaults for your target, select the Use Default Settings option button. If necessary, select the target type from the drop-down list. If you want debugging information included in this target, select the Debug Build check box; otherwise, clear this check box.

–Or–

If you want to base the new target on an existing target in your project, select the Copy Settings option button, and then select the existing target from the drop-down list.

5. Choose OK.

6. In the Targets dialog box, choose OK.

The new target that you just created is available in the Target drop-down list on the project window. You can now build your new target by choosing it from the list and then choosing Rebuild All from the Project menu.

▶ **To delete a target definition**

1. From the Project menu, choose Targets.

   The Targets dialog box appears.

2. In the Target list, select the target that you want to delete.

3. Choose Delete.

   A confirmation message box appears.

4. Choose Yes to confirm the deletion.

5. Choose OK.

If the name you have chosen for a target does not describe its purpose adequately, you can change the name.

▶ **To rename a target definition**

1. From the Project menu, choose Targets.

   The Targets dialog box appears.

2. In the Target list, select the target that you want to rename.

3. Choose Rename.

   The Rename Target dialog box appears, with the existing target name under the label Old Target Name.

4. Type the new name in the New Target Name box.

5. Choose OK.

Using Groups in a Project

When you create a new project, Visual C++ adds one group to the project, called Source Files. For many projects, this one group is sufficient. You can, however, create other groups in your project. You can use groups to recognize explicitly logical grouping of files within the hierarchy of the project. You could create a group to contain all your user interface source files, for instance. You could also create groups to contain other files related to your project, such as specifications, documentation, or test suites. These files are represented by a different icon, as shown in Table 2.1 on page 27.

You can add a group only at the project level. You cannot add a group under another group.

▶ **To add a group**

- From the Project menu, choose New Group.

You can rename any group that you have created.

▶ **To rename a group**

1. Select the group in the project window.
2. From the Edit menu, choose Properties (ALT+ENTER).

   –Or–

   Click the right mouse button to display the shortcut menu, and choose Properties.
3. On the General tab, type the new name for the group in the Group Name text box.

Note You cannot rename the Dependencies group that Visual C++ creates automatically after scanning your source files for dependencies.

▶ **To remove a group**

1. Select the group in the project window.
2. From the Edit menu, choose Delete (DEL).

Removing a group removes all the files in the group from the list of project files.

You can also drag graphical representations of files from one group to any other group in your project. You can use this method either to copy or to move files. In addition, you can add files to your project using File Manager.

Note These methods only alter the lists of files in your project; they do not physically change the locations of files on your system. In particular, dragging files from the File Manager to your project simply adds the filenames to the project list; it does not add files to your project directory.

▶ **To move files from one group to another**

1. In the project window, select the files that you want to move. (Holding down the CTRL or SHIFT key allows you to select multiple files in the project window.)

2. With the mouse, drag the files onto the destination project group. You can drag them onto the project group node or the file nodes in the group.

   –Or–

   From the Edit menu, choose Cut (CTRL+X). Then select the destination group in the project window, and from the Edit menu, choose Paste (CTRL+V).

▶ **To copy files to a group**

1. In the project window, select the files that you want to copy. (Holding down the CTRL or SHIFT key allows you to select multiple files in the project window.)

2. Hold down CTRL and drag the files onto the project group. You can drag them onto the project group node or the file nodes in the group.

   –Or–

   From the Edit menu, choose Copy (CTRL+C). Then select the destination group in the project window, and from the Edit menu, choose Paste (CTRL+V).

▶ **To move or copy files or groups from one project to another**

1. In the project window, select the files or groups that you want to move or copy. (Holding down the CTRL or SHIFT key allows you to select multiple files in the project window.)

2. From the Edit menu, choose Cut (CTRL+X) if you want to move the files or groups, or Copy (CTRL+C) if you want to copy the files or groups.

3. Close the current project.

4. Open the destination project.

5. Select the group to receive the files if you are moving or copying files, or the project if you are moving or copying groups.

6. From the Edit menu, choose Paste (CTRL+V).

Tip If you press CTRL and click a selection, this toggles the selection state. You can use this method to quickly remove a file from a multiple selection.

If you move or copy selections which include files in Dependency groups, Visual C++ explicitly moves or copies only the source files. Visual C++ automatically updates the dependencies before building the project, however, and they appear then in the appropriate groups.

Setting Options Within a Project

Setting options at the project level is sufficient for most projects. Within a project, you can set different options for various targets, either those created by default or targets that you have explicitly created. In most cases, you have at least two targets for each platform: Debug and Release.

Projects also represent a hierarchical structure of options for each target. The options set at the project level apply to all files within the project. You can set options specific only to individual files, however, if you need to compile files with options different from the project options. For instance, if you set Default optimizations for the project, all files contained within the project use Default optimizations. You can, however, set specific optimizations—or no optimizations at all—for any individual files in the project. The options that you set at the file level in the project override options set at the project level.

You can set some types of options, such as linking, only at the project level.

You can set options at the following levels within a project:

- Project level. Options set at this level apply to all actions. Any options set for the project apply to every file in the project unless overridden at the file level.
- File level. Options set at this level apply to file-level actions, such as compiling. Any options set for the file apply only to that file and override any options set at the project level.

Selecting the Directories for Output Files

You can select the directories in which to put the intermediate and final output files for each target. By putting these files in different directories, you can maintain copies of the same files built in different ways—for instance, a debug and a release version of your target file.

▶ **To select output directories**

1. From the Project menu, choose Settings.

   The Project Settings dialog box appears, as shown in Figure 2.2.

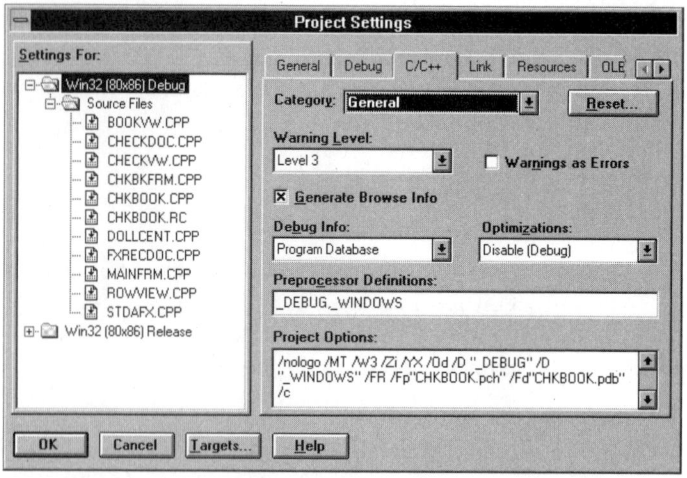

Figure 2.2   Project Settings Dialog Box

2. From the pane at the left of the Project Settings dialog box, select the node for which you want to set directories. If you select the project node, you can set both intermediate and target directories; if you select a file, you can set only the intermediate directory.

3. Select the General tab from the tabs at the top of the dialog box.

   The General tab is one of several which contain all the options for the project. It specifies how the project uses the Microsoft Foundation Class Library (MFC) and which directories the project uses for intermediate and target files.

4. Type the directory name for the intermediate files (.OBJ files, for instance) in the Intermediate Files text box.

5. If you are setting directories for the project level, type the directory name for the target files (.EXE files, for instance) in the Output Files text box.

6. Choose OK.

Specifying Project Settings

You can set options for a project only when the project is open.

▶ **To specify project settings**

1. From the Project menu, choose Settings.

   The Project Settings dialog box appears, as shown in Figure 2.2.

2. From the pane at the left of the dialog box, select the project-level node for the target. You can also select multiple project-level nodes for targets, and set options common to all the targets.

3. From the tabs at the top of the dialog box, select the type of options that you want to set.

4. Set the options you want on the selected tab. From the C/C++ and Link tabs, you can select from the Category list at the top of the tab to set options in various categories, if necessary.

   When you have completed setting the options on a tab, you can select another and set additional options. CTRL+TAB displays the next tab, and CTRL+SHIFT+TAB displays the previous tab.

5. When you have completed setting options, choose OK.

Setting File Options

A file inherits the options settings from the project. For each individual file, however, you can set options that are different from, or in addition to, the project's options.

▶ **To set file options in the current target**

1. Select the file or files in the project window.

2. Click the right mouse button to display the shortcut menu and choose Settings.

   The Project Settings dialog box appears, as shown in Figure 2.2, with the files selected in the left pane.

3. From the tabs at the top of the dialog box, select the type of options that you want to set.

4. Set the options you want on the selected tab. From the C/C++ compiler tab, you can select from the Category list to set options in various categories, if necessary.

   For more information on compiler options, see option descriptions in Chapter 20, "Setting Compiler Options."

   When you have completed setting the options on a tab, you can select another and set additional options.

5. When you have completed setting options, choose OK.

Note If you set options incompatible with the project type that you chose when you created your project, you may not get the result that you desire or expect.

You can also set common options across multiple targets. Within the targets in your project, you can select any combinations of groups or files.

▶ **To set file options in multiple targets**

1. From the Project menu, choose Settings.

   The Project Settings dialog box appears, as shown in Figure 2.2.

2. In the left pane of the dialog box, select the targets, groups, or files. Click the plus signs or double-click the node names to expand the graph of project files if necessary, and use the SHIFT and CTRL keys in conjunction with the mouse to make multiple selections.

3. From the tabs at the top of the dialog box, select the type of options that you want to set. The visible tabs depend on the files, groups, or targets that you have selected. Only those tabs with options common to the selections appear.

4. Set the desired options on the selected tab. From the C/C++ compiler tab, you can select from the Category list to set options in various categories, if necessary. Only the options common to all the selections are enabled.

   For more information on compiler options, see option descriptions in Chapter 20, "Setting Compiler Options."

   When you have completed setting the options on a tab, you can select another and set additional options.

5. When you have completed setting options, choose OK.

Note If you set options incompatible with the project type that you chose when you created your project, you may not get the result that you want or expect.

Excluding Files from a Target

You may want to exclude some files from a target build in your project. You may want to exclude files with platform-specific code from targets for other platforms, or you may want to exclude files that you use to test or debug your application from release targets.

▶ **To exclude one or more files from a target build**

1. From the Project menu, choose Settings.

   The Project Settings dialog box appears.

2. In the left pane, expand the graph for the desired target by clicking the plus signs or by double-clicking the node names.

3. Select the file(s) to exclude. You can make multiple selections by holding down the CTRL or SHIFT keys while clicking filenames in the graph.

4. Select the General tab.

5. Select the Exclude File From Build check box.

6. Choose OK.

Visual C++ now excludes the selected files when you build the selected target. The files are still included in other targets, however, unless you explicitly exclude them there as well.

The project window displays information on its graph about the files in the project. It displays icons for various types of files in the project, and it changes the icon for a file if it is currently excluded from a target.

Table 2.1 shows the icons and their meanings.

Table 2.1   File Icons in the Project Window

Icon	Meaning
	Visual C++ can use this file in a build, and it is included in the build for this target.
	Visual C++ can use this file in a build, but it is not included in the build for this target.
	Visual C++ cannot use this file in a build.

Files in the last category might include documentation or specifications, for instance.

Using External Projects

You can open an existing makefile in Visual C++ as an external project. They are called external projects because you must use external methods to set project options, rather than using the methods available within Visual C++.

If your external project generates an executable file compatible with the Microsoft Visual C++ Version 2.0 debugging format, you can debug it from within Visual C++.

Opening an External Project

Opening an external project creates a project target file, with the extension .VCP, for the project. This file stores any options that you select for the project. If you subsequently open the project again, Visual C++ restores all the environment settings that you selected for that project. It also opens the browse information file for the project, if one exists and it has the base name of the project and the extension .BSC.

▶ **To open an external project**

1. From the File menu, choose Open (CTRL+O).

   Toolbar: 🖻

   The Open dialog box appears.

2. Select the drive and directory containing the project that you want to open.

3. Select the .MAK file for the project from the File Name list and choose OK, or double-click the filename in the list. Alternatively type the name of the makefile in the text box.

Note The default selection in the List Files Of Type drop-down list is Main Files, which includes project .MAK files. If you want to see .MAK files only, select Project from the drop-down list. Visual C++ also recognizes files named MAKEFILE as makefiles. If the makefile does not end in .MAK or have the name MAKEFILE, you can also select Project from the Open As drop-down list in the Open dialog box to open any file as a makefile.

Visual C++ opens a project window for the external project, which shows the project-level node only. You cannot expand this node. You cannot use the menu commands to add groups or add or delete files from this project.

Setting Options for External Projects

Visual C++ creates a project configuration file, with extension .VCP, for an external project. This file stores any options that you select for the project.

▶ **To set options for an external project**

1. From the Project menu, choose Settings.

   The Project Settings dialog box appears. It displays the tabs with options for the project.

2. Select the General tab from the tabs at the top of the dialog box.

3. In the pane at the left of the dialog box, select the desired target or targets. If you select only one target, you can set all options for that target. If you select multiple targets, you can set only options common to all targets selected.

   From the subsequent options, select the ones that apply or fill in the appropriate information in the text boxes.

   Build Command Line
   The command line that the operating system executes for this project when you choose Build from the Project menu. By default, the system executes Microsoft NMAKE with the /F option followed by the name of the external makefile.

Rebuild All Options

The options added to the command line when you select Rebuild All on the Project menu. By default, /A for Microsoft NMAKE is added.

Output File Name

The name of the file that is created when you build the project. This could be an application or static library, for instance.

Browse Info File Name

Name of the browse information file to create for this project. It must have the extension .BSC.

ClassWizard File Name

Name of the ClassWizard file that has MFC information for this project.

Platform

The system architecture and/or processor type for which the project is being created.

4. Select the Debugging Options tab from the tabs at the top of the dialog box.

5. Enter the information required for debugging in the text boxes. Visual C++ uses this information when you choose commands such as Go or Step Into on the Debug menu.

Executable for Debug Session

The name of the program that the external makefile builds if you are debugging an executable program, or the name of the executable file that calls a DLL if you are debugging a DLL. If you are debugging an executable file on a remote machine, this executable file on the local machine contains the symbolic debugging information.

Working Directory

The working directory that the application uses when it runs. This may be a different directory from the output files directory in the project. It could contain test cases, for instance.

Program Arguments (for .EXE files)

Arguments which need to be passed to the executable file when it starts.

Additional DLLs

Any additional DLLs that the program may load when executing. Visual C++ loads the symbols for these DLLs before they are called. Because the symbols are available as soon as you being debugging, this enables you to set breakpoints in DLLs before the DLLs are entered. You can set a breakpoint at DLLMain,for instance.

Remote Executable File Name

The name for the executable file that you are debugging on a remote machine. The location for this executable file is specified relative to the remote machine.

6. Choose OK.

Using Precompiled Headers

You can greatly speed compile time by compiling any C or C++ files—including inline code—only once into a precompiled header file (.PCH) and thereafter using the precompiled header for each build. The Visual C++ compiler allows two ways to create and use precompiled header files. The Precompiled Headers category on the C/C++ tab simplifies either approach.

The simplest way to use precompiled headers is to create a new application using AppWizard. It sets default compiler options to create a precompiled header file, STDAFX.PCH, from STDAFX.H for use by all the skeleton files it creates.

If you do not use AppWizard to create your application, you can select the Precompiled Headers category on the C/C++ tab in the Project Settings dialog box and select the Automatic Use Of Precompiled Headers option to create an easy-to-use precompiled header file. For more information, see "Precompiled Headers" on page 300 in Chapter 20 or the "/Yd" option on page 361 in Appendix A.

Building a Project

From Visual C++, you can build or rebuild the program or library that a project defines. When you build a project, Visual C++ processes only the files in the project that have changed since the last build. When you rebuild a project, Visual C++ processes all the files in the project. You can choose to build either a single target, the current target, or you can choose multiple targets to build in one operation.

When you create a project, Visual C++ sets default options for targets. The debug targets contain full symbolic debugging information that can be used by the integrated debugger in Visual C++ or by other debuggers that use the Microsoft debug format. It also turns off all optimizations, because they generally make debugging more difficult. The release targets do not contain any symbolic debugging information, and they use any optimizations that you have set after creating the targets. Depending on your installation and the choices you made when you created your project, you may have other default targets with other options, or you may have created other targets with other options. Each target also specifies the directories in which the intermediate and final files are created.

If you have excluded files from the current target, as described in the section "Excluding Files from a Target" on page 26, different icons for those excluded files are displayed in the project window, as shown in Table 2.1.

Building the Current Target

You can choose the current target that you want to build. This is the target that you build when you choose Build *target* from the Project menu.

▶ **To select a target**

- From the Target drop-down list on the project window, select a target.

▶ **To build a project**

- From the Project menu, choose Build *Target* (SHIFT+F8), where *Target* represents the program or library defined by the project.

  Toolbar: 🖼️

▶ **To rebuild a project**

- From the Project menu, choose Rebuild All (ALT+F8).

  Toolbar: 🖼️

Information about the build is displayed in the Output window. It displays information from the build tools and lists any errors or warnings that occur during the build. If no errors are reported, the build completed successfully. If errors are reported, you need to debug them. For information on debugging build errors, see "Debugging Compiler and Linker Errors" on page 182 in Chapter 14.

Since the build occurs in the background, you can continue to use Visual C++ during the build. Some menu commands and toolbar buttons are disabled during a build. You cannot close the current project, for instance. If you use the tabs at the bottom of the Output window to view the previous output from another tool while you are running the current build, you can click the Build tab to return to the build output.

An audible message notifies you when the build is complete. The audible message corresponds to one of three standard system events in Windows:

System Event	Indicates
Asterisk	Build has completed without errors or warnings
Question	Build has completed with warnings
Exclamation	Build has completed with errors

If you have a sound card installed, you can use the Sound application in the Windows NT Control Panel to assign these system events to different sounds. Otherwise, all audible events issue a beep.

In some cases, you may need to stop building your project before the process finishes.

▶ **To stop a build**

- From the Project menu, choose Stop Build (CTRL+BREAK).

  Toolbar: ▣

Visual C++ stops the currently executing tool if possible; otherwise, it stops the build as soon as the currently executing tool finishes.

Building Multiple Targets

Any project can have more than one target. Instead of selecting each target in turn, and building it as the current target using the Build *target* command on the Project menu, you can choose to build more than one of your project's targets using the Batch Build command on the Project menu.

▶ **To build multiple targets**

1. From the Project menu, choose Batch Build.

   The Batch Build dialog box appears.

2. Select the targets that you want to build from the Targets list.

3. Choose Build to build only those components of each target that are out of date, or Rebuild All to build all components for each target.

   The results for each target are separated in the Output window by a line containing the name of the target being built.

▶ **To stop building multiple targets**

- From the Project menu, choose Stop Build (CTRL+BREAK).

  Toolbar: ▣

Visual C++ stops the currently executing tool if possible; otherwise, it stops the build as soon as the currently executing tool finishes. The build of the target currently in progress ends. A message box appears asking if you wish to continue building the remaining targets. If you answer yes, then the batch build continues from the next target in the list. If you answer no, then the entire batch build is stopped.

If you stop the batch build, the targets remaining to be built, including the one which was stopped, are selected in the Targets list of the Batch Build dialog box. If the batch build runs to completion without being stopped, the current target is selected.

Building a Single File Without a Project

You can create a single source file and then build an NT Console application directly from that source file. This is generally useful only for relatively simple applications.

▶ **To build a console application from a single source file**

1. Create or open a source file in a text editor window.

2. From the Project menu, choose Build (F8).

   Visual C++ displays a message box asking if you would like to create a default project.

3. Choose Yes.

   The Save As dialog box appears if you have not yet given the source file a name.

4. If necessary, give the source file a new name with the extension .C, .CXX, or .CPP.

   If you don't use one of these file extensions, Visual C++ does not build anything, because it does not recognize the source file to build in the project.

5. Choose OK.

Visual C++ creates a default project using the base name of the source file as the base name for the project. It uses default settings for a Console application for the project and builds the application.

Running a Program

When you have completed building your project, you can start applications from Visual C++. You can also run applications and dynamic-link libraries in the integrated debugger.

▶ **To run an executable program**

- From the Project menu, choose Execute *Target* (CTRL+F5), where *Target* represents the program defined by the project.

  Toolbar:

▶ **To run an application in the integrated debugger**

- From the Debug menu, choose Go (F5) or Step Into (F8).

  Toolbar: ▣↓ ⟨▣⟩

If you are debugging a DLL, you need to prepare for your debugging session as described in "Debugging DLLs" on page 210 in Chapter 14. For more information on debugging your programs, see Chapter 14, "Using the Debugger."

CHAPTER 3

Using the Text Editor

Visual C++ provides an integrated text editor to manage, edit, and print source files. Most of the procedures involved in using the editor, such as file and text handling and moving around in a file, should seem familiar if you have used other Windows-based text editors. With the editor, you can:

- Perform advanced find and replace operations.
- Specify syntax coloring.
- Customize tab stops in a source file.
- Use toolbar shortcuts for various commands.
- Get context-sensitive Help from within a source file.
- Use multiple levels of undo and redo.
- Open multiple windows for debugging, monitoring variables, disassembling code, displaying source files, and viewing project and program structure.
- Open multiple views of the same file.
- Use bookmarks for quick navigation in files.
- Select and manipulate column blocks.
- Take advantage of other ease-of-use features, such as a list of recently opened files at the bottom of the File menu, parsing text around the insertion point as the initial search string in a Find operation, and keyboard shortcuts.

Tip While using the source code editor, in many instances you can click the right mouse button to display a shortcut menu of frequently used commands. The commands available depend on what the pointer is pointing at and whether you are in edit or debug mode. For example, if you click while pointing at the name of an include file while in edit mode, the shortcut menu shows a command to open that file, as well as Cut, Copy, Paste, ClassWizard, and Properties commands.

Managing Files

The Visual C++ text editor File menu has several commands for standard file management, such as creating, opening, saving, and printing source files.

Creating a File

The New command creates a new source file. Creating a source file does not affect other source files you may have open.

▶ **To create a new source file**

1. From the File menu, choose New (CTRL+N).

   The New dialog box appears.

2. Select Code/Text, then choose OK.

   Toolbar: 🔳

3. From the File menu, choose Save (CTRL+S).

   Toolbar: 💾

   The Save As dialog box appears.

4. In the Directories box, double-click a directory where you want to store the source file (or move down a path to the appropriate directory).

5. Type a filename in the File Name box, then choose OK. The default extension given to a file is the last extension used when you saved a file. You can type another extension or select one from the List Files Of Type box.

New files are labeled Text*n* until they are saved. The *n* is a sequential number.

The maximum number of bytes in a line is 251.

Before you can save or close an individual window it must be active. To make a window active, either switch to the window (by clicking anywhere in it) or choose the window name or number from the Window menu. You can use the Save All command to save all open windows.

Opening a Source File

When you open a source file, its name is added to the Window menu. You cannot use the Open command on the File menu to open another copy of an open source file.

▶ **To open a file**

1. From the File menu, choose Open (CTRL+O).

   Toolbar: 📂

   The Open dialog box appears.

2. Select the drive and directory where the file is stored. The default is the current drive and directory.

3. Set the types of files to display in the List Files Of Type box. Files with the chosen extension are displayed in the File Name box.

    This box serves as a filter to display all files with a given extension. For example, Projects (*.mak) displays all files with the .MAK extension. The drop-down box initially lists commonly-used file extensions. The default shows the .mak, .c, .cpp, .cxx, .h, and .rc extensions.

    Alternatively, you can specify wildcard patterns in the File Name box to display file types. The new wildcard pattern is retained until the dialog box is closed. You can also use any combination of wildcard patterns, delimited by semicolons. For example, typing "*.INC; *.H; *.CPP" displays all files with these extensions.

4. In the File Name box, select a filename, then choose OK.

    –Or–

    Double-click the filename.

Tip   The names of the four most recently opened files are displayed at the end of the File menu. To open one of these files, choose its name from the menu.

You can also open a file by using the File Manager to display the file icon, then dragging and dropping it into Visual C++.

You can also open a file by clicking its icon in the project window.

▶   **To set read only options**

1. Make the file active by clicking the source window.

2. From the Edit menu, choose Properties (ALT+ENTER).

    The Text File Properties page opens.

3. Select the Read Only check box.

    Note   The Read Only check box only affects the editing session; it does not affect the read/write status of the file on disk.

Saving Files

Each source window associated with a source file can retain its own fonts, sizing, and other window attributes. When you make changes to a source window, the Save button on the toolbar becomes available (not dimmed) to indicate that the information in the source window and source file differs. An asterisk (*) also appears in the title bar if the file has changed since it was last saved.

▶ **To save a file**

1. Switch to the source window.

2. From the File menu, choose Save (CTRL+S).

    Toolbar: 🖫

3. If your file is unnamed, the environment displays the Save As dialog box. In the File Name box, type the filename.

4. In the Drives and Directories boxes, select a drive and directory.

5. Choose OK.

If the file has already been named, the Save command saves changes without displaying the Save As dialog box.

▶ **To save all open files**

• From the File menu, choose Save All.

You can also save another copy of an existing file. This procedure is useful for maintaining revised copies of a file while keeping the original unchanged.

▶ **To save a new file or another copy of an existing file**

1. Make the file active by clicking the source window.

2. From the File menu, choose Save As (F12).

    The Save As dialog box appears.

3. Type a filename and extension in the File Name box.

4. Choose the drive and the directory where you want to save the file.

5. Choose OK.

▶ **To set Save options**

1. From the Tools menu, choose Options.

    The Options dialog box appears.

2. Select the Editor tab. Then select the desired save option.

    ▪ To save open files before running any tool, select the Save Before Running Tools check box.

    ▪ To always prompt before saving a file, select the Prompt Before Saving Files check box.

Printing

You can print highlighted text or the contents of a source window, print a complete file, customize your print job, and print help topics.

▶ **To print highlighted text**

1. Select the text you want to print.

2. From the File menu, choose Print (CTRL+P).

   The Print dialog box appears. Under Print Range, Selection is automatically selected for you.

3. Choose OK.

Text is printed in the default font for the printer if the default editor font is used. Otherwise, the text prints with the selected editor font if that font is available on the printer.

The Print command also prints the contents of an active window, such as the Output window. An active window is the window with the current focus.

▶ **To print the contents of an active window**

1. From the File menu, choose Print.

   The Print dialog box appears.

2. Under Print Range, select the All option button.

3. Choose OK.

▶ **To print a complete source file**

1. From the File menu, choose Print (CTRL+P).

   The Print dialog box appears.

2. Under Print Range, select the All option button.

3. Choose OK.

You can customize your print jobs by adding headers and footers and by adjusting margins.

▶ **To customize a print job**

1. From the File menu, choose Page Setup.

2. Type the header or footer text, codes, or both.

To Print	Use
Filename	&f
Page number of current page	&p
Current system time	&t
Current system date	&d
Left aligned	&l
Centered	&c
Right aligned	&r

3. Under Margins, type measurements.

▶ **To print the contents of the current help topic**

- From the File menu in the Help window, choose Print Topic.

  Only one help topic can be printed at a time.

Moving Around in Source Files

The Visual C++ text editor provides a variety of means to move around in source files. In addition to the regular cursor and page controls, Visual C++ provides commands to:

- Move to a specific line number.
- Find the matching brace or parenthesis.
- Find the enclosing **#if** conditional statements.
- Set bookmarks.

▶ **To move to a line**

1. From the Search menu, choose Go To (CTRL+G).

   The Go To dialog box appears.

2. In the Line box, type a line number.

3. Choose OK.

   If you type a line number greater than the last line in your source file, the editor moves to the end of the file.

You can move to the matching brace in a block or determine if you have a matching brace to enclose a block with the Match Brace command.

▶ **To move to a matching brace**

1. Place the insertion point immediately in front of a brace.

2. From the Search menu, choose Match Brace (CTRL+]).

    The insertion point moves forward or backward to the matching brace. Choosing the command again returns the insertion point. If a matching brace cannot be found, the editor beeps. This also works for parentheses and square brackets.

You can also move to the enclosing **#if** block in your source code with the Next and Previous **#if** command keystrokes. This method works for all #if conditionals, which includes **#if**, **#ifdef**, **#else**, **#endif**.

▶ **To move to the enclosing #if**

1. Place the insertion point on a line.

2. Find the enclosing statement you want.

    ■ Press CTRL+< to place the insertion point on the line containing the **#if** keyword that encloses the current line.

    ■ Press CTRL+> to place the insertion point on the line containing the **#endif**, **#else**, or **#elif** line that encloses the current line.

Note You can use the SHIFT+CTRL+> or SHIFT+CTRL+< shortcut to select text from the current cursor position to the enclosing **#ifdef** or **#endif**, **#else**, or **#endif**, respectively.

Using Bookmarks

You can set a bookmark to mark frequently accessed lines in your source file. Once a bookmark has been set at a line, you can use menu or keyboard commands to move to it. You can clear a bookmark when you no longer need it.

Note Bookmarks are not saved between editing sessions.

▶ **To set a bookmark**

1. Move the insertion point to the line where you want to set a bookmark.

2. From the Search menu, choose Toggle Bookmark (CTRL+F2). The line is highlighted or marked in the margin if you have set a selection margin.

▶ **To move to the next bookmark after the insertion point**

• From the Search menu, choose Next Bookmark (F2).

▶ **To move to the previous bookmark before the insertion point**

• From the Search menu, choose Previous Bookmark (SHIFT+F2).

▶ **To clear a bookmark**

1. Move the insertion point to the bookmark.

2. From the Search menu, choose Toggle Bookmark (CTRL+F2).

▶ **To remove all bookmarks in a source file**

• From the Search menu, choose Clear All Bookmarks.

Controlling the Source Window

The Visual C++ text editor features a number of options that control the display of source windows. You can switch between windows, split window views, and make windows read-only.

Since an opened file cannot be "reopened," you cannot use the Open command to display the same file in another window. To open a new window to view the same contents as the active window, use the Split command. This procedure is helpful if you want to simultaneously view two parts of the same file.

▶ **To create a new window for an open source file**

1. Make the source window active by clicking it.

2. From the Window menu, choose the New Window command.

   A second copy of the source file is displayed with a *:n* suffix. As you open more windows on the source file, the value of *n* is increased. You can scroll and split each window independently. You can make changes to the source file from any window.

▶ **To split a source window**

1. Click the source file window or use the Window menu to make the source window active.

   If there are multiple windows open on the source file, select one of them.

2. From the Window menu, choose Split.

   The split bar is displayed.

3. Drag the split bar to the desired location.

Tip You can also split a source window by clicking the split bar at the top of the vertical scrollbar and dragging it down to the location you want.

The Read Only command makes the current window or any duplicates of the window read only. When you choose this command, the file cannot be edited.

▶ **To make a source window read only**

1. Click the source file window or use the Window menu to make the source window active.

   If there are multiple windows open on the source file, select one of them.

2. From the Edit menu, choose Properties (ALT+ENTER).

   The Text File Properties page is displayed.

3. Select the Read Only check box.

   To undo the command, select it again.

   READ in the Status Bar indicates that a source file is read only.

   If you open a read-only disk file, the Read Only check box is automatically checked. To edit a version of the file, clear the Read Only check box, make your edits, and then save the file under a different name.

Note The Read Only check box only affects the editing session; it does not affect the read/write status of the file on disk.

▶ **To switch to a source window**

- Do one of the following:
  - Click anywhere in the window.
  - Choose the window name from the Window menu.
  - Press CTRL+F6 to cycle through the active source windows one at a time.
  - Press CTRL+TAB to switch to the last active window (release the CTRL key to switch to the window).

All files are automatically closed when you quit Visual C++ (you are prompted to save any altered files). You can also close any individual source file without quitting the application.

▶ **To close a source file**

1. Switch to the source window.

2. Then, either:

   ▪ From the File menu, choose Close (CTRL+F4). This action closes the active window and any additional views of the window.

   –Or–

   ▪ Double-click the window's Control-menu box if the window is not maximized. When you double-click the Control-menu box, the window is closed but additional views of the window remain open.

Before you can close a window, it must be active. To make the window active, either click the window or choose the window name or number from the Window menu.

Editing Text with the Visual C++ Text Editor

The Visual C++ text editor allows you to cut, copy, and paste text using menu commands and shortcuts as well as the drag-and-drop editing mechanism. An undo buffer is provided to allow undoing and redoing of selected editing actions.

Cutting, Copying, Pasting, and Deleting Text

The Cut command removes selected text from the active window and places it on the Clipboard. The Copy command duplicates selected text from the active window and places it on the Clipboard. From the Clipboard, you can then paste the text to another location, file, or application. The Delete command deletes text without copying it to the Clipboard. As with all editing actions, however, you can undo a delete with the Undo command on the Edit menu.

▶ **To transfer text**

1. Select the text you want to transfer.

2. From the Edit menu, choose the Cut or Copy command.

Command	Shortcut
Cut	CTRL+X or SHIFT+DEL
Copy	CTRL+C or CTRL+INS
Paste	CTRL+V or SHIFT+INS

Tip To cut the current line, press CTRL+Y.

3. Place the insertion point in any source window where you want to insert the text.

4. From the Edit menu, choose the Paste command.

The Delete command (DEL) on the Edit menu deletes selected text. The deleted text is not placed onto the Clipboard and cannot be pasted.

Tip To undo the last edit, press CTRL+Z or ALT+BACKSPACE. To redo the last undo, press CTRL+A.

Using Drag-and-Drop Editing

Drag-and-drop editing is the easiest way to move or copy a selection of text a short distance in a file or between files.

▶ **To move text using drag-and-drop editing**

1. Select the text you want to move.
2. Point to the selected text, and then hold down the mouse button.

   The drag-and-drop pointer appears.
3. Drag the dotted insertion point to the new location and release the mouse button.

▶ **To copy text using drag-and-drop editing**

1. Select the text you want to copy.
2. Hold down the CTRL key, point to the selected text, and then hold down the mouse button.

   The drag-and-drop pointer appears. You can release the CTRL key.
3. Drag the dotted insertion point to the new location and release the mouse button.

Tip To undo the last edit, press CTRL+Z or ALT+BACKSPACE. To redo the last undo, press CTRL+A.

Undoing and Redoing Editing Actions

The Undo command on the Edit menu allows you to "undo" previous editing actions. The number and scope of editing actions you can undo is determined by the size of the Undo buffer.

▶ **To undo an editing action**

- From the Edit menu, choose Undo (CTRL+Z or ALT+BKSP).

  Toolbar: 🔄

The Redo command "undoes" the action of an Undo command. Redo is unavailable unless an Undo command has been chosen.

▶ **To redo an undo action**

- From the Edit menu, choose Redo (CTRL+A).

  Toolbar: 🔁

Note The number and scope of Redo commands is limited by the size of the buffer.

Specifying Column Blocks for Editing

You can select columnar blocks of text to cut, copy, delete, indent, and unindent.

▶ **To specify a block of text for editing**

1. Find the text you want to select. Hold down the ALT key until you click the left mouse button to begin the selection.

2. Release the ALT key and drag the mouse to specify the text to be selected.

   When the left mouse button is released, the block of text is selected and the text is available for cut, copy, delete, and indent operations.

Tip You can also place the Visual C++ text editor in column select mode by pressing CTRL+SHIFT+F8. This mode is active only during the next immediate selection.

To cancel column select mode, press the ESC key.

Finding and Replacing Text

The Visual C++ text editor offers advanced find and replace capabilities. You can search for text in a single source file or use the Find In Files command to search for text in multiple files.

You can search for literal text strings or use regular expressions to find words or characters. You can even use tagged regular expressions for searching and replacing.

Finding Text in a Single File

The Find command searches the active window for a text string. You can:

- Find a whole word match. This "find" matches all occurrences of a text string not preceded or followed by an alphanumeric character or the underscore (_).

- Find a case-sensitive match. This "find" searches for text that matches the capitalization of the text string.
- Use a general-pattern search using regular expressions. This "find" uses special character sequences—regular expressions—to search for text.
- The Set Bookmarks On All command sets a bookmark at each occurrence of the text string or regular expression. You can then choose the Next Bookmark command from the Search menu to move to each bookmark in your file.

▶ **To find a text string**

1. Position the insertion point where you want to start your search.

   The editor uses the location of the insertion point to select a default search string.

2. From the Search menu, choose Find (ALT+F3).

   The Find dialog box appears.

3. Type the search text or a regular expression in the Find What box.

4. Select any of the Find options.

5. To begin your search, choose Find Next or Set Bookmarks On All. The find dialog box disappears when the search begins. To repeat a find operation, you can use the shortcut keys or toolbar buttons.

Action	Shortcut
Find next, searching forward in the file	F3
Find next, searching backward in the file	SHIFT+F3

The drop-down list box connected to the Find What text box records the last 16 text items you searched for. Select the drop-down arrow to the right of the text box or press ALT+DOWN ARROW to open the list.

▶ **To begin a find without the Find dialog box**

- Type or select a search string in the toolbar list box, then press ENTER or click the Find Next button.

  Toolbar: 🔍

  –Or–

- Select a text string in a source file, then press CTRL+F3.

Note   You can use regular expressions with a find from the toolbar if you have previously selected the Regular Expression check box in the Find dialog box.

The following are keyboard shortcuts for the Find box on the standard toolbar:

Action	Shortcut
Put the selected source-file text in the Find box and search for it	CTRL+F3
Select text string in Find text box	CTRL+F or ALT+A
Search forward	RETURN or F3
Search backward	SHIFT+RETURN or SHIFT+F3
Get help on selected keyword	F1
Go to definition	F11
Go to reference	SHIFT+F11

Finding Text in Multiple Files

The Find In Files command on the Search menu searches multiple text files for a text string. You can:

- Find a whole word match. This "find" matches all occurrences of a text string not preceded or followed by an alphanumeric character or the underscore (_).

- Find a case-sensitive match. This "find" searches for text that matches the capitalization of the text string.

- Use a general-pattern search using regular expressions. This "find" uses special character sequences—regular expressions—to search for text.

▶ **To find a text string in multiple source files**

1. From the Search menu, choose Find In Files.

   Toolbar: 🔍

   The Find In Files dialog box appears.

2. Select the files that you want to search. You can use the controls in the dialog box to change drives and directories, and you can select files from multiple drives and directories.

   To add a file to the Selected Files list to be searched, you can select it in the File Name list and choose Add. Alternatively, you can double-click it.

   To remove a file from the Selected Files list, you can select it and then click Remove. Alternatively, you can double-click it. The Remove All button removes all the filenames from the Selected Files list.

   Visual C++ retains the contents of the Selected Files list between uses of the Find in Files command in any single session.

3. Type the search text or a regular expression in the Find What box.

   Visual C++ retains up to 16 previous search strings in any single session. Select the drop-down arrow to the right of the text box or press ALT+DOWN ARROW to open the list. You can select any entry from the list by clicking it.

4. If necessary, select one or more find options. For example, if you typed a regular expression in the Find What text box, you must select Regular Expression.

5. Click Find to begin the search.

   When you perform this type of search, the Output window displays the list of file locations where the text string was located. Each occurrence has the fully qualified filename, followed by the line number of the occurrence and the line containing the match.

6. To open a file containing a match, double-click the entry in the Output window, or move the insertion point to the entry and press ENTER.

   An editor window containing the file opens, and the line containing the selected match is highlighted. You can then jump to other occurrences of the text string by choosing the Next Error/Tag (F4) or Previous Error/Tag (SHIFT+F4) command from the Search menu or by double-clicking the specific entries in the Output window.

When you jump to a found string location specified in the Output window, the corresponding source file is loaded, if it is not already open in the editor.

The Find In Files Output window is a virtual window that is maintained even when not displayed. You can display the output from the last multiple-file search done during the current Visual C++ session by choosing the Output command from the Window menu or choosing the Find In Files tab in the Output window.

The drop-down list box connected to the Find What box records the last 16 text items you searched for.

Replacing Text

The Replace command searches the active window for a text string and replaces it with another text string. You can:

- Find a whole word match. This "find" matches all occurrences of a text string not preceded or followed by an alphanumeric character or the underscore (_).

- Find a case-sensitive match. This "find" searches for text that matches the capitalization of the text string.

- Use a general-pattern search using regular expressions. This "find" uses special character sequences—regular expressions—to search for text.

▶ **To replace text**

1. Position the insertion point where you want to start your search.

   The editor uses the location of the insertion point to select a default search string.

2. From the Search menu, choose Replace.

   The Replace dialog box appears.

3. Type the search text or a regular expression in the Find What box. If you type a regular expression, select the Regular Expression check box.

4. Type the replacement text in the Replace With box.

5. Select any of the Replace options.

   Begin replacing text by choosing Find Next or Replace All.

The drop-down list box connected to the Find What text box on the toolbar records the last 16 text items you searched for. Click the drop-down arrow to the right of the text box or press ALT+DOWN ARROW to open the list.

Using Regular Expressions

A regular expression is a search string that uses special characters to match a text pattern in a file.

▶ **To use a regular expression**

• Type a regular expression in the Find What text box.

The following table lists valid regular expressions.

Regular Expression	Description
.	Any single character.
*	None or more of the preceding character or expression. For instance, ba*c matches bc, bac, baac, baaac, and so on.
+	At least one or more of the preceding character or expression. For instance, ba+c matches bac, baac, baaac, but not bc.
^	The beginning of a line.
$	The end of a line.
[ ]	Any one of the characters contained in the brackets, or any of an ASCII range of characters separated by a hyphen. For instance, b[aeiou]d matches bad, bed, bid, bod and bud, and r[eo]+d matches red, rod, reed and rood, but not reod or roed. x[0-9] matches x0, x1, x2, and so on. If the first character in the brackets is ^ (caret), then the regular expression matches any characters except those in the brackets.

Regular Expression	Description
[^]	Any character except those following the ^ character (caret) in the brackets, or any of an ASCII range of characters separated by a hyphen. For instance, x[^0-9] matches xa, xb, xc, and so on, but not x0, x1, x2, and so on.
\{\}	Any sequence of characters between the escaped braces. For instance, \{ju\}+fruit finds jufruit, jujufruit, jujujujufruit, and so on. Note that it will not find jfruit, ufruit, or ujfruit because the sequence ju is not in any of those strings.
\{c\!c\!c\}	Any one of the characters separated by the alternation symbol (\!). For instance, \{j\!u\}+fruit finds jfruit, jjfruit, uufruit, and so on.
\~	Not the following character. b\~ad matches bbd, bcd, bdd, and so on, but not bad.
\(\)	Indicates a tagged expression to retain for replacement purposes. If the expression in the Find What text box is \(lpsz\)BigPointer, and the expression in the Replace With box is \1NewPointer, all selected occurrences of lpszBigPointer are replaced with lpszNewPointer. Each occurrence of a tagged expression is numbered according to its order in the Find What text box, and its replacement expression is \n, where 1 corresponds to the first tagged expression, 2 to the second, and so on. You can have up to 9 tagged expressions.
\:e	Predefined expression, where :e can be:
	:a Any alphanumeric character.
	:b Any white-space character.
	:c Any alphabetic character.
	:d Any decimal digit.
	:f Any part of a filename.
	:h Hexadecimal number.
	:i Microsoft C/C++ identifier.
	:n Unsigned number.
	:p Any directory path.
	:q Any quoted string.
	:w Any English word.
	:z Any unsigned decimal integer.
\	Removes pattern match characteristic in the Find What text box from the special characters listed above. For instance, 100$ matches 100 at the end of a line, but 100\$ matches the character string 100$ anywhere on a line.

Note You can use regular expressions with a search in a single source file with the Find button on the toolbar if you have previously selected Regular Expression in the Find or Replace dialog box.

Recording and Playing Stored Keystrokes

The Visual C++ text editor provides the facility to record and play back keystrokes. This feature allows you to automate a repetitive keyboard task. The playback will be available until a new set of keystrokes is recorded or the editing session is ended.

Recorded keystrokes are played back only into a single editor view. If a new editor view is activated while recording a macro, the recorder will remain in record mode and continue recording keystrokes. However, when the recorded keystrokes are played back, all the recorded keystrokes are played back into the single target text editor view.

Note The only commands that are recordable are editor commands associated with keystrokes. Find/Replace is *not* supported in keystroke recording. During recording, all mouse-driven selections in text windows are disabled.

▶ **To record keystrokes**

1. From the Tools menu, choose Record Keystrokes (CTRL+SHIFT+R).

2. Record editor keystrokes as desired. During record, all mouse-driven selections are disabled.

3. When finished with the keystroke recording, from the Tools menu, choose Stop Recording (CTRL+SHIFT+R).

   Toolbar: ▣

▶ **To play back keystrokes**

- From the Tools menu, choose Playback Recording (CTRL+SHIFT+P). The recorded keystrokes are played back into the last active editor window.

Setting Visual C++ Text Editor Options

Many parts of Visual C++ can be customized to suit your programming needs. You can:

- Set preferences for file saving.
- Enable or disable virtual spaces in the text editor.
- Set and use the selection margin.
- Modify tab, font, and syntax color settings.

Setting Save Preferences

You can set save preferences—such as whether to be prompted before saving a file —in the Options dialog box. As a default, Visual C++ saves all changed files before you build an application.

▶ **To change the default save behavior**

1. From the Tools menu, choose Options.

   The Options dialog box appears.

2. Select the Editor tab.

3. To change the default, clear the Save Before Running Tools check box.

4. To be prompted to save files before a build, select Prompt Before Saving Files, then choose OK.

Enabling Virtual Spaces in the Editor

The Visual C++ text editor can treat text selection and space insertion in one of two ways. When the virtual spaces option is enabled, spaces are inserted between the end of the line and the insertion point before new characters are added to the line. When the virtual spaces option is not enabled, the editor behaves like Microsoft Word for Windows and the insertion point is set to the end of the line.

▶ **To enable virtual spaces**

1. From the Tools menu, choose Options.

   The Options dialog box appears.

2. Select the Editor tab.

3. Select the Virtual Spaces check box.

4. Choose OK.

Setting and Using the Selection Margin

The selection margin is an area to the left of each line of text. You can use the mouse in this area to select text. The selection margin also displays information about source lines. Breakpoints, bookmarks, the instruction pointer, and the tag pointer are all indicated by colored widgets in the selection margin.

▶ **To set the selection margin**

1. From the Tools menu, choose Options.

   The Options dialog is displayed.

2. Select the Editor tab.

3. Select the Selection Margin check box.

4. Choose OK.

When the mouse is moved over the margin, the cursor changes to an up-and-right-pointing select arrow (a mirror image of the standard select arrow).

▶ **To use the selection margin**

- Do one of the following:

  ▪ Clicking the left mouse button in the margin selects the entire line to the right of the click. Dragging the mouse cursor in the selection margin selects multiple consecutive lines.

  ▪ Clicking the left mouse button or dragging the mouse cursor with the SHIFT key held down extends the selection.

  ▪ Holding down CTRL and clicking anywhere in the selection margin selects the entire file. (This is equivalent to choosing the Select All command on the Edit menu).

Setting Tabs

The editor supports tab stops in a source file. You can set the number of spaces a tab consists of, then either save them as tabs or spaces when you save the file. You can also toggle the display of tab symbols in a source file.

▶ **To change tab settings**

1. From the Tools menu, choose Options.

   The Options dialog box appears.

2. Select the Editor tab.

3. Under Tab Settings, in the Tab Stops box, type the number of spaces to be used as a tab stop. The default is four spaces.

4. Select the Keep Tabs option to treat each tab as a single tab character when the file is saved.

   Alternatively, select Insert Spaces to convert each tab to the number of spaces set in the Tab Stops box.

5. Choose OK.

Even with the Keep Tabs option checked, the editor converts tabs to multiple spaces when the file is open. You may notice that deleting a tab requires removing spaces rather than a single tab. The spaces are converted to tabs only when the file is saved to disk.

▶ **To display or hide tab symbols**

- Press CTRL+ALT+T.

  Tab symbols are displayed as >> whenever there is a tab in a source file. The CTRL+ALT+T keyboard shortcut is the only means of toggling the display of tab symbols.

You can press the TAB key to insert a single tab anywhere in your source file. You can also move a block of lines one tab to the right or left.

▶ **To insert tabs in front of a group of lines**

1. Select the group of lines.
2. Press TAB.

▶ **To delete tabs preceding a group of lines**

1. Select the group of lines.
2. Press SHIFT+TAB.

Note   SHIFT+TAB only returns to previous tab stops.

Setting the Font and Font Size

You can change the text font and font size with the Fonts command. You can change the font for a window or make a font the default for all windows. You may find different fonts in various windows give visual clues about the function of the windows—the default setting for source windows, a different font for the Watch window, and so on. You can use fonts and font size to better manage your window display.

▶ **To change a font type and font size**

1. From the Tools menu, choose Options.

   The Options dialog box appears.

2. Select the Fonts tab.

3. Select the font from the Font box. The text sample in the Sample box will change to the font you selected. Select the Show Proportional Fonts check box to display the available proportional fonts.

4. Select the size in points from the Size box. The text sample in the Sample box will change to the font size you selected.

The currently used default font for all your editor windows is indicated below the Default Font label. You can change the default font by selecting a font and a point size from the Font and Size list boxes and then choosing the Change Default button.

Text within the source window can be only one font and size. Multiple fonts cannot be displayed in the same source window. However, each source window can contain a different font and size, even when source windows with different fonts are attached to the same source file.

Changing Syntax Colors

Using different colors for various language elements such as functions and variables gives you immediate visual cues about the structure of your source code. You can change the default colors of these elements as well as the color of other text such as reserved words, breakpoints, errors, and bookmarks. You can also turn off syntax coloring for all source files. These changes are global and affect all source files with extensions recognized by Visual C++.

▶ **To change syntax coloring in an individual source file**

1. Click the source file window or use the Window menu to make the source window active.

   If there are multiple windows open on the source file, select one of them. Syntax coloring changes will appear in all windows opened on the source file.

2. From the Edit menu, choose Properties (ALT+ENTER).

   The Text File Properties page is displayed. The Language list box displays the current setting for syntax coloring. The three choices: are C, C++, and None.

3. Select C or C++ to set syntax coloring for that source file, or select None to turn syntax coloring off.

Note Global syntax coloring must be enabled before you can set the Syntax Coloring properties for any specific file. To enable global syntax coloring, select the Colors tab in the Options dialog box on the Tools menu and then select the Display Syntax Coloring check box.

▶ **To enable syntax coloring for user-defined types**

1. Create a text-only file USERTYPE.DAT containing a list of user-defined type names in the same directory as MSVC.EXE.

Note You must save USERTYPE.DAT as a text-only file. You can use the Visual C++ editor or Windows Notepad to create this file. The file should contain a list (one per line) of the user-defined strings that should be colored.

---

2. Click the source file window or use the Window menu to make the source window active.

   If there are multiple windows open on the source file, select one of them. Syntax coloring changes will appear in all windows opened on the source file.

3. From the Edit menu, choose Properties (ALT+ENTER).

   The Text File Properties page is displayed. The Language list box displays the current setting for syntax coloring. The three choices: are C, C++, and None.

4. Select C or C++ to set syntax coloring for that source file. Or select None to turn syntax coloring off.

The USERTYPE.DAT file is read when Visual C++ is initialized. It cannot be renamed, nor can it be reloaded during an editing session. The syntax coloring mechanism checks the USERTYPE.DAT file last. Thus, all previously defined coloring schemes take precedence over the user-defined types.

Tip   For any source file in Visual C++, you can specify which syntax coloring to apply—C or C++—or to turn off syntax coloring altogether. To do so, open the Text File Properties page for a source file and select C, C++, or None in the Language drop-down list box. This feature is especially useful if you have C++ code in a header file with an .H extension (to which the development environment automatically attaches C syntax coloring), or if you have C or C++ source code with filename extensions that Visual C++ doesn't recognize. You should be cautious when using nonstandard extensions, however. The file extensions of some source files (.CPP, .CXX, and .C) are used by the development environment to determine whether the C++ or C compiler is used during the build.

C H A P T E R   4

Working with Resources

In Visual C++, a resource is an interface element that the user gleans information from or manipulates to perform an action. Some basic resources are created for your project by AppWizard. These resources can be modified, and other resources can be created, using the various resource editors described in chapters 5 through 11. These editors have some shared basic procedures, such as how you create, open, and delete a resource, and there are common operations for working with symbols (resource identifiers) as well.

You can work with resources that were not developed in the Visual C++ environment or are not part of your current project. For example, you can:

- Work with nested and conditionally included resource files.
- Update existing resources or convert them to Visual C++ format.
- Import or export graphics resources to or from your current resource file.
- Include shared or read-only identifiers (symbols) that can't be modified by Visual C++.
- Include resources in your executable file (.EXE) that don't require editing (or that you don't want to be edited) during your current project, such as resources that are shared between several projects.
- Include resource types not supported by Visual C++.
- View existing symbols and modify symbol names and other values.

Note   Visual C++ includes sample resources that you can use in your own application. For information about using these, see "COMMON.RES Sample Resources" in Part 2 of *Programming with the Microsoft Foundation Class Library*.

The Visual C++ Files

You can save your application resource files as one of the following file extensions:

- .C, .CXX, and .CPP (application source file)
- .H (application include file)
- .RC (listing of resources)
- .RES (compiled resource file)
- .BMP, .DIB, .ICO, and .CUR (bitmap, device-independent bitmap, icon, and cursor)

Visual C++ also works with several additional files during your resource editing session:

Filename	Description
RESOURCE.H	Header file generated by Visual C++; contains symbol definitions.
projectname.APS	Binary version of the current resource file; used by Visual C++ for quick loading.
projectname.CLW	File containing information about the current project; used by ClassWizard.
projectname.MAK	File containing project compilation instructions.
projectname.VCP	A project configuration file.

Using Existing Resource Files Not Created with AppWizard

▶ **To update an existing resource (.RC) file for use with Visual C++**

1. Make a backup copy of your existing .RC file.
2. Add the .RC file to your project.
3. Open the resource file in Visual C++.

   Note Visual C++ uses the include path set using the Directories tab in the Options dialog box. In addition, relative include paths for a Visual C++ resource file must be based on the directory where the .RC file is currently located.

4. Save the Visual C++ version of the resource file.

Reading in and then saving resource files not created by AppWizard has two results that are important to be aware of:

- Visual C++ makes several changes to how your resource files are organized so that you can work with all your resources in one place.

- Several resource-related features supported by the Microsoft Foundation Class Library (MFC) are automatically available when your resource script file includes the library file AFXRES.H. For more information on how to manually add framework support to existing .RC files, see "Keeping ClassWizard Updated When Code Changes" on page 155 in Chapter 12.

Converting Existing Resource Files to Visual C++ Format

Saving a non-AppWizard resource (.RC) file for the first time in Visual C++ has several important consequences:

- Resources contained in files that were added to your old .RC file with include statements are written back to disk as part of the main Visual C++ resource file.

  For example, if your old project had dialog boxes in a separate .DLG file, this separate file is no longer needed since Visual C++ moves the dialog boxes into the main .RC file.

  However, if you have resource files containing resources that you do not want to edit in Visual C++, or that you want to continue to store in a separate resource file (such as a version resource file), move the resource to a separate file and add it back by using the Set Includes command on the Resource menu. For more information, see "Using Advanced Resource File Techniques" on page 73.

- Any symbol definitions included in your old .RC file are marked as read-only symbols by Visual C++ the first time you save the .RC file. To make the symbols available for modification and editing, remove them from the included header file and place them in the resource header, RESOURCE.H.

- Symbols that are defined with expressions rather than integers and used in the resource file are evaluated by Visual C++, but they are then written to the Visual C++ symbols header (.H) file as simple integers. To preserve the expressions for calculated symbol values, include them in a read-only symbols header file. For more information on using read-only symbols, see "Using Shared (Read-Only) or Calculated Symbols" on page 74.

- Conditional compilation statements in your old .RC file are evaluated by Visual C++ the first time the file is read in, but they are not written back to disk when you save the .RC file.

Note To preserve conditional compilation statements you should place the sections of your old .RC file containing these statements in a separate file, then include the file using the Set Includes command on the Resource menu.

- Comments in your old .RC file are not preserved.

In most cases, Visual C++ makes it easy and convenient to work with all your resources and symbols in a single Visual C++ file. However, Visual C++ also supports a nested resource file structure, conditionally included resource files, and expressions as symbol values if your project requires it. For more information, see "Using Advanced Resource File Techniques" on page 73.

Features Supported Only in Microsoft Foundation Class Library Resource Files

Normally when you build an MFC application for Windows from scratch using AppWizard, you start by generating a basic set of files, including a resource file, that contain the core features of the Microsoft Foundation classes. However, if you are editing a resource file for an application for Windows that is not based on MFC, the following features specific to the framework are not available in Visual C++:

- ClassWizard (Chapter 12)
- Menu prompt strings
- List Contents for combo-box controls

You can, however, add framework support to existing resource script files that do not have it.

▶ **To add framework support to .RC files that do not already have it**

1. From the Resource menu, choose Set Includes.

   The Set Includes dialog box appears.

2. In the Read-Only Symbol Directives box, replace the include statement for WINDOWS.H with the following:

   ```
   #include "afxres.h"
   ```

3. You may also need to add additional include files using the Compile-Time Directives box. For more information on include files, see the *Class Library Reference*.

4. Choose OK.

5. Close the resource file and then reopen it for the changes to take effect.

Using the Resource Editors

The Visual C++ resource editors are powerful and easy to use, providing the functionality you need to create and modify application resources. Your main tasks in using the resource editors generally consist of creating new resources, modifying existing resources, and deleting old resources. The resource editors are functionally consistent for ease of use.

Visual C++ lets you edit all of the Microsoft Windows resources that your application can use:

- Accelerator tables
- Bitmaps (toolbar buttons)
- Cursors
- Dialog boxes
- Icons
- Menus
- String tables
- Version information

Each resource is displayed in an appropriate editor. For example, graphical resources like toolbar buttons, cursors, and icons are modifiable bitmaps. The accelerator tables, string tables, and version information consist of formatted text. Dialog boxes are a combination of graphical components and text strings. Menus consist of text strings that appear in the menu bar. When you create or open a resource, the appropriate editor for it is selected automatically.

Tip   While working with resources, in many instances you can click the right mouse button to display a shortcut menu of frequently used commands. The commands available depend on what the pointer is pointing at. For example, if you click while pointing at a toolbar, the shortcut menu shows a list of toolbars that you can toggle on or off and commands to open the Toolbars dialog box and the Customize dialog box.

For information about using each of the resource editors, see the appropriate chapter in this book.

Common Resource Edit Procedures

The resource editors have many commands in common. For example, once you learn how to create and open a dialog box, you know the steps to creating and opening any of the other resources. The most common resource editing activity is either creating a new resource or opening an existing resource for editing.

▶ **To view the resource browser window**

- With the *PRJNAME*.MAK project window open, double-click the *PRJNAME*.RC item. The resource browser window appears (Figure 4.1).

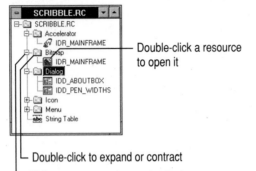

Double-click a resource to open it

Double-click to expand or contract

Click once to expand or contract

Figure 4.1   Resource Browser Window

When the resource browser window is first displayed, each of the resource categories is condensed. You can expand any category by clicking its "+" sign.

While viewing the resource browser window, standard Edit menu commands such as Undo, Cut, Copy, Paste, and Delete are available by using either the menu commands or the accelerator keys.

▶ **To create a new resource**

1. From the Resource menu, choose New (CTRL+R).
2. Select a resource from the Resource Type list box and choose OK.

   –Or–

- Click the corresponding toolbar button, as shown in Table 4.1:

Table 4.1   Toolbar New Resource Buttons

Resource	Button
Dialog box	🔲
Menu	🔲
Cursor	🔲
Icon	🔲
Bitmap	🔲
String table	🔲
Accelerator table	🔲
Version information	🔲

When a resource is created, Visual C++ assigns it a unique symbol name and value. If you need to change the symbol value, you can use the ID box on the resource's properties page. For more information on the properties page, use the Help button.

Tip The Properties window displays a thumbnail view of each graphical resource as you select its entry in the resource browser. To open the Properties window, from the Edit menu, choose Properties (ALT+ENTER). Click the pushpin button at the top left of the Properties window to keep it visible when it does not have focus.

▶ **To copy an existing resource**

1. In the resource browser window, select the resource you want to copy.

2. From the Edit menu, choose Copy (CTRL+C) and then Paste (CTRL+V).

▶ **To open an existing resource for editing**

1. In the resource browser window, select the resource you want to edit.

2. Press ENTER.

    –Or–

    Double-click the resource.

    The resource editor window opens for editing.

▶ **To save an edited resource (.RC) file**

1. From the File menu, choose Save.

    The resource is saved using its current name.

    –Or–

1. From the File menu, choose Save As.

2. In the Drives list box, select the target drive.

3. In the Directories list box, select the directory path.

4. Type the File Name for the file.

5. Choose OK.

    The resource is saved using the Save As name.

▶ **To delete an existing resource**

1. In the resource browser window, select the resource you want to delete.

2. From the Edit menu, choose Delete (DEL).

    The resource is deleted.

The easiest way to copy resources from either an existing resource or an executable file to your current resource file is to have both .RC files open in Visual C++ at the same time. Then use drag-and-drop to move items from one resource browser window to another (see Figure 4.2).

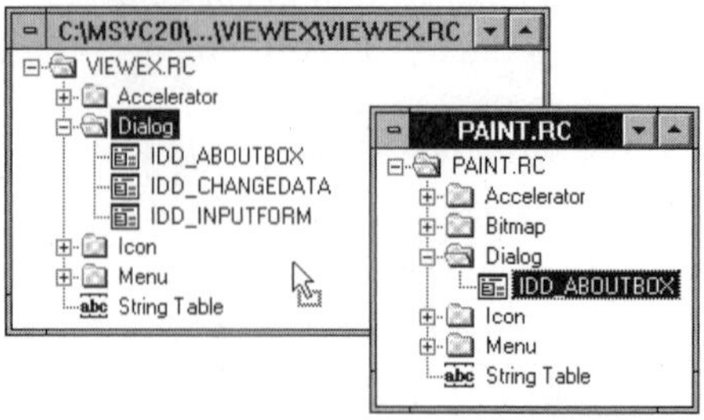

Figure 4.2   Using Drag-and-Drop to Copy Resources Between Files

Note Visual C++ includes sample resource files that you can use in your own application. For more information, see "COMMON.RES Sample Resources" in Part 2 of *Progtramming with the Microsoft Foundation Class Library*.

▶ **To copy resources from one file to another**

1. Open both files. Make sure both resource browser windows are visible.

2. In the resource browser window of the "from" file, select the resource you want to copy.

3. Hold down the CTRL key and drag the resource to the resource browser window of the "to" file.

    Dragging the resource without holding down the CTRL key moves the resource rather than copies it.

Note To avoid conflicts with symbol names or values in the existing file, Visual C++ may change the transferred resource's symbol value, or symbol name and value, when you copy it to the new file.

▶ **To import a separate bitmap, icon, or cursor file into your current resource file**

1. From the Resource menu, choose Import.

    The Import Resource dialog box appears.

2. Choose the name of the .BMP, .ICO, or .CUR file you want to import. When you choose OK, the file is added to the current resource file.

Tip   You can also copy a bitmap, icon, or cursor into your current resource file by dragging it from File Manager and dropping it into the Visual C++ resource browser window.

▶ **To export a bitmap, icon, or cursor as a separate file**

1. Select the bitmap, icon, or cursor you want to export. Visual C++ exports the graphic selected in the resource browser window or the graphic in the currently active image editor window.

2. From the <u>R</u>esource menu, choose <u>E</u>xport.

3. If you do not want to accept the current filename, type a new one.

4. Choose OK. The graphics file is saved on the disk.

Working with Symbols

A symbol is a resource identifier that consists of a text string (name) mapped to an integer value. Symbols provide a descriptive way of referring to resources and user-interface objects, both in your source code and while you're working with them in the resource editors.

When you create a new resource or resource object, Visual C++ provides a default name for the resource (for example, IDC_RADIO1) and assigns a value to it. The name-plus-value definition is stored in the Visual C++-generated file RESOURCE.H.

In working with symbols from within Visual C++, you can:

- Change the symbol associated with a resource or object.
- Change a symbol's name or value in the Symbol Browser (if the symbol hasn't been used yet).
- Change a symbol's name in the Properties window (if the symbol is already in use by a single object).
- Use the Symbol Browser to browse existing symbols, add new symbols, and change or delete unused symbols.

Note   When you are copying resources or resource objects from one .RC file to another, Visual C++ may change the transferred resource's symbol value, or symbol name and value, to avoid conflicts with symbol names or values in the existing file.

Changing a Symbol or Symbol Name

When you create a new resource or resource object, Visual C++ assigns it a default name—for example, IDD_DIALOG1. Use the resource's properties page to change the default symbol name or to change the name of any symbol already associated with a resource.

▶ **To change a resource's symbol name**

1. In the resource browser window, select the resource.

2. From the Edit menu, choose Properties (ALT+ENTER) to move directly to the resource's properties page.

3. In the ID box, type a new symbol name or select from the list of existing symbols. If you typed a new symbol name, Visual C++ assigns it a value automatically.

You can use the Symbol Browser to change the name of symbols not currently assigned to a resource. For more information, see "Changing Unassigned Symbols" on page 71.

Changing a Symbol's Numerical Value

Usually you can let Visual C++ assign the numerical value associated with the symbol names you define. However, there may be times when you need to change the symbol value associated with a resource—for example, when you want a group of controls or a series of related strings in the string table to have sequential IDs.

For symbols already associated with a single resource, use the resource's properties page to change the symbol value. For symbols associated with more than one resource or object, make the changes directly in RESOURCE.H using a text editor.

▶ **To change a symbol value assigned to a single resource or object**

1. Select the resource.

2. From the Edit menu, choose Properties (ALT+ENTER).

3. In the properties page ID box, type the symbol name followed by an equal sign and an integer. For example,

```
IDC_EDITNAME=5100
```

−Or−

1. Open the Symbol Browser, select the symbol you want to change, and choose Change.

   The Change Symbol dialog box appears.

2. Choose View Use.

   The resource and its properties page is displayed.

3. In the properties page ID box, type the symbol name followed by an equal sign and an integer. For example,

   ```
   IDC_EDITNAME=5100
   ```

The new value is stored in the symbol header file the next time you save the project. Only the symbol name remains visible in the ID box; the equal sign and value are not displayed after they are validated.

▶ **To change the numeric value of a symbol assigned to more than one resource or object**

1. End your editing session by closing the current resource file.

2. Open RESOURCE.H in a source window and make the necessary changes.

3. Save RESOURCE.H.

   The next time you open the project's .RC file, Visual C++ uses the new symbol values.

Note While editing RESOURCE.H, take special care not to define duplicate symbols. Visual C++ can detect duplicate symbols only if all symbols are created by Visual C++.

You can use the Symbol Browser to change the value of symbols not currently assigned to a resource. For more information, see "Changing Unassigned Symbols" on page 71.

Managing Symbols with the Symbol Browser

As your application grows in size and sophistication, so do the number of resources and symbols that must be created. Keeping track of large numbers of symbols scattered throughout several files can be difficult. The Symbol Browser (Figure 4.3) simplifies symbol management by offering a central tool through which you can:

- Quickly browse existing symbol definitions to see the value of each symbol, a list of symbols being used, and the resources assigned to each symbol.

- Create new symbols.

- Change the name and value of a symbol that is not in use.

- Delete a symbol if it is not being used.

- Move quickly to the appropriate Visual C++ resource editor where the symbol is being used.

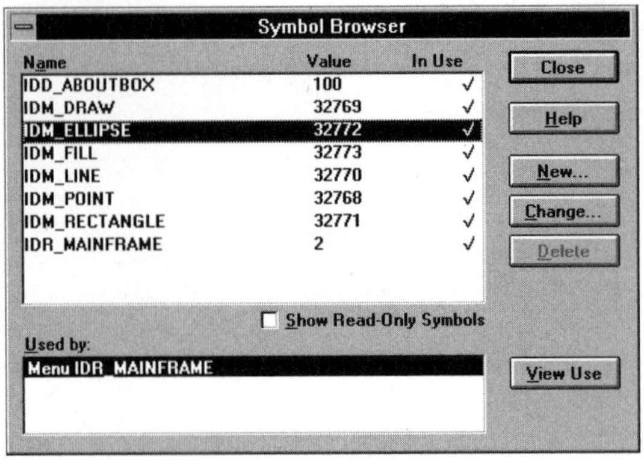

Figure 4.3   Symbol Browser

▶ **To open the Symbol Browser dialog box**

- From the Resource menu, choose Symbols.

  Toolbar: ▮ID=▮

Creating New Symbols

When you are beginning a new project, you may find it convenient to map out the symbol names you need before creating the resources they will be assigned to.

▶ **To create a new symbol using the Symbol Browser**

1. In the Symbol Browser dialog box, choose New.

   The New Symbol dialog box appears.

2. In the Name box, type a symbol name.

3. Accept the symbol value assigned by Visual C++ or, in the Value box, type a new value.

4. Choose OK to place the new symbol into the symbol list. The symbols appear in alphabetical order.

   If you type a symbol name that already exists, a message box appears stating that a symbol with that name is already defined. You cannot define two or more symbols with the same name, but you can define different symbols with the same numeric value. For more information, see "Symbol Name Restrictions" and "Symbol Value Restrictions," both on page 72.

Changing Unassigned Symbols

While in the Symbol Browser, you can edit or delete existing symbols that are not already assigned to a resource or object. You can change existing symbols that are in use in only one place by using the Change command to move to the appropriate resource's properties page or by moving to the properties page directly. You cannot change read-only symbols. A check mark in the In Use column of the Symbol Browser indicates that the symbol is being used. If Show Read-Only Symbols is selected, read-only symbols are also displayed. Editable symbols are displayed as bold text, and read-only symbols are displayed as normal text.

For more information on changing the name or value of a symbol already in use, see "Changing a Symbol or Symbol Name" on page 68.

▶ **To change an unassigned symbol using the Symbol Browser**

1. In the Name box, select the unassigned symbol you want and choose Change.

    The Change Symbol dialog box appears.

2. Edit the symbol's name or value in the boxes provided.

3. Choose OK.

▶ **To delete an unassigned symbol using the Symbol Browser**

*   Select the unassigned symbol that you want to delete, and choose Delete (DEL).

Note   Before deleting an unused symbol in a resource file, make sure it is not used elsewhere in the program or by resource files included at compile time.

Opening the Resource Editor for a Given Symbol

When you are browsing symbols in the Symbol Browser, you may want more information on how a particular symbol is used. The View Use command provides a quick way to get this information.

▶ **To move to the resource editor where a symbol is being used**

1. In the Name box of the Symbol Browser, select the symbol you want.

2. In the Used By box, select the resource type that interests you.

3. Choose View Use.

    The resource appears in the appropriate editor window.

Symbol Name Restrictions

All symbol names must be unique within the scope of the application. This prevents conflicting symbol definitions in the header files. Legal characters for a symbol name include A-Z, a-z, 0-9, and the underscore (_). Symbol names cannot begin with a number and are limited to 247 characters. Symbol names are case insensitive, but the case of the first symbol definition is preserved.

Symbol names can be used more than once in your application. For example, if you are writing a data-entry program with several dialog boxes containing a text box for a person's Social Security number, you may want to give all the related text boxes a symbol name of IDC_SSN. To do this, you can define a single symbol and use it as many times as needed.

While it is not required, symbol names are often given descriptive prefixes which indicate the kind of resource or object they represent. The Microsoft Foundation Class Library (MFC) uses the following symbol naming conventions:

Category	Prefix	Use
Resources	IDR_	Accelerator or menu (and associated resources)
	IDD_	Dialog
	IDC_	Cursor
	IDI_	Icon
	IDB_	Bitmap
Menu items	IDM_	Menu item
Commands	ID_	Command
Controls and child windows	IDC_	Control
Strings	IDS_	String in the string table
	IDP_	String-table string used for message boxes

For more information on framework naming conventions, see "Technical Note 20" in *Microsoft Foundation Class Library Technical Notes*.

Symbol Value Restrictions

In Visual C++, a symbol value can be any integer expressed in the normal manner for **#define** preprocessor directives. Here are some examples of symbol values:

```
18
4001
0x0012
-3456
```

Note Symbol values for resources (accelerators, bitmaps, cursors, dialogs, icons, menus, string tables, and version information) must be decimal numbers in the range from 0 to 32767 (but cannot be hexadecimal). Symbol values for parts of resources (such as dialog box controls or individual strings in the string table) can be from 0 to 65534 or from -32768 to 32767.

Some number ranges are used by Visual C++ and MFC for special purposes. For more information, see "Technical Note 20" in *Microsoft Foundation Class Library Technical Notes*.

In Visual C++, you cannot define a symbol value using other symbol strings. For example, the following symbol definition is not supported:

```
#define IDC_MYEDIT  IDC_OTHEREDIT  //not supported
```

You also cannot use preprocessor macros with arguments as value definitions. For example,

```
#define  IDD_ABOUT  ID(7) //not supported
```

is not a valid expression in Visual C++ regardless of what ID evaluates to at compile time.

Your application may have an existing file containing symbols defined with expressions. For more information on how to include the symbols as read-only symbols, see "Using Shared (Read Only) or Calculated Symbols" on page 74.

Using Advanced Resource File Techniques

You can use the Set Includes command on the Resource menu to modify Visual C++'s normal working arrangement of storing all resources in the project .RC file and all symbols in RESOURCE.H. For more information on symbols, see "Working with Symbols" on page 67.

In the Set Includes dialog box, use the Symbol Header File box to change the name of the header file where Visual C++ stores the symbol definitions for your resource file.

Use the Read-Only Symbol Directives box to include header files that contain symbols that should not be modified during a Visual C++ editing session. For example, you can use the Read-Only Symbol Directives box to include a symbol file that has been created to be shared among several projects. This box is also used to include MFC .H files.

Use the Compile-Time Directives box to include resource files that:

- Are created and edited separately from the resources in your main resource file.
- Contain compile-time directives, such as directives that conditionally include resources.
- Contain resources in a custom format.

The Compile-Time Directives box is also used to include standard MFC resource files.

Once you've made changes to your resource file using the Set Includes dialog box, you need to close the file and then reopen it for the changes to take effect.

Changing the Name of the Symbols Header File

Normally Visual C++ saves all symbol definitions in RESOURCE.H. However, you may need to change this include filename so that you can, for example, work with more than one resource file in the same directory.

▶ **To change the name of the resource symbol header file**

1. From the Resource menu, choose Set Includes.

   The Set Includes dialog box appears.

2. In the Symbol Header File box, type the new name for the include file.

3. Choose OK.

Using Shared (Read-Only) or Calculated Symbols

The first time Visual C++ reads a non-Visual C++ resource file, it marks all included header files as read-only. Subsequently, you can use the Set Includes command on the Resource menu to add additional read-only symbol header files.

One reason you may want to use read-only symbol definitions is for symbol files that you plan to share among several projects.

You would also use included symbol files when you have existing resources with symbol definitions that use expressions rather than simple integers to define the symbol value. For example,

```
#define   IDC_CONTROL1 2100
#define   IDC_CONTROL2 (IDC_CONTROL1+1)
```

Visual C++ will correctly interpret these calculated symbols as long as:

- The calculated symbols are placed in a read-only symbols file.
- Your resource file contains resources to which these calculated symbols are already assigned.

▶ **To include shared (read-only) symbols in your resource file**

1. From the Resource menu, choose Set Includes.

   The Set Includes dialog box appears.

2. In the Read-Only Symbol Directives box, use the #include compiler directive to specify the file where you want the read-only symbols to be kept. (The file should not be called RESOURCE.H, since that is the filename normally used by Visual C++'s main symbol header file.)

   Important What you type in the Read-Only Symbol Directives box is included in the resource file exactly as you type it. Make sure what you type does not contain any spelling or syntax errors.

   You should use the Read-Only Symbol Directives box to include files with symbol definitions only. Do not include resource definitions; otherwise, duplicate resource definitions will be created when it is saved.

   ---

3. Place the symbols in the file you specified.

   The symbols in files included in this way are evaluated each time you open your resource file, but they are not rewritten on the disk by Visual C++ when you save your file.

Including Resources From Other Files

Normally it is easy and convenient to work with Visual C++'s default arrangement of all resources in one .RC file. However, you can add resources in other files to your current project at compile time. Use the Set Includes dialog box's Compile-Time Directives box.

There are several reasons to place resources in a file other than Visual C++'s main resource file:

- To include resources that have already been developed and tested and need no further modification.
- To include resources that are being used by several different projects, or that are part of a source code version-control system, and thus must exist in a central location where modifications will affect all projects.
- To include resources (such as RCDATA resources) that are in a custom format.

- To include statements in your resource file that execute conditionally at compile time using compiler directives such as #ifdef and #else. For example, your project may have a group of resources that are bracketed by #ifdef _DEBUG ... #endif and are thus included only if the constant _DEBUG is defined at compile time.

- To include statements in your resource file that modify resource-file syntax by using #define to implement simple macros.

If you have sections in your existing resource files that meet any of these conditions, you should place the sections in one or more separate .RC files and include them in your project using the Set Includes dialog box. The *projectname*.RC2 file created by AppWizard in the RES subdirectory of a new project is used for this purpose.

▶ **To include resource files that will be added to your project at compile time**

1. Place the resources in a resource script file with a unique filename. (Do not use *projectname*.RC, since this is the filename used for Visual C++'s main resource file.)

2. From the Resource menu, choose Set Includes.

   The Set Includes dialog box appears.

3. In the Compile-Time Directives box, use the #include compiler directive to include the new resource file in the main Visual C++ resource file.

   The resources in files included in this way are made a part of your executable file at compile time. They are not available for editing or modification when you are working on your project's main .RC file. You need to work on included resource files in a separate Visual C++ resource script file.

CHAPTER 5

Using the Dialog Editor

The Visual C++ dialog editor allows you to place and arrange controls in a dialog-box template and to test the dialog box. The editor thus shows you the dialog box exactly as the user will see it. While using the dialog editor, you can define message handlers and manage data gathering and validation with the Visual C++ ClassWizard.

With the dialog editor, you can:

- Modify the dialog properties.
- Add, select, move, size, and arrange controls.
- Delete and copy controls.
- Change the tab order of controls.
- Define accelerator keys.
- Create a form-view dialog box.
- Test a dialog box.

You can also use the Visual C++ dialog editor to create and edit templates used with form views and dialog bars. A form view is a template for a program window whose client area contains dialog-box controls. For more information, see "Creating a Form View Dialog Box" on page 91.

Tip While using the dialog editor, in many instances you can click the right mouse button to display a shortcut menu of frequently used commands. The commands available depend on what the pointer is pointing at. For example, if you click while pointing at a dialog box, the shortcut menu shows the ClassWizard and Properties commands.

For information about common resource edit procedures such as creating new resources, opening existing resources, and deleting resources, see Chapter 4, "Working with Resources."

Modifying the Dialog Properties

When a dialog box is created, Visual C++ assigns it a unique symbol name, ID value, and caption. If you need to change these values, use the Dialog Properties page, which you can open using the Properties command on the Edit menu.

To change the symbol name (and accept the default ID value), type the symbol name in the ID text box.

To change the symbol name and ID value, type the symbol name followed by an equal sign and a new value. For example,

```
IDD_DIALOG1=1001
```

To modify the caption, type the name you want in the Caption text box.

For more information on the Dialog Properties page, choose the Help button near the top left corner of the Properties window.

Controlling the Properties Window

You have two display choices with the Properties window to suit your working style or the nature of the resource editing task. Use the "pushpin" command button in the upper-left corner of the Properties window to control how it is displayed.

Pushpin Up:

Pushpin Down:

When the button is in the down position, the Properties window stays visible even when you are working in another window. This is convenient if, during an editing session, you want to move back and forth frequently between setting properties and editing objects. Pressing ENTER after you change a value in the Properties window returns you to the editing window but leaves the Properties window visible.

When the button is in the up position, you can dismiss the active Properties window by pressing ENTER or ESC. This is useful if you want to concentrate on working in an editing window but need to bring up the Properties window briefly to change one or two values.

Types of Controls

The dialog editor lets you create dialog boxes that include the standard control types shown on the Controls toolbar in Figure 5.1:

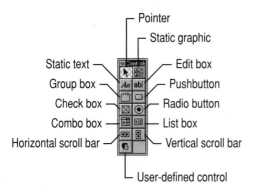

Figure 5.1   The Dialog Controls Toolbar

By default the Controls toolbar is displayed when the dialog editor is open, but you can modify this behavior.

▶   **To hide the Controls toolbar**

- Click the close box in the upper left corner of the Controls toolbar.

▶   **To show the Controls toolbar**

1. From the Tools menu, choose Toolbars.
2. Select the Controls check box, then choose Close.

Adding Controls

You add controls to a dialog box by selecting the control you want from the Controls toolbar. When displayed, the toolbar stays positioned above other open windows in your workspace.

The fastest way to add controls to a dialog box, reposition existing controls, or move controls from one dialog box to another is to use the drag-and-drop method described in Using Drag-and-Drop Editing in Chapter 3 on page 45. When you add a control to a dialog box with drag and drop, the control is given a standard height appropriate to that type of control.

You can also add a new control by clicking the Controls toolbar button for the control you want and:

- "Drawing" the control in the dialog box. This is a good method when you want to specify the initial size of the object.

- Clicking in the dialog box at the location you want. This is an alternative method to dragging and dropping.

When you add a control to a dialog box or reposition it, its final placement may be determined by whether or not you have Snap To Grid turned on. For information about Snap To Grid and other placement and alignment tools, see "Arranging Controls" on page 87.

▶ **To add a control to a dialog box using the drag-and-drop method**

1. Drag a control from the Controls toolbar to the dialog editor window (Figure 5.2).

   As you drag the control into the dialog box, a dotted outline of the control indicates its position.

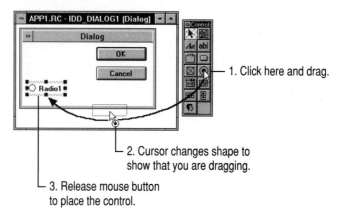

Figure 5.2   **Dragging a Control from the Controls Toolbar**

2. When the dotted outline of the control is in the position you want, release the mouse button. The control is given a standard size appropriate to that type of control.

▶ **To add a control to a dialog box using the point-and-click method**

1. On the Controls toolbar, click the button for the control you want.

   To add multiple controls of the same type, hold down the CTRL key while making your selection.

2. Move the pointer to the dialog box and click at the position(s) you want. The control is given a standard size appropriate to that type of control.

3. Press ESC when you are finished placing controls.

▶ **To add a control by "drawing" it with the pointer**

1. On the Controls toolbar, click the control you want.

   To add multiple controls of the same type, hold down the CTRL key while making your selection.

2. Place the pointer where you want the upper-left corner of the control to be located.

3. Drag the pointer to the right and downward; a dotted outline of the control appears.

4. When the control is the size you want, release the mouse button.

5. Press ESC when you are finished placing controls.

When you have added a control to the dialog box, you can change its caption or any other of its properties in the Properties window.

Selecting Controls

To move, copy, delete, or align controls, you select them and then perform the operation you want. In most cases, you need to select more than one control to use the sizing and alignment tools on the Dialog toolbar.

When a control is selected, it has a shaded border around it with solid (active) or hollow (inactive) "sizing handles," small squares that appear in the selection border.

When you are sizing or aligning multiple controls, the dialog editor uses the "dominant control" to determine how the other controls are sized or aligned. When multiple controls are selected, the dominant control has solid sizing handles; all the other selected controls have hollow sizing handles.

▶ **To select a control**

- Point to the control you want and click. The currently selected object (control or dialog box) is deselected.

  –Or–

- Use TAB to move forward or SHIFT+TAB to move backward through the controls in the dialog box.

▶ **To select more than one control**

1. From the Controls toolbar, select the pointer tool.

2. Drag to draw a selection box around the controls you want to select (Figure 5.3). Controls partially outside the selection box are not selected.

   When you release the mouse button, all controls inside the selection box are selected.

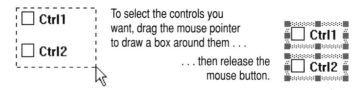

Figure 5.3   Selecting Multiple Controls

Once you have selected one or more controls, you can remove or add individual controls without disturbing the selection as a whole.

▶ **To alter an existing selection**

• Hold down the SHIFT key and click the control you want to remove from or add to the existing selection.

▶ **To change the dominant control when more than one control is selected**

• Hold down the CTRL key and click the control you want to use to influence the size or location of the others.

   The sizing handles change from hollow to solid. All further resizing or alignment is based on this control.

Moving Controls

You can use the following procedures to move one or more controls from one location to another in a dialog box or from one dialog box to another. If Snap To Grid is on, the control snaps to the alignment grid. For information on other ways to align multiple controls, see "Aligning Controls" on page 88.

▶ **To move a control within a dialog box**

• Drag the control to its new location.

   –Or–

- For a single control, select the control and use the arrow keys to move the control one dialog unit (DLU) at a time. A DLU is based on the size of the dialog-box font, normally 8-point MS Sans Serif. A horizontal DLU is the average width of the dialog-box font divided by four. A vertical DLU is the average height of the font divided by eight.

▶ **To move a control from one dialog box to another**

- If both dialog boxes are visible, drag the control to its new location. (Hold down the CTRL key while dragging if you just want to copy the control.)

  –Or–

- Use the Cut and Paste commands on the Edit menu. The control is placed in the same position as in the original dialog box.

Tip   In rare cases, you may need to place a control outside a dialog box. To do this, hold down the ALT key while dragging the control.

Deleting and Copying Controls

Use Edit menu commands to delete and copy controls.

▶ **To delete a control**

1. Select the control.
2. From the Edit menu, choose Cut (CTRL+X) or Delete (DEL).

▶ **To copy a control**

- Drag the control while holding down the CTRL key.

  –Or–

- Use the Copy (CTRL+C) and Paste (CTRL+V) commands on the Edit menu.

When you paste a control into a new dialog, it is placed in the same position it had in the old dialog box.

Sizing Individual Controls

Use the sizing handles to resize a control. When the pointer is positioned on a sizing handle, it changes shape to indicate the direction in which the control will be resized (see Figure 5.4). Active sizing handles are solid; if a sizing handle is hollow, the control cannot be resized along that axis.

When you change the size of a control, its final shape may be affected by whether or not you have Snap To Grid turned on. For more information, see "Using Snap to Grid" on page 88.

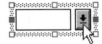

Figure 5.4   Sizing a Control

▶ **To size a control**

1. Click the control or select it with the TAB key.

2. Use the sizing handles to change the size of the control:

    ▪ Sizing handles at the top and sides change the horizontal or vertical size.

    ▪ Sizing handles at the corners change both horizontal and vertical size.

    –Or–

    Use the SHIFT key plus the arrow keys to resize the control one DLU at a time.

You can automatically change the size of a control so that it is the appropriate size for its text caption.

▶ **To resize a control to fit its caption**

1. Select the control.

2. From the Layout menu, choose Size to Content (F7).

When you select a drop-down combo box or drop-down list box to size it, only the right and left sizing handles are active (Figure 5.5). Use these handles to set the width of the box as it is initially displayed.

You can also set the vertical size of the drop-down portion of the box.

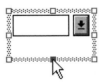

Click the button to change to drop-down view . . .

. . . then drag the sizing handle to change the size of the drop-down box.

Figure 5.5   Sizing the Drop-down Portion of a Combo Box

▶ **To set the size of the combo box drop-down area**

1. Click the drop-down arrow at the right of the combo box (see Figure 5.5).

   The outline of the control changes to show the size of the combo box with the drop-down area extended.

2. Use the bottom sizing handle to change the initial size of the drop-down area.

3. Click the drop-down arrow again to close the drop-down portion of the combo box.

You can resize a group of controls based on the size of the dominant control. You can also resize a control based on the dimensions of its caption text.

▶ **To make controls the same width, height, or size**

1. Select the controls you want to resize.

2. Make sure the correct dominant control is selected. The final size of the controls in the group depends on the size of the dominant control. For more information on selecting the dominant control, see "Selecting Controls" on page 81.

3. Choose one of the following tools on the Dialog toolbar:

   - Make Same Width (CTRL+MINUS SIGN)

     Toolbar: ⊞

   - Make Same Height (CTRL+BACKSLASH)

     Toolbar: ⊞

   - Make Same Size (CTRL+EQUAL SIGN)

     Toolbar: ⊞

Changing the Tab Order

Tab order is the order in which the TAB key moves the input focus from one control to the next within a dialog box. Usually the tab order proceeds from left to right in a dialog box, and from top to bottom. Each control has a properties page with a Tabstop check box used to determine whether a control actually receives input focus or not.

Even controls that do not have the Tabstop property set need to be part of the tab order. This can be important, for example, when you define mnemonics for controls that do not have captions. Static text that contains a mnemonic for a related control must immediately precede the related control in the tab order.

Note If your dialog box contains overlapping controls, changing the tab order may change the way the controls are displayed. Controls that come first in the tab order are always displayed on top of any overlapping controls that follow them in the tab order.

▶ **To change the tab order for all controls in a dialog box**

1. From the Layout menu, choose Tab Order (CTRL+D).

   A number at the upper left of each control shows its place in the current tab order.

2. Set the tab order by clicking each control in the order you want the TAB key to follow.

3. Press ENTER to exit Tab Order mode.

▶ **To change the existing tab order**

To change the existing tab order, specify the starting control; that is, select the control *prior to* the one where you want the changed order to begin. The selected control determines the number of the control you click next. For example, if you are in Tab Order mode and control number 3 is selected, the next control you click is set to number 4.

1. From the Layout menu, choose Tab Order (CTRL+D).

2. Specify where the change in order will begin. To do this, hold down the CTRL key and click the control *prior to* the one where you want the changed order to begin.

   For example, if you want to change the order of controls 7 through 9, select control 6 first.

   Note To set a specific control to number 1 (first in the tab order), double-click the control.

3. Reset the tab order by clicking the controls in the order you want the TAB key to follow.

4. Press ENTER to exit Tab Order mode.

Defining Accelerator Keys

Normally keyboard users move the input focus from one control to another in a dialog box with the TAB and arrow keys. However, you can define a mnemonic key that allows users to choose a control by pressing a single key.

Note All the mnemonics within a dialog box should be unique.

▶ **To define a mnemonic key for a control with its own visible caption (push buttons, check boxes, and radio buttons)**

1. Select the control.

2. From the Edit menu, choose Properties (ALT+ENTER) to open the control's properties page.

3. In the Caption box, type an ampersand (&) in front of the letter you want as the mnemonic for that control.

   An underline appears in the displayed caption to indicate the mnemonic key.

▶ **To define a mnemonic for a control without a visible caption**

1. Make a caption for the control by using a static text control. In the static text caption, type an ampersand (&) in front of the letter you want as the mnemonic.

2. Make sure the static text control immediately precedes the control it labels in the tab order.

Arranging Controls

The dialog editor provides layout tools that align and size controls automatically. For most tasks, you can use the Dialog toolbar (Figure 5.6). All commands are also available on the Layout menu and most have shortcut keys.

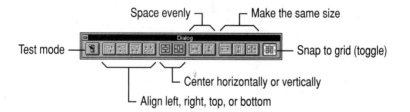

Figure 5.6   Dialog Toolbar

Many layout commands are available only when more than one control is selected. For information on selecting more than one control, see "Selecting Controls" on page 81.

The location, height, and width of the current control is displayed in the lower-right corner of the Visual C++ status bar (Figure 5.7). When more than one control is selected, the position indicators show the position of the dominant control (the control with solid sizing handles). When the dialog box is selected, the status bar displays the position of the dialog box and its height and width.

┌─ Height and width of object

⊹ 129, 6   ⊡ 50×14

└─ Position of selected object relative to
upper-left corner of containing window

Figure 5.7   Dialog Editor Position Indicators

The location and size of a dialog box, as well as the location and size of controls within it, are measured in dialog box units (DLUs).

Using Snap to Grid

When you are placing or arranging controls in a dialog box, you can use the layout grid for more precise positioning. When the grid is turned on, controls appear to "snap to" the dotted lines of the grid as if magnetized. You can turn this "snap to grid" feature on and off and change the size of the layout grid cells.

▶ **To turn Snap To Grid on or off**

1. From the Layout menu, choose Grid Settings.

2. Select or clear the Snap To Grid check box.

   You can still control Snap To Grid in individual dialog editor windows using the Snap To Grid button on the Dialog toolbar.

▶ **To change the size of the layout grid**

1. From the Layout menu, choose Grid Settings.

2. Type the height and width in DLUs for the cells in the grid. The minimum height or width is 4 DLUs. For more information on DLUs, see "Moving Controls" on page 82.

Aligning Controls

Once controls are in place, the dialog editor offers a variety of ways to refine their positions. You can:

- Align a group of controls along their left, right, top, or bottom edges.

- Align a group of controls on their center, either horizontally or vertically.

- Even the spacing between a group of three or more controls.

- Center one or more controls in the dialog box, vertically or horizontally.
- Automatically give push buttons a standard position along the bottom or on the right of the dialog box.

▶ **To align controls**

1. Select the controls you want to align.
2. Make sure the correct dominant control is selected. The final position of the group of controls depends on the position of the dominant control. For more information on selecting the dominant control, see "Selecting Controls" on page 81.
3. From the Layout menu, choose Align Controls, and then choose one of the following alignments:

   - The Left command aligns the selected controls along their left side (CTRL+LEFT ARROW).

     Toolbar:

   - The Right command aligns the selected controls along their right side (CTRL+RIGHT ARROW).

     Toolbar:

   - The Top command aligns the selected controls along their top edges (CTRL+UP ARROW).

     Toolbar:

   - The Bottom command aligns the selected controls along their bottom edges (CTRL+DOWN ARROW).

     Toolbar:

▶ **To align controls on their center, vertically or horizontally**

1. Select the controls you want to center.
2. Make sure the correct dominant control is selected. The final position of the group of controls depends on the position of the dominant control. For more information on selecting the dominant control, see "Selecting Controls" on page 81.
3. From the Layout menu, choose Align Controls, and then choose Vert. Center (F9) or Horiz. Center (SHIFT+F9).

▶ **To even the spacing between controls**

1. Select the controls you want to rearrange.

2. From the Layout menu, choose Space Evenly, and then choose one of the following spacing alignments:

   ▪ Across (ALT+LEFT ARROW or ALT+RIGHT ARROW). Controls are spaced evenly between the leftmost and the rightmost control selected.

     Toolbar: ⊬⊣

   ▪ Down (ALT+UP ARROW or ALT+DOWN ARROW). Controls are spaced evenly between the topmost and the bottommost control selected.

     Toolbar: ⊤

▶ **To center controls in the dialog box**

1. Select the control or controls you want to rearrange.

2. From the Layout menu, choose Center In Dialog, and then choose one of the following arrangements:

   ▪ Vertical (CTRL+F9)

     Toolbar: ⊟

     Controls are centered vertically in the dialog box.

   ▪ Horizontal (CTRL+SHIFT+F9)

     Toolbar: ▦

     Controls are centered horizontally in the dialog box.

▶ **To arrange push buttons along the right or bottom of the dialog box**

1. Select one or more push buttons.

2. From the Layout menu, choose Arrange Buttons, and then choose one of the following arrangements:

   ▪ Right (CTRL+B)

   ▪ Bottom (CTRL+SHIFT+B)

   The selected buttons are positioned in a standard arrangement along the bottom or right side of the dialog box. If a control other than push buttons is selected, its position is not affected.

Using Custom Controls

A custom control is a special-format dynamic-link library (DLL) or object file used to add additional features and functionality to the user interface of the Windows NT operating system. A custom control can be a variation on an existing Windows dialog-box control (for example, a text box suitable for use with Windows for Pen Computing) or a totally new category of control.

Working with User-Defined Controls

The dialog editor Controls toolbar button for user-defined controls is shown below. The dialog editor user-defined controls let you use existing custom controls regardless of their format.

Toolbar:

With user-defined controls, Visual C++ allows you to:

- Set the location in the dialog box.
- Enter a caption.
- Identify the name of the control's Windows class (your application code must register the control by this name).
- Type a 32-bit hexadecimal value that sets the control's style.

When you are designing a dialog box that contains custom controls, the custom control is displayed as a gray square. In test mode the custom control also is displayed as a gray square, and its run-time behavior is not simulated.

▶ **To edit user-defined control properties**

1. Select the control.
2. From the Edit menu, choose Properties (ALT+ENTER).
3. Type or modify the information as appropriate.

Creating a Form View Dialog Box

You can use the dialog editor to create a template that is used as a "form view," a **CView**-compatible window that contains dialog-box controls. An application that might need a form view is one in which the primary program function is data entry. In this case, the program's main view contains nothing but dialog-box controls for entering data.

To construct a form view, you create a dialog box as you normally would but set several style properties differently. You then incorporate the form view into your program using the Microsoft Foundation Class Library **CFormView** class. You can use the same procedure to create a template for use with the **CDialogBar** class. For more information, see the *Class Library Reference*.

▶ **To create a dialog box template for use with the CFormView or CDialogBar class**

1. Use the dialog editor in the usual way to create a dialog-box template with the controls arranged as you want them to appear in the form view.

2. From the Edit menu, choose Properties (ALT+ENTER).

3. Select the Styles tab and set the following properties:

   ▪ In the Style box, select Child.

   ▪ In the Border box, select None.

   ▪ Clear the Visible check box.

4. Select the General tab, and clear the dialog-box template's caption.

5. Incorporate the template into your program using the **CFormView** class.

Testing a Dialog Box

You can simulate the run-time behavior of a dialog box from within the dialog editor without compiling your program. This gives you immediate feedback on how the layout of controls appears and performs and thus speeds up the user-interface design process.

When you are in test mode you can:

▪ Type text, select from combo-box lists, turn options on and off, and choose commands.

▪ Test the tab order.

▪ Test the grouping of controls such as radio buttons or check boxes.

▪ Test the dialog box's keyboard shortcuts (for controls that have mnemonic keys defined for them).

Note Connections to dialog-box code made using ClassWizard are not simulated during dialog-box test mode.

When you test a dialog box, it is usually displayed at a location relative to the main Visual C++ program window. If the dialog box's Absolute Align property is selected, the dialog box is displayed at a position relative to the upper-left corner of the screen.

▶   **To test a dialog box**

1. From the Resource menu, choose Test (CTRL+T).

    Toolbar:

2. To end the test session, do one of the following actions:

    ▪   Press ESC.

    ▪   Close the dialog box using its control-menu box (ALT+F4).

    ▪   Choose a push button with a symbol name of IDOK or IDCANCEL.

C H A P T E R   6

Using the Menu Editor

Menus allow you to arrange commands in a logical, easy-to-find fashion. With the Visual C++ menu editor, you create and edit menus in Visual C++ by working directly with a menu bar that closely resembles the one in your finished application.

With the menu editor, you can:

- Create standard menus and commands.
- Create shortcut (pop-up) menus.
- Assign shortcut keys, accelerator keys, and status bar prompts to menus and commands.
- Move menus or commands from one place to another.

In addition, you can use ClassWizard to hook menu items to code. For more information on connecting interface objects to message handling functions, see Chapter 12, "Using ClassWizard."

Tip While using the menu editor, in many instances you can click the right mouse button to display a shortcut menu of frequently used commands. The commands available depend on what the pointer is pointing at. For example, if you click while pointing at a menu item, the shortcut menu shows Cut, Copy, Paste, and View As Popup commands, as well as commands to open ClassWizard and the properties page for the selected item.

For information about common resource edit procedures such as creating new resources, opening existing resources, and deleting resources, see Chapter 4, "Working with Resources."

Figure 6.1 identifies the terms used to describe menu editing in the procedures that follow.

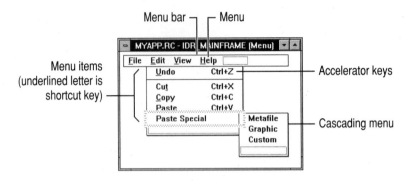

Figure 6.1   Menu Terminology

Creating Menus or Menu Items

You can create menus on the menu bar, cascading menus, and menu commands.

▶ **To create a menu on the menu bar**

1. Select the new-item box (an empty rectangle) on the menu bar (see Figure 6.2). You can also move to the new-item box with the TAB (move right) and SHIFT+TAB (move left) keys or the right and left arrow keys.

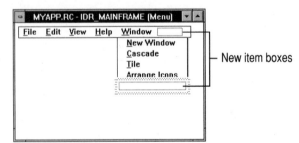

Figure 6.2   Menu Editor New-Item Boxes

2. Type the name of the menu. When you start typing, focus automatically shifts to the Menu Item Properties page, and the text you type appears both in the Caption box and in the menu editor window.

   You can define a mnemonic key that allows the user to select the menu with the keyboard. Type an ampersand (&) in front of a letter to specify it as the mnemonic. Make sure all the mnemonics on a menu bar are unique.

   Once you have given the menu a name on the menu bar, the new-item box shifts to the right, and another new-item box opens below for adding menu items.

   Note   To create a single-item menu on the menu bar, clear the Pop-up check box on the Menu Item Properties page.

▶ **To create a menu item**

1. First, create a menu according to the steps outlined in the previous procedure.

2. Select the menu's new-item box.

   –Or–

   Select an existing menu item and press INS. The new-item box is inserted before the selected item.

3. Type the name of the menu item. When you start typing, focus automatically shifts to the Menu Item Properties page, and the text you type appears in the Caption box.

   You can define a mnemonic key that allows the user to select the menu command. Type an ampersand in front a letter to specify it as the mnemonic. The mnemonic allows the user to select the menu command by typing that letter.

4. In the ID box, type the menu item ID, or select an existing command identifier. If you don't specify an ID, Visual C++ will generate an ID for you based on the command name.

5. On the properties page, select the menu item styles that apply.

   For information on what each menu item style means, choose the Menu Item Properties page Help button.

   Button: 🔘

6. In the Prompt box on the properties page, type the prompt string you want to appear in your application's status bar. This feature is only available with Microsoft Foundation Class Library resource script (.RC) files.

   This creates an entry in the string table with the same resource identifier as the menu item you created.

7. Press ENTER to complete the menu item. The new-item box is selected so you can create additional menu items.

▶ **To create a cascading (hierarchical) menu**

1. Select the new-item box on the menu where you want the cascading menu to appear. Then type the name of the menu item that, when selected, will cause the cascading menu to appear.

   When you start typing, focus automatically shifts to the Menu Item Properties page, and the text you type appears in the Caption box

   –Or–

   Select an existing menu item that you want to be the parent item of the cascading menu, and press ALT+ENTER.

2. On the properties page, select the Pop-up check box. This marks the menu item with the cascading menu symbol (▶), and a new-item box appears to its right.

3. Add additional menu items to the cascading menu according to the instructions in the previous procedure.

Selecting Menus and Menu Items

▶ **To select a menu and display its menu items**

- Click the menu caption on the menu bar or the parent item of the cascading menu. Then click the menu item you want.

  –Or–

- Move to the menu caption with the TAB (move right) and SHIFT+TAB (move left) keys or the right and left arrow keys.

▶ **To select one or more menu items**

1. Click the menu or cascading menu you want.

   Its menu items are displayed.

2. Click to select a menu item, or press the SHIFT key while clicking to select multiple menu items. Holding down the SHIFT key and clicking an already-selected menu item deselects it.

   –Or–

   With the pointer outside the menu, drag to draw a selection box around the menu items you want to select.

Creating Shortcut Menus

Shortcut menus display frequently used commands with a right mouse click. They can be context sensitive to the location of the pointer. Using shortcut menus in your application requires building the menu itself and then connecting it to application code.

Once you have created the menu resource, your application code needs to load the menu resource and use the TrackPopupMenu command to cause the menu to appear. Once the user has dismissed it by clicking outside it, or has clicked on a command, that function will return. If the user chooses a command, that command message will be sent to the window whose handle was passed.

▶ **To create a shortcut menu**

1. Create a menu bar with an empty title.

2. Define the shortcut menu items using the properties window.

3. Save the menu dialog.

▶ **To connect a shortcut menu to your application**

- Add the following code to your source file:

```
CMenu menu;
menu.LoadMenu(IDR_MENU1);
GetsubMenu(0)._TrackPopupMenu(IDM_LEFTALIGN, \
  x, y, theApp.m_pMainWnd);
```

Moving and Copying Menus and Menu Items

▶ **To move or copy menus or menu items using drag-and-drop**

1. Drag (or to copy, hold down the CTRL key and drag) the item you want to move to:

    ▪ A new location on the current menu.

    ▪ A different menu. (You can navigate into other menus by dragging the cursor over them.)

2. Drop the menu item when the insertion guide (see Figure 6.3) shows the position you want.

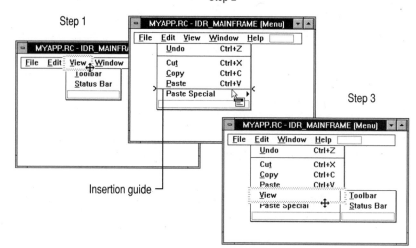

Figure 6.3   Moving a Menu to a Cascading Menu

▶ **To move or copy menus or menu items using the menu commands**

1. Select one or more menus or menu items.

2. From the Edit menu, choose Cut (to move) or Copy (to copy). You can also use the keyboard shortcuts for Cut (CTRL+X or SHIFT+DEL) and Copy (CTRL+C or SHIFT+INS).

3. If you are moving the items to another menu resource or resource script file, make that menu editor window active.

4. Select the position of the menu or menu item you want to move or copy to.

5. From the Edit menu, choose Paste (CTRL+V). The moved or copied item is placed before the item you select.

Note   You can also drag, copy, and paste to other menus in other menu windows.

Viewing the Menu Resource as a Pop-up Menu

Normally, when you are working in the menu editor, a menu resource is displayed as a menu bar. However, you may have menu resources that are added to the application's menu bar while the program is running. To see what a menu resource looks like as a pop-up menu, use the menu editor's View As Popup command on the Resource menu.

▶ **To view a menu resource as a pop-up menu**

- From the Resource menu, choose View As Popup.

  To change back to the menu-bar view, choose View As Popup again.

Associating a Menu Item with an Accelerator Key

Many times you want a menu item and a keyboard combination to issue the same program command. You do this by assigning the same resource identifier to the menu item and to an entry in your application's accelerator table. You then edit the menu item's caption to show the name of the accelerator key.

▶ **To associate a menu item with an accelerator key**

1. In the menu editor, select the menu item you want. From the Edit menu, choose Properties (ALT+ENTER) or double-click the item.

2. In the Caption box, add the name of the accelerator key to the menu caption:

   - Following the menu caption, type the escape sequence for a TAB (\t), so that all the menu's accelerator keys are left-aligned.

   - Type the name of the modifier key (CTRL, ALT, or SHIFT) followed by a plus sign and the name, letter, or symbol of the additional key.

   For example, to assign CTRL+O to the Open command on the File menu, you modify the menu item's caption so that it looks like this:

   ```
   Open\tCtrl+O
   ```

   The menu item in the menu editor is updated to reflect the new caption as you type it.

3. Create the accelerator-table entry in the accelerator editor and assign it the same identifier as the menu item. Use a key combination that you think will be easy to remember.

   For more information on creating and naming accelerator resources, see Chapter 7, "Using the Accelerator Editor."

Associating a Menu Item with a Status Bar Prompt

Your application can display descriptive text for each of the menu items that may be selected. MFC can handle this for you if you have a string in the string table whose ID is the same as the command. You do this by assigning a text string to each menu item using the Menu Item Properties page.

▶ **To associate a menu item with a status bar text string**

1. Select the menu item.

2. In the Prompt box, type the associated status bar text.

C H A P T E R   7

Using the Accelerator Editor

An accelerator table is a Windows resource that contains a list of accelerator keys (also known as shortcut keys) and the command identifiers that are associated with them. A program can have more than one accelerator table.

Normally, accelerators are used as keyboard shortcuts for program commands that are also available on a menu or toolbar. However, you can use the accelerator table to define key combinations for commands that don't have a user-interface object associated with them.

You can use ClassWizard to hook accelerator key commands to code. For more information on ClassWizard, see Chapter 12, "Using ClassWizard."

With the accelerator editor, you can:

- Add, delete, change, and browse the accelerator key assignments in your project.
- View and change the resource identifier associated with each entry in the accelerator table. The identifier is used to reference each accelerator table entry in program code.
- Associate an accelerator key with a menu item.

Tip While using the accelerator editor, in many instances you can click the right mouse button to display a shortcut menu of frequently used commands. The commands available depend on what the pointer is pointing at. For example, if you click while pointing at an accelerator entry, the shortcut menu shows the Cut, Copy, New Accelerator, ClassWizard, and Properties commands.

Note Windows does not allow the creation of empty accelerator tables. If you create an accelerator table with no entries, it is deleted automatically when you exit Visual C++.

For information about common resource edit procedures such as creating new resources, opening existing resources, and deleting resources, see Chapter 4, "Working with Resources."

Editing an Accelerator Table

▶ **To add an entry to an accelerator table**

1. Select the new-item box at the end of the list, or press INS.

2. Type the accelerator key to define it. (Pressing INS, or typing the key name with the new-item box selected, moves the focus to the Accel Properties page automatically. What you type is entered in the key box.)

Note Make sure all accelerators you define are unique. When duplicate accelerator keys are assigned, only the first one works correctly.

▶ **To delete an entry from an accelerator table**

1. Select the entry you want to delete. Hold down the CTRL or SHIFT key while clicking to select multiple entries.

2. From the Edit menu, choose Delete (DEL).

▶ **To move or copy an accelerator table entry from one resource script file to another**

1. Open the accelerator editor windows in both resource script files.

2. Select the entry you want to move.

3. Drag the entry to its new location.

   –Or–

   Use the Copy (or Cut) and Paste commands on the Edit menu.

Note When you copy—rather than move—an entry, duplicate accelerator keys are created. Visual C++ does not prompt you to resolve accelerator key conflicts.

Setting Accelerator Properties

The Accel Properties page allows you to control the features of each accelerator key. By default, the properties page is dismissed when it does not have focus. If you want the properties page to remain on the screen, even when it does not have focus, click the pushpin at the upper left corner of the window.

The following are legal entries in the Key box of an accelerator properties page:

- An integer between 0 and 255 in decimal, hexadecimal, or octal format. The setting of the Type property determines if the number is an ASCII or virtual key value.

  Single-digit numbers are always interpreted as the corresponding key, rather than as ASCII values. To enter an ASCII value from 0 to 9, precede it with two zeros (for example, 006).

- A single keyboard character. Uppercase A–Z or the numbers 0–9 can be either ASCII or virtual key values; any other character is ASCII only.

- A single keyboard character in the range A–Z (uppercase only), preceded by a caret (^)—for example, ^C. This enters the ASCII value of the key when it is pressed with the CTRL key held down.

Note When entering an ASCII value, the CTRL and SHIFT modifiers on the properties page are not available. You cannot use a control-key combination entered with a caret to create a virtual accelerator key.

- Any valid virtual key identifier. The Key box on the properties page contains a list of standard virtual key identifiers.

Tip Another way to define an accelerator key is to choose the Next Key Typed button and then press any of the keys on the keyboard.

Associating an Accelerator Key with a Menu Item

Many times you want a menu item and a keyboard combination to issue the same program command. You do this by assigning the same resource identifier to the menu item and to an entry in your application's accelerator table. You then edit the menu item's caption to show the name of the accelerator. For more information on menu items and accelerator keys, see "Associating a Menu Item with an Accelerator Key" on page 100 in Chapter 6.

C H A P T E R   8

Using the String Editor

A string table is a Windows resource that contains a list of IDs, values, and captions for all the strings of your application. For example, the status bar prompts are located in the string table. An application can have only one string table.

The Visual C++ string editor allows you to edit a program's string table resource. In a string table, strings are grouped into segments, or blocks, of 16 strings each. The segment a string belongs to is determined by the value of its identifier; for example, strings with identifiers of 0 to 15 are in one segment, strings with values of 16 to 31 are in a second segment, and so on. Thus, to move a string from one segment to another you need to change its identifier.

Individual string segments are loaded on demand in order to conserve memory. For this reason, programmers usually try to group strings into logical groupings of sixteen or less and then to use each group or segment only when it's needed.

With the string editor, you can:

- Find a string in the string table.
- Add a string table entry.
- Delete individual strings.
- Move a string from one segment to another.
- Move a string from one resource script to another.
- Change a string or its identifier.
- Add formatting or special characters to a string.

Figure 8.1 shows the string editor.

ID	Value	Caption
IDR_MAINFRAME	2	VIEWEX Windows Application
IDR_TEXTTYPE	3	\nText\nSimple Text
IDR_INPUTTYPE	5	\nInput\nInput Form View
IDR_SPLIT2TYPE	6	\nBoth\nSplitter Frame with both
IDR_SPLIT3TYPE	7	\nTri\nThree-way Splitter Frame
AFX_IDS_APP_TITLE	57344	VIEWEX Windows Application

VIEWEX.RC - [String Table]

Figure 8.1   The String Editor

Tip While using the string editor, in many instances you can click the right mouse button to display a shortcut menu of frequently used commands. The commands available depend on what the pointer is pointing at. For example, if you click while pointing at a string table entry, the shortcut menu shows the Cut, Copy, New String, and Properties commands.

Note Windows does not allow the creation of empty string tables. If you create a string table with no entries, it is deleted automatically when you exit Visual C++.

For information about common resource edit procedures such as creating new resources, opening existing resources, and deleting resources, see Chapter 4, "Working with Resources."

Finding a String

The string editor includes a Find command to let you quickly locate strings in the string table by either their caption or resource identifier.

▶ **To find a string in the string table**

1. Open the string table by double-clicking its icon in the resource browser window.

2. From the Search menu, choose Find (ALT+F3).

   The Find dialog box appears.

3. In the Find What box, type the caption text or resource identifier of the string you want to find. Select or clear the Match Case check box as appropriate.

4. Choose Find Next.

   If a string or its identifier in the string table matches what you typed, it is selected.

Adding or Deleting a String

Once the string editor window is displayed, you can add or delete entries in the string table. String table segments are separated by a horizontal line in the string editor window.

▶ **To add a string table entry**

1. Select the new-item box (an empty rectangle) at the end of a string segment.

2. Type the new string.

   Focus shifts to the String Properties page as you start typing, the text is entered in the Caption box, and the string is given the next identifier in sequence.

   –Or–

1. Select an existing entry in the string table.
2. From the Resource menu, choose New String.

   A new string is created and given the next available identifier after the currently selected string. The String Properties page opens.
3. Type the new string in the Caption box.

Note   Null strings are not allowed in Windows string tables. If you create an entry in the string table that is a null string, the entry is deleted when you close the string editor.

▶ **To delete a string in the string table**

1. Select the string you want to delete.
2. From the Edit menu, choose Delete (DEL).

Moving a String from One Segment to Another

▶ **To move a string from one segment to another**

1. Select the string you want to move.
2. From the Edit menu, choose Properties (ALT+ENTER).

   The String Properties page opens.
3. Change the string's value in the ID box so that it falls in the range you want.

   For example, to move a string with a name of IDS_MYSTRING and a value of 100 to a segment in the 200 range, type the following in the ID box:

   IDS_MYSTRING=201

4. Press ENTER to record the change.

Moving a String from One Resource Script File (.RC) to Another

▶ **To move a string from one resource script (.RC) file to another**

1. Open the string editor windows in both resource script files.
2. Use the drag-and-drop method described in "Using Drag-and-Drop Editing" on page 45 in Chapter 3.

   –Or–

   Use the Cut and Paste commands on the Edit menu.

> **Note** If the moved string's symbol name or value conflicts with an existing identifier in the destination file, the symbol name is changed (if a symbol by that name already exists) or the symbol value is changed (if a symbol with that value already exists).

Changing a String or Its Identifier

▶ **To change a string or its identifier**

1. Select the string you want to edit.

2. From the Edit menu, choose Properties and modify the string in the Caption box.

3. In the ID box, modify the string's identifier:

   - Type a new symbol name or choose one from the list.

   - Change a string's value by typing the symbol name followed by an equal sign and the new value; for example

   ```
   IDS_ERROR_MSG=2350
   ```

For more information on editing symbols, see Chapter 13, "Browsing Through Symbols."

Adding Formatting or Special Characters to a String

▶ **To add formatting or special characters to a string**

- Use the standard escape sequences shown in Table 8.1.

   Table 8.1   Formatting and Special Characters in Strings

To Get This	Type This
New line	\n (or press CTRL+ENTER when typing the string)
Carriage return	\r
Tab	\t (or press CTRL+TAB when typing the string)
Backslash (\)	\\
ASCII character	\ddd (octal notation)
Alert (bell)	\a

CHAPTER 9

Using the Graphic Editor

The Visual C++ graphic editor has a rich set of tools for drawing bitmaps, icons, and cursors, as well as features to support the creation of toolbar bitmaps and the management of icon and cursor images.

With the graphic editor, you can:

- Create and edit bitmaps in 256 colors.
- Use a full complement of drawing tools.
- Easily copy images from one bitmap to another.
- Use custom brushes for special effects.
- Draw cursors and icons with transparent and inverse-color regions.
- Edit bitmaps for toolbar buttons.

Most editing procedures are the same for bitmaps, icons, and cursors. This chapter first shows the procedures common to all graphical resources. Later sections detail procedures and graphic-editor capabilities specific to icons, cursors, and toolbar-button images.

Note Many of the graphic editor's functions require a mouse or other pointing device.

Tip While using the graphic editor, in many instances you can click the right mouse button to display a shortcut menu of frequently used commands. The commands available depend on what the pointer is pointing at. For example, if you click while pointing at the bitmap folder, the shortcut menu shows the New and New Bitmap commands.

For information about common resource edit procedures such as creating new resources, opening existing resources, and deleting resources, see Chapter 4, "Working with Resources."

Windows and Tools for Editing Graphics

You edit bitmaps, icons, and cursors in the image editor window, using the tools on the Graphics toolbar (Figure 9.1).

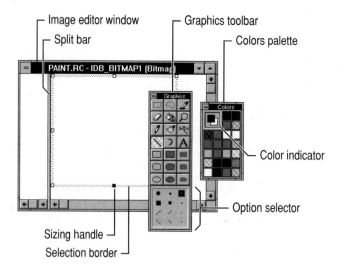

Figure 9.1   Image Editor Window, Graphics Toolbar, and Colors Palette

The Image Editor Window

The image editor window shows two views of an image. A split bar separates the two panes. You can drag the split bar from side to side to change the relative sizes of the panes. The active pane displays a selection border, as shown in Figure 9.1.

The Graphics Toolbar

The Graphics toolbar has two parts, which are shown in Figure 9.1:

- The toolbar, which contains 21 tools for drawing, painting, entering text, erasing, and manipulating views

- The option selector, which you click to select brush widths and other drawing options

To use the toolbar, Colors palette, and option selector, you click the desired tool, color, or option.

The Colors Palette

The Colors palette has two parts, which are shown in Figure 9.1:

- The color indicator, which shows the foreground and background colors and (for icons and cursors) selectors for "screen" and "inverse" color

- The Colors palette, which you click to select the foreground and background colors

The Status Bar

The Status bar, at the bottom of the frame window, displays two panes when an image editor window is open. When the pointer is over an image, the left pane shows the cursor's current position, in pixels, relative to the upper-left corner of the image. During a dragging operation such as selecting, moving, or drawing a rectangle, the right pane shows the size, in pixels, of the affected area.

The Image Menu

The Image menu, which appears only when the graphic editor is active, has commands for editing images, managing color palettes, and setting image editor window options.

Editing Graphical Resources

There are several editing operations involved in using the graphic editor. This section describes these graphics-editing tasks:

- Setting bitmap properties

- Setting foreground and background colors, and choosing opaque and transparent backgrounds

- Drawing and erasing

- Drawing lines and closed figures

- Cutting, copying, clearing, and moving selected parts of a bitmap

- Filling an area of a bitmap with a color or quickly "picking up" a color from the bitmap to use it elsewhere

- Inverting the colors in a selection

- Creating a custom brush

- Flipping or resizing a bitmap

You can also import existing bitmaps, icons, and cursors and add them to your project, and you can open files that are not part of a project for "stand-alone" editing. For more information on importing resources, see "Common Resource Edit Procedures" on page 63 and "Working with Symbols" on page 67, both in Chapter 4.

Note Most graphic-editor operations are the same for all kinds of graphical resources. Unless the text states otherwise, the procedures described in this section can be performed on bitmaps, cursors, or icons.

Setting Bitmap Properties

You use the Properties window to change most resource properties. Exceptions are new icons or cursors for additional target devices. For more information, see "Setting a Cursor's Hot Spot" on page 130 and see Appendix O, "Initializing and Configuring Visual C++" in Books Online.

Tip By default the Properties window is hidden whenever it does not have focus. To keep the Properties window in view when it does not have focus, click the "pushpin" command button in the upper-left corner of the Properties window.

▶ **To change a bitmap's properties**

1. Open the bitmap whose properties you want to change.

2. From the Edit menu, choose Properties (ALT+ENTER) to open its properties page.

3. Change any or all of these properties on the General tab:

   - In the ID box, modify the resources's identifier. For a bitmap, Visual C++ by default assigns the next available identifier in a series: IDB_BITMAP1, IDB_BITMAP2, and so forth. Similar names are used for icons and cursors.

   - In the Width and Height boxes, modify the bitmap's width and height (in pixels). The default value for each is 48.

     If you change the dimensions of a bitmap using the properties page, the image is cropped or "blank" space is added to the right of or below the existing image.

   - In the Colors list box, select Monochrome, 16, or 256. If you have already drawn the bitmap with a 16-color palette, selecting Monochrome causes Visual C++ to substitute black and white for the colors in the bitmap. Contrast is not always maintained: for example, adjacent areas of red and green are both converted to black.

- In the File Name box, modify the name of the file in which the bitmap is to be stored. By default, Visual C++ assigns a base filename created by removing the first four characters ("IDB_") from the default identifier and adding the extension .BMP.

- Select the Save Compressed check box to cause Visual C++ to save the bitmap in a compressed format.

4. Change any or all of the color properties on the Palette tab:

- Double-click to select a color and display the Custom Color Selector dialog box.

- Define the color by typing RGB or HSL values in the appropriate text boxes, or by moving the cross hairs on the color box.

For more information, see "Changing Colors" on page 132.

Showing and Hiding the Graphics Toolbar

Since many of the drawing tools are available from the keyboard, sometimes it is useful to hide the Graphics toolbar.

▶ **To show or hide the Graphics toolbar**

1. Place the cursor over the toolbar area and click the right mouse button.

   A shortcut menu appears.

2. From the shortcut menu, choose Graphics.

Selecting Foreground and Background Colors

Except for the eraser, these tools draw with the current foreground or background color when you press the left or right mouse button, respectively.

▶ **To select a foreground color**

- With the left mouse button, click the color you want on the Colors palette.

▶ **To select a background color**

- With the right mouse button, click the color you want on the Colors palette.

Freehand Drawing and Erasing

The graphic editor's freehand drawing and erasing tools all work in the same way: you select the tool and, if necessary, select foreground and background colors and size and shape options. You then move the cursor to the bitmap and click or drag to draw and erase.

When you have selected the eraser tool, brush tool, or airbrush tool, the option selector displays that tool's options.

Tip Instead of using the eraser tool, you may find it more convenient to draw in the background color with one of the drawing tools.

Selecting and Using a Drawing Tool

The various drawing tools are easily selected using the Graphics toolbar. Table 9.1 shows each toolbar button and its related drawing tool.

Table 9.1   Drawing Tools and Their Buttons

Drawing Tool	Toolbar Button
Eraser	
Pencil	
Brush	
Airbrush	

▶ **To select and use a drawing tool**

1. Click a button on the Graphics toolbar:

   - The eraser tool (SHIFT+P) "paints over" the image with the current background color when you press the left mouse button. When you press the right mouse button, it replaces the current foreground color with the current background color.

   - The pencil tool (P) draws freehand in a constant width of one pixel.

   - The brush tool's (D) shape and size are determined by the option selector.

   - The airbrush tool (A) randomly distributes color pixels around the center of the brush.

2. If necessary, select colors and a brush:

   - In the Colors palette, click with the left button to select a foreground color or with the right button to select a background color.

   - On the options selector of the Graphics toolbar, click a shape representing the brush you want to use. Your selection is highlighted.

3. Point to the place on the bitmap where you want to start drawing or painting. The brush or cursor appears on the bitmap.

4. Press the left mouse button (for the foreground color) or the right mouse button (for the background color), and hold it down as you draw.

5. Release the mouse button.

▶ **To resize the brush tool or eraser tool to a single pixel**

- Press the period (.).

▶ **To change the size of the brush, airbrush, or eraser**

- Press the PLUS SIGN (+) key to increase the size or the MINUS SIGN (−) key to decrease it.

  −Or−

- Press the period (.) to choose the smallest size.

  −Or−

- Choose a brush in the option selector.

Drawing Lines and Closed Figures

The Visual C++ tools for drawing lines and closed figures all work in the same way: you put the insertion point at one point and drag to another. For lines, these points are the endpoints. For closed figures, these points are opposite corners of a rectangle bounding the figure.

Lines are drawn in a width determined by the current brush selection, and framed figures are drawn in a width determined by the current width selection. Lines and all figures, both framed and filled, are drawn in the current foreground color if you press the left mouse button or in the current background color if you press the right mouse button.

▶ **To draw a line**

1. From the toolbar, select the line tool (L).

   Toolbar:

2. If necessary, select colors: in the Colors palette, click with the left button to select a foreground color or with the right button to select a background color.

3. If necessary, select a brush: in the option selector, click a shape representing the brush you want to use. Your selection is highlighted.

4. Place the pointer at the line's starting point.

5. Drag to the line's endpoint.

The various closed-figure drawing tools are easily selected using the Graphics toolbar. Table 9.2 shows each toolbar button and its related drawing tool.

Table 9.2   Closed-Figure Drawing Tools and Their Buttons

Closed-Figure Drawing Tool	Toolbar Button
Framed rectangle	
Filled rectangle	
Framed round rectangle	
Filled round rectangle	
Framed ellipse	
Filled ellipse	

▶   **To draw a closed figure**

1. From the Graphics toolbar, select a closed-figure drawing tool:

   - The framed-rectangle tool (R) draws a rectangle framed with the foreground or background color.

   - The filled-rectangle tool (SHIFT+R) draws a rectangle filled with the foreground or background color.

   - The framed-round-rectangle tool (N) draws a rectangle with rounded corners framed with the foreground or background color.

   - The filled-round-rectangle tool (SHIFT+N) draws a rectangle with rounded corners filled with the foreground or background color.

   - The framed-ellipse tool (E) draws an ellipse framed with the foreground or background color.

   - The filled-ellipse tool (SHIFT+E) draws an ellipse filled with the foreground or background color.

2. If necessary, select colors: on the Colors palette, click with the left button to select a foreground color or with the right button to select a background color.

3. If necessary, select a line width: on the option selector, click a shape representing the brush you want to use. Your selection is highlighted.

4. Move the cursor to one corner of the rectangular area in which you want to draw the figure.

5. Drag the to the diagonally opposite corner.

Filling Bounded Areas

The graphic editor provides the fill (or "paint-bucket") tool for filling any enclosed bitmap area with the current drawing color or the current background color.

▶ **To use the fill tool**

1. From the Graphics toolbar, choose the fill tool (F).

   Toolbar:

2. If necessary, choose drawing colors: in the Colors palette, click with the left button to select a foreground color or with the right button to select a background color.

3. Move the fill tool to the area you want to fill.

4. Click the left or right mouse button to fill with the foreground color or the background color, respectively.

Picking Up Colors

The color-pickup tool makes any color on the bitmap the current foreground color or background color, depending on whether you press the left or the right mouse button.

▶ **To pick up a color**

1. From the Graphics toolbar, select the color-pickup tool (COMMA).

   Toolbar:

   The pointer changes to the "eyedropper."

2. Select the color you want to pick up from the Colors palette or from the Palette tab of the properties page. After you pick up a color, the graphic editor reactivates the most recently used tool.

3. Draw using the left mouse button for the foreground color, or the right mouse button for the background color.

▶ **To cancel the color-pickup tool**

- Choose another tool or press ESC.

Selecting an Area of the Bitmap

The selection tool defines an area of the bitmap that you can cut, copy, clear, resize, invert, or move. You can also create a custom brush from the selection. For more information, see "Creating a Custom Brush" on page 123.

▶ **To select an area of the bitmap**

1. In the Graphics toolbar, click the selection tool (S).

   Toolbar: ▣

2. Move the insertion point to one corner of the bitmap area that you want to select. Cross hairs appear when the insertion point is over the bitmap

3. Drag the insertion point cursor to the opposite corner of the area you want to select. A rectangle shows which pixels will be selected. All pixels within the rectangle, including those "under" the rectangle, are included in the selection.

4. Release the mouse button. The "selection border"—a rectangular frame— encloses the selected area. Now any operation you perform will affect only the pixels within the rectangle.

▶ **To select the entire bitmap**

- Click the bitmap outside the current selection.

  –Or–

- Press ESC.

  –Or–

- Choose another tool on the toolbar.

Cutting, Copying, Clearing, and Moving

You can perform standard editing operations—cutting, copying, clearing, and moving—with the selection, whether the selection is the entire bitmap or just a part of it. Because the graphic editor uses the Windows Clipboard, you can transfer images between Visual C++ and other applications for Windows, such as Microsoft® Paintbrush™ and Microsoft Word for Windows.

In addition, you can resize the selection, whether it includes the entire bitmap or just a part. For more information on resizing, see "Resizing a Bitmap" on page 124.

▶ **To cut the current selection and copy it onto the Clipboard**

- From the Edit menu, choose Cut (CTRL+X).

  Toolbar: 🖾

  The original area of the selection is filled with the current background color, and the selection is now in the Clipboard.

▶ **To clear the current selection without copying it onto the Clipboard**

- From the Edit menu, choose Delete (DEL).

  The original area of the selection is filled with the current background color.

▶ **To paste the Clipboard contents into the bitmap**

1. From the Edit menu, choose Paste (CTRL+V).

   Toolbar: 🖾

   The Clipboard contents, surrounded by the selection border, appear in the upper-left corner of the pane.

2. Position the pointer within the selection border and drag the image to the desired location on the bitmap.

3. To anchor the image at its new location, click outside of the selection border or choose a new tool.

▶ **To move the selection**

1. Position the pointer inside the selection border or anywhere on it except the sizing handles.

2. Drag the selection to its new location.

   The original area of the selection is filled with the current background color.

3. To anchor the selection in the bitmap at its new location, click outside the selection border or choose a new tool.

▶ **To copy the selection**

1. Position the cursor inside the selection border or anywhere on it except the sizing handles.

2. Hold down the CTRL key as you drag the selection to a new location.

   The area of the original selection is unchanged.

3. To copy the selection into the bitmap at its current location, click outside the selection cursor or choose a new tool.

▶ **To draw with the selection**

1. Position the cursor inside the selection border or anywhere on it except the sizing handles.

2. Hold down the SHIFT key as you drag the selection.

   Copies of the selection are left along the dragging path. The more slowly you drag, the more copies are made.

Choosing Opaque and Transparent Backgrounds

When you move or copy a selection from a cursor or icon, any pixels in the selection that match the current background color are by default "transparent": they do not obscure pixels in the target location. A custom brush behaves the same way. For more information on custom brushes, see "Creating a Custom Brush" on page 123.

▶ **To toggle the background-color transparency**

- Press O.

  –Or–

- In the Graphics toolbar option selector, click the appropriate button:

  ▪ Opaque background: the existing image is obscured by all parts of the selection.

    Toolbar:

  ▪ Transparent background: the existing image shows through parts of the selection that match the current background color.

    Toolbar:

You can change the background color while a selection is already in effect to change which parts of the image are transparent.

Flipping the Selection

▶ **To flip the selection along the horizontal axis**

- From the Image menu, choose Flip Horizontal (X).

▶ **To flip the selection along the vertical axis**

- From the Image menu, choose Flip Vertical (Y).

▶ **To rotate the selection 90°**

- From the Image menu, choose Rotate 90° (Z).

Inverting Colors in the Current Selection

So that you can tell how a bitmap would appear with inverted colors, Visual C++ provides a convenient way to invert colors in the selected part of the bitmap.

▶ **To invert colors in the current selection**

- From the Image menu, choose Invert Colors.

Creating a Custom Brush

A custom brush is a rectangular portion of a bitmap that you "pick up" and use like one of the graphic editor's ready-made brushes. All operations you can perform on a selection, you can perform on a custom brush as well.

▶ **To create a custom brush**

1. Select the part of the bitmap that you want to use for a brush. For more information, see "Selecting and Using a Drawing Tool" on page 116.
2. Press CTRL+B.

Pixels in a custom brush that match the current background color are normally "transparent": they do not paint over the existing image. You can change this behavior so that background-color pixels paint over the existing image.

You can use the custom brush like a "stamp" or a "stencil" to create a variety of special effects.

Using a Custom Brush

▶ **To draw custom brush shapes in the background color**

1. Select an opaque or transparent background. For more information, see "Choosing Opaque and Transparent Backgrounds" on page 122.
2. Set the background color to the color in which you want to draw.
3. Position the custom brush where you want to draw.
4. Press the right mouse button.

   Any opaque regions of the custom brush are drawn in the background color.

▶ **To double or halve the custom brush size**

- Press the PLUS SIGN (+) to double the brush size, or the MINUS SIGN (−) to halve it.

▶ **To cancel the custom brush**

- Press ESC or choose another drawing tool.

Resizing a Bitmap

The behavior of the graphic editor while resizing a bitmap depends on whether the selection includes the entire bitmap or just part of it:

- When the selection includes only a part of the bitmap, Visual C++ shrinks the selection by deleting rows or columns of pixels and filling the vacated regions with the current background color, or it stretches the selection by duplicating rows or columns of pixels.

- When the selection includes the entire bitmap, Visual C++ either shrinks and stretches the bitmap, or crops and extends it.

There are two mechanisms for resizing a bitmap: the resizing handles and the properties page. You can drag the sizing handles to change the size of all or part of a bitmap. Sizing handles that you can drag are solid, like those on the lower right corner and the midpoints of the right and bottom sides of the bitmaps. You cannot drag handles that are hollow. You can use the properties page to resize only the entire bitmap, not a selected part.

Note If you have the Tile Grid option selected (see Grid Settings command on the Image menu), then resizing snaps to the next tile grid line. If only the Pixel Grid option is selected, resizing snaps to the next available pixel. Usually, only the Pixel Grid option is selected.

Resizing an Entire Bitmap

▶ **To resize an entire bitmap using the properties page**

1. From the Edit menu, choose Properties (ALT+ENTER) to open the properties page.

2. Type the desired dimensions in the Width and Height boxes.

   If you are increasing the size of the bitmap, the graphic editor extends the bitmap to the right or downward, or both, and fills the new region with the current background color. The image is not stretched.

   If you are decreasing the size of the bitmap, the graphic editor crops the bitmap on the right or bottom edge, or both.

You can use the Width and Height properties to resize only the entire bitmap, not to resize a partial selection.

▶ **To crop or extend an entire bitmap**

1. Select the entire bitmap.

   If a part of the bitmap is currently selected and you want to select the entire bitmap, click anywhere on the bitmap outside the current selection border, press ESC, or choose another drawing tool.

2. Drag a sizing handle until the bitmap is the desired size.

Normally, the graphic editor crops or enlarges a bitmap when you resize it by moving a sizing handle. If you hold down the SHIFT key as you move a sizing handle, the graphic editor shrinks or stretches the bitmap.

▶ To shrink or stretch an entire bitmap

1. Select the entire bitmap.

    If a part of the bitmap is currently selected and you want to select the entire bitmap, click anywhere on the bitmap outside the current selection border, press ESC, or choose another drawing tool.

2. Hold down the SHIFT key and drag a sizing handle until the bitmap is the desired size.

▶ To shrink or stretch part of a bitmap

1. Select the part of the bitmap you want to resize. For more information, see "Selecting an Area of the Bitmap" on page 120.

2. Drag one of the sizing handles until the selection is the desired size.

Managing the Graphic Editor Workspace

By adjusting the graphic editor workspace to fit your needs and preferences, you can work more effectively and comfortably. This section describes procedures for:

- Selecting and sizing image-editor panes
- Changing the magnification of image editor windows
- Displaying and hiding pixel grids

Using Image-Editor Panes

Normally the image editor window displays a bitmap in two panes separated by a split bar. One view is actual size, and the other is enlarged (the default enlargement factor is 6). The views in these two panes are updated automatically: changes you make in one pane are immediately shown in the other. The two panes make it easy for you to work on an enlarged "picture" of your bitmap, in which you can distinguish individual pixels and, at the same time, observe the effect of your work on the actual-size view of the image.

If the bitmap is 200 x 200 pixels or larger, however, only one pane is displayed initially. Move the split bar to display both panes.

You can use the two panes in other ways. For example, you might enlarge the smaller pane and use the two panes to show different regions of a large bitmap.

You move the split bar to change the relative sizes of the panes. The split bar can move all the way to either side if you want to work on only one pane.

▶ **To select an image-editor pane**

- Press TAB or F6, or click anywhere on the pane. The selection border then shows that the pane is active.

▶ **To size the image-editor panes**

1. Position the pointer on the split bar.

   The pointer turns into a two-headed arrow.

2. Drag the split bar to the right or to the left.

Zooming In and Out

By default, the graphic editor displays the view in the left pane at actual size and the view in the right pane at 6 times actual size. There are two ways to change the magnification factor—the ratio between actual and displayed size—of the image you are editing and to toggle between an actual-size view and an enlarged view:

- The Zoom tool lets you select a magnification factor and choose in advance the portion of the image that appears in the "zoomed" view.

- Zoom Under Cursor, available from the keyboard only, centers the part of the image that is under the cursor in the image-editor pane.

▶ **To zoom in or out on an image-editor pane**

1. On the toolbar, click the Zoom tool.

   Toolbar:

2. Position the pointer over the pane you want to zoom in or out on.

   If you are zooming in on an actual-size view and the magnified view will not fit in the pane, a tracking rectangle shows the part of the bitmap that will appear in the magnified view. Position the tracking rectangle over the area you want to view.

3. Click to zoom.

   If you have used the Zoom Decrease or Zoom Increase command to change the zoom factor for the active pane, the current factor is used. Otherwise the default factor of 6 is used. For more information on magnification, see "Changing the Magnification Factor" on page 127.

   The pointer changes to the tool it was before you selected the Zoom tool.

▶ **To zoom in on the part of the image under the cursor**

1. On the toolbar, click the Zoom tool.

   Toolbar: 🔍

2. Position the pointer on the point that you want to have centered in the zoomed view.

3. Press M to toggle the magnification factor.

Changing the Magnification Factor

The magnification factor is the ratio between the actual size of the bitmap and the displayed size. The default is 6, and the range is from 1 to 8.

▶ **To change the magnification factor**

1. Select the image-editor pane whose magnification factor you want to change.

2. On the toolbar, click the Zoom tool.

   Toolbar: 🔍

   The cursor changes to the Zoom tool, and magnification-factor options appear in the option selector on the Graphics toolbar. If the current magnification factor matches an option, that option is highlighted.

3. Click the desired magnification factor.

   –Or–

1. Select the image-editor pane whose magnification factor you want to change.

2. Press > (SHIFT+PERIOD) to increase the magnification factor, or press < (SHIFT+COMMA) to decrease the magnification factor.

Displaying and Hiding the Pixel Grid

For all image-editor panes with a magnification factor of 4 or greater, you can display a grid that delimits the individual pixels in the image. For more information, see "Changing the Magnification Factor" above.

▶ **To display or hide the pixel grid**

1. From the Image menu, choose Grid Settings.

2. In the Grid Settings dialog box, select the Pixel Grid box to display the grid, or clear the box to hide the grid.

3. Choose OK.

   –Or–

- Press G to toggle the grid display.

You can also display a tile grid to simplify editing toolbar graphics. For more information, see "Setting the Tile Grid Dimensions" on page 130.

Creating a New Icon or Cursor

Icons and cursors are like bitmaps, and you edit them in the same ways. But icons and cursors have attributes that distinguish them from bitmaps. For example, each icon or cursor resource can contain multiple images for different display devices. In addition, a cursor has a "hot spot"—the location Windows NT uses to track its position.

Creating a New Image

When you create a new icon or cursor, the graphic editor first creates an image for the VGA. The image is initially filled with the "screen" (transparent) color. If the image is a cursor, the hot spot is initially the upper-left corner (coordinates 0,0).

By default, the graphic editor supports the creation of images for the following devices:

Device	Colors	Width	Height
EGA/VGA	16	32	32
Monochrome	2	32	32
CGA	2	32	16

You can create images for other devices if you first create descriptions for those devices in the Registry. For more information on adding a device description to the Windows NT Registry, see Appendix O, "Initializing and Configuring Visual C++," in Books Online.

Selecting a Display Device

When you create a new icon or cursor image, you need to designate the target display device (see Figure 9.2). When the icon or cursor resource is opened, the image most closely matching the current display device is opened by default.

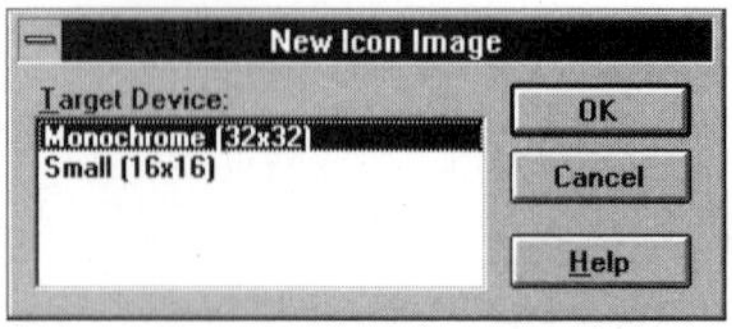

Figure 9.2   New Icon Image Dialog Box

▶ **To select a display device**

1. On the control bar of the image editor window, click the New Icon Image button.

Button:

2. Select a display device image from the list box.

Drawing with Screen and Inverse Colors

The initial icon or cursor image has a transparent attribute. Although icon and cursor images are rectangular, many do not appear so because parts of the image are "transparent": the underlying image on the screen shows through the icon or cursor. And when you drag an icon, parts of the image may appear in an inverted color. You create these effects by choosing screen- and inverse-color options from the color indicator on the Colors palette (see Figure 9.3).

The screen and inverse "colors" you apply to icons and cursors either shape and color the derived image or designate inverse regions. The colors indicate parts of the image possessing those attributes. You can change the colors that represent the screen- and inverse-color attributes for your convenience in editing. These changes do not affect the appearance of the icon or cursor in your application.

—— Screen color

—— Inverse color

Figure 9.3   Selectors for Screen Color and Inverse Color

▶ **To create transparent or inverse regions in an icon or cursor**

1. On the Colors palette, click a selector:

   - The screen-color selector:
   - The inverse-color selector:

2. Apply the screen or inverse color.

▶ **To change the colors representing screen color and inverse color**

1. Select either the screen-color selector or the inverse-color selector.

2. Choose a color from the Colors palette.

   The complementary color is automatically designated for the other selector.

> **Tip** If you double-click the screen color or inverse-color indicator, the Custom
> Color Selector dialog box appears.

Setting a Cursor's Hot Spot

The hot spot is the point to which Windows refers in tracking the cursor's position.
By default, the hot spot is set to the upper-left corner (coordinates 0,0). The Cursor
Properties page and the image-editor control bar show the hot spot coordinates.

▶ **To set a cursor's hot spot**

1. On the control bar of the image editor window, click the Hot Spot button.

   Button:

2. Click the pixel you want to designate as the cursor's hot spot.

Editing Toolbar Graphics

The Visual C++ graphic editor has special features to simplify creation of tiled
graphics for toolbar buttons. All the button bitmaps for a toolbar are taken from one
bitmap, which must contain one image for each button. All images must be the same
size: the default is 16 x 15 pixels. Images must be side by side in the bitmap.
Typically the order of the images in the bitmap is the order in which they are drawn
on the screen. For more information, see the class **CToolBar** in the *Class Library
Reference*.

Each button has one image. The various button states and styles (pressed, up, down,
disabled, disabled down, and indeterminate) are generated from that one image.
Although bitmaps can be any color, best results are achieved with images in black
and shades of gray.

Setting the Tile-Grid Dimensions

The graphic editor can superimpose a tile grid on the view of a bitmap. The tile grid
delimits sections of the bitmap in dimensions you specify so that you can properly
position tiled images within the bitmap. When the tile grid is displayed, the sizing
handles on the selection border behave differently from when the tile grid is not
displayed. When you drag the sizing handles, the bitmap is resized in increments of
the tile dimensions. For more information on resizing, see "Resizing a Bitmap" on
page 124.

▶ **To set the tile-grid dimensions**

1. From the Image menu, choose Grid Settings.

   The Grid Settings dialog box appears.

2. Select the Pixel Grid check box if it is not already checked.

   You cannot set the Tile Grid dimensions if the Pixel Grid check box is not selected.

3. Select the Tile Grid check box.

4. If necessary, edit the Width and Height settings.

   Typically, these settings are the same as the width and height of your button bitmaps.

5. Choose OK.

The image editor window now displays a tile grid.

▶ **To toggle the display of the tile grid**

• Press CTRL+G.

Note   When the tile grid is displayed and you drag the sizing handles, the bitmap is resized in increments of the tile dimensions.

Creating a New Toolbar Button

▶ **To create a new toolbar button**

1. Move the focus to the resource browser window.

2. Double-click the Bitmap folder.

3. Double-click IDR_MAINFRAME to open the toolbar image.

4. Display the tile grid.

5. If necessary, select a background color for the new button.

6. To resize the bitmap, drag the sizing handle on the right side of the bitmap to the right (see Figure 9.4). The bitmap's width is increased by an amount equal to the tile grid's Width setting.

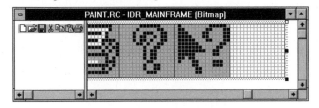

Figure 9.4   Resizing the Toolbar Bitmap

7. If the new button is to be added at a position other than the right end of the bitmap, make room for it:

  - Select the rightmost button images, including the one at the new button's position (see Figure 9.5).

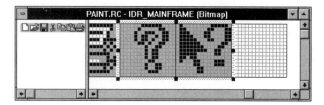

Figure 9.5   Selecting Button Images

  - Drag the selection to the right, using the tile grid to align the images (see Figure 9.6).

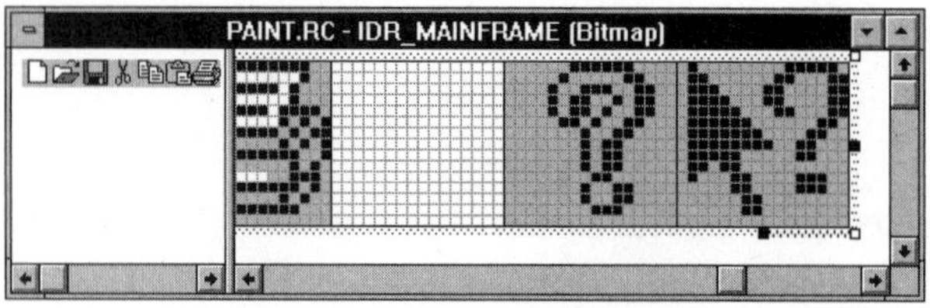

Figure 9.6   Moving the Selected Button Images

Tip Before selecting and dragging, use the Image menu to adjust the Grid Settings so that Pixel Grid and Tile Grid are active.

---

8. Draw the new button image in the space you have created.

9. From the File menu, choose Save (CTRL+S).

Changing Colors

The graphic editor's Colors palette initially displays 24 "ready-made" colors: 16 standard colors and 8 dithered colors. In addition to the ready-made colors, you can create your own custom colors. Colors palette selections can be saved on disk and individually reloaded as needed. The "last used" Colors palette definition is saved in the Registry and automatically loaded the next time you start Visual C++.

The Palette tab in the Properties window displays up to 256 colors. Changing any of the colors on the Palette tab will immediately change the corresponding color in the bitmap. The colors on the Palette tab are always solid colors and can indicate any color your video card is capable of displaying.

Note   The Palette tab in the Properties window displays for bitmaps only.

▶ **To change colors on the Colors palette or Palette tab**

1. From the Image menu, choose Adjust Colors.

   −Or−

   Double-click one of the colors on the Colors palette.

   −Or−

   Double-click one of the colors on the Palette tab of the Bitmap Properties page.

   The Custom Color Selector dialog box appears (see Figure 9.7).

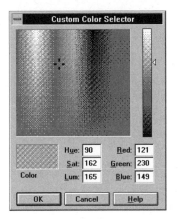

Figure 9.7   Custom Color Selector Dialog Box

2. Define the color by typing RGB or HSL values in the appropriate text boxes, or by moving the cross hairs on the color box.

3. Set the luminance by moving the slider on the luminance bar.

4. Many custom colors are dithered. If you want the solid color closest to the dithered color, double-click the Color preview window. (If you later decide you want the dithered color, move the slider or the cross hairs again to restore the dithering.)

5. Choose OK to add the new color.

Saving and Loading Colors Palettes

You use commands on the Image menu save or load a palette.

▶ **To save a custom Colors palette**

1. From the Image menu, choose Save Palette.

2. Use the Save Palette Colors dialog box to navigate directories, and type a filename.

▶ **To load a custom Colors palette**

1. From the Image menu, choose Load Palette.

2. Use the Load Palette Colors dialog box to navigate directories and choose a filename.

Tip Since the graphic editor has no means to restore the default Colors palette, save the default Colors palette under a name such as STANDARD.PAL or DEFAULT.PAL so that you can easily restore the defaults.

CHAPTER 10

Using the Binary Data Editor

The binary data editor allows you to edit a resource at the binary level in either hexadecimal or ASCII format. You should use the binary editor only when you need to view or make minor changes to custom resources or resource types not supported by Visual C++.

Caution Editing nondata resources in the binary data editor can corrupt the resource. A corrupted resource can cause Visual C++ and Windows NT to behave in unexpected ways.

Tip While using the binary data editor, in many instances you can click the right mouse button to display a shortcut menu of frequently used commands. The commands available depend on what the pointer is pointing at. For example, if you click while pointing at the binary data editor with selected hex values, the shortcut menu shows the Cut, Copy, and Paste options.

Creating a New Data Resource or Custom Resource

You create new custom or data resources by placing them in a separate file using normal .RC file syntax, then including the file with the Set Includes command on the Resource menu.

▶ **To create a new custom or data resource**

1. In Visual C++, create an .RC file that contains the custom or data resource.

   Custom data can be entered in an .RC file as null-terminated quoted strings, or as integers in decimal, hexadecimal, or octal format. For more information, see the Software Development Kit documentation.

2. From the Resource menu, choose Set Includes.

   The Set Includes dialog box appears.

3. In the Compile-Time Directives box, type an include statement that gives the name of the file containing your custom resource. For example:

```
#include mydata.rc
```

Make sure the syntax and spelling of what you enter is correct. The contents of the Compile-Time Directives box is inserted into the resource script file exactly as you type it.

4. Choose OK to record your changes. The custom or data resource is included in your application at compile time.

Opening a Binary Resource for Editing

▶ **To open a resource for binary editing**

1. Move to the resource browser window.

2. Find the resource type you want to edit. Double-click to expand that resource directory, if necessary.

3. Select the specific resource you want to edit.

4. From the Resource menu, choose Open Binary Data.

   The binary data window appears (Figure 10.1).

If you want to use the binary data editor on a resource already being edited in another Visual C++ editor window, close the other editor window first.

Note If you use the resource browser window to open a resource whose format Visual C++ does not recognize (such as a VERSION, RCDATA, or custom resource), the resource is automatically opened in the binary data editor.

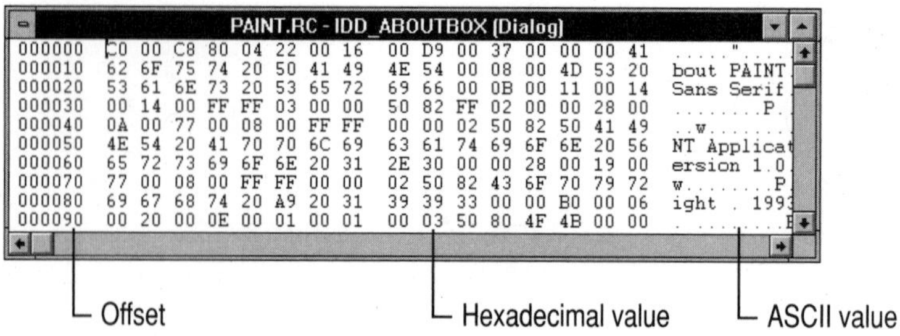

Figure 10.1 Binary Data Editor

Editing Binary Data

▶ **To edit a resource in the binary data editor**

1. Select the byte you want to edit.

   The TAB key moves the focus between the hexadecimal and ASCII sections of the editor window. PAGE UP and PAGE DOWN move you through the resource one screen at a time. You can also move to the top of the resource with CTRL+HOME and to the end with CTRL+END.

2. Type the new value, or paste a value you have copied.

C H A P T E R   1 1

Using the Version Information Editor

Version information is company and product identification, a product release number, and a copyright and trademark notification. The version information editor is a simple tool for creating and maintaining this data. Although the version information resource is not required by an application, it is a useful place to collect this information that identifies the application.

A single version information resource can contain multiple string blocks, each representing a different language or character set. All you need do is define the character sets and languages that are specific to your product.

With the version information editor, you can add or delete string blocks, and you can modify individual string values.

Note The Windows standard is to have only one version resource named VS_VERSION_INFO.

If you wish to access the version information from within your program, your application can make use of the **GetFileVersionInfo** function and the **VerQueryValue** function. For additional information on how to access version information, see the online *Microsoft Win32 Programmer's Reference, Volume 2*.

Tip While using the version information editor, in many instances you can click the right mouse button to display a shortcut menu of resource specific commands. For example, if you click while pointing at a block header entry, the shortcut menu shows the New String Block and Delete String Block commands.

For information about common resource edit procedures such as creating new resources, opening existing resources, and deleting resources, see Chapter 4, "Working with Resources."

Editing the Version Information

Figure 11.1 shows the version information resource (Figure 11.1).

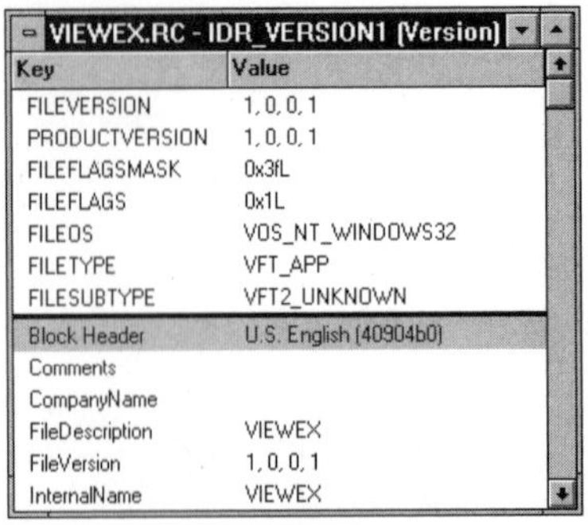

Key	Value
FILEVERSION	1, 0, 0, 1
PRODUCTVERSION	1, 0, 0, 1
FILEFLAGSMASK	0x3fL
FILEFLAGS	0x1L
FILEOS	VOS_NT_WINDOWS32
FILETYPE	VFT_APP
FILESUBTYPE	VFT2_UNKNOWN
Block Header	U.S. English (40904b0)
Comments	
CompanyName	
FileDescription	VIEWEX
FileVersion	1, 0, 0, 1
InternalName	VIEWEX

Figure 11.1   Version Information Resource

The version information resource has a single fixed information block (at the top of the resource) and one or more string information blocks (at the bottom of the resource). The top block has both editable numeric fields and selectable drop-down lists. The bottom string block has editable text fields.

The information sequence of the string block can be sorted by clicking on either the Key or Value field. This automatically rearranges the information into the selected sequence.

▶ **To edit a version information resource**

- Click the mouse on the item you want to edit. The selected text box or drop-down list opens up for modification.

Note   When editing the File Flags property page, the DEBUG flag cannot be set for .RC files because Visual C++ 2.0 sets that flag with an **#ifdef** in the resource script, based on the **_DEBUG** build flag.

▶ **To add new string blocks**

1. With a version information resource open, from the Resource menu, choose New String Block.

   This appends an additional string information block into the current version information resource and opens the Block Header Properties page.

2. On the Block Header Properties page, choose the appropriate language and character set for the new block.

▶   **To delete string blocks**

1. With a version information resource open, highlight one of the Block Headers.

2. From the <u>R</u>esource menu, choose <u>D</u>elete String Block.

    This deletes the selected header and leaves the remaining version information intact.

CHAPTER 12

Using ClassWizard

ClassWizard is like a programmer's assistant: it makes it easier for you to do certain routine tasks such as creating new classes, defining message handlers, overriding MFC virtual functions, and gathering data from controls in a dialog box, form view, or record view. ClassWizard is for use only with MFC applications.

With ClassWizard, you can:

- Create new classes derived from any of the main framework base classes that handle Windows messages and recordsets.
- Browse the Windows messages associated with windows, dialog boxes, controls, menu items, and accelerators.
- Create new message-handling member functions.
- See which messages have message handlers already defined and jump to the handler program code.
- Define member variables that automatically initialize, gather, and validate data entered into dialog boxes or form views.
- Add OLE Automation methods and properties.

One of ClassWizard's main tasks is to work with Microsoft Foundation Class Library (MFC) "message maps." A message map is a message-dispatch table that associates Windows messages with class member functions. This eliminates the cumbersome switch statements needed in traditional programming for Windows.

Important ClassWizard only works with the special-format message-map and data-map sections of your header and implementation files. ClassWizard also works with OLE Automation maps and database field maps. The Microsoft Foundation Class Library uses this information for message handling and dialog data exchange and validation. For more information, see "Adding a New Class" on page 145.

ClassWizard is used with Microsoft Foundation Class Library version 3 projects. For information on how to convert other projects (including Microsoft Foundation

Class Library version 1 projects) for use with ClassWizard, see "Technical Note 19" in *Microsoft Foundation Class Library Technical Notes*.

Adding a New User-Interface Class

Use ClassWizard to add error-free class declarations to your project for classes that contain message-handling functions.

Note ClassWizard is only for use with user-interface classes derived from **CCmdTarget** that handle messages or manage dialog-box controls. To add a new class that does not handle messages, create the class directly in the text editor. (The exception to this rule is class **CRecordset**, for database support.)

ClassWizard allows you to create classes derived from the Microsoft Foundation classes shown in Table 12.1:

Table 12.1   Types of Classes Created in ClassWizard

Class	Description
CButton	Button control
CCmdTarget	Base class for objects that can receive and respond to messages. It is the result of a selection based on a table query.
CComboBox	List box with static or edit control
CDialog	Dialog box
CDocument	Class for managing program data
CEdit	Rectangular child window for text entry
CFormView	Window that can contain dialog-box controls
CFrameWnd	Single document interface (SDI) frame window
CListBox	List box
CMDIChildWnd	Multiple document interface (MDI) child frame window
CMDIFrameWnd	Main multiple document interface (MDI) frame window
CRecordset	Class for accessing a database table or query
CRecordView	Window containing dialog box controls mapped to recordset fields
CScrollBar	Scroll bar
CScrollView	Scrolling window, derived from **CView**
CStatic	A simple text field, box, or rectangle used to label, box, or separate other controls
CView	Class for displaying program data
CWnd	Custom window
splitter	An MDI child window that the user can split into multiple panes

For more information on these classes, see the *Class Library Reference*.

When you use ClassWizard to create a new class derived from one of the framework classes listed above, it automatically places a complete and functional class in the header (.H) and implementation (.CPP) files you specify. ClassWizard keeps track of the class's message-handling and data-exchange members, so that you can update the class at a later time.

Adding a New Class

When you use ClassWizard to create a new class, it adds skeletal information on the new class to both the header and implementation files. If you specify filenames that don't yet exist, ClassWizard creates the new files and adds them to your project.

▶ **To add a new class to your project using ClassWizard**

1. From the Project menu, choose Class<u>W</u>izard (CTRL+W).

   Toolbar: 🖾

   Note   For classes associated with a dialog-box resource—classes derived from **CDialog**, **CFormView**, **or CRecordView**—create the resource in the dialog editor before you use ClassWizard to create the class.

   ---

2. Choose Add Class.

   The Add Class dialog box appears. If you are currently editing a dialog box that is not yet associated with a class, the Add Class dialog box appears automatically.

3. Type the name of your new class in the Class Name box and, in the boxes provided, type the names of the header and implementation files where the class is to be defined, or use the defaults supplied.

   By default, ClassWizard assigns the same name to .H and .CPP files.

4. In the Class Type list box, select the name of the class type from which your current class is to be derived (see Table 12.1).

5. Choose OLE Automation if you want to expose the capabilities of this class through OLE Automation.

   If you select this option, the newly created class will be available as a programmable object by Automation client applications, such as Microsoft Visual Basic™ or Microsoft Excel.

6. Choose OLE Createable if you want to allow other applications to create objects of this class by using OLE Automation.

   With this option selected, an OLE client application can create one of these objects at any time. This option is enabled only if you choose OLE Automation.

   External name is used by the client application to specify the object to be created. The external name is system wide and must be unique.

7. Choose Create Class to create the class in the files you specified.

Tip Use the OLE Events tab in Class Wizard to add OLE2 events that are initiated when certain actions occur.

Use the OLE Automation tab to add OLE automation methods and properties to an existing class. These methods and properties define a dispatch interface that OLE automation clients can use.

For more information about creating database classes (CRecordView, CRecordset) and OLE classes, see the article "ClassWizard" in *Programming with the Microsoft Foundation Classes*.

Importing a Class

If you add a message-handling class to your current project by copying code from another project, you can update ClassWizard so that it recognizes the new class.

Note If the new code you have copied contains more than two or three new message-handling classes, you can save time by rebuilding the ClassWizard file completely rather than importing each new class individually. For more information, see "Rebuilding the ClassWizard (.CLW) File" on page 156.

▶ **To import a class from another project**

1. If the code you are importing doesn't already have ClassWizard comments in it, manually add the special-format comments ClassWizard uses to locate message-map entries. For more information, see "Keeping ClassWizard Updated When Code Changes" on page 155.

2. Choose Add Class from any of ClassWizard's dialog box tabs. When the Add Class dialog box appears, choose Import Class.

3. In the Import Class dialog box, type the name of the new class and the name of the header and implementation files where the class source code can be found. You can also use the Browse buttons to locate the files.

   By default, the header file and the implementation file have the same name as the class file.

4. Choose OK to add the new class to the ClassWizard file.

Mapping Messages to Functions

ClassWizard lets you browse the messages associated with a user-interface object in your application and quickly define message-handling functions for them. ClassWizard also automatically updates the message-dispatch table, or message map, and your class header file when you use ClassWizard to define message-handling functions.

Table 12.2 shows the types of objects you work with in ClassWizard and the types of messages associated with them.

Table 12.12   User-Interface Objects and Associated Messages

Object ID	Messages
Class name, representing the containing window (see Table 12.1)	Windows messages appropriate to a **CWnd**-derived class: a dialog box, window, child window, MDI child window, or topmost frame window
Menu or accelerator identifier	**COMMAND** message (executes the program function) **UPDATE_COMMAND_UI** message (dynamically updates the menu item)
Control identifier	Control notification messages for the selected control type

Adding a Message Handler

After creating a class with ClassWizard, or importing an existing class, you can use ClassWizard to browse the messages or control notifications associated with each object and to create handler routines (member functions) as appropriate.

The general procedure for using ClassWizard to define a message or command handler is as follows:

▶ **To define a message handler with ClassWizard**

1. From the resource browser window, select the menu, accelerator, or dialog resource that has the user-interface object you want to work with.

2. From the Project menu, choose ClassWizard (CTRL+W).

   Toolbar:

3. ClassWizard displays information about the currently selected class name or the class you last edited with ClassWizard, and about the user-interface object that is currently selected.

4. In the Object IDs box, select the name of the user-interface object you want to define a message handler for. Table 12.2 shows the types of objects that will appear in the Object IDs box and the messages appropriate to each type.

5. In the Messages box, select the message for which you want to define a handler and choose Add Function (or double-click the message name).

You can only select messages that do not already have a handler defined. A message with a handler already defined is marked with a small hand next to it.

Note The messages you see in the Messages box are those most appropriate to your class. If your class is a dialog class, form view, or record view, then the messages will normally include window messages but not menu commands. To list menu commands as well as window messages, open ClassWizard with the focus on a menu or accelerator resource.

In addition, you can change the set of messages you handle by selecting the Class Info tab and selecting a new set of messages in the Message Filter box. For information on handling custom messages, see "Technical Note 6" in *Microsoft Foundation Class Library Technical Notes*.

Tip Selecting a message displays a brief description of it at the bottom of the MFC ClassWizard dialog box. You can get a more complete description of the message by pressing F1.

---

6. For messages that don't already have a predefined name for the handler function, the Add Member Function dialog box appears. Type the member function name you want and press ENTER, or press ENTER to accept the name proposed by ClassWizard. This returns you to the ClassWizard Message Maps tab.

A picture of a hand appears next to the message name to show that a member function is defined to handle the message. The name of the new message-handling function appears in the Member Functions box.

At this point you have several options. You can:

- Add more message handlers.
- Choose Edit Code to jump to the empty ClassWizard-created function in your source code and begin defining the function's behavior.
- Choose OK to automatically update your source code with selected member functions and close ClassWizard. You can return to ClassWizard any time during the development process.
- Choose Cancel to avoid updating your source code with the selected member functions. Note that ClassWizard does not remove the functions and code it previously added.

When you choose OK or Edit Code, ClassWizard updates your source code as follows:

- A function declaration is inserted into the header file.
- A complete, correct function definition with a skeletal implementation is inserted into the implementation file.
- The class's message map is updated to include the new message-handling function.

Shortcut for Defining Message Handlers for Dialog Buttons

To define a message handler for a dialog button, you can use the following convenient shortcut to bypass the intermediate steps described in the previous procedure.

▶ **To define a message handler for a dialog button**

1. In the dialog editor, select a button.
2. While holding down the CTRL key, double-click the button.

   ClassWizard automatically creates a message handler in the class associated with the dialog box. The message handler is named according to the control ID of the dialog button. Finally, ClassWizard jumps to the newly created function in your source code.

Shortcut for Defining Member Variables for Dialog Controls

To define a member variable for a dialog control, you can use the following convenient shortcut to bypass explicitly invoking ClassWizard from the dialog editor.

▶ **To define a member variable for a dialog control**

1. In the dialog editor, select a control.
2. While holding down the CTRL key, double-click the dialog control. The Add Member Variable box appears.
3. Fill out the Add Member Variable dialog box. For more information, see "Defining Member Variables" on page 152.
4. Choose OK. ClassWizard returns you to the dialog editor.

Tip To jump from a dialog button to its existing handler, hold down the CTRL key while double-clicking the button.

Deleting a Message Handler

Once you have defined a message handler with ClassWizard, you can also use ClassWizard to delete it. However, you must remove the function definition, as well as any references to the function, from the implementation file yourself. ClassWizard never makes changes to your implementation code—only to the message and data maps.

▶ **To delete a message-handling function**

1. In the ClassWizard dialog box, select the Message Maps tab.

2. In the Class Name box, select the class containing the message-handling function you want to delete.

3. In the Member Functions box, select the name of the member function to delete.

4. Choose Edit Code to open the implementation file containing the member function. Delete the function header and function body, or copy it to a file not in the current project.

5. Return to ClassWizard and choose Delete Function. This deletes the member function entries from the message-map for that class in both the header and implementation files.

Editing a Message Handler

Once you have defined a procedure with ClassWizard you can use the Edit Code command to jump to the member function definition and begin to add or modify code.

▶ **To jump to a member function definition**

1. In the ClassWizard dialog box, select the Message Maps tab.

2. In the Class Name box, select the class containing the message-handling function you want to edit.

3. In the Member Functions box, select the function you want to edit.

4. Choose Edit Code, or double-click the function name.

   ClassWizard moves to the beginning of the member function.

Overriding a Virtual Function

ClassWizard can override virtual functions defined in a base class. The mechanism is very similar to creating message handlers for Windows messages. ClassWizard lists and then lets you override the common virtual functions that appear above the //implementation line in the sources.

▶ **To override a virtual function in one of your classes**

1. On the Message Maps tab, select the name of the class in which you want to override a virtual function.

2. In the Object IDs box, select the class name again. This displays a list of virtual functions you can override and a list of Windows messages. The virtuals come before the messages and appear in mixed case.

3. In the Messages box, select the name of the virtual function you want to override.

4. Choose Add function. This creates the function and displays its name in the Member Functions box. The names of virtual overrides are preceded by a gray glyph containing the letter "V" (handlers have a "W").

5. Choose Edit Code to jump to the Windows message code.

Working with Dialog-Box Data

ClassWizard offers an easy way to take advantage of the dialog data exchange (DDX) and dialog data validation (DDV) capabilities of MFC.

To use DDX, you define member variables in the dialog-box, form view, or record view class and associate each of them with a dialog-box control. The framework transfers any initial values to the controls when the dialog box is displayed. It then updates the variables with user-entered data when the user chooses OK to dismiss the dialog box.

With DDV, dialog-box information entered by the user is validated automatically. You can set the validation boundaries: the maximum length for string values in an edit-box control or the minimum or maximum numeric values when you expect a number to be entered. You can also use ClassWizard to connect dialog-box controls to your own custom data-validation routines.

Dialog Data Exchange

ClassWizard lets you create variables that use the framework's automatic dialog data exchange capabilities. For each dialog-box control you want to set an initial value for or gather data from, use ClassWizard to define a data member in the dialog class. The framework then transfers the initial value of each variable to the dialog box when it is created and updates each member variable when the dialog box is dismissed.

Note You can also use **CWnd::UpdateData** to transfer data back and forth between controls and member variables while a dialog box is open.

Defining Member Variables

▶ **To define data members for dialog data exchange**

1. Create your dialog box, place in it the controls you want, and set the appropriate control styles in the Properties window. Then use ClassWizard to define a new dialog box class. For more information on adding a class, see "Adding a New User-Interface Class" on page 144.

2. In the MFC ClassWizard dialog box, select the Member Variables tab.

Note For a recordset class, the Update Cols button refreshes the current static list with the current database list. If a member has been assigned to a deleted column, it may be deleted.

The Bind All button creates an initial recordset with a default member name for every column in the table.

---

3. In the Control IDs box, select the control for which you want to set up DDX and choose Add Variable. The Add Member Variable dialog box appears.

4. In the Member Variable Name box, type the name of the new variable. ClassWizard provides the m_ prefix to identify it as a member variable.

5. In the Category box, select whether this variable is a Value variable or a Control variable.

   For standard Windows controls, choose Value to create a variable that contains the control's text or status as typed by the user. The framework automatically converts the control's data to the data type selected in the Variable Type box (see Table 12.3).

   You can also choose Control in the Properties drop-down list to create a Control variable that gives you access to the control itself (see Table 12.4).

6. In the Variable Type box, choose from a list of variable types appropriate to the control (see Table 12.3 and Table 12.4).

Once you've defined a DDX Value variable for a standard Windows control, the framework automatically initializes and updates the variable for you.

Table 12.3 shows the type of DDX value variables ClassWizard initially provides. To create additional variable types, see "Technical Note 26" in *Microsoft Foundation Class Library Technical Notes*.

Table 12.3   DDX Variable Types for the Value Property

Control	Variable Type
Edit box	**CString, int, UINT, long, DWORD, float, double**
Normal check box	**BOOL**
Three-state check box	**int**
Radio button (first in group)	**int**
Nonsorted list box	**CString, int**
Drop list combo box	**CString, int**
All other list box and combo box types	**CString**

The following additional notes apply to using DDX Value variables:

- Possible values for three-state check boxes are 0 (off), 1 (on), and 2 (indeterminate).

- Values for a group of radio buttons range from 0 for the first button in the group to $n-1$ for a group with n buttons. A value of -1 indicates that no buttons are selected.

- When you are using a group of check boxes or radio buttons with a DDX variable, make sure the Auto property is set for all the controls in the group.

- Set the Group property for the first radio button in a group, and make sure all the other radio buttons immediately follow the first button in the tab order.

- To use an integer value with a combo box or list box, make sure the Sort property is turned off on the Properties window Styles tab.

Note You can now use ClassWizard to bind a member variable to the value of a scroll bar control, using the Value property and the **int** data type, as well as to a **CScrollBar** object, using the Control property. The Value property binds the value of a scroll bar control (the position of the scroll box, or "thumb"). ClassWizard enables DDX for a scroll bar by calling **DDX_Scroll** in your DoDataExchange override.

If your DoDataExchange function contains a call to **DDX_Scroll**, you must additionally set the scroll bar range before that call, as shown in the following code:

```
void CMyDlg::DoDataExchange( CDataExchange* pDX )
{
    CScrollBar* pScrollBar = (CScrollBar*)GetDlgItem( IDC_SCROLLBAR1 );
    pScrollBar->SetScrollRange( 0, 100 );
    CDialog::DoDataExchange( pDX );
    //{{AFX_DATA_MAP(CMyDlg)
    DDX_Scroll(pDX, IDC_SCROLLBAR1, m_nScroll );
    //}}AFX_DATA_MAP
}
```

Table 12.4 shows the type of DDX Control variables you can define with ClassWizard.

Table 12.4   DDX Variable Types Defined with the Control Property

Control	Variable Type
Edit box	**CEdit**
Check box	**CButton**
Radio button	**CButton**
Pushbutton	**CButton**
List box	**CListBox**
Combo box or drop list combo box	**CComboBox**
Static text	**CStatic**
Scroll bar	**CScrollBar**

Setting Initial Values for Member Variables

You can set the initial value of DDX variables by editing the initialization code that ClassWizard places in the constructor for the dialog-box class. (ClassWizard does not disturb these initialization statements once they have been put in place.) The framework transfers the values to the dialog box when it is created.

To see what the user typed once the dialog box is dismissed, access the values of the DDX variables just as you would any C++ member variable.

Dialog Data Validation

By default, ClassWizard supports the types of data validation shown in Table 12.5, but you can add additional types (see "Technical Note 26" in *Microsoft Foundation Class Library Technical Notes*).

Table 12.5   DDV Variable Types

Variable Type	Data Validation
CString	Maximum length
Numeric (**int**, **UINT**, **long**, **DWORD**, **float**, **double**)	Minimum value, maximum value

You can define the maximum length for a **CString** DDX variable or the minimum or maximum values for a numeric DDX variable at the time you create it.

At run time, if the value entered by the user exceeds the range you specify, the framework automatically displays a message box asking the user to reenter the value. The validation of DDX variables takes place all at once when the user chooses OK to accept the entries in the dialog box.

Custom Data Exchange and Validation

Although you can write a dialog-box class that gathers and validates its own dialog-box data using custom message handlers, you may find that you have routines for data exchange and validation (containing your own variable types and data formats) that you want to use over and over. You can extend the ClassWizard user interface to reuse your own DDX and DDV routines. For more information on this subject, see "Technical Note 26" in *Microsoft Foundation Class Library Technical Notes*.

Keeping ClassWizard Updated When Code Changes

It's very likely that as your program develops you'll need to delete or modify a class, to delete some resources and add others, or to move a class from one source file to another. ClassWizard is designed to keep in sync with your code as you make these changes: it asks you for the updated information when you next edit the affected class.

ClassWizard stores the information about your application's classes in a file with the file extension .CLW. To accommodate source files that have changed, ClassWizard displays the Repair Class Information dialog box whenever it finds that the information in the .CLW file is out of date.

The Repair Class Information dialog box has two main functions:

- Delete obsolete classes from the ClassWizard file
- Update the ClassWizard file with the new name or location of classes that you have changed or moved

Deleting Classes

When you delete a class from your header and implementation files, the information in the .CLW file needs to be updated as well. The next time you select that class in ClassWizard, you are prompted to update the information in the ClassWizard file.

▶ **To delete a message-handling class created with ClassWizard**

1. From the Project menu, choose Files.

   The Project Files dialog box appears.

2. Select and remove the class header and implementation files from the Files In Group list.

3. Close the Project files dialog box.

4. From the <u>P</u>roject menu, choose Class<u>W</u>izard (CTRL+W). In the Class Name box, select the class you have modified.

   ClassWizard displays the Repair Class Information dialog box.

5. Choose Remove.

   The class is deleted from the ClassWizard file.

Renaming or Moving Classes

When you change the name of a class or move it from one implementation file to another, you're prompted to update the information in the .CLW file the next time you edit the class in ClassWizard.

▶ **To change the name of a class or move it from one file to another**

1. Make the desired changes to your source files.

   Note When you change the name of a class, remember to change it everywhere, including in the special-format comments ClassWizard uses. For example, `//{{AFX_MSG_MAP(OldClass)` becomes `//{{AFX_MSG_MAP(NewClass)`

   ---

2. From the Project menu, choose ClassWizard. In the Class Name box, choose the class you want to change from the list.

   ClassWizard displays a message box warning you that the old class could not be found. When you choose OK, the Repair Class Information dialog box appears.

3. In the Class Name, Header File, and Implementation File boxes, supply the new information about the class. If necessary, use the appropriate Browse command to look for the correct name of the header or implementation file.

4. Choose OK to update the ClassWizard file.

Rebuilding the ClassWizard (.CLW) File

If you have made numerous changes to your code or have added a large number of existing user-interface classes to your current project, you may find it convenient to rebuild the ClassWizard file from scratch rather than update it one class at a time. To do this, you delete your project's ClassWizard (.CLW) file and use ClassWizard to generate a new one. The newly-generated .CLW file contains information about all the classes that have the special-format ClassWizard comments.

▶ **To rebuild the ClassWizard file**

1. Delete your project's current .CLW file.

2. Open the project resource file so that information about your program's resources can be added to the file as well.

3. From the Project menu, choose ClassWizard (CTRL+W).

   Toolbar: ![icon]

   A message box is displayed asking if you want to rebuild the ClassWizard file from your source files. Choose Yes.

4. The Select Source Files dialog box appears. Use the File Name box and the Add, Add All, and Delete commands to create a list of source files in the Files in Project box.

5. When the list of project files is complete, choose OK.

   ClassWizard generates a new .CLW file.

CHAPTER 13

Browsing Through Symbols

Browse windows display information about the symbols in your program. When you build a project, by default, the compiler creates a file with the information about the symbols in your project. This file has the project's base name and the extension .BSC. You can also browse through any .BSC file created with the BSCMAKE.EXE utility located in the directory with other Visual C++ executables.

You view browse information in browse windows, which have different appearances and different controls depending on the type of information that they are displaying. In browse windows, you can examine:

- Information about all the symbols in any source file
- The source code line in which a symbol is defined
- Each source code line where there is a reference to a symbol
- The relationships between base classes and derived classes
- The relationships between calling functions and called functions

Working with Browse Information Files

A browse information file stores information about the symbols in your program. The browse window displays this information and allows you to move readily among instances of the symbols in your source code.

Creating a Browse Information File

You must create a browse information file (.BSC file) in order to use the browse windows. By default, Visual C++ creates a browse information file whenever you build a project. If you turn off those default settings—in order to speed up your builds, for instance—you can use Browse Info tab in the Project Settings dialog box to turn the settings on again.

▶ **To enable automatic creation of a browse information file**

1. Open the project, if it is not open.

2. From the Project menu, choose Settings.

   The Project Settings dialog box appears.

3. Select the Browse Info tab.

4. Clear the Update Browse Info File Only On Demand check box. Microsoft Visual C++ builds the browse information file each time you change a source file and build your project.

Opening and Closing Browse Information Files

When you open a project, Visual C++ automatically opens the browse information file associated with the project for all browse queries. You can use a browse window to get information on a symbol in the project.

You can explicitly close the information file currently open.

▶ **To close an information file**

- From the Project menu, choose Close *filename*.

Using an Information File Not Associated with the Current Project

You can open a browse information file for any project besides the currently open project. You then can use a browse window to get information on a symbol in that project.

▶ **To open an information file not associated with the current project**

1. From the File menu, choose Open.

2. In the List Files Of Type list box, select Browse Info Files (*.bsc).

3. Select the desired drive, directory, and browse information file.

An alternative method for opening a browse information file is to drag the browse information file icon over the Visual C++ icon in the File Manager.

Note If a query causes Visual C++ to open a source file for you, it opens the source file used to create the currently open browse information file, regardless of whether the source file is in the currently open project or not.

Browsing the Current Information File

Whenever you open a project, Visual C++ always opens the browse information file for the project if it exists. If you have explicitly closed the browse information file, Visual C++ opens the information file for the project whenever you complete a query command. You can also open another browse information file explicitly, using the Open command on the File menu.

▶ **To query the current information file about a symbol**

1. Use one of the following methods to specify the symbol:

   - Move the insertion point to the symbol in a source file or the left browse window pane.

   - Type the symbol in the Find text box on the Standard toolbar. CTRL+F or ALT+A moves the focus to the text box.

   - Select the symbol from the drop-down list if you have previously entered the symbol in the list box on the Standard toolbar. CTRL+F or ALT+A moves the focus to the edit box.

   - Select the symbol from any pane in a browse window.

   You can also use the asterisk wildcard at the end of a character string to match any symbols starting with those characters. If you want to view multiple files using the File Outline, you can enter a filename specification with an asterisk wildcard at the end of the filename (oc*.cpp, for instance), at the end of the filename extension (ocwin.c*), or at the end of both (oc*.*).

2. From the Search menu, choose Browse (CTRL+F11).

   The Browse dialog box appears.

3. If the insertion point was not on a symbol, and you did not select a symbol from the drop-down list on the Standard toolbar, enter a symbol name in the Query on Name text box.

4. Select a query from the list.

   A browse window with the controls specific to that query appears, and displays the default query for the symbol for the selected query type.

▶ **To query the current information file from a source file**

1. Specify the symbol by moving the insertion point to the symbol in a source file.

2. Press one of the following keys:

Key	Action
F11	Opens the file containing the definition of the symbol and selects the symbol in the definition.
SHIFT+F11	Opens the file containing the first reference to the symbol and selects the symbol.
CTRL+F11	Opens the Browse dialog box. You select the desired query.

Symbol Type Abbreviations in the Browse Window

When you display symbols in the browse window, they are preceded by abbreviations denoting the type of symbol. The browse window uses the following abbreviations:

Abbreviation	Meaning
c	class
f	function
d	data
m	macro
t	non-class type
V	Virtual function or data member
S	Static function or data member

Using the Browse Toolbar

You can use the controls on the Browse toolbar to launch a query about a symbol whenever you have an open browse information file. The active controls at any point are not grayed; the inactive controls are grayed.

You can customize the Browse toolbar to display the controls of your choice, using the Customize command on the Tools menu. With the Customize dialog box, you can add tools to an existing toolbar or create a new toolbar. For more information, see "Creating a Custom Toolbar" on page 254 or "Modifying a Toolbar" on page 255, both in Chapter 17.

The Browse tools include the following:

Button	Action
	Opens the file containing the definition of the symbol and selects the symbol in the definition.
	Opens the file containing the first reference to the symbol and selects the symbol.
	Jumps to the next definition or reference to the symbol. After the last, it returns to the first.
	Jumps to the previous definition or reference to the symbol. After the last, it returns to the first.
	Returns the insertion point to its location before the last query, and restores the previous query in the browse window.
	Displays the browse window with the file outline.
	Displays the browse window with the definition and references for the selected symbol.
	Displays the browse window with the graph of classes derived from the selected class.
	Displays the browse window with the graph of base class(es) for the selected class.
	Displays the browse window with the graph of functions that the selected function calls.
	Displays the browse window with the graph of functions that call the selected function.

Building Your Project More Quickly

In a large project, creating a browse information file (.BSC file) can take a significant amount of time. Whenever Visual C++ builds a new project, it automatically creates a browse information file. By default, it also automatically builds the browse information file each time it builds or rebuilds the current project.

You can build your project more quickly by disabling the automatic update of the browse information file temporarily. The compiler continues to generate the intermediate .SBR files, but it does not use them to create the browse information file for the project.

The Browse Info tab in the Project Settings dialog box gives you an option to control building the browse information file. You can choose either to build your browse information file when it is out of date, or only when you request it.

▶ **To build the browse information file only when it is out of date**

1. Open the project if it is not currently open.

2. From the Project menu, choose Settings.

   The Project Settings dialog box appears.

3. Select the Browse Info tab.

4. Clear the Update Browse Info File Only On Demand check box.

Now, every time you build or rebuild the project, Visual C++ builds the browse information file.

▶ **To build the browse information file on demand**

1. Open the project if it is not currently open.

2. From the Project menu, choose Settings.

   The Project Settings dialog box appears.

3. Select the Browse Info tab.

4. Select the Update Browse Info File Only On Demand check box.

Now, whenever you want to bring the information file up to date, you must explicitly choose the Build Browse Info File command on the Project menu.

Displaying the Symbols in a File

You can display an outline of all the symbols in a specific source file or in multiple source files, and filter the types of information displayed.

▶ **To display all the symbols in a file**

1. Open the source file that you want to examine. If it is already open, click that window to move the focus there.

   –Or–

   Select the file in the *project*.MAK window.

2. Press CTRL+F11 to display the Browse dialog box, and select File Outline from the list.

Toolbar:

The File Outline browse window appears, with classes and functions displayed at the top of the leftmost pane, as shown in Figure 13.1.

Figure 13.1   Browse window with File Outline

Window Element	Function	Actions
Left pane	Displays the functions and classes in the file by default.	Click to select a symbol from the list. Double-click to open source at the definition.
Right pane	Displays definitions and references for the item currently selected in the left pane.	Double-click the location specified for the definition or reference to open source at the definition or reference.
Pushpin	Determines whether or not the window disappears after it loses focus.	Click to push or pull pin.
Help button	Displays help for the window	Click for help.
Filter buttons	Filter the browse query to display selected types of information. See "Filtering Browse Information for Files" for more information.	Click to toggle filter.

The left pane displays the following information about symbols:

Left entries	Middle entry	Right entry
Applicable filter types from the selected filters and virtual or static member indicator	Symbol name	Type of symbol if the symbol name is ambiguous about type

▶ **To display all the symbols in multiple files**

1. From the Search menu, choose Browse (CTRL+F11).

   The Browse dialog box appears.

2. In the Query on Name text box, enter a filename specification with an asterisk wildcard at the end of the filename (oc*.cpp, for instance), at the end of the filename extension (ocwin.c*) or at the end of both (oc*.*).

   Note If you type a filename specification followed by the asterisk wildcard, but without an extension (oc*, for instance), Visual C++ reports that it cannot find the file.

   ---

3. Select File Outline from the list.

   Toolbar: ▣

The File Outline browse window appears, with classes and functions displayed at the top of the leftmost pane, as shown in Figure 13.1.

Filtering Browse Information for Files

You can choose to filter the types of information displayed from the selected file

▶ **To filter query information**

- Click the desired button to display the indicated result.

Button	Keyboard	Display Result
Classes	ALT+C	Classes
Functions	ALT+U	Functions
Data	ALT+A	Data symbols
Macros	ALT+M	Macros
Types	ALT+Y	Non-class types

Displaying Class Information

You can view C++ class hierarchies as graphs. You can select a class and display either of the following two types of graphs for class hierarchies:

Derived Class Graph: All the classes that inherit attributes from the selected class.

Base Class Graph: All the classes from which the selected class inherits attributes, up to its ultimate base class, or base classes, if it has multiple inheritance.

In each graph, a node represents a class.

Displaying the Graph of Classes Derived from a Class

▶ **To display a derived class graph**

1. Move the insertion point to the class name in a source file. If you have previously entered the class name in the list box on the Standard toolbar, you can select it from the drop-down list.

2. From the Search menu, choose Browse (CTRL+F11).

   The Browse dialog box is displayed.

3. Double-click Derived Classes and Members in the list.

The Derived Classes and Members window appears, with the selected class displayed at the top of the leftmost pane, as shown in Figure 13.2.

▶ **To quickly display a derived class graph**

1. Move the insertion point to the class name in a source file.

2. Click the Derived Class Graph button on the Browse toolbar.

The Derived Classes and Members window appears.

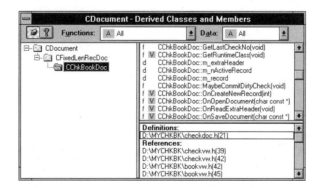

Figure 13.2   Derived Classes and Members Window

Window Element	Function	Action
Left pane	Displays graph of derivations.	Click the plus or minus sign to expand or contract graph. Click the node or title to select it and display the corresponding information in the right pane. Double-click a symbol to open source at definition.
Top right pane	Displays member functions and member variables of the class selected in the left pane.	Double-click to open source at definition.
Bottom right pane	Displays definitions and references for the item currently selected in either the left or top right panes.	Double-click to open source at the definition or a specific reference.
Pushpin	Determines whether or not the window disappears after it loses focus.	Click to push or pull pin.
Help button	Displays help for the window	Click for help.
Filter lists	Filter the browse query to display selected types of information. See Filtering Browse Information for Classes for more information.	Select filter types from the lists.

Displaying the Base Class Graph for a Class

▶ **To display the base class graph**

1. Move the insertion point to the class name in a source file. Alternatively, you can select the class name. If you have entered the class name in the list box on the Standard toolbar, you can select it from the drop-down list.

2. From the Edit menu, choose Browse (CTRL+F11).

   The Browse dialog box is displayed.

3. Double-click Base Class Graph in the list.

The Base Classes and Members window appears, with the selected class displayed in at the top of the leftmost pane, as shown in Figure 13.3.

▶ **To quickly display a base class graph**

1. Move the insertion point to the class name in a source file.

2. Click the Base Classes and Members button on the Browse toolbar.

The Base Classes and Members window appears.

Figure 13.3   Base Classes and Members Window

Window Element	Function	Action
Left pane	Displays graph of derivations.	Click the plus or minus sign to expand or contract graph. Click the node or title to select it and display the corresponding information in the right panes. Double-click a symbol to open source at definition.
Top right pane	Displays member functions and member variables of the class selected in the left pane.	Click to display definition and references in bottom right pane. Double-click to open source at definition.
Bottom right pane	Displays definitions and references for the item currently selected in either the left or top right panes.	Double-click to open source at the definition or a specific reference.
Pushpin	Determines whether or not the window disappears after it loses focus.	Click to push or pull pin.
Help button	Displays help for the window	Click for help.
Filter lists	Filter the browse query to display selected types of information. See Filtering Browse Information for Classes for more information.	Select filter type from the lists.

If the class has multiple inheritance, and one base class is represented more than one time on more than one inheritance path, the second and each subsequent instance of its title is displayed with an ellipsis (**...**) following it. You cannot expand such nodes.

Filtering Browse Information for Classes

You can choose to filter information displayed about functions and data in the selected class.

▶ **To filter browse information**

- From the Functions drop-down list, select the desired filter:

Entry	Display Result
All	All member functions
Virtual	Virtual member functions only
Static	Static member functions only
Non-Virtual	Non-virtual member functions only
Non-Static	Non-static member functions only
Non-Static Non-Virtual	Non-static, non-virtual member functions only
None	No member functions

You can also press ALT+U to open the list, and then use the up and down arrow keys to choose an entry. Pressing ENTER selects that filter.

- From the Data drop-down list, select the desired filter:

Button	Display Result
All	All member data
Static	Static member data only
Non-Static	Non-Static member data only
None	No member data

You can also press ALT+A to open the list, and then use the up and down arrow keys to choose an entry. Pressing ENTER selects that filter.

The graphic symbols displayed in the drop-down list identify corresponding entries in the top right pane of the browse window.

Displaying Function Information

You can display as a graph the relationships among functions in your program. You can select a function and display either of the following two types of graphs for function relationships:

- Call Graph: All the functions that the selected function calls.
- Callers Graph: All the functions that call the selected function.

In each graph, a node represents a function.

Displaying a Call Graph

A call graph displays all the functions that a selected function calls.

▶ **To display the graph of all functions that a selected function calls**

1. Move the insertion point to the function name in a source file. If you have entered a function name in the list box on the Standard toolbar, you can select it from the drop-down list.

2. From the Search menu, choose Browse (CTRL+F11).

   The Browse dialog box is displayed.

3. Double-click Call Graph in the list.

▶ **To quickly display the graph of all functions that a selected function calls**

1. Move the insertion point to the function name in a source file.

2. Click the Call Graph button on the Browse toolbar.

   If the function name is a member function that appears in more than one class or is an overloaded function, the Resolve Ambiguities dialog box appears. Select the symbol that you want from the list.

The Call Graph window appears, with the selected function displayed at the top of the left pane, as shown in Figure 13.4.

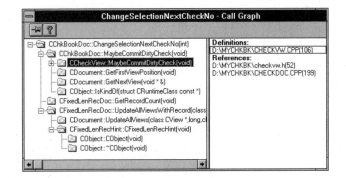

Figure 13.4   Call Graph Window

Window Element	Function	Action
Left pane	Displays graph of functions that the selected function calls.	Click the plus or minus sign to expand or contract graph. Click the node or title to select it and display the corresponding information in the right pane. Double-click to open source at the definition or a specific reference.
Right pane	Displays definitions and references for the item currently selected in the left pane.	Double-click to open source at the definition or a specific reference.
Pushpin	Determines whether or not the window disappears after it loses focus.	Click to push or pull pin.
Help button	Displays help for the window	Click for help.

Displaying a Graph of Calling Functions

A callers graph displays all the functions that call a selected function.

▶ **To display the graph of all functions that call a selected function**

1. Move the insertion point to the function name in a source file. Alternatively, you can select the function name. If you have entered a function name in the list box on the Standard toolbar, you can select it from the drop-down list.

2. From the Search menu, choose Browse (CTRL+F11).

   The Browse dialog box is displayed.

3. Double-click Callers Graph in the list.

▶ **To quickly display the graph of all functions that call a selected function**

1. Move the insertion point to the function name in a source file.

2. Click the Callers Graph button on the Browse toolbar.

   If the function name is a member function that appears in more than one class or is an overloaded function, the Resolve Ambiguities dialog box appears. Select the symbol that you want from the list.

The Callers Graph window appears, with the selected function displayed at the top of the left pane, as shown in Figure 13.5.

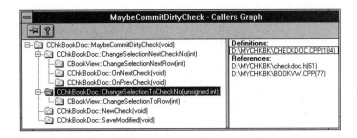

Figure 13.5   Callers Graph Window

Window Element	Function	Action
Left pane	Displays graph of functions that call the selected function.	Click the plus or minus sign to expand or contract graph. Click the node or title to select it and display the corresponding information in the right pane. Double-click to open source at the definition or a specific reference.
Right pane	Displays definitions and references for the item currently selected in the left pane.	Double-click to open source at the definition or a specific reference.
Pushpin	Determines whether or not the window disappears after it loses focus.	Click to push or pull pin.
Help button	Displays help for the window	Click for help.

Finding Definitions and References

The browse windows makes it easy to move from one location of a symbol in a file to another location in another file. For instance, if you are in a source file examining the use of a symbol, you can immediately jump to the definition of that symbol. Or if you have changed the definition of a symbol, you can jump to every place in every file where the symbol is used.

Note The browse information file is based on the state of the source files at the time of the last build. If you edit source files and then go to a definition or a reference, the location in the browse information file may no longer be accurate.

If a definition is listed as <Unknown>, it is probably located in a library for which you are not provided the source code. For example, the Windows API functions are defined in source code that is not provided with Visual C++.

Displaying a Symbol Definition

▶ **To display the definition of a symbol**

1. Use one of the following methods to specify the symbol:

   - Move the insertion point to the symbol in a source file.

   - Type the symbol in the Find text box on the Standard toolbar.

   - Select the symbol from the drop-down list if you have previously entered the symbol in the list box on the Standard toolbar.

   You can also use the asterisk wildcard at the end of a character string to match any symbols starting with those characters.

2. From the Search menu, choose Browse (CTRL+F11).

   The Browse dialog box is displayed.

3. Double-click Definitions And References in the list.

   If the symbol is a member appearing in more than one class, the Resolve Ambiguities dialog box appears. Select the unambiguous symbol from the list.

The Definitions And References window appears, with the selected function displayed at the top of the left pane, as shown in Figure 13.6.

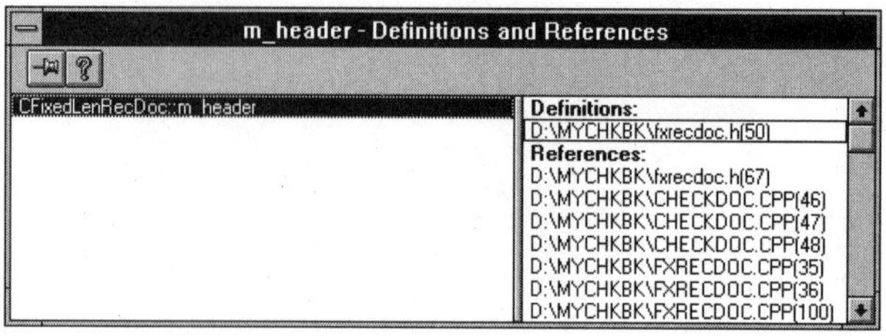

Figure 13.6   Definitions and References Window

Window Element	Function	Actions
Left pane	Displays the selected symbol or a list of the matching symbols if you used a wildcard.	Click to select a symbol from the list. Double-click to open source at the definition.
Right pane	Displays definitions and references for the item currently selected in the left pane.	Double-click the location specified for the definition or reference to open source at the definition or reference.
Pushpin	Determines whether or not the window disappears after it loses focus.	Click to push or pull pin.
Help button	Displays help for the window	Click for help.

▶ **To quickly display the definition of a symbol**

1. Move the insertion point to the symbol in a source file.

2. Click the Definition/Reference button on the Browse toolbar.

Visual C++ opens the source file with the definition, and highlights the definition.

Displaying Symbol References

▶ **To display a reference to a symbol**

1. Use one of the following methods to specify the symbol:

   • Move the insertion point to the symbol in a source file.

   • Type the symbol in the Find text box on the Standard toolbar. You can append the asterisk wildcard to a character string to match any symbols starting with those characters.

   • Select the symbol from the drop-down list if you have previously entered the symbol in the list box on the Standard toolbar.

2. From the Search menu, choose Browse (CTRL+F11).

   The Browse dialog box is displayed.

3. Double-click Definitions and References in the list.

   If the symbol is a member appearing in more than one class, the Resolve Ambiguities dialog box appears. Select the symbol that you want from the list.

The Definitions and References window appears, with the selected symbol displayed at the top of the left pane, as shown in Figure 13.6.

Window Element	Function	Action
Left pane	Displays the selected symbol or a list of the matching symbols if you used a wildcard. If the symbol is not fully qualified, it is followed by the symbol's type.	Click to select a symbol from the list. Double-click a symbol to open source at its definition.
Right pane	Displays definitions and references for the item currently selected in the left pane.	Double-click the location specified for any reference or definition to open source at that reference or definition.
Pushpin	Determines whether or not the window disappears after it loses focus.	Click to push or pull pin.
Help button	Displays help for the window	Click for help.

▶ **To quickly display the reference to a symbol**

1. Move the insertion point to the symbol in a source file.

2. Click the Reference button on the Browse toolbar.

Visual C++ opens the source file with the first reference, and highlights the reference.

Jumping to a Definition or Reference

After you have moved the insertion point to a symbol, you can use the following methods to jump to the next reference to a symbol, the next definition of a symbol, the previous reference to a symbol, or the previous definition of a symbol.

▶ **To jump to another definition or reference**

Key	Toolbar Button	Search Menu	Jumps to
CTRL+NUMPad +		Next Definition –Or– Next Reference	The next definition or reference
CTRL+NUMPad –		Previous Definition –Or– Previous Reference	The previous definition or reference
CTRL+NUMPad *		Pop Context	The previous context and query

You can jump to the definition of a symbol or to the first reference to a symbol directly from any occurrence of the symbol in a source file.

▶ **To jump to a reference or definition from a source file**

1. Use one of the following methods to specify the symbol:

    ▪ Move the insertion point to the symbol in a source file.

    ▪ Select the symbol in the source file.

2. Press one of the following keys:

Key	Action
F11	Opens the file containing the definition of the symbol and selects the symbol in the definition.
SHIFT+F11	Opens the file containing the first reference to the symbol and selects the symbol.

Modifying the Browse Window Display

A browse window appears in response to queries, and by default, disappears when you move the focus away from the window. You can maintain the browse window in view with the pushpin button at the top of the window. Fixing a browse window on your display with the pushpin has these two effects:

- The browse window remains visible even if you move the focus to another window, to edit a source file, for instance.

- The browse window remains on top of all other Visual C++ windows.

▶ **To keep a browse window visible**

- Click the pushpin button at the top of the window.

▶ **To change the size of a pane in a browse window**

- With the mouse pointer, point to the split bar between panes, and drag the split bar to its new location.

▶ **To move the focus from pane to pane in a browse window**

- Press TAB to move to the next pane.

- Press SHIFT+TAB to move to the previous pane.

Nodes in a graph display a plus sign or minus sign in the left margin of the graph. If a plus sign is next to a node, you can expand that node If a minus sign is next to a node, you can contract that node.

▶ **To expand or contract a node in a graph**

- Click the PLUS SIGN (+) or MINUS SIGN (–), or select the node with the arrow keys and press ENTER.

C H A P T E R   1 4

Using the Debugger

Visual C++ provides an integrated debugger to debug programs and OLE applications, manage breakpoints, control threads, and perform many other debugging functions. The debugger allows you to examine the state of an executable program, dynamic-link library, or OLE client or server at any point as it runs.

Debugging is a two-phase process. First, you correct errors that prevent you from building your program—mistaken language syntax, undeclared variables, misspelled keywords, and the like—and then you use the debugger to detect and correct logic errors and behavioral anomalies in your program.

With the debugger you can:

- Control and manage breakpoints in advanced ways.
- Control multiple debug windows displaying such things as memory values, register values, and assembly language code.
- Control threads in multiple-threaded environments.
- Remotely debug programs operating on other operating systems.
- Completely control debugging DLLs and OLE2 applications.
- Analyze a living program with "Just-in-Time" debugging rather than conduct a postmortem examination after it dies.

The debugger allows you to control the execution of your program, and examine the program state at various points in its execution. In the debugger, you can specify the conditions under which to stop the execution of your program. These conditions are known as breakpoints. After setting breakpoints, you start execution of your program under the control of the debugger.

If you choose to step through your program, you can either enter the code for the function when it is called in a statement, using the Step Into command on the Debug menu, or skip over the code for the function, using the Step Over command. You can similarly exit from a called function with the Step Out command, which returns you to the statement where the function was called.

When you stop debugging, either by exiting the program or by selecting the Stop Debugging command, the project retains any breakpoints that you have set. If you close the project, it stores the breakpoints, and restores them when you open the project again. Your debugging can thus span sessions.

When the program is stopped, you can use the debug windows and dialog boxes to examine the state of your program.

Tip   While in debug mode, in many instances you can click the right mouse button to display a shortcut menu of frequently used commands. The commands available depend on what the pointer is pointing at. For example, if you click while pointing at a source file, the shortcut menu shows several commands, including Toggle Breakpoint and QuickWatch.

Understanding Debugging Windows, Dialog Boxes, and Toolbars

Visual C++ displays information in a series of windows that you can view as you debug a program. You can use commands from the Debug menu to access the debugging windows.

Table 14.1 lists the debugging windows and the information they show.

Table 14.1   Debugging Windows

Window	Information
Watch	Displays values of variables and expressions in the Watch window. Watch expressions can be entered and edited directly in the Watch window text box.
Locals	Displays values of local variables within the function currently being stepped through.
Registers	Displays current contents of the general purpose and CPU status registers. The format is specified on the Debug tab in the Options dialog box.
Memory	Displays current contents of memory; the format and location are specified on the Debug tab in the Options dialog box.
Output	This window displays output during a debugging session, such as output from **OutputDebugString** function calls (or the class library **afxDump**), thread termination codes, and first-chance exception notification. This window also displays information about the build process, including any compiler errors.

Table 14.1   Debugging Windows (*continued*)

Window	Information
Call Stack	Displays all the functions that have been called but have not returned. The options are specified on the Debug tab in the Options dialog box.
Disassembly	Displays associated assembly-language and source code for straight disassembly debugging and mixed-mode debugging. The format is specified on the Debug tab in the Options dialog box.

You can size and minimize any of these undocked windows during debugging so that you can see various types of information at one time. These windows also behave like source windows, allowing you to copy and print information from them. Printing is not available in the Disassembly, Call Stack, Memory, or Registers windows.

Tip   You can use the right mouse button to instantly access the shortcut menus for a particular window. Each shortcut menu contains a list of useful commands appropriate to the current window.

For more information on using Visual C++ windows, see "Working with Document Windows" on page 245 and "Working with Docking Tool Windows" on page 247, both in Chapter 17.

Visual C++ also uses a series of dialog boxes to manipulate breakpoints, variables, threads, and exceptions for debugging. You can use commands from the Debug menu to access the debugging dialog boxes.

Table 14.2 lists the debugging dialog boxes and the information they show.

Table 14.2   Debugging Dialog Boxes

Window	Information
QuickWatch	Displays variables and expressions. You can also use the QuickWatch dialog box to quickly view and modify variables and expressions.
Breakpoints	Displays the list of all breakpoints assigned to your project. You can also use the Breakpoints dialog box to create new breakpoints.
Exceptions	Displays the list of system exceptions assigned to your project. You can also use the Exceptions dialog box to control exceptions.
Threads	Displays the list of application threads available for debugging. You can also use the Threads dialog box to control which thread is currently active.

Table 14.3 lists the buttons available in the debugging category of toolbars and their equivalent menu actions.

Table 14.3   Debugging Toolbar Buttons

Button	Equivalent menu action
	Runs the current dialog box to test appearance and behavior.
	Starts or continues the current program.
	Restarts the current program.
	Stops debugging the current program.
	Sets or clears a breakpoint.
	Steps into the next statement.
	Steps over the next statement.
	Steps out of the current function.
	Runs the current program to the line containing the cursor.
	Shows variables and expressions quickly.
	Clears all breakpoints.
	Sets or clears a breakpoint.
	Activates or deactivates the Output window.
	Activates or deactivates the Watch window.
	Activates or deactivates the Locals window.
	Activates or deactivates the Registers window.
	Activates or deactivates the Memory window.
	Activates or deactivates the Call Stack window.
	Activates or deactivates the Disassembly window.

Debugging Compiler and Linker Errors

The first phase of debugging is to fix language syntax errors. The Output window shows a list of all errors that prevent a program from being built, including filename, line number, and error number. The Output window behaves like a source window, allowing you to copy and print information from the window. If displayed, the status bar gives a summary of the current error.

If you don't understand the error message, move the insertion point to the error number and press F1 to display online information about it.

▶ **To move through the list of errors**

- From the Search menu, choose Next Error/Tag (F4) to highlight the error following the current error.

  –Or–

- From the Search menu, choose Previous Error/Tag (SHIFT+F4) to highlight the error preceding the current error.

  –Or–

- In the Output window, double-click an error, or select an error and press ENTER.

  As each error is highlighted in the Output window, the corresponding line containing the error is highlighted in the source window.

You can move to any line number in a source file.

▶ **To move to a specific line**

1. From the Search menu, choose Go To (CTRL+G).

   The Go To dialog box appears.

2. In the Line Number box, type a line number.

3. Choose OK.

If you type a line number greater than the last line in your source file, the editor moves to the end of the file.

Using Breakpoints

Breakpoints specify to the debugger where or when to break execution of a program —that is, stop the program temporarily. You can then examine the state of your program, examine or modify variables, examine the call stack, and so on. You can set multiple breakpoints in your program.

Breakpoints are useful when you have a general idea of where a bug occurs in a program. The debugger runs until it reaches the breakpoint, then stops. At this point you can step to the next line of code or trace through a function until you find the problem. While the program is paused at a breakpoint, you can also examine variable values using the QuickWatch dialog box or examine other program elements in any of the debugging windows (Watch, Locals, Registers, Memory, Call Stack, or Disassembly).

The Toggle Breakpoints button on the toolbar simply sets or clears a breakpoint at the insertion point. The Breakpoints dialog box allows you to set more complex breakpoints, such as breaking if an expression is true or breaking on a window message.

The Breakpoints dialog box keeps a list of all breakpoints assigned to your project. Breakpoints can be set in any of your project source files or in executable files or DLLs.

All breakpoints active in the Source, Call Stack, and Disassembly windows are saved as part of the project information when a project is closed. These breakpoints become active when the project is reopened. A project is closed when you choose Close from the File menu, when you open or create another project, or when you quit Visual C++.

Note Hard address breakpoints are saved with the project but they are disabled when the project is reopened.

Setting a Breakpoint with the Toolbar

The Toggle Breakpoints button on the toolbar simply sets or clears a breakpoint at the insertion point. You can set breakpoints in the source, Call Stack, and Disassembly windows.

▶ **To set a breakpoint using the toolbar**

1. Move the insertion point to the line where you want the program to break.
2. Click the Toggle Breakpoints button: 🖐️

   The line is highlighted (or a widget is displayed in the margin), indicating that the breakpoint is set.

▶ **To remove a breakpoint using the toolbar**

1. Move the insertion point to the line containing the breakpoint.
2. Click the Toggle Breakpoints button: 🖐️

Warning Setting a breakpoint on a local variable may be very slow if you are remotely debugging the application.

▶ **To remove a breakpoint**

1. From the Debug menu, choose Breakpoints (CTRL+B).
2. In the Breakpoints box, select the breakpoint you want to remove.
3. Choose Delete to remove the selected breakpoint. Or choose Clear All to remove all of the listed breakpoints.
4. Choose Close.

Break At a Location

The Breakpoint dialog box default type is "Break At Location."

▶ **To set a breakpoint at a location**

1. Position the insertion point on a line in a source file.

2. From the <u>D</u>ebug menu, choose <u>B</u>reakpoints (CTRL+B).

   The Breakpoints dialog box appears and the line number for the line with the insertion point automatically appears in the Location box. You can also type a function name here to specify the location.

3. Choose Add to add this location as a breakpoint.

   The Breakpoints box shows the currently active breakpoints.

4. Choose Close.

Tip   You can also type a function name or location in the find box on the toolbar and press F9. The F9 shortcut is also usable in the Call Stack and Disassembly window. The entire procedure also has the following shortcuts:

Toolbar shortcut: 🖑

Keyboard shortcut: F9

You can also type a location directly into the Location box in the Breakpoints dialog box. You can type a function name or a line number. If you omit the line number, the first executable line in the function is assumed.

The following examples illustrate the syntax:

Format	Example	Description
.line number	`.35`	Sets a breakpoint at line 35 in the current source file
filename!.line number	`MyApp.cpp!.35`	Sets a breakpoint at line 35 in MYAPP.CPP
function name	`CMyWindow::OnCall`	Sets a breakpoint at the beginning of this function

Two of the breakpoint types evaluate whether an expression is true or has changed. When the expression evaluates correctly, the program pauses at the location specified.

You can also break at any location when an expression is true, or when an expression has changed.

▶ **To break at a location when an expression is true, or when an expression has changed**

1. Position the insertion point on a line in a source file.

2. From the Debug menu, choose Breakpoints (CTRL+B).

   The line number for the line with the insertion point automatically appears in the Location box.

3. In the Type box, choose Break At Location If Expression Is True or Break At Location If Expression Has Changed.

4. Specify an expression in the Expression box.

5. Optionally, type the length of the expression in bytes in the Length box.

6. Choose Add to add this location as a breakpoint.

   The Breakpoints box shows the currently active breakpoints.

7. Choose Close.

Tip An error occurs when an expression contains an out-of-scope variable. To ensure that potentially out-of-scope variables are always in scope, use the context operator {fn, s, e}. Typically, just {fn} is enough to adequately scope the variable. Note that the context operator has the same precedence as the cast operator, and can therefore be used as follows: {fn1}(i+j) - {fn2}k.

To detect when an expression has changed, you must type an expression that evaluates to a memory location (an L-value) in the Expression box when you set the breakpoint.

If you choose Break When Expression Has Changed, you may also need to edit the value in the Length box. The default length is 1, which indicates 1 times the size of the expression's type. If you are dereferencing a pointer, for instance, you must also type the length of this memory location (in bytes) in the Length box. Otherwise the length refers to the length of the pointer.

General Syntax for Breakpoint Locations

The general syntax for breakpoint locations has the following form:

[[*fn*],[*s*],[*e*]].*line*

   or

[[*fn*],[*s*],[*e*]]*label, symbol* or *address*

where

Syntax	Description
{}	The context operator, with the context specified by the following three elements
fn	The name of a function
s	The name of a source file, with drive and path if necessary
e	The name of an executable file or DLL
line	A line number in a source file
label, *symbol*, *address*	Any symbol, label or address that evaluates to an address

If you use this form, you must also type the braces enclosing *fn*, *s*, and *e* forming the context operator. If you omit any of those elements, you must include the commas.

This general syntax form can be abbreviated, as shown in the shortened forms in the previous table.

You can also set breakpoints in the following forms:

Format	Example	Description
offset	`0x1002A`	Sets a breakpoint at the specified offset in memory.
offset	`Traverse`	Sets a breakpoint at function Traverse.
.line number	`.35`	Sets a breakpoint at line 35 in the current source file.
filename!.line number	`MyApp.cpp!.35`	Sets a breakpoint at line 35 in MYAPP.CPP.
function name	`CMyWindow::OnCall`	Sets a breakpoint at the beginning of this function.

context operator	`{,foo.c,}.45`
	`{foo,foo.c,`
	`foo.dll}MyLabel`
		Sets a breakpoint using the context operator.

These forms of breakpoints are most useful if you are viewing mixed source and assembly language code. Use the Disassembly command on the Debug menu to display source code in this form.

Break on Expression

Two of the breakpoint types evaluate only whether an expression is true or has changed. When the expression evaluates correctly, the program pauses immediately.

To detect when an expression has changed, you must type an expression that evaluates to a memory location (an L-value) in the Expression box when you set the breakpoint.

If you choose Break When Expression Has Changed, you may also need to edit the value in the Length box. The default length is 1, which indicates 1 times the size of the expression's type. If you are dereferencing a pointer, for instance, you must also type the length of this memory location (in bytes) in the Length box. Otherwise the length refers to the length of the pointer.

When you set a breakpoint on an expression, Visual C++ will use debug registers:

1. If there are debug registers left (there are only four available on 80386 and later chips) *and*

2. if the item(s) is static data (DGROUP) based.

If emulation is used rather than debug registers, the execution speed of the program being debugged is significantly slowed down and at times the debuggee or debugger may seem hung while executing code in the debuggee (for example, single stepping). The program, however, is not hung. Emulation requires that after each instruction is executed, the address in question must be examined manually by the debugger.

Note   The debugger does not dereference pointers automatically.

▶   **To break when an expression is true or when an expression has changed**

1. From the Debug menu, choose Breakpoints (CTRL+B).

2. In the Type box, select Break When Expression Is True or Break When Expression Has Changed.

3. Specify an expression in the Expression box.

   If you chose Break When Expression Has Changed, the expression must evaluate to a memory location.

4. If you chose Break When Expression Has Changed and you are evaluating an expression which points to a memory location, you must also type in the Length box the length in bytes of the memory location specified by the expression.

5. Choose Add to add this location as a breakpoint.

   The Breakpoints box shows the currently active breakpoints.

6. Choose Close.

Warning   Setting a breakpoint on a local variable may be very slow if you are remotely debugging the application.

Tip   An error occurs when an expression contains an out-of-scope variable. To ensure that potentially out-of-scope variables are always in scope, use the context operator {fn, s, e}. Typically, just {fn} is enough to adequately scope the variable. Note that the context operator has the same precedence as the cast operator, and can therefore be used as follows: {fn1}(i+j) - {fn2}k.

Understanding Breakpoint Expressions

Breakpoint expressions can be any valid C or C++ expressions. They can also contain the BY, WO, or DW cast operators, which return the byte, word, or doubleword at the given address.

Constants are treated as decimal numbers unless they begin with a leading '0' (octal) or '0x' (hexadecimal).

The expressions listed below are all valid for breakpoints of type Break When Expression Is True:

- `frame.size < 10`
- `i == 100`
- `i == 100 || j > 10`
- `work.rate  *  hours  >= 1000`

The expressions listed below are all valid for breakpoints of type Break When Expression Has Changed:

- `*p`
- `frame.size`
- `next->node`

You can also type a starting address, such as an offset or a register, in the Expression box. In this case, you must also specify in the Length box the number of bytes to examine for changes.

If you want to watch the address contained in a pointer, you must give the pointer's address. In other words, for a pointer p, the breakpoint occurs when p is assigned to, *p breaks when *p is assigned to.

Break at WndProc Procedures

The breakpoint type "Break At WndProc If Message Is Received" lets you set a breakpoint that tests messages received by any exported Windows function. You can select whether to break on a specific message or on any message from a class of messages or from several classes of messages.

▶ **To set a breakpoint on a message**

1. From the Debug menu, choose Breakpoints (CTRL+B).

2. In the Type box, select Break At WndProc If Message Is Received.

3. In the WndProc box, type the name of the Windows callback function that you want tested for messages.

   If you are setting a breakpoint during a debug session, the list contains all of the exported functions in your project; otherwise it is blank.

4. Choose the Messages button to open the Messages dialog box.

5. Select the Selection option button.

6. In the Selection box, select the message.

7. Choose OK to close the Messages dialog box.

8. Choose Close to close the Breakpoints dialog box.

You can follow a similar procedure to set a breakpoint on one or more classes of messages.

▶ **To set a breakpoint on any message in one or more classes**

1. From the Debug menu, choose Breakpoints (CTRL+B).

2. In the Type box, select Break At WndProc If Message Is Received.

3. In the WndProc box, type the name of the exported Windows function.

4. Choose the Messages button to open the Messages dialog box.

5. Select the Class option button.

6. In the Class box, select one or more message classes.

7. Choose OK to close the Messages dialog box.

8. Choose Close to close the Breakpoint dialog box.

If you set a breakpoint using either of these two procedures, the program will pause execution at the specified window procedure when a message matching the qualifications is received.

Controlling Program Execution

Once a breakpoint is reached and the program stops, you can control program execution with commands on the Debug menu. Table 14.4 lists the Debug menu commands and their actions.

Table 14.4   Debug Menu Commands that Control Execution

Debug Menu Command	Action
Go	Executes code from the current statement until a breakpoint is reached or the end of the program is reached. (This command is equivalent to the Go button on the toolbar.)
Restart	Resets execution to the first line of the program. It reloads the program into memory and discards the current values of all variables (breakpoints and watch expressions still apply). It automatically halts at the **main()** or **WinMain()** function.
Stop Debugging	Terminates the debugging session and returns to a normal editing session.
Break	Breaks the program at its current location.
Step Into	Single-steps through instructions in the program and enters each function call that is encountered.
Step Over	Single-steps through instructions in the program. If this command is used when you reach a function call, the function is executed without stepping through the function instructions.
Step Out	Executes the program out of a function call and stops on the instruction immediately following the call to the function. This allows you to step into a function without having to step all the way through it. This allows you to quickly finish executing the current function after determining that a bug is not present in the function.
Run to Cursor	Executes the program as far as the line that currently has the cursor. This is equivalent to setting a temporary breakpoint at the cursor location.
Set Next Statement	Sets an instruction pointer to the line containing the cursor. (This is displayed on the shortcut menu in the Disassembly and Source Windows while debugging).

Executing to a Location

▶ **To execute until a breakpoint is reached**

- From the Debug menu, choose Go (F5).

    Toolbar: 📲

▶ **To execute to the cursor**

1. Open a source file and move the insertion point to the location where you want the debugger to break.

2. From the Debug menu, choose Run To Cursor (F7).

Tip   The F7 key is also active in the Call Stack and Disassembly windows and the Find box on the standard toolbar.

▶ **To go to the current location**

1. Open a source file and move the insertion point to the location where you want the debugger to go to.

2. Press CTRL+SHIFT+F7.

Tip You can use this procedure to skip a certain section of code—for instance, a section of code that contains a known bug—so that you can continue debugging other sections. You can also use this procedure to return to an earlier statement to retest your application using different values for some variables, for example.

You can step through your program one statement at a time, starting from a breakpoint, using the Step Into command or the Step Into button on the toolbar.

▶ **To run the program and execute the next statement (Step Into)**

1. Open a source file and set a breakpoint.

2. From the Debug menu, choose Go (F5).

    When the program comes to the breakpoint, the debugger pauses execution.

3. From the Debug menu, choose Step Into (F8).

    Toolbar: 🔘

    Whether it is in the current function or in a call to another function, the debugger executes the next statement, then pauses execution.

4. Repeat Step 3 to continue executing the program one statement at a time.

Stepping Over or Out of Routines

You can step through your program one statement at a time in a chosen function, starting from a breakpoint, without entering any other functions, by using the Step Over command. You can also exit from a function immediately and return to the line where the function was called by using the Step Out command.

▶ **To run the program and execute the next statement only in the current function**

1. Open a source file and set a breakpoint.

2. From the Debug menu, choose Go (F5).

    Toolbar: 🔘

    When the program comes to the breakpoint, the debugger pauses execution.

3. From the Debug menu, choose Step Over (F10).

    Toolbar: 🔘

    The debugger executes the next function but pauses again after the function returns.

4. Repeat Step 3 to continue executing the program a statement at a time.

   Shortcut: CTRL+F10

You can stop the debugger after it has executed the return statement in a function. It stops on the line following the function call.

▶ **To run the program and stop execution after the current function returns to the calling function**

1. Open a source file and set a breakpoint in the function.
2. From the Debug menu, choose Go (F5).

   Toolbar:

   When the program comes to the breakpoint, the debugger pauses execution.
3. From the Debug menu, choose Step Out (SHIFT+F7).

   Toolbar:

   The debugger continues execution until it has completed execution of the return from the current function, then pauses.

Interrupting Your Program

There may be times when you cannot set a breakpoint to halt the program, such as when your program encounters an infinite loop. In such cases, you can interrupt your program by choosing Break on the Debug menu. This action returns control to Visual C++ and opens the Disassembly window. You can then use the Go, Step Into, or the Step Over commands to regain control of your program.

Under Win32s™, you must use the shortcut key CTRL+SHIFT+F11 on the remote machine to return control to Visual C++.

Note   You should take care when interrupting execution. If you interrupt execution while Windows or other system code is executing the results can be unpredictable.

Viewing and Modifying Variables

When you are stopped at a breakpoint, you can view variables in your program. You can also modify variables to test different strategies or recover from bugs.

This section describes how to view and modify variables using the following debugging features:

- Displaying the Watch window
- Formatting Watch variables
- Displaying Local variables

- Using QuickWatch
- Watching expressions
- Modifying a variable
- Expanding and collapsing variables
- Using the Call Stack window
- Using the Registers window
- Using the Memory and Disassembly windows

Displaying the Watch Window

You can use the Watch command on the Debug menu to display the Watch window or to bring it to the foreground. The Watch window displays variables and watch expressions. A watch expression is any expression you want to see evaluated as the program progresses. For more information on watch expressions, see "Watching Expressions" on page 198. The Watch window is an editable window that has all the drag-and-drop and cut-and-paste features of any editable window in the Visual C++ environment.

▶ **To display a variable or watch expression in the Watch window**

1. From the Debug menu, choose Watch (ALT+3).

2. Type the variable name or watch expression in the Watch window text box and press ENTER.

If the variable that you want to display is a structure, object, array, or pointer of any type, it is marked with a plus sign (+) in the left margin of the window. You can expand the structure by double-clicking the variable. An expanded variable is marked with a minus sign (−) in the left margin. You can collapse an expanded variable by double-clicking it. You can also expand or contract a structure by selecting it and pressing the ENTER key.

The Watch window and the QuickWatch dialog box show variables in their default format. However, you can display variables in different formats by inserting special symbols.

▶ **To remove a variable or watch expression in the Watch window**

1. From the Debug menu, choose Watch (ALT+3).

2. Select the line containing the variable name or watch expression and press DEL.

Tip Use the Remove Watch button in the Watch window to remove the variable or watch expression on the current line. This command button action is equivalent to the CTRL+Y key combination.

Formatting Watch Variables

You can use formatting symbols to change the display format of variables in the Watch window. The value initially displayed depends on the setting specified in the Debug dialog box under the Tools Options menu. To change the format, follow the variable name with a comma and a letter or letters:

Symbol	Format	Value	Display
d,i	Signed decimal integer	0xF000F065	-268373915
u	Unsigned decimal integer	0x0065	101
o	Unsigned octal integer	0xF065	0170145
x,X	Hexadecimal integer	61541 (dec.)	0x0000F065
l,h	long or short prefix for: d, i, u, o, x, X		
f	Signed floating-point	3./2.	1.500000
e	Signed scientific-notation	3./2.	1.500000e+000
g	Shorter of e and f	3./2.	1.5
c	Single character	0x0065	'e'
s	String	szHello	"Hello world"

For instance, if the value of x is 0x0065, you can type x,c in the watch window and press ENTER for the following result:

```
x,c = 'e'
```

You can display the contents of memory locations with the following formatting symbols:

Symbol	Format	Value	Display
ma	64 ASCII characters	esp	0x0012ffac .4...0...".0W&.......1W&.0.:W..1...." ..1.JO&.1.2..".1...0y....1
m[b]	16 bytes in hexadecimal, followed by 16 ASCII characters	esp	0x0012ffac B3 34 CB 00 84 30 94 80 FF 22 8A 30 57 26 00 00 .4...0...".0W&..
mw	8 words	esp	0x0012ffac 34B3 00CB 3084 8094 22FF 308A 2657 0000
md	4 double words	esp	0x0012ffac 00CB34B3 80943084 308A22FF 00002657

With the memory location formatting symbols, you can type any value or expression that evaluates to a location.

To display the value of a character array as a string, precede the array name with an ampersand (&):

```
&yourname = 0x32E7:0x4706 "John Jacob Googleheimer Smith"
```

Also, a character from the list can follow an expression:

```
rep+1,x
alps[0],mb
xloc,g
count,d
```

To watch the value at an address or the value pointed to by a register, use the BY, WO, or DW operator. Follow the operator with a variable, register, or constant.

- BY returns the contents of the byte pointed to.
- WO returns the contents of the word pointed to.
- DW returns the contents of the doubleword pointed to.

If the BY, WO, or DW is followed by a variable, then the environment watches the byte, word, or doubleword on address contained in the variable.

You can also use the context operator { } to display the contents of any location.

Note With structures, arrays, pointers and objects, you can use formatting symbols only on the unexpanded variables. Double-click the result, displayed as {...}, to expand the variable. The specified formatting applies to all members.

Tip The ALT+F9 shortcut key toggles between decimal and hexadecimal display formats in the Call Stack, Watch, Locals and QuickWatch windows.

Displaying Local Variables

You can use the Locals command on the Debug menu to display the Locals window or to bring it to the foreground. The Locals window displays values and types for all local variables for the currently active function. You can drag information out of the Locals window for copying to another window. You can also change the value of a variable in the Locals window directly by typing a new value over the currently displayed value.

▶ **To display the local variables in the Locals window**

- From the Debug menu, choose Locals (ALT+3).

Tip   The display of local variables is available only for the parts of your program that have been built with debugging information.

Using QuickWatch

You can use QuickWatch to view variables and expressions quickly. Unlike watch expressions, which are stored in the Watch window, the values of QuickWatch variables and expressions appear only in the QuickWatch dialog box. You can easily add them to the Watch window from the QuickWatch dialog box.

QuickWatch is useful in exploratory debugging where you are checking a number of variables that are suspect. You can also use the QuickWatch dialog box to examine one-time changes of variables or as a quick expression evaluator.

The QuickWatch window also contains the following commands:

Zoomin   Expand or contract an array or structure.

Recalc   Re-evaluate the expression in the Expression text box.

Assign   Assign the value in the New Value text box to the expression in the Expression text box.

Note   The QuickWatch dialog box provides support for the automatic downcast of pointers in OLE and MFC debugging. The QuickWatch dialog box automatically detects when a pointer is pointing to a subclass of the type it is required to point to, and when expanded, Visual C++ will add an extra member (that looks like another base class) which indicates the derived-most type. For example, if you are displaying a pointer to a **CObject** and the pointer really points to a **CComboBox**, the QuickWatch expression evaluator will recognize this and introduce a pseudo member so you can access the **CComboBox** members.

▶   **To view a variable's value or an expression's result using QuickWatch**

1. Place the insertion point on a variable or expression in your code.
2. From the <u>D</u>ebug menu, choose QuickWatch (SHIFT+F9).

   Toolbar:

Tip   The Expression drop-down list box contains the most recently used QuickWatch expressions.

▶ **To add a variable or expression to the Watch window from QuickWatch**

1. Place the insertion point on a variable or expression in your code.

2. From the Debug menu, choose QuickWatch (SHIFT+F9).

   Toolbar: ⌨️

3. Choose Add Watch.

   The Watch window opens if it is not currently open.

Watching Expressions

You can use the Watch window to display variables you want to view or expressions that you want to see evaluated as the program progresses. Values or expressions that you type into the Watch window are evaluated only while the program is in a debug session.

▶ **To add a variable or expression to the Watch window**

1. While the program is paused between steps or at a breakpoint, move the insertion point to Watch window text box.

2. Type the variable name or expression.

3. Press ENTER.

   The variable or expression is evaluated immediately. If the expression or variable cannot be evaluated, an error message will appear in the window next to it.

You can also copy and paste variable names from your program source files into the Watch window. You must always press ENTER after pasting to evaluate the variable or expression.

You can also use the QuickWatch dialog box to add variables to the Watch window.

▶ **To delete a variable or expression from the Watch window**

1. Move the insertion point to the line containing the variable or expression.

2. Select the entire variable name or expression, or the current line or multiple lines, using either the mouse or the SHIFT and arrow keys.

3. Press DEL or use the Remove Watch button in the Watch window.

   Shortcut: CTRL+Y

   Tip You can also use the Watch button in the Watch window to quickly remove the selected variable.

Modifying a Variable

While the program is paused at a breakpoint or between steps, you can change the value of any non-**const** variable in your program. This gives you the flexibility to try out changes and see their results in real time or to recover from some logic error and continue. You can modify the variable in either the Watch window or the Locals window directly. You can also modify the variable in your program by using the QuickWatch dialog box.

▶ **To modify the value of a Watch window or Locals window variable**

1. In the Watch window text box or the Locals window, select the variable value (*not* the variable name) you want to modify and press DEL.

   –Or–

   Place the insertion point at the end of the variable value and use the BACKSPACE key to delete the value.

2. Type the new value.

3. Press ENTER.

You can also use the QuickWatch dialog box to modify a variable.

▶ **To modify the value of a variable using the QuickWatch dialog box**

1. Place the insertion point on a variable or expression in your code.

2. From the Debug menu, choose QuickWatch (SHIFT+F9).

   Toolbar: 🔍

   The QuickWatch dialog box appears with the variable or expression you want.

3. Type a new value or expression in the New Value box.

4. Choose Modify Value.

Tip To change the value of a structure or array, modify the individual fields or elements. You cannot change an entire array or structure at once. You cannot directly edit strings.

Expanding and Collapsing Variables

In the Watch window, the Locals window, and the QuickWatch dialog box, variables that contain more than one element—such as arrays, structures, classes or enumerated types—are displayed with either a + or – sign preceding them.

The + symbol indicates that the variable contains elements and can be expanded. The – symbol indicates that the variable is fully expanded and can be collapsed.

▶ **To expand or collapse a variable**

1. Move the insertion point to the line containing the variable.

2. Press ENTER.

   –Or–

   Double-click the variable.

Using the Call Stack Window

During a debug session, you can view the functions that have been called but have not returned. The Call Stack command on the Debug menu displays a window that lists the function calls that led to the current statement. Each call is optionally shown with the arguments and types passed to it. The currently executing function is listed first.

▶ **To observe the behavior of a function call**

1. Place the insertion point at the desired location in the function.

2. From the Debug menu, choose Run to Cursor (F7) to execute your program to the location of the insertion point.

   The Locals window is updated automatically to show the local variables for the function or procedure.

3. From the Debug menu, choose Call Stack (CTRL+K).

   The calls are listed in the calling order, with the current function (the most deeply nested) at the top.

Tip You can use the shortcut key F7 in the Call Stack window to execute to the return address. You can use the shortcut key F9 in the Call Stack window to set or remove a breakpoint at the return address.

Navigating to the Source Window

While the Call Stack or Locals window is open, you can select any function name shown in the Calls list and press ENTER, or double-click the function name. The function's code will be displayed in the source or Disassembly window. The Locals and other debugging windows will reflect the current function view. This does not change the program counter location; it only changes the view.

Controlling Call Stack Display

The default format for displaying functions is to include both values and types on the display line. The Debug tab in the Options dialog box controls the display of call stack information in the Call Stack window.

Tip   The box at the top of the Locals window contains a Locals For drop-down box that contains a list of Call Stack functions. If you select one of these functions, the debugging window views are changed to reflect the new view.

▶ **To change the call stack display formats**

1. From the Tools menu, choose Options.

2. Select the Debug tab.

3. Under Call Stack Window, select the Parameter Values or Parameter Types check box for the display you want.

Tip   You can use the right mouse button shortcut menu to quickly display or hide the parameter types and values.

Using the Registers Window

The Registers window displays the names and current values of the native CPU registers and flags. It also displays the floating-point stack. You can change the value of any register or flag in the Registers window while the program is being debugged.

▶ **To change the value of any register in the Registers window**

1. Use the TAB key or mouse to move the insertion point to the beginning of a register value.

2. Insert the new value by over-typing the current value.

3. Press ENTER.

Important   Changing register values may affect the next execution command. Be especially careful with EIP and EBP registers.

Table 14.5 lists the flag values displayed in the Registers window and their respective set values for Intel x86 processors.

Table 14.5   Register Window Flags

Flag	Set
Overflow	O=1
Direction	D=1
Interrupt	I=1
Sign	S=1
Zero	Z=1
Auxiliary Carry	A=1
Parity	P=1
Carry	C=1

▶   **To set or clear a flag in the Registers window**

1. Move the insertion point to the flag.
2. Double-click the flag value.

Using the Memory and Disassembly Windows

You can open the Memory window with the Memory command on the Debug menu to display memory locations starting at a specified address (0x00010000 by default). You can scroll through the information in the Memory window to view any memory locations in the program's available address space. Options on the Debug tab in the Options dialog box control the starting address, the display format, the number of values to display on each line, and other parameters.

Selecting Addresses in the Memory and Disassembly Windows

You can set the address for the Memory window display by directly editing the memory address.

▶   **To change a memory address directly**

1. Move the insertion point to a memory address.
2. Type a new memory address over the currently displayed address.

    The Memory window now displays the new address.

▶ **To go to a specific address in the Memory or Disassembly window**

1. Make the Memory or Disassembly window the active window.
2. From the Search menu, select Go To (CTRL+G).

    The Go To dialog box is displayed.
3. Type the address or expression in the Line text box.
4. Choose OK.

Tip   You can drag and drop a new address from any location into the Memory or Disassembly window to set a new address.

Viewing Memory at a Dynamic Address

You can set a dynamic starting point for the memory window display by entering an expression in the Options dialog box. You specify these dynamic starting points with "live expressions."

▶ **To create a live expression**

1. From the Tools menu, choose Options.

    The Options dialog box opens.
2. Select the Debug tab.
3. Type the address expression in the Address text box.

    For example, to cause the Memory window to display memory contents starting at the address of a pointer variable *pPtr type `*pPtr`.
4. Select the Re-evaluate Expression check box.
5. Choose OK.

Many items are more easily viewed using live expressions. For example, on an Intel x86 system, you can examine what is currently on top of the stack by entering ESP as the live expression. Or you could also specify a pointer variable as the address expression, then follow the pointer in the Memory window as it increments through an array.

Tip   An easy way to view the memory at any address is to drag and drop a symbol or address to the address column in the Memory window.

Changing Memory Contents Directly

You can also change memory contents directly.

▶ **To change the contents of a memory location**

1. Move the insertion point to the desired memory address, either by using the mouse or by tabbing.

2. Type the new memory contents over the existing contents.

    The Memory window ignores any characters that are not compatible with the current display format.

Tip You can drag and drop a new address from any location into the Memory or Disassembly window to set a new address range, or you can type a new address in the address column.

Setting Memory Window Options

You can change the format and starting location of data displayed in the Memory window by using the Options dialog box while the debugger is paused at a break or between tracing steps.

▶ **To change the Memory window display formats**

1. From the Tools menu, choose Options.

    The Options dialog box opens.

2. Select the Debug tab.

3. Under Memory Window, select the appropriate check box for the display desired.

4. Choose OK.

Controlling the Memory and Disassembly Window Display

The default format for displaying numbers is decimal. Memory locations are usually more useful when displayed in hexadecimal (base 16) format rather than decimal (base 10).

▶ **To change the display format in the Memory window**

1. From the Tools menu, choose Options.

    The Options dialog box opens.

2. Select the Debug tab.

3. Select the appropriate format from the Format drop-down list.

4. Choose OK.

Tip   The ALT+F9 shortcut key toggles between decimal and hexadecimal display formats in the Call Stack, Watch, Locals, and QuickWatch windows.

Viewing Assembly Code

The Disassembly command on the Debug menu opens the Disassembly window which displays the assembly code associated with source code currently being debugged.

When you step through your source code using the Step Into command or the Step Into button on the toolbar, the debugger steps through single assembly-language statements.

▶ **To view assembly code**

- From the Debug menu, choose Disassembly (ALT+7).

Tip   You can use CTRL+F7 to quickly switch between the Source and Disassembly windows. This shortcut key positions the Disassembly window display corresponding to the current source line or it positions the Source window at the source line corresponding to the current instruction displayed in the Disassembly window.

Controlling Assembly Code Display

The default format for displaying assembly code is to annotate the disassembled code with source code and to display code bytes and symbols. The Debug tab in the Options dialog box controls the display of assembly code in the Disassembly window.

▶ **To change the disassembly display formats**

1. From the Tools menu, choose Options.

    The Options dialog box opens.

2. Select the Debug tab.

3. Under Disassembly Window, select the appropriate check box for the display you want.

4. Choose OK.

Advanced Debugging

This section describes the advanced debugging features of Visual C++:

- Debugging exceptions
- Exceptions and debugger actions
- Debugging threads
- Debugging DLLs
- Debugging OLE2 applications
- Enabling Just-In-Time debugging
- Debugging remote applications
- Using I/O Redirection

Debugging Exceptions

You can use the Exceptions dialog box, accessed from the Debug menu, to specify debug actions for system and user-defined exceptions in your program. Exceptions can occur inside or outside exception handlers (sections of code containing structured exception handling statements).

Using the Exceptions dialog box, you can list each exception in your program that might occur and determine beforehand what actions the debugger will take when that exception occurs. The debugger can take one of two actions: Stop Always or Stop If Not Handled.

By default, a list of system exceptions is provided in the Exceptions list box on the Exceptions dialog box. You can modify this list, deleting system exceptions or adding your own exceptions. This information is saved in the *project*.VCP file (where *project* represents your project name) and persists with the project.

Each exception has a unique number. System exceptions are defined in WINBASE.H with the prefix of EXCEPTION (for example EXCEPTION_ACCESS_VIOLATION).

For any exception not in the exception list, the action is Stop If Not Handled, which is also the default for most exceptions in the list.

▶ **To add a new exception to the exception list**

1. From the Debug menu, choose Exceptions.

   The Exceptions dialog box opens.

2. In the Number box, type the DWORD exception number for the user-defined exception.

3. Optionally, type the name of the exception in the Name box.

4. Optionally, select an action to apply to the exception from the Action options.

5. Optionally, choose Add.

6. Choose OK.

You can also easily change any parameter associated with an exception.

▶   **To change an existing exception in the exception list**

1. From the Debug menu, choose Exceptions.

   The Exceptions dialog box opens.

2. Select the exception in the Exceptions list box.

3. Change any of the parameters, such as the action.

4. Optionally, choose the Change button.

5. Choose OK.

Or you can delete any exception from the Exceptions list.

▶   **To remove an exception from the exception list**

1. From the Debug menu, choose Exceptions.

   The Exceptions dialog box opens.

2. Select the exception in the Exceptions list box.

3. Choose the Remove button.

   When an exception is deleted from the Exceptions list, its action reverts to Stop If Not Handled.

4. Choose OK.

If you wish to restore system exceptions to the list, use the Reset button.

▶   **To restore all default system exceptions to the exceptions list**

1. From the Debug menu, choose Exceptions.

   The Exceptions dialog box opens.

2. Choose the Reset button.

   All default system exceptions are restored to the Exceptions list without disturbing any of the user-defined exceptions that have been added.

3. Choose OK.

Exceptions and Debugger Actions

The debugger takes one of its two actions when it is notified of an exception. The debugger may be notified one or two times when an exception is thrown. It is always notified the first time, before the program gets a chance to handle the exception. When the program continues, if the exception is not handled, the debugger is notified again. For each exception, you can choose whether to stop in the debugger at each of these notifications. The Action group in the Exceptions dialog box contains two options:

Stop Always
> When the exception occurs, stop at the first-chance notification and at the last-chance notification, if there is one. When the debugger stops the first time, you have the opportunity to change some element in the program (the EIP register for instance) to fix the cause of the exception.
>
> When you continue the program after a first-chance notification, a dialog box appears asking if you want to pass the exception to the program being debugged. If you choose Yes, the program's exception handlers are invoked. Choosing No dismisses the exception and assumes that you fixed it in the debugger.
>
> If the exception is not then properly handled (either by your debugger fix or by the program's exception handler), the debugger will stop again. If you continue the program at this point, the exception is dismissed, on the assumption that you fixed it in the debugger. If you didn't fix it in the debugger, it will occur again as another first-chance exception.

Stop If Not Handled
> When the exception occurs, don't stop at the first-chance notification; instead pass the exception to the program, send a notification line to the Output window, and stop only at last-chance notification. That is, if the program's exception handlers fail or the program does not have a handler for the exception, then stop in the debugger. If you continue the program at this point, the exception is dismissed, on the assumption that you fixed it in the debugger. If you didn't fix it in the debugger, it will occur again as another first-chance exception.

Note When a Visual C++ program does a throw and the throw is not caught, Visual C++ normally calls **terminate**(). However, if the program is being debugged, Visual C++ notifies you that the exception was not caught. At this point, you can look at your program to see what happened. If Visual C++ called **terminate**(), then your program would no longer be available for debugging.

Debugging Threads

You can use the Visual C++ debugger to debug multithreaded applications. If the application you are debugging has more than one thread, use the Threads dialog box, accessed from the Debug menu, to choose a single thread to debug in the Visual C++ debugger.

The Threads dialog box displays a list of all threads that currently exist for the application. From this list you can:

- Set focus on a thread (make it the active thread that the debugger will recognize) by selecting a single thread and choosing the Set Focus button.
- Suspend a thread by selecting the thread and choosing the Suspend button.
- Resume execution of a suspended thread by selecting the thread and choosing the Resume button.

The Thread list in the Threads dialog box displays status information on each thread as follows:

Thread ID
   This is the DWORD that uniquely identifies the thread. When you set focus on a thread, it is displayed in the Thread list with an asterisk next to its identifier.

Suspend
   This can be a value from 0 to 127.

Priority
   This can be one of seven priorities:

   - Idle
   - Lowest
   - Below Normal
   - Normal
   - Above Normal
   - Highest
   - Time Critical

Location
   This is the current address of the thread, displayed either as a function name or as an address. If Function is selected, the current function name is displayed if known by the debugger. If no function is known, the address is displayed. If Address is selected, the current address is always displayed.

Note If you are showing thread locations by Name instead of by Address, then each thread will normally be shown with the function name in which its EIP currently resides. However, if the EIP is in a location where Visual C++ has no symbols (for example, in the NT kernel), then Visual C++ will show, in brackets, the name of the topmost function on the stack for which Visual C++ has symbols.

Debugging DLLs

There are two basic approaches that you can take to debugging a dynamic-link library (DLL). You can use either of the following two methods:

- If you are writing both the DLL and the executable file which calls the DLL, you can open the project which builds the executable file. Then, on the Debug tab in the Project Settings dialog box, you specify any arguments required by the executable program, and any DLLs that it calls. You need to specify only the DLLs which you want to set breakpoints in or step into.

  If you use this method, you must build both the executable program and the DLL.

- If you are writing only the DLL, you can open the project which builds the DLL. Then, on the Debug tab in the Project Settings dialog box, you specify the executable program which calls the DLL, and any additional DLLs that it calls. You need to specify only the DLLs which you want to set breakpoints in or step into.

  This is the method to use if you are writing a DLL that Microsoft Excel, for instance, is going to call.

▶ **To debug a DLL using the project for the executable program**

1. Ensure that the DLL has been built as a debug version with symbolic debugging information.

2. From the Project menu, choose Settings.

   The Project Settings dialog box appears.

3. Select the Debug tab.

4. If the executable program requires any command-line arguments when it starts up, type those arguments in the Program Arguments text box.

5. Type the name of the DLL (or DLLs) that you want to debug in the Additional DLLs text box.

6. Choose OK. The information is now stored with your project.

7. Set breakpoints at the points where you want to determine the state of your DLL or executable file. You can open a file for the DLL and set breakpoints in that file, even though it is not a part of the project for the executable file.

8. Start the debugger by selecting one of the commands from the Debug menu (Go, or one of the Step commands).

▶ **To debug a DLL using the project for the DLL**

1. If you are developing the executable program, open the project for the executable program and build it.

2. Ensure that the DLL has been built as a debug version with symbolic debugging information.

3. From the <u>P</u>roject menu, choose <u>S</u>ettings.

   The Project Settings dialog box appears.

4. Select the Debug tab.

5. Type the name of the executable program which calls the DLL in your project in the Executable For Debug Session text box.

6. Type the name of any additional DLL (or DLLs) that you want to debug in the Additional DLLs text box.

7. Choose OK. The information is now stored with your project.

8. Set breakpoints at the points in the source files for your DLL where you want to determine the state of your DLL.

9. From the Debug menu, choose Go (F5) to start the debugger.

▶ **To debug a DLL created with an external project**

1. From the <u>P</u>roject menu, choose <u>S</u>ettings.

   The Project Settings dialog box appears.

2. Select the Debug tab.

3. In the Executable For Debug Session text box, type the name of the DLL that your external makefile builds.

4. Ensure that the DLL has been built as a debug version with symbolic debugging information.

5. Follow one of the two procedures immediately preceding this one to debug the DLL.

Debugging OLE2 Applications

The Visual C++ debugger supports debugging OLE2 client and server applications. You can seamlessly step across and into OLE2 clients and servers with the ability to step across OLE2 Remote Procedure Calls.

▶ **To debug an OLE2 Client or Server Application**

1. Open the project for the OLE2 application and build a version of the OLE2 application with symbolic debugging information.

2. From the <u>T</u>ools menu, choose <u>O</u>ptions.

3. Select the Debug tab.

4. Ensure that the OLE RPC Debugging check box is checked.

   Note You must have Windows NT administrator privileges to enable the OLE RPC check box.

5. Choose OK. The information is now stored with your project.

6. Set breakpoints at the points in the source files for your OLE2 application where you want to determine the state of the application.

7. From the Debug menu, choose Go (F5) to start the debugger.

All regular debugging facilities are available as you debug your OLE2 application. As you step into OLE2 applications, a second instance of the debugger is spawned upon entry.

Note The QuickWatch dialog box provides support for the automatic downcast of pointers in OLE and MFC debugging. The QuickWatch dialog box automatically detects when a pointer is pointing to a subclass of the type it is required to point to and when expanded, Visual C++ will add an extra member (that looks like another base class) which indicates the derived-most type. For example, if you are displaying a pointer to a **CObject** and the pointer really points to a **CComboBox**, the QuickWatch expression evaluator will recognize this and introduce a fake member so you can access the **CComboBox** members.

Enabling Just-In-Time Debugging

The Visual C++ debugger can be set to replace any application error debugger. For example, you can specify that Visual C++ rather than Dr. Watson should be launched when an application error occurs. This just-in-time debugging mode is set with the Debug tab in the Options dialog box.

Note You must have Windows NT administrator privileges to enable Just-In-Time debugging.

▶ **To enable Just-In-Time debugging**

1. From the Tools menu, choose Options.

2. Select the Debug tab.

3. Select the Just-In-Time Debugging check box.

4. Choose OK.

A check indicates that Visual C++ will be the default application error debugger. If the check box is cleared, any other available analyzer will be used.

Debugging Remote Applications

You can use Visual C++ to remotely debug programs running on Intel and Win32s platforms. Conceptually, you use the host machine to control a small remote monitor on the remote machine. The debug commands are entered on the host machine and communicated with the remote machine via an appropriate connection.

Remote Intel platforms are connected with a serial connection between the machines.

There are three phases to remote debugging:

- Setting up the remote monitor
- Configuring the remote connection
- Debugging the program using standard Visual C++ techniques

Tip When you are remotely debugging an application, you should try to minimize the amount of information that needs to be sent across the remote connection. One way to minimize the amount of information that needs to be sent and to speed up debugging is to close any unused debugger windows.

Setting up the Remote Debug Monitor

The remote monitor is a small program that resides on the target machine. It controls the execution of the remote program and the communication with the Visual C++ debugger.

▶ **To install the remote debug monitor**

- For an NT remote machine, the remote monitor consists of the following files: MSVCMON.EXE, TLN0COM.DLL, and DMN0.DLL. These files must be copied manually to the remote machine.
- For a remote Win32s machine, the remote debug monitor is automatically installed during setup.

Configuring the Remote Connection

Once remote debugging is enabled, you must specify the type of connection between the host and target machines. The number and type of connections available is determined by the target platform. For example, Intel platforms have only serial connections. Other remote platforms may have other types of connections.

▶ **To configure the remote connection**

1. From the Tools menu, choose Options.
2. Select the Debug tab.
3. Select the Remote Debugging check box.
4. Choose Connection.

   The Connections dialog box is displayed.
5. Choose the appropriate connection type from the connection list.

6. Choose Settings.

   The appropriate settings dialog box is displayed. For a serial connection, the Serial Communication Settings dialog box is displayed. In Win32s, the Win32 Serial Settings dialog box is displayed.

7. Set the appropriate communication settings.

8. Choose OK.

9. Verify that the Remote Executable Path And File Name box on the Debug tab in the Project Settings dialog box has the correct entry.

10. Start the remote debug monitor (MSVCMON.EXE) on the remote machine.

11. Begin debugging using any Visual C++ debugging commands and procedures.

Using I/O Redirection

You can use I/O redirection while debugging within Visual C++. The debugger supports full I/O direction in the same way as Windows NT CMD.EXE.

▶ **To set I/O redirection**

1. From the Project menu, choose Settings.

2. Select the Debug tab.

3. Specify any I/O redirection required in the Program Arguments text box.

4. Set other debug options as desired.

The table below lists the format and meaning of the available I/O redirection commands. Any permutation of commands is also allowed.

Format	Action
<file	Read stdin from file
>file	Send stdout to file
>>file	Append stdout to file
2>file	Send stderr to file
2>>file	Append stderr to file
2>&1	Send stderr (2) output to same location as stdout (1)
1>&2	Send stdout (1) output to same location as stderr (2)

Note You cannot set redirection commands from the command line of Visual C++.

C H A P T E R   1 5

Profiling Code

The profiler in Visual C++ is a powerful analysis tool you can use to examine the run-time behavior of your programs. By using the information given by the profiler, you can find out which sections of your code are working efficiently and which need to be examined more carefully. The profiler can also give you diagnostic information that shows areas of code that are not being executed.

Because profiling is a tuning process, you should use the profiler to make your programs run better, not to find bugs. Once your program is fairly stable, you should start profiling to find out where to devote your attention to optimize your code. Use the profiler to determine whether an algorithm is effective, a function is being called frequently (if at all), or a piece of code is being covered by software testing procedures.

The profiler is run from within the Visual C++ development environment, but can also be run from the command line. For information on using the profiler from the command line, see Appendix C, "Profiler Reference." Appendix C includes descriptions of the PREP, PROFILE, and PLIST command-line tools and the profiler batch files. To learn more about profiling, see Chapter 11, "Profiling Techniques," in *Programming Techniques*. For information on profiling your applications on Win32s, see "Profiling Under Win32s" on page 224.

The following topics are covered in this chapter:

- Setting up the profiler
- Building code for profiling
- Running the profiler
- Types of profiling
- Selective profiling
- Other profiler features
- Profiling under Win32s

Setting Up the Profiler

The profiler uses the INIT environment variable to find TOOLS.INI, which contains information used by the profiler. Typically, the Setup program creates TOOLS.INI and sets INIT for you. If not, use the System icon in the Control Panel to set this variable.

For information on using TOOLS.INI to narrow profiling regions, see "Modifying TOOLS.INI" on page 221.

Building Code for Profiling

Before using the profiler, you must build the current project with profiling enabled (equivalent to LINK /PROFILE). If you want to do line profiling, you also need to include debugging information.

Note Setting your build options to enable profiling turns off incremental linking. To reenable incremental linking, turn off the Enable Profiling option described below.

▶ **To build your project for profiling**

1. From the Project menu, choose Settings.
2. Select the Link tab.
3. From the Categories drop-down box, choose General.
4. Select the Enable Profiling check box. This also enables .MAP file generation.
5. Select the Generate Debug Info check box, if it isn't already selected.
6. Select the C/C++ tab.
7. From the Debug Info drop-down box, select Program Database or Line Numbers Only.
8. Choose OK.
9. From the Project menu, choose Build.

When the build is complete, the project is ready to be profiled.

Note If you are function profiling, the profiler ignores debug information, so you can skip steps 5–7.

Running the Profiler

In Visual C++, choose Profile from the Tools menu. A dialog box appears as shown in Figure 15.1.

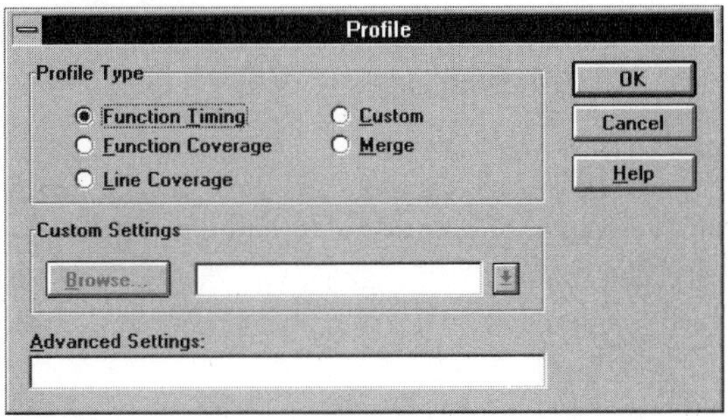

Figure 15.1   Visual C++ Profile Dialog Box

Note If you haven't built your current project with profiling enabled, this dialog box will not appear, and an error message will let you know that you need to rebuild your project. See "Building Code for Profiling" on page 216 for more information.

From this dialog box you can perform these kinds of profiling:

- Function Timing
- Function Coverage
- Line Coverage

You can also:

- Merge multiple profiling sessions
- Use Custom Settings to run a profiler batch file, allowing you to perform other functions, including:
    - Function Counting
    - Line Counting
- Provide additional profiler options through Advanced Settings

Types of Profiling

The profiler can analyze the execution of your code with two levels of detail: function or line. Function profiling is good for detecting inefficient code and is faster than line profiling, because there is less information to collect. Line profiling can be useful for checking the validity of an algorithm, because it shows how many times each line is executed in response to certain input data, and you can see which lines aren't executed at all.

In many cases, you will want to profile only part of your project, such as a single function or library. To learn how to specify when to start and stop profiling certain areas, see "Selective Profiling" on page 221.

Function Profiling

The profiler provides three ways to profile by function:

- Function timing lists time spent in functions together with "hit count"—the number of times the function was called.
- Function counting lists only hit counts, but it is faster than function timing.
- Function coverage lists functions that are or are not executed.

Debugging information is not required for function timing, function counting, or function coverage. The profiler reads the project's .MAP file to match addresses with function names. It also creates a modified executable module and saves it in a temporary file with an _XE or _LL extension. This modified file contains "thunks" (substitutions for function calls), enabling the profiler to count and time the functions.

Function Timing

The Function Timing option in the Profile dialog box profiles the current project, recording how many times each function was called (hit count) as well as how much time was spent in each function and called functions.

Here is a sample of the data function timing can give you:

```
Func           Func+Child        Hit
Time    %        Time      %     Count  Function
- - - - - - - - - - - - - - - - - - - - - - - - - - - - - - - - - - - - -
2.606  48.1      2.606    48.1       2  _SetCursor@4 (user32.def)
```

Function Counting

Function counting records how many times each function was called (hit count). To start a function counting profile run, use a custom batch file that specifies the source module and lines to profile.

Function counting can be accessed by choosing Custom from the Profile dialog box, then selecting the FCOUNT.BAT batch file (typically found in \MSVC20\BIN) in the Custom Settings box.

Function counting is similar to function timing, but only hit counts (greater than zero) are recorded, so profiled program execution is slightly faster. Here is a sample output line with column headings:

```
 Hit
Count    %   Function
----------------------
      1  25.0 _LoadCursorA@8 (user32.def)
```

Function Coverage

The Function Coverage option in the Profile dialog box profiles the current project, recording whether a function was called.

Function coverage profiling is useful for determining which sections of your code are *not* being executed. The profiler lists all profiled functions, with an asterisk marking those that were executed. The profiling overhead for function coverage matches the overhead for function counting. Here is a sample function coverage report:

```
Covered Function
----------------
    .   _InitInstance (generic.obj)
    .   _LoadAcceleratorsA@8 (user32.def)
    *   _LoadCursorA@8 (user32.def)
    .   _LoadIconA@8 (user32.def)
    .   _SendMessageA@16 (user32.def)
    *   _SetCursor@4 (user32.def)
    .   _SetDlgItemTextA@12 (user32.def)
```

Line Profiling

With the profiler's two line profiling options, you can see which source lines are being executed.

- Line counting shows you how many times each line was executed.

- Line coverage shows you which lines were executed at least once.

Line profiling uses debugging information in your executable file to trigger the profiler, so it does not need a .MAP file.

Line Counting

Line counting records how many times each line was called (hit count). To start a line count profile, use a custom batch file that specifies the source module and lines to profile.

Line counting can be accessed by choosing Custom from the Profile dialog box, then selecting the LCOUNT.BAT batch file (typically found in \MSVC20\BIN) in the Custom Settings box.

Here is a sample of the output of a line counting profile run:

```
        Hit
Line count    %   Source
------------------------
   1:                 // test.c
   2:
   3:                 #include <windows.h>
   4:
   5:                 void WasteTime(HANDLE hInstance, HWND hWnd)
   6:     1   0.0 {
   7:                     LONG lCount, lX;
   8:                     HCURSOR hOldCursor;
   9:     1   0.0     hOldCursor = SetCursor(LoadCursor(NULL,
                          IDC_WAIT));
  10:     1   0.0     for(lCount = 0; lCount < 1000L; lCount++) {
  11:  1000  49.9         lX = 57L;
  12:  1000  49.9     }
  13:     1   0.0     SetCursor(hOldCursor);
  14:     1   0.0 }
```

Note that all included source lines are printed, even if they're not executed.

Line count profiling is very slow because the profiler inserts a debugging breakpoint for every source code line, and these breakpoints remain for the duration of the profile session. To speed up profiling, reduce the number of lines selected for profiling. For more information, see "Selective Profiling" on page 221.

Line Coverage

The Line Coverage option in the Profile dialog box profiles the current project, recording whether a line was executed.

Line coverage profiling is useful for determining which sections of your code are *not* being executed. The profiler lists all profiled lines, with an asterisk marking those that were executed. The profiling overhead for line coverage is lower than for line counting, because the profiler only needs to stop at a line once. Here is a sample line coverage report:

```
Line Covered  Source
---------------------
    1:             // waste.c
    2:
    3:             #include <windows.h>
    4:
    5:             void WasteTime(HANDLE hInstance, HWND hWnd)
    6:      *       {
    7:                 LONG lCount, lX;
    8:                 HCURSOR hOldCursor;
    9:      *         hOldCursor = SetCursor(LoadCursor(NULL, IDC_WAIT));
   10:      *         for(lCount = 0; lCount < 1000L; lCount++) {
   11:      *             lX = 57L;
   12:      *         }
   13:      *         if(lCount == 0) {
   14:      .             lCount = 1; // should never execute
   15:                 }
   16:      *         SetCursor(hOldCursor);
   17:      *       }
```

Note that all included source lines are printed, even if they're not executed.

Line coverage profiling is much faster than line count profiling because the profiler can remove the inserted breakpoints when those lines are first executed.

Selective Profiling

It usually doesn't make much sense to profile an entire program. In most applications for Windows, the majority of the application's time is spent waiting for messages, which is not very useful information. Often, only one section of a program, such as repagination, might be performing poorly. Narrowing the region of code being profiled can speed up execution of profiler sessions.

To narrow the area being profiled, see the following sections:

- Modifying TOOLS.INI
- Specifying Functions to Profile
- Specifying Lines to Profile
- Choosing Starting Functions for Profiling

Modifying TOOLS.INI

When setting up the profiler, the Visual C++ Setup program creates a TOOLS.INI file in the install directory (\MSVC20 by default). The directory containing TOOLS.INI should be pointed to by the INIT environment variable.

The [profiler] section of TOOLS.INI specifies libraries and object files for the profiler to ignore. By default, TOOLS.INI excludes the Win32 libraries, MFC libraries, and C run-time libraries shipped with Visual C++.

The following lines (taken from the default TOOLS.INI) exclude the common dialog and GDI libraries from profiling:

```
[profiler]
exclude:comdlg32.lib
exclude:gdi32.lib
```

Specifying Functions to Profile

By default, all functions in all modules are profiled, except those listed in the [profiler] section of TOOLS.INI. You can exclude and include functions from profiling using options in the Advanced Settings box of the Profile dialog box. For example, to exclude all functions in MYOBJ.OBJ except the MyFunc function, use these options:

```
/EXC MYOBJ.OBJ /INC MyFunc
```

Note Do not insert spaces in the text following /INC.

For more information on excluding and including functions, see the list of options for "PREP" on page 390 in Appendix C.

Specifying Lines to Profile

By default, all lines in all modules are profiled, except those listed in the [profiler] section of TOOLS.INI. You can exclude and include areas of code from profiling using options in the Advanced Settings box of the Profile dialog box. For example, if you want all lines in the TEST module, specify the object-file name with these options:

```
/EXCALL /INC test.obj
```

If you need specific lines, specify the source module with line numbers like this:

```
/EXCALL /INC test.c(5-14)
```

Note Do not insert spaces in the text following /INC.

For more information on excluding and including lines, see the list of options for "PREP" on page 390 in Appendix C.

Choosing Starting Functions for Profiling

The /SF option lets you profile only a selected function and the functions it calls. This enables you to easily isolate a routine and its children for analysis.

To profile only MyFunc and the functions it calls, enter the following in the Advanced Settings box of the Profile dialog box:

```
/SF MyFunc
```

Using function selection can give you more useful results than function exclusion/inclusion, but function selection can be slower.

Note   When you specify a C++ function name to the profiler, you must provide its decorated name. The easiest way to get that name is to look it up in the project's .MAP file. For more information on C++ decorated names, see Appendix J, "Decorated Names."

Other Profiler Features

Several other profiler features can be accessed from the Profile dialog box. These features allow you to perform advanced operations such as merging multiple profile sessions, calling customized profiler batch files, and adding special command-line options.

Merging Profiler Output

The Merge option in the Profile dialog box starts another profiler run of the same type as the most recent profiler run. The results of this profile session are merged with the previous session, and the Profile tab of the Output window shows the results of the merge.

This option lets you obtain more accurate results by letting you combine profiling information from several sessions into a composite report.

For more information on merging profiler output, see "Combining PROFILE Sessions" in Chapter 11 of *Programming Techniques*.

Running a Custom Batch File

When a batch file is executed using the Custom option in the Profile dialog box, Visual C++ substitutes the project's program name for the %1 parameter. You can specify your program's command-line arguments in the Program Arguments box on the Debug tab in the Project Settings dialog box.

For more information on creating and running profiler batch files, see "Profiler Batch Processing" on page 387 in Appendix C.

Advanced Profiler Settings

The Advanced Settings box in the Profile dialog box lets you specify additional command-line options for PREP Phase I.

For more information, see "PREP" on page 390 in Appendix C.

Profiling Under Win32s

When developing an application for Win32s, you may find that your code performs differently than under Windows NT. To help optimize your code for Win32s, profile it using PROFW32S, a special version of the profiler that runs under Win32s.

Installing the Win32s Profiler

The Microsoft Win32s Setup program (SETUP.EXE) installs all the necessary profiler files for Win32s and correctly configures the profiler for your selected environment.

If you have already installed Win32s but did not choose to install the profiler at that time, you can run the Setup program again and install just the profiler components.

Win32s Profiling Procedure

The Visual C++ Profile dialog box is not supported under Win32s. Instead, run PREP and PLIST directly from the command line on the host (Windows NT) system, then run the Win32s profiler, PROFW32S, from the Program Manager or File Manager on the Win32s target system.

For more information on profiling from the command line, see Appendix C, "Profiler Reference."

C H A P T E R   1 6

Using Spy++

Spy++ (SPYXX.EXE) is a Win32-based utility that gives you a graphical view of the system's processes, threads, windows, and window messages. With Spy++, you can:

- View outlines that show relationships among system "objects," including processes, threads, and windows.
- Select a window from the outline view or by direct mouse positioning.
- Get quick access to detailed information on selected objects.
- Open online Help for window messages.
- Choose from a variety of easy-to-use message viewing options with parameter decoding.

Tip While using Spy++, in many instances you can click the right mouse button to display a shortcut menu of frequently used commands. The commands available depend on what the pointer is pointing at. For example, if you click while pointing at a windows message, the shortcut menu lets you get help on that message or find out the properties of that message.

There are two other utilities similar to Spy++ that are included in Visual C++: PView, which lets you view details on processes and threads, and DDESPY.EXE, a monitoring program for Dynamic Data Exchange (DDE) messages. These utilities are documented in Books Online.

Starting Spy++

To start Spy++, from the Windows Program Manager, double-click the Spy++ icon in the Visual C++ program group.

Note Only one copy of Spy++ can be run at a time. Attempting to run additional copies of Spy++ will bring the currently running Spy++ to the front.

Remember that Spy++ is a "read-only" program. Using Spy++ does not change program operation, but can slow program execution.

Working in Spy++

Spy++ has a toolbar and hyperlinks to help you work faster. It also provides a Refresh command to update the active view, a Window Finder Tool to make spying easier, and a font dialog box to customize view windows.

The Spy ++ Toolbar

The toolbar appears beneath the menu bar. It provides shortcut commands for opening new views, starting or stopping the message stream display, changing message stream options, clearing a message stream window, and finding a window.

You can hide or display the toolbar with the Toolbar command on the View menu. When this command is selected, the toolbar appears. When it is turned off (cleared), the toolbar is hidden.

Button	Effect
🖼	Creates a window to display window messages. This button calls up the Message Options dialog box to let you select the window whose messages will be displayed. See "The Messages View" on page 230.
☐	Creates a window to display a tree view of all windows and controls active in the system. See "The Windows View" on page 229.
⊕	Creates a window to display a tree view of all processes active in the system. See "The Processes View" on page 229.
◉	Creates a window to display a tree view of all threads active in the system. See "The Threads View" on page 230.
▤ or ▤	Starts or suspends displaying the message stream. This button is available only when a Messages window is active (has the focus).

Button	Effect
🖽	Displays the Message Options dialog box. Use this dialog box to select windows and message types for viewing. This button is available only when a Messages window is active (has the focus). See "Choosing Message Options" on page 232.
✖	Clears the contents of the active Messages window. This button is available only when a Messages window is active (has the focus).
🔍	Opens the Find Window dialog box, which lets you select a window to view messages or find properties. See "The Window Finder Tool."

The Window Finder Tool

The Window Finder Tool lets you view messages or find properties of a selected window.

▶ **To select a visible window to spy on**

1. Arrange your windows so that both Spy++ and the subject window are visible.

2. From the Spy menu, choose Find Window (CTRL+F) to open the Find Window dialog box.

   Toolbar: 🔍

3. Drag the Finder Tool to the desired window. Window details are shown as you drag the tool.

   –Or–

   If you know the window handle of the window you want (for example, from the debugger), type it in the Handle box.

4. Under Show, choose Properties or Messages to select what kind of information to display.

5. Choose OK.

Expanding Spy++ Trees

You can expand and contract individual items or the entire tree in the Windows, Processes, and Threads views by clicking on the icons in the window or by using the tree menu. The + and – icons act as they do in the Visual C++ project window. The Tree menu contains four commands:

Menu Command	Description
Expand One Level	Expands the currently selected item to the next level.
Expand Branch	Fully expands the currently selected item.
Expand All	Fully expands all items in the window.
Collapse	Fully collapses the currently selected item.

Refreshing the View

Spy++ takes a "snapshot" of the system tables and refreshes a view based on this information. It is important that you periodically refresh your system views. If you have a Spy++ view open and haven't refreshed the view, you won't see those processes, threads, and windows that are subsequently initialized. Also, you can see items that no longer exist. The Refresh command is available for all views except the Messages view. To refresh the currently active view, choose Refresh (F5) from the Window menu.

WinHelp Jumps

From the Messages view, you can get help on any of the displayed messages by right-clicking on the message and choosing the Help On *message* command from the shortcut menu. From the Message Properties dialog box, you can use the Message Help button to open WinHelp.

Changing Fonts

You can change the font and font size for Spy++ windows.

▶ **To change font options**

1. From the Options menu, choose Font.

    The Font dialog box appears.

2. Choose a font and font size.

3. Choose OK.

Selecting the Save Settings As Default box will cause all future windows to use this font.

Spy++ Views

When Spy++ starts, it opens a window titled "Windows 1," which shows a tree view of all windows and controls active in the system. There are also three other "views" available in Spy++: Messages, Processes, and Threads.

The Windows View

The Windows view shows only windows. Figure 16.1 shows the Spy++ representation of the Windows view with all levels expanded.

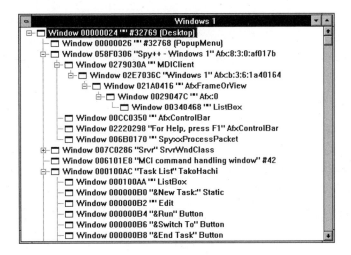

Figure 16.1   The Spy++ Windows view

The current desktop window is shown at the top of the tree. All other windows are children of the desktop, and are listed according to the standard window hierarchy, with sibling windows ordered by depth. You can collapse or expand the whole tree by clicking the – or + symbol for the top level window.

The Windows view is most useful if you need to find a particular window. If you start with a tree expanded at the second level (all windows that are children of the desktop), then you can identify a desired desktop-level window by its class name and title. Once you've found the desktop-level window, you can expand the level to find a specific child window.

The Processes View

Microsoft Windows supports multiple processes. Each process can have one or more threads, and each thread can have one or more associated top-level windows. Each top-level window can own a series of windows. A + symbol indicates that a level is already collapsed. Click the + symbol to expand the level. The collapsed view consists of one line per process.

Use the Processes view if you want to examine a particular system process, which usually corresponds to an executing program. Processes are identified by module names, or they are designated "system processes." To find a process, collapse the tree and search through the list.

The Threads View

The Threads view is a flat listing of all threads with associated windows. Processes are not included. You'll see later that you can easily navigate to the process that owns a selected thread. Use the Threads view to search for a particular thread.

The Messages View

Each window has an associated message stream. You can view this message stream in the Messages view. Figure 16.2 shows the Spy++ representation of the Messages view window.

```
┌─────────────────── Messages [Window 00BE0452] ────────────────┬─┐
│ 00BE0452 S .WM_ICONERASEBKGND hdc:00C3004B                     │▲│
│ 00BE0452 R .WM_ICONERASEBKGND                                  │ │
│ 00BE0452 S .WM_WINDOWPOSCHANGED lpwp:002C00E4                   │ │
│ 00BE0452 ..WM_MOVE xPos:309 yPos:690                            │ │
│ 00BE0452 R ..WM_MOVE                                            │ │
│ 00BE0452 S ..WM_SIZE fwSizeType:SIZE_MINIMIZED nWidth:36 nHeigh │ │
│ 00BE0452 R ..WM_SIZE                                            │ │
│ 00BE0452 R .WM_WINDOWPOSCHANGED                                 │ │
│ 00BE0452 S .WM_NCACTIVATE fActive:True                          │ │
│ 00BE0452 R .WM_NCACTIVATE                                       │ │
│ 00BE0452 S .WM_ACTIVATE fActive:WA_INACTIVE fMinimized:True hwnd│ │
│ 00BE0452 R .WM_ACTIVATE                                         │ │
│ 00BE0452 S .WM_ACTIVATEAPP fActive:False dwThreadID:000000CF    │ │
│ 00BE0452 R .WM_ACTIVATEAPP                                      │ │
│ 00BE0452 R WM_SYSCOMMAND                                        │ │
│ 00BE0452 P WM_PAINTICON                                         │▼│
└─┴─────────────────────────────────────────────────────────────┴─┘
```

Figure 16.2   The Spy++ Messages View

You can create a Messages view for a thread or process as well. This allows you to view messages sent to all windows owned by a specific process or thread, which is particularly useful for capturing window initialization messages.

Opening a Messages Window

You can open a Messages view either directly or indirectly.

▶ **To select a window, process, or thread for message log viewing**

1. Move the focus to the appropriate view window.

2. Find the name of the window, process, or thread that you want to examine, and select it.

3. From the Spy menu, choose Messages (CTRL+M) to open a Messages view. The Message Options dialog box appears.

   –Or–

   Click the right mouse button to display the shortcut menu. Choose Messages. Spy++ begins logging messages for the selected object.

For a more direct way to select a window for message stream viewing, use the following procedure.

▶ **To select a visible window for message log viewing**

1. Arrange your windows so that both Spy++ and the subject window are visible.

2. From the Spy menu, choose Messages (CTRL+M) to open a Messages view.

   Toolbar: 🖳

   The Message Options dialog box appears as shown in Figure 16.3. The Windows tab is selected by default.

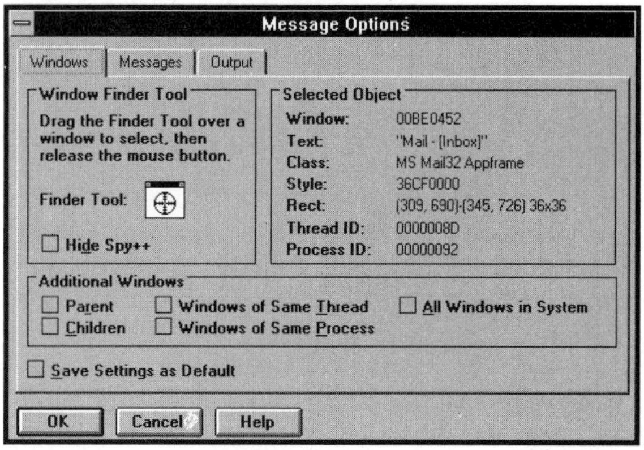

Figure 16.3   Message Options dialog box with a window selected

3. Drag the Finder Tool to the desired window. Under Selected Object, window details are shown as you drag the tool.

4. Choose OK.

You can also use the Window Finder Tool to select a window for viewing.

Tip If you select the Hide Spy++ check box when using the Window Finder Tool, the main Spy++ window disappears. This makes it easier to use the Finder Tool to select another window. The Spy++ window reappears when you choose the OK or Cancel button.

The resulting Message Log window is shown in Figure 16.2. Note that the first column contains the window handle, and the second column contains a message code (explained in "Message Codes," on page 241). Decoded message parameters and return values are on the right.

Controlling the Messages View

With Spy++, you have considerable control over the content of the Messages view. You can start and stop displaying the messages at any time, and you can specify:

- Which message types you want to see.
- Which windows you want to monitor.
- The display format for message lines.

These settings are available from the Message Options dialog box and apply only to the selected Messages view.

Starting and Stopping the Message Log Display

When a Messages view window is active, a Start or Stop Logging choice appears on the Spy++ Messages menu, and the Start/Stop Logging toolbar button becomes active.

▶ **To suspend the message log display**

- From the Messages menu, choose Stop Logging (F8).

  Toolbar: 🔲

▶ **To start the message log display**

- From the Messages menu, choose Start Logging (F8).

  Toolbar: 🔲

Choosing Message Options

The Options command on the Messages menu opens the Message Options dialog box, which has three tabs to select from: Windows, Messages, and Output.

The Windows Tab

The Windows tab contains the Window Finder Tool, as described on page 227. Other options on the Windows tab include:

Option	Description
All Windows in System	Display messages for all windows.
Parent	Display messages for the selected window and its immediate parent window.
Children	Display messages for the selected window and all its child windows, including nested child windows.
Windows of Same Thread	Display messages for the selected window and all other windows owned by the same thread.
Windows of Same Process	Display messages for the selected window and all other windows owned by the same process.
Save Settings as Default	Save the preceding settings for new message stream windows. These settings are saved when Spy++ quits.

The Messages Tab

You can use the Messages tab to select message types for viewing. Typically you first select message groups, then you can fine-tune the selection by selecting individual message types. The All button selects all message types, and the None button clears all types.

Note that the last three entries in the left column under Message Groups do not map to specific entries under Messages To View. These include:

- WM_USER: with a code greater than WM_USER
- Registered: registered with the **RegisterWindowMessage** call
- Unknown: unknown messages in the range 0 to (WM_USER – 1)

If you select these "groups," the selection is applied directly to the message stream.

When you create a new Messages window, it can display all messages. When you filter messages from the Messages tab, that filter only applies to new messages, not messages that have already been displayed in the Windows view.

A grayed check box under Message Groups indicates that the Messages To View list box has been modified for messages in that group; not all of the message types in that group are selected.

The Output Tab

You can use the Output tab to select the following options:

Option	Description
Message Nesting Level	Prefix nested messages with one period per level.
Raw Message Parameters	Display the hexadecimal **wParam** and **lParam** values.
Decoded Message Parameters	Display the results of message-specific decoding of the **wParam** and **lParam** values.
Raw Return Values	Display the hexadecimal **lResult** return value.
Decoded Return Values	Display the results of message-specific decoding of the **lResult** return value.
Lines maximum	Limit the number of lines that are retained in the currently selected Messages view.
Save Settings as Default	Save the preceding settings for new message stream windows. These settings are saved when you quit Spy++.

Spy++ Properties

You can find out more about entries in the property with properties dialog boxes. To open a properties dialog box, do one of the following:

- Double-click an item in one of the views.

- Click the item, then choose Properties from the View menu or press ALT+ENTER.

- Point at the item and click the right mouse button, then choose Properties from the shortcut menu.

The appropriate properties dialog box appears as shown in Figure 16.4.

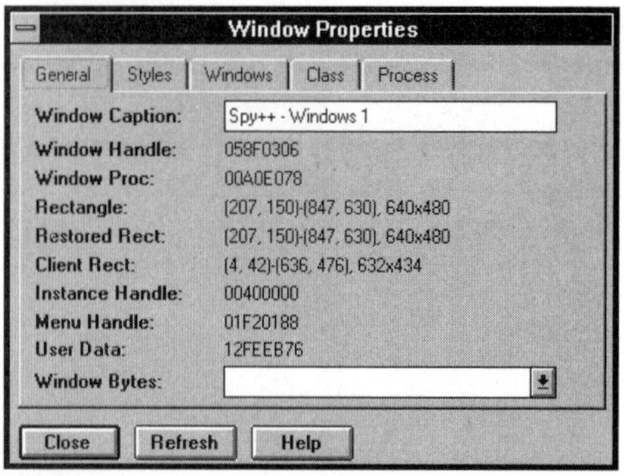

Figure 16.4   Window Properties dialog box

Properties dialog boxes are not modal, so you can click on other items in view windows and the dialog box will update to show information on the selected item.

Window Properties

If you double-click a hexadecimal window ID, Spy++ displays a Window Properties dialog box.

The Window Properties dialog box contains 5 tabs: General, Styles, Windows, Class, and Process. Click the title of the tab to display that tab's options.

The options on the General tab are:

Entry	Description
Window Caption	The text in the window caption.
Window Handle	The unique ID of this window. Window handle numbers are reused; they identify a window only for the lifetime of that window.
Window Proc	The virtual address of the window procedure function for this window. This field also indicates whether this window is a Unicode window.`
Rectangle	The bounding rectangle for the window. The size of the rectangle is also displayed. Units are pixels in screen coordinates.
Restored Rect	The bounding rectangle for the window when it is restored. The size of the rectangle is also displayed. This rectangle will differ from Rectangle only when the window is maximized or minimized. Units are pixels in screen coordinates.
Client Rect	The bounding rectangle for the window client area. The size of the rectangle is also displayed. Units are pixels relative to the top left of the window.
Instance Handle	The instance handle of the application. Instance handles are not unique.
Control ID or Menu Handle	If the window being displayed is a child window, the Control ID label is displayed. Control ID is an integer that identifies this child window's control ID. If the window being displayed is not a child window, the Menu Handle label is displayed. Menu Handle is an integer that identifies the handle of the menu associated with this window.
User Data	Application-specific data that is attached to this window structure.
Window Bytes	The number of extra bytes associated with this window. The meaning of these bytes is determined by the application. Expand the list box to see the byte values in DWORD format.

The options on the Styles tab are:

Entry	Description
Window Styles	A combination of window style codes.
Extended Styles	A combination of extended window style codes.

The options on the Windows tab are:

Entry	Description
Next Window	The handle of the next sibling window in the same sequence shown in the window tree view ("none" if there is no next window).
Previous Window	The handle of the previous sibling window in the same sequence shown in the window tree view ("none" if there is no previous window).
Parent Window	The handle of this window's parent window ("none" if there is no parent).
First Child	The handle of this window's first child window, in the sequence shown in the Window Tree view ("none" if there are no child windows). Click on this value to view the properties of the first child window.
Owner Window	The handle of this window's owner window. An application's main window typically owns system-modal dialog windows, for example ("none" if there is no owner).

The options on the Class tab are:

Entry	Description
Class Name	The name (or ordinal number) of this window class.
Class Styles	A combination of class style codes.
Class Bytes	Application-specific data associated with this window class.
Class Atom	The atom for the class returned by the RegisterClass call.
Instance Handle	The instance handle of the module that registered the class. Instance handles are not unique.
Window Bytes	The number of extra bytes associated with each window of this class. The meaning of these bytes is determined by the application. Expand the list box to see the byte values in DWORD format.
Window Proc	The current address of the WndProc function for windows of this class.
Menu Name	The name of the main menu that is associated with windows of this class ("none" if there is no menu).

Entry	Description
Icon Handle	The handle for the icon that is associated with windows of this class ("none" if there is no icon).
Cursor Handle	The handle for the cursor that is associated with windows of this class ("none" if there is no cursor).
Bkgnd Brush	The handle for the background brush that is associated with windows of this class, or one of the predefined COLOR_* colors for painting the window background ("none" if there is no brush).

The options on the Process tab are:

Entry	Description
Process ID	The ID of the process that owns the thread that created this window. Click on this value to view the properties of this process.
Thread ID	The ID of the thread that created this window. Click on this value to view the properties of this thread.

Note A process gets a copy of a window class on startup. The process can then modify this copy without affecting other applications. Thus the class structure contains a pointer (Process ID) back to its process.

Process Properties

The Process Properties dialog box contains three tabs: General, Memory, and Page File. Click the title of a tab to display its options.

The options on the General tab are:

Entry	Description
Module Name	The name of the module.
Process ID	The unique ID of this process. Process ID numbers are reused, so they identify a process only for the lifetime of that process. The Process object type is created when a program is run. All the threads in a process share the same address space and have access to the same data. Click on this value to view the properties of this process.
CPU Time	Total CPU time spent on this process and its threads. Equal to User Time plus Privileged Time.
User Time	The cumulative elapsed time that this process's threads have spent executing code in User Mode in non-idle threads. Applications execute in User Mode, as do subsystems such as the window manager and the graphics engine.

Entry	Description
Privileged Time	The total elapsed time this process has been running in Privileged Mode in non-idle threads. The service layer, the Executive routines, and the Kernel execute in Privileged Mode. Device drivers for most devices other than graphics adapters and printers also execute in Privileged Mode. Some work that Windows does for your application may appear in other subsystem processes in addition to Privileged Time.
Elapsed Time	The total elapsed time this process has been running.
Priority Base	The current base priority of this process. Threads within a process can raise and lower their own base priority relative to the process's base priority.

The options on the Memory tab are:

Entry	Description
Virtual Bytes	The current size (in bytes) of the virtual address space the process is using. Use of virtual address space does not necessarily imply corresponding use of either disk or main memory pages. However, virtual space is finite, and using too much may limit the ability of the process to load libraries.
Peak Virtual Bytes	The maximum number of bytes of virtual address space the process has used at any one time.
Working Set	The set of memory pages touched recently by the threads in the process. If free memory in the computer is above a threshold, pages are left in the Working Set of a process even if they are not in use. When free memory falls below a threshold, pages are trimmed from Working Sets. If they are needed, they will be soft-faulted back into the Working Set before they leave main memory.
Peak Working Set	The maximum number of pages in the working set of this process at any point in time.
Paged Pool Bytes	The current amount of paged pool the process has allocated. Paged pool is a system memory area where space is acquired by operating system components as they accomplish their appointed tasks. Paged pool pages can be paged out to the paging file when not accessed by the system for sustained periods of time.
Nonpaged Pool Bytes	The current amount of nonpaged pool allocated by the process. Nonpaged pool is a system memory area where space is acquired by operating system components as they accomplish their appointed tasks. Nonpaged pool pages cannot be paged out to the paging file; they remain in main memory as long as they are allocated.
Private Bytes	The current number of pages this process has allocated that cannot be shared with other processes.

The options on the Page File tab are:

Entry	Description
Page File Bytes	The current number of pages that this process is using in the paging file. The paging file stores pages of data used by the process but not contained in other files. The paging file is used by all processes, and lack of space in the paging file can cause errors while other processes are running.
Peak Page File Bytes	The maximum number of pages that this process has used in the paging file.
Page Faults	The number of Page Faults by the threads executing in this process. A page fault occurs when a thread refers to a virtual memory page that is not in its working set in main memory. Thus, the page will not be retrieved from disk if it is on the standby list and hence already in main memory, or if it is being used by another process with which the page is shared.

Thread Properties

The Thread Properties dialog box contains one tab: General. The options on the General tab are:

Entry	Description
Module Name	The name of the module.
Thread ID	The unique ID of this thread. Note that thread ID numbers are reused; they identify a thread only for the lifetime of that thread.
Process ID	The unique ID of this process. Process ID numbers are reused, so they identify a process only for the lifetime of that process. The Process object type is created when a program is run. All the threads in a process share the same address space and have access to the same data.
Current Priority	The current dynamic priority of this thread. Threads within a process can raise and lower their own base priority relative to the base priority of the process.
Base	The current base priority of this process.
Thread State	The current state of the thread. A Running thread is using a processor; a Standby thread is about to use one. A Ready Thread is waiting to use a processor because one is not free. A thread in Transition is waiting for a resource to execute, such as waiting for its execution stack to be paged in from disk. A Waiting thread does not need the processor because it is waiting for a peripheral operation to complete or a resource to become free.
Wait Reason	This is applicable only when the thread is in the Wait state. Event Pairs are used to communicate with protected subsystems.
Start Address	Starting virtual address for this thread.

Entry	Description
CPU Time	Total CPU time spent on this process and its threads. Equal to User Time plus Privileged Time.
User Time	The total elapsed time that this thread has spent executing code in User Mode. Applications execute in User Mode, as do subsystems like the window manager and the graphics engine.
Privileged Time	The total elapsed time that this thread has spent executing code in Privileged Mode. When a Windows system service is called, the service will often run in Privileged Mode to gain access to system-private data. Such data is protected from access by threads executing in User Mode. Calls to the system may be explicit, or they may be implicit, such as when a page fault or an interrupt occurs.
Elapsed Time	The total elapsed time (in seconds) this thread has been running.
Context Switches	The number of switches from one thread to another. Thread switches can occur either inside a single process or across processes. A thread switch may be caused by one thread asking another for information, or by a thread being preempted when a higher priority thread becomes ready to run.

Message Properties

The Message Properties dialog box contains one tab: General. The options on the General tab are:

Entry	Description
Window Handle	The unique ID of this window. Window handle numbers are reused; they identify a window only for the lifetime of that window. Click this value to view the properties of this window.
Nesting Level	Depth of nesting of this message, where 0 is no nesting.
Message	Number, status, and name of the selected windows message.
lResult	The value of the lResult parameter, if any.
wParam	The value of the wParam parameter, if any.
lParam	The value of the lParam parameter, if any. This value is decoded if it is a pointer to a string or structure.

Message Codes

Each message line shown in Figure 16.2 contain a 'P,' 'S,' 's,' or 'R' code. These codes have the following meanings:

Code	Meaning
P	The message was posted to the queue with the **PostMessage** function. No information is available concerning the ultimate disposition of the message.
S	The message was sent with the **SendMessage** function. This means that the sender doesn't regain control until the receiver processes and returns the message. The receiver can, therefore, pass a return value back to the sender.
s	The message was sent, but security prevents access to the return value.
R	Each 'S' line has a corresponding 'R' (return) line that lists the message return value. Sometimes message calls are nested, which means that one message handler sends another message.

C H A P T E R   1 7

Customizing Visual C++

Visual C++ allows you to customize various aspects of its layout and operation. You can:

- Arrange the layout of windows and toolbars.
- Assign shortcut keys to commands.
- Add your tools to the Tools menu.
- Specify directories for build utilities, include files and libraries.

Visual C++ allows you to arrange the display area in the way that best suits your preferences and work habits. Some arrangements are maintained with each project. In a project, for instance, you can size editor windows, move them to convenient locations and automatically save these locations with your project.

Other arrangements are maintained globally for Visual C++. For instance, you can display some windows in one layout while you are editing your files or building your project and another layout when you are debugging.

Some of the windows in Visual C++ can either be fixed along the Visual C++ window border or be allowed to move anywhere on your display. These windows are called docking windows.

Some of the commands in Visual C++ are assigned shortcut keys by default. For instance, to print the source file an editor window that currently has the focus, you can press CTRL+P. Other commands do not have any default shortcut key assigned to them. In Visual C++, you can:

- Delete existing assignments for shortcut keys.
- Replace default shortcut keys with different ones.
- Assign shortcut keys to commands that have none by default.
- Assign multiple shortcut keys to a command.

Using these assignments, you can choose your own set of shortcut keys, ones which are familiar and natural for you to use, or which have some easily remembered values.

Visual C++ provides online help for language keywords and for function calls. In some cases, these language elements may have entries in more than one help file. You can specify which help files to search for help, and you can also specify the order in which to search the help files for any language element.

Note You can also customize other aspects of Visual C++. To find out about customizing text editor windows and their use of fonts or colors, see Chapter 3, "Using the Text Editor." To find out about customizing settings for debugging, see Chapter 14, "Using the Debugger."

Working with Windows

Visual C++ has two types of windows, which it treats in different ways:

Type	Attributes	Layout associated with:
Document windows	Position and size only within the Visual C++ application window. Can be maximized and minimized.	Project.
Docking tool windows and toolbars	Fix in *docks* along the borders of the Visual C++ application window, or float anywhere on your display. Toolbars are docking tools windows. All docking tool windows except toolbars can convert to document window characteristics.	Either editing or debugging.

The layout for window types—that is, their visibility, position and size—is associated either with a project in the case of document windows, or with editing or debugging operations in the case of tool windows and toolbars. Once you have chosen a layout, that layout is persistent. If you close a project and later open it again, the document windows have the last layout that you used: The same windows are open, and they have the same sizes and positions. When you create layouts of tool windows or toolbars, either for editing or debugging, those layouts are used for all subsequent sessions until you explicitly change them again.

Both window types can display shortcut menus with commands appropriate for the window in its current state. The shortcut menu for editor windows, which are document windows, displays the Cut, Copy, and Paste commands while editing, but Toggle Breakpoint and QuickWatch while debugging. You click the right mouse button in the window to display the shortcut menu.

There is also a shortcut menu associated with the dock along the border of the Visual C++ application window. If you click the right mouse button in the dock area or on a toolbar, the menu displays commands to show or hide all the docking tool windows, and to customize toolbars. The various shortcut menus are shown in Figure 17.1.

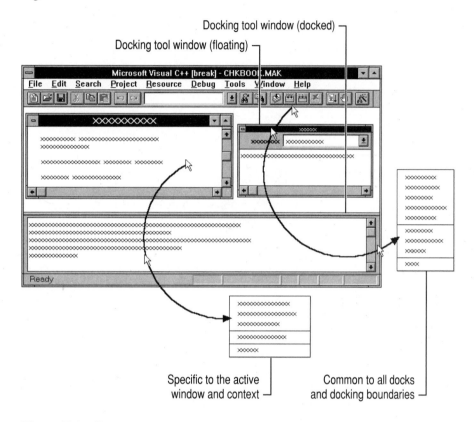

Figure 17.1   Shortcut menus displayed with the right mouse button

Working with Document Windows

The following windows are document windows:

- Project window
- Editor windows, either for text or resources
- Resource browser window

These document windows are associated with the project workspace. Visual C++ records their positions, sizes, selections made in them, window splits, and so on when you close a project. When you open the project again, it restores these characteristics.

Document windows also can display a shortcut menu with commands appropriate for the window in its current state. You click the right mouse button in the document window to display the shortcut menu.

Positioning Document Windows

You can position the document windows for a project to suit your preferences. Visual C++ then retains these positions when you close the project. If you open the project again, it restores these window positions, opens the necessary files and displays their contents in the windows with any window splits and selections that you have made.

▶ **To move a window**

- Move the mouse pointer into the title bar and drag the window to the desired location.

▶ **To size a window**

- Move the mouse pointer onto the window border and drag the window border to the desired size.

▶ **To display the shortcut menu**

- Move the mouse pointer onto the window and click the right mouse button.

▶ **To tile windows**

- From the Windows menu, choose Tile Horizontally.

    Toolbar: 🗔

    –Or–

- From the Windows menu, choose Tile Vertically.

    Toolbar: 🗔

▶ **To overlap windows**

- From the Windows menu, choose Cascade.

    Toolbar: 🗔

▶ **To split a window**

1. Click the Split button on the Window toolbar.

    Toolbar: 🗔

2. Drag the split bar in the window to the desired location and click the left mouse button.

Selecting Document Windows to Display When Opening a Project

You can specify whether to display project documents when you open a project. The default choices upon opening are to:

- Open project documents that you previously had open in the project.
- Close non-project documents when you open a project.

If you open documents in the project, you can close the project, and open it later with all those documents open, or with no documents open.

▶ **To open project documents when you open a project**

1. From the Tools menu, choose Options.

   The Options dialog box appears.

2. Select the Workspace tab.

3. To open project documents, select the Restore Window Layout When Opening Project check box.

   To not open project documents, clear the Restore Window Layout When Opening Project check box.

Working with Docking Tool Windows

You can fix docking tool windows in *docks* along the borders of the Visual C++ application window, or you can use various commands to convert them to floating windows, and then size and position them anywhere on your display.

The following are docking tool windows:

- Output
- Watch
- Locals
- Registers
- Memory
- Call Stack
- Disassembly

You can use the Options dialog box of the Tools menu to give these docking tool windows the characteristics of document windows. By default, the Disassembly window has the characteristics of a document window.

You can show the Output window in one layout while editing and in another layout while debugging. The other tool windows are available only while debugging.

Note The choice and layout of docking tool windows are always associated with editing or debugging, even if you have given them the characteristics of document windows.

You can show the Output window in one layout while editing and in another layout while debugging. The other docking tool windows are available only while debugging.

Showing and Hiding Docking Tool Windows

You can show or hide the Output window at any time. You can show or hide the debugging windows only while you are debugging.

▶ **To show a docking tool window**

- From the Debug menu, choose the tool window that you want to show.

  –Or–

- From the Window menu, choose Output (ALT+1).

  –Or–

- Move the mouse pointer over the border of a tool window, click the right mouse button, and choose the unchecked window that you want to show from the shortcut menu.

  –Or–

- Press the following shortcut key or click the corresponding button:

Window	Shortcut Key	Button
Output	ALT+1	
Watch	ALT+2	
Locals	ALT+3	
Registers	ALT+4	
Memory	ALT+5	
Call Stack	ALT+6	
Disassembly	ALT+7	

The desired window appears in its default location, or in the last location that you assigned it, if you assigned it one.

▶ **To hide a docking tool window**

- Move the mouse pointer the border of a tool window, click the right mouse button, and choose the checked window that you want to hide.

  –Or–

- Move the mouse pointer over a floating tool window, click the right mouse button, and choose Hide from the shortcut menu.

  –Or–

- Click the control box on the upper left corner of the floating window.

  –Or–

- Move the focus to the window, and from the <u>W</u>indow menu, choose <u>H</u>ide (SHIFT+ESC).

Positioning Docking Tool Windows

The window positions for docking tool windows are not associated with the current project, but are the same no matter which project you open. The locations can be different depending on whether you are editing or debugging. You can create one layout with your choice of docking tool windows for editing, and another layout with a different choice of docking tool windows for debugging. When you switch from editing to debugging, the layout automatically changes.

Docking tool windows can have either of the following two display modes in Visual C++:

Floating In its floating mode, a docking tool window has a thin title bar, can appear anywhere on your display, and is always on top of all other Visual C++ windows. Figure 17.2 shows a floating tool window.

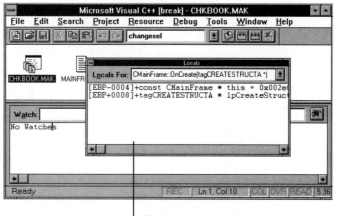

— Floating Locals window

Figure 17.2   Floating Locals Window

Docked   In its docked mode, a docking tool window is fixed to a dock along the border of the main Visual C++ window. Figure 17.3 shows a docked tool window.

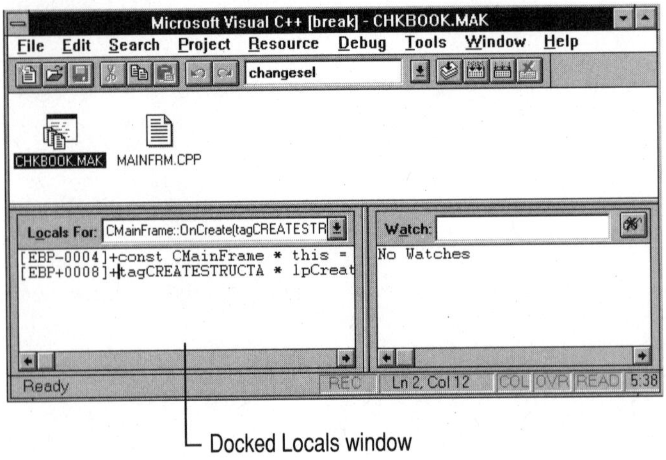

— Docked Locals window

Figure 17.3   Docked Locals Window

You can specify whether tool windows appear as docking windows or as floating windows.

▶ **To change a docked window to a floating window**

1. Position the mouse pointer in a blank area on the window border.

2. Drag the window away from the dock, and move it to the desired position.

   –Or–

- Double-click the window border.

▶ **To dock a floating window**

1. Position the mouse pointer in a blank area of a toolbar or in the title bar of a tool window.

2. Drag the window to any of the four window borders of the Visual C++ application window.

   –Or–

- Double-click the window title bar.

Tool windows stretch to fill the entire border to which you drag it, as shown in Figure 17.4; toolbars change to a single row or column and take the space required by their tools.

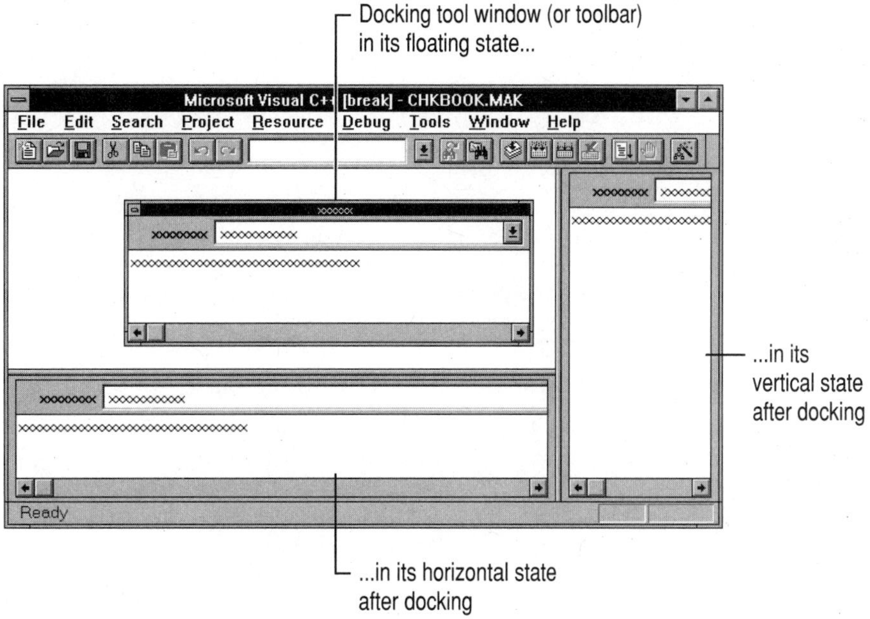

Figure 17.4   Window in floating and docked states

▶ **To position a floating window over a dock area**

1. Position the mouse pointer in the title bar of a tool window.

2. Hold down the CTRL key and drag the window over any dock area of the Visual C++ application window.

The window moves into position over the dock, but remains a floating window.

Both docked windows and floating windows also can display shortcut menus with commands appropriate for the window in its current state. You can click the right mouse button in the window to display the shortcut menu.

Sizing Docking Tool Windows

You can resize any floating tool window in any direction. You can also size tool windows when they are docked by moving its split bar or bars. If two or more tool windows are in the same dock, you can size them by moving the split bar between them.

▶ **To resize a docking tool window**

1. Move the mouse pointer over the window split bar in a docked window or over the window border in a floating window.

   The mouse pointer turns into a sizing arrow.

2. Drag the split bar or border to resize the window.

Changing a Docking Tool Window to Document Window Characteristics

You can use the Options dialog box of the Tools menu or the keyboard to give the docking tool windows the characteristics of document windows.

Even though toolbars are docking windows, you cannot give them document window characteristics.

▶ **To specify whether a tool window is a docking or a document window**

1. From the Tools menu, choose Options.

   The Options dialog box appears.

2. On the Workspace tab, select the windows that you want to be docking tool windows from the Docking Views list.

   Alternatively, clear the check box for docking tool windows that you want to have the characteristics of document windows.

▶ **To quickly switch between docking and document characteristics in a tool window**

1. Move the insertion point into the window, either when it is a docking window or a document window.

2. Click the right mouse button inside the window, click the right mouse button and select Docking View, or press ALT+F6.

If the tool window has the characteristics of a document window, it changes to have the characteristics of a docking window and is docked. If the window is docked, it takes on the characteristics of a document window.

Note The choice and layout of docking tool windows are always associated with editing or debugging, even if you have given them the characteristics of document windows.

Working with Toolbars

Toolbars contain buttons that correspond to menu commands in Visual C++. A toolbar provides a quick and convenient method for executing commands that you use often.

When it starts for the first time, Visual C++ displays the Standard toolbar, with default choices of commands. If you are not satisfied with the default choices, you can choose other toolbars to display, as well as which command buttons to display on any toolbar.

Because toolbars are docking windows, you can either fix a toolbar along the border of the Visual C++ window, or you can turn it into a floating window that can move anywhere on your display.

In addition to the default toolbars, Visual C++ displays toolbars that reflect the currently open editors. For example, if you open the resource file for your project, and open a bitmap resource, Visual C++ displays the toolbars associated with the Image editor. The state of the program determines whether the tools on any given toolbar are currently enabled or disabled.

Toolbars are not associated with the current project, but appear in the same locations no matter which project you open. They can have different locations and positions depending on which editors are open, whether you are debugging, and so on. You can create one layout with your choice of toolbars for editing, for instance, and another layout with a different choice of toolbars for debugging. When you switch from editing to debugging, the layout automatically changes.

Showing and Hiding Toolbars

Visual C++ has several predefined toolbars. When you start Visual C++ for the first time, it puts one of these predefined toolbars on its dock. You can choose, however, which toolbars you want to show at any time.

▶ **To show or hide a toolbar using the main menu**

1. From the Tools menu, choose Toolbars.

   The Toolbars dialog box appears.

2. To show toolbars, select the check boxes for the toolbars that you want to appear.

   To hide toolbars, clear the check boxes for the toolbars that you want to hide.

   Each shown toolbar appears immediately. It appears in its default location, or in the last location that you assigned it, if you assigned it one. Each hidden toolbar disappears immediately.

▶   **To show a toolbar using the shortcut menu**

1. Move the mouse pointer over a toolbar, either floating or docked, and click the right mouse button.

    The shortcut menu appears. The toolbars with checks appearing next to them are currently displayed.

2. To show toolbars, select the check boxes for the toolbars that you want to appear.

    To hide toolbars, clear the check boxes for the toolbars that you want to hide.

    Each shown toolbar appears immediately. It appears in its default location, or in the last location that you assigned it, if you assigned it one. Each hidden toolbar disappears immediately.

▶   **To hide a toolbar using control box on the toolbar window**

•   Click the control box on the upper left corner of the window.

Creating a Custom Toolbar

You can create a new toolbar and add any tool button to it. You can create either a toolbar with a name of your choice, or allow Visual C++ to give it the default title Toolbar, followed by a number.

▶   **To create a named toolbar**

1. From the Tools menu, choose Toolbars.

    The Toolbars dialog box appears.

2. Choose New.

    The New Toolbar dialog box appears.

3. Type the name of your custom toolbar in the Toolbar Name text box.

4. Choose OK.

    Two windows appear:

    ▪   At the upper left of your Visual C++ window, a new toolbar window with the name that you specified appears.

    ▪   The Customize dialog box appears, with the Toolbars tab visible.

        This dialog box gives you choices for categories of toolbar buttons. The categories are listed in the Categories list box. When you select a category, the Tools frame contains all the buttons in the selected category. Each button represents a command.

5. Select a category in the Categories list box.

6. Drag the desired buttons from the selected category onto the custom toolbar.

7. Repeat Steps 5 and 6 until you have all the buttons you want on your toolbar.

8. Click Close on the Customize dialog box.

▶ **To quickly create a toolbar with a default name**

1. From the Tools menu, choose Customize.

   The Customize dialog box appears, with the Toolbars tab visible.

   This dialog box gives you choices for categories of toolbar buttons. The categories are listed in the Categories list box. When you select a category, the Tools frame contains all the buttons in the selected category. Each button represents a command.

2. Select a category in the Categories list box.

3. Drag the first button from the selected category onto any area of your display (except an existing toolbar).

   The first button creates a toolbar named Toolbar*n*, where *n* is 1, 2, 3, 4, and so on.

4. Repeat Steps 2 and 3 until you have all the buttons you want on your toolbar. Modify step 3 to drag the button onto the toolbar that you have just created.

5. Click Close on the Customize dialog box.

Modifying a Toolbar

You can easily add buttons to a toolbar, remove buttons from a toolbar, arrange buttons on a toolbar, copy toolbar buttons, or rename a custom toolbar.

▶ **To add buttons to a toolbar**

1. From the Tools menu, choose Customize.

   The Customize dialog box appears, with the Toolbars tab visible.

   This dialog box gives you choices for categories of toolbar buttons. The categories are listed in the Categories list box. When you select a category, the Tools frame contains all the buttons in the selected category. Each button represents a command.

2. Select a category in the Categories list box.

3. Drag a button from the selected category onto the toolbar.

4. Repeat Steps 2 and 3 until you have all the buttons you want on your toolbar.

5. Choose Close on the Customize dialog box.

▶ **To remove buttons from a toolbar**

1. From the Tools menu, choose Customize.

   The Customize dialog box appears, with the Toolbars tab visible.

2. Drag the button that you want to remove away from the toolbar.

3. Choose Close on the Customize dialog box.

▶ **To move buttons on a toolbar**

1. From the Tools menu, choose Customize.

   The Customize dialog box appears, with the Toolbars tab visible.

2. Drag the button that you want to move to its new location on the same toolbar or to a location on another displayed toolbar.

3. Choose Close on the Customize dialog box.

▶ **To quickly move buttons on a toolbar**

- Hold down the ALT key and drag the button that you want to move to its new location on the same toolbar or to a location on another displayed toolbar.

▶ **To copy buttons from a toolbar**

1. From the Tools menu, choose Customize.

   The Customize dialog box appears, with the Toolbars tab visible.

2. Hold down the CTRL key.

3. Drag the button that you want to copy to its new location on the same toolbar or to a location on another displayed toolbar.

4. Choose Close on the Customize dialog box.

▶ **To quickly copy buttons on a toolbar**

- Hold down the ALT+CTRL key combination and drag the button that you want to copy to its new location on the same toolbar or to a location on another displayed toolbar.

Note If you hold down the CTRL key, or a CTRL key combination, and drag a button onto an area where there is no existing toolbar, Visual C++ creates a new toolbar with a default name.

▶ **To insert a space between buttons on a toolbar**

1. From the Tools menu, choose Customize.

   The Customize dialog box appears, with the Toolbars tab visible.

2. To insert a space before a button that is not followed by a space, drag the button before which you want to insert the space toward the right, or down for vertical toolbars, until it overlaps the next button about halfway.

   To insert a space before a button that is followed by a space and retain the space following the button, drag the button until the right or bottom edge is just touching the next button or just overlaps it.

   To insert a space before a button that is followed by a space and close up the following space, drag the button completely past its original position but not past the next button.

3. Choose Close on the Customize dialog box.

▶ **To close up a space between buttons on a toolbar**

1. From the Tools menu, choose Customize.

   The Customize dialog box appears, with the Toolbars tab visible.

2. Drag the button on one side of the space toward the button on the other side of the space, but not past it.

   If there is no space on the side of the button that you dragging away from, and you drag the button more than halfway past the adjacent button, Visual C++ also inserts a space on the opposite side of the button that you are dragging.

3. Choose Close on the Customize dialog box.

▶ **To rename a custom toolbar**

1. From the Tools menu, choose Toolbars.

   The Toolbars dialog box appears.

2. Select the toolbar that you want to rename from the Toolbars list.

3. Type the new name for the toolbar in the Toolbar Name text box.

4. Choose Close.

Resetting a Toolbar

If you have modified a predefined toolbar, either by adding or removing buttons, you can readily return it to its default state.

▶ **To reset a toolbar**

1. From the Tools menu, choose Toolbars.

   The Toolbars dialog box appears.

2. From the list of toolbars, select the one that you want to reset.

3. Choose Reset.

Deleting a Toolbar

You can delete any custom toolbar that you have created.

▶ **To delete a toolbar**

1. From the Tools menu, choose Toolbars.

   The Toolbars dialog box appears.

2. From the list of toolbars, select the one that you want to delete.

   You cannot delete any of the predefined toolbars.

3. Choose Delete.

Docking Toolbars

Toolbars can have either of the following two display modes in Visual C++:

Floating In its floating mode, a toolbar has a thin title bar, can appear anywhere on your display, and is always on top of all other Visual C++ windows. You can modify its size or position when it is floating. Figure 17.5 shows a floating toolbar.

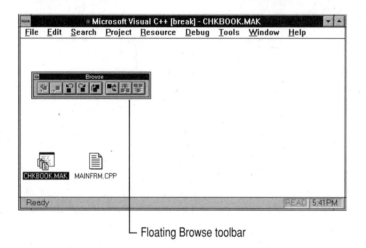

— Floating Browse toolbar

Figure 17.5   Floating Toolbar

Docked In its docked mode, a toolbar is fixed to a dock along the border of the main Visual C++ window. You cannot modify its size when it is docked. Figure 17.6 shows a docked toolbar.

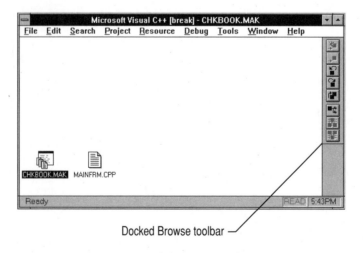

Docked Browse toolbar —

Figure 17.6   Docked Toolbar

When Visual C++ starts up in its default configuration after installation, it displays the Standard toolbar on the top dock of the main Visual C++ window, as shown in Figure 17.7.

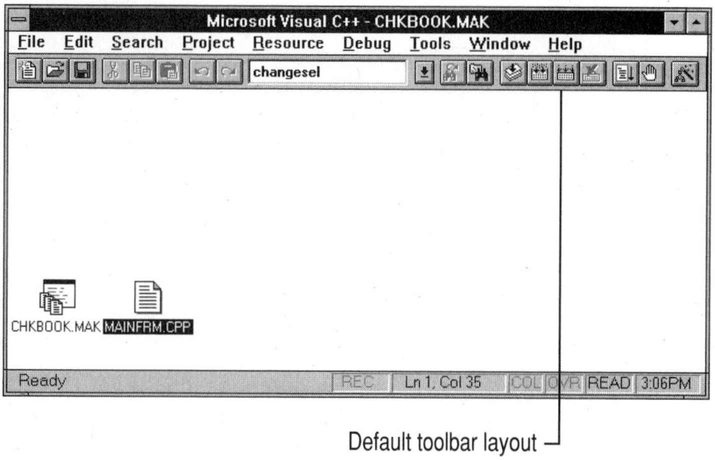

Default toolbar layout ⏌

Figure 17.7   Default toolbar layout

You can also dock any of the standard toolbars that you choose to display, or any of the custom toolbars that you create. You can remove any toolbar from the dock, which automatically converts it into a floating toolbar.

▶ **To remove a toolbar from a dock**

1. Position the mouse pointer in a blank area in the toolbar.

2. Drag the toolbar away from the dock, and move it to the desired position, either on the desktop or in another dock.

▶ **To dock a floating toolbar**

1. Position the mouse pointer over the toolbar title bar or in a blank area in the toolbar.

2. Drag the toolbar to any of the four window borders of the Visual C++ application window.

   When the mouse pointer reaches the boundary of the docking area, the toolbar window assumes a shape appropriate for the docking location. Along the top and bottom borders, it becomes a single horizontal row of buttons; along the sides, it becomes a single vertical row.

▶ **To quickly move toolbars off and on the toolbar dock**

- Position the mouse pointer in a blank area in the toolbar, or in the title bar of a floating toolbar, and double-click.

  If you double-click a toolbar in a toolbar dock, it moves to its previous floating position.

  If you double-click the title bar of a floating toolbar, it moves to the last toolbar dock on which it was displayed. If the toolbar has not been docked before, it moves to a new row in the toolbar dock below the menu bar.

▶ **To move a floating toolbar over a dock area**

1. Position the mouse pointer in a blank area of the toolbar or in its title bar.
2. Hold down the CTRL key and drag the toolbar over any dock area of the Visual C++ application window.

The toolbar moves into position over the dock, but remains a floating toolbar.

Sizing Toolbars

You can resize any floating toolbar. The toolbar changes the row and column arrangement to accommodate whatever new orientation that you give the toolbar window. The window takes the least amount of space necessary to display all its buttons, in whatever orientation you give it.

Note   You cannot change the size or orientation of docked toolbars.

▶ **To resize a toolbar**

1. Move the mouse pointer over the toolbar window border.

   The mouse pointer turns into a two-headed arrow.

2. Drag the border to resize the window.

Customizing the Keyboard

You can use the Keyboard tab on the Customize dialog box to establish your choice of shortcut keys for any of the commands in Visual C++. You can assign more than one shortcut key for any command. You can select the editor for which the shortcut key is valid.

▶ **To assign a shortcut key**

1. From the Tools menu, choose Customize.

   The Customize dialog box appears.

2. Select the Keyboard tab, if it is not visible.

3. From the Editor drop-down list, select the editor in which the shortcut key invokes the command.

4. From the Categories list, select the category of command that contains the command to which you want to assign a shortcut key.

5. From the Commands list, select the command to which you want to assign a shortcut key. When you select the command, a description of its effect appears in the Description box, and the currently assigned shortcut keys appear in the Current Keys list.

6. Move the insertion point to the Press New Shortcut Key box, and press the desired shortcut key or key combination.

   If you press a key or key combination which is invalid, no key is displayed and the Assign key is inactive. You cannot assign key combinations with TAB, ESC, or F1, or combinations such as CTRL+ALT+DELETE, which Windows NT uses.

7. Choose the Assign button.

   You can repeat steps 3 through 7 until you have made all your desired key assignments. You can also delete or change key assignments.

8. Choose the Close button.

All your shortcut key assignments are now in effect.

▶ **To delete a shortcut key**

1. From the Tools menu, choose Customize.

   The Customize dialog box appears.

2. Select the Keyboard tab, if it is not visible.

3. From the Editor drop-down list, select the editor in which the shortcut key invokes the command.

4. From the Categories list, select the category of command that contains the command from which you want to delete a shortcut key.

5. From the Commands list, select the command from which you want to delete a shortcut key. When you select the command, a description of its effect appears in the Description box, and the currently assigned shortcut keys appear in the Current Keys list.

6. Select the shortcut key to delete in the Current Keys list.

7. Choose the Remove button.

   You can repeat steps 3 through 7 until you have made all your desired key assignments. You can also assign new keys or change key assignments.

8. Choose the Close button.

All your shortcut key deletions are now in effect.

▶ **To reset all shortcut keys to their default values**

1. From the Tools menu, choose Customize.

    The Customize dialog box appears.

2. Select the Keyboard tab, if it is not visible.

3. Choose the Reset All button.

4. Choose the OK button.

All commands now have their original, default shortcut key assignments.

Customizing the Tools Menu

You use the Tools tab in the Customize dialog box to add, delete, and edit Tools menu items. You can add frequently used utilities to the Tools menu and run them within Visual C++.

Adding Commands to the Tools Menu

You can add up to eight commands to the Tools menu. A tool can be any program that you can run in Windows NT, such as native Windows NT programs, Windows 3.1 programs, MS-DOS® programs, POSIX programs, or OS/2® programs.

To become familiar with the steps in adding a command to the Tools menu, use the Notepad accessory that comes with Windows NT.

▶ **To add a command to the Tools menu**

1. From the Tools menu, choose Customize.

    The Customize dialog box appears.

2. Select the Tools tab.

3. Choose Add.

    The Add Tool dialog box appears.

4. Type NOTEPAD.EXE in the Command text box.

    You can also click the Browse button, select the appropriate drive and directory, and then select NOTEPAD.EXE from the list of filenames.

5. Choose OK.

    The Tools tab reappears.

    You can change the default menu name by editing the Menu Text text box. You can also add arguments to be passed to the program by typing them in the Arguments text box (see "Using Argument Macros" on page 264) or set the initial directory for your program by typing it in the Initial Directory text box.

> **Note** If the program you are adding to the Tools menu has a .PIF file, the startup directory specified by the .PIF file overrides the directory specified in the Initial Directory text box.

6. Choose Close.

   The command now appears on the Tools menu. To run the program, choose it from the menu.

Editing a Tools Menu Command

▶ **To edit a Tools menu command**

1. From the Tools menu, choose Customize.

   The Customize dialog box appears.

2. Select the Tools tab.

3. Under Menu Contents, select the menu command you want to edit.

4. Perform one or more of the following actions:

   - To move the selected command up one position in the menu, choose Move Up.

   - To move the selected command down one position, choose Move Down.

   - To change the menu title, the command line (tool path and file name), command-line arguments, or the initial directory, type the new information in the appropriate text box.

   If you want to specify a letter in the menu title as an access key (a menu accelerator key), precede that letter in the Menu Text text box with an ampersand (&). The first letter in the title is the keyboard access key by default.

   If you want to be prompted for command-line arguments each time you run the tool, select the Ask For Arguments check box.

5. Choose OK.

▶ **To remove a command from the Tools menu**

1. From the Tools menu, choose Customize.

   The Customize dialog box appears.

2. Select the Tools tab.

3. Under Menu Contents, select the command you want to delete from the Menu Contents list.

4. Choose Remove to remove the program from the list.

5. Choose OK.

Tools Options

The Tools tab in the Customize dialog box includes three check boxes that let you customize options that apply to the active tool in the Menu Contents list. The check boxes are described in the following paragraphs.

Option	Result
Ask for Arguments	When this check box is selected, an argument dialog box will appear when you run the tool and the arguments you type in will be passed to the program.
Redirect to Output Window	When this check box is selected, the standard I/O output from the tool will appear in the Output window. A separate virtual output window is maintained for each tool whose output has been redirected to the Output window. The names of these tools appear in a tab at the bottom of the output window when you run them. You can switch between virtual Output windows by clicking the tabs at the bottom of the Output window. See "Using Error Syntax for Tools" in the following section to learn about additional capabilities gained by redirecting tool output to the Output window.
Close Window on Exit	When this check box is selected, the Command window automatically closes when the tool has finished executing. This applies to character-mode applications only.

Using Argument Macros

You can specify arguments for any program that you add to the Tools menu by entering the arguments in the Arguments text box. To help you integrate your tools with the current status of the Visual C++ environment, Visual C++ provides a set of 12 argument macros (see Table 17.1).

Table 17.1 Visual C++ Argument Macros

Macro Name	Expands to a String Containing
$File	The complete filename of the current source (defined as *drive+path+filename*), blank if a nonsource window is active.
$FileName	The filename of the current source (defined as *filename*), blank if a nonsource window is active.
$FileDir	The directory of the current source (defined as *drive+path*), blank if a nonsource window is active.
$Proj	The current project base name (defined as *filename*), without the .MAK extension, blank if no project is currently open.
$ProjDir	The directory of the current project (defined as *drive+path*), blank if no project is currently open.
$Cmdline	The command-line arguments passed to the application (obtained from the General properties page from Settings command of the Project menu).
$Line	The current cursor line position within the active window.

Table 17.1   Visual C++ Argument Macros (*continued*)

Macro Name	Expands to a String Containing
$Col	The current cursor column position within the active window.
$CurText	The current text (the word under the current cursor position, or a single-line selection if there is one).
$Dir	The current working directory (defined as *drive+path*).
$Target	The current project target name (defined as *drive+path+filename*).
$RC	A resource file (*.RC). For Visual C++ projects, this is the first resource file in the project list. For external projects, it is **$Target.RC**. If there is no resource file or there is no active project, **$RC** is blank.

Macro recognition is not case sensitive. All path macros end in a backslash (\).

To use a macro as an argument, type the macro name in the Arguments text box. Or, for macros that expand to a directory, you can type the macro name in the Initial Directory box. As an example, the following procedure demonstrates how to add the **$File** argument macro to the Windows Notepad accessory (installed in a previous procedure).

▶ **To add the $File macro to an installed tool and then run it**

1. From the Tools menu, choose Customize.

   The Customize dialog box appears.

2. Choose the Tools tab.

3. Under Menu Contents, select the command you want to edit.

   In this case, select the Notepad accessory installed earlier.

4. In the Arguments text box, type $File.

5. Choose OK to close the Customize dialog box.

6. Open any source file or make an open source file active by clicking it.

7. From the Tools menu, choose Notepad.

   The Windows Notepad editor opens with the active Visual C++ source file as its text file.

Using Error Syntax for Tools

When you redirect the output from a tool to the Output window by selecting the Redirect to Output Window check box for the tool in the Tools dialog box, you gain access to the Output window's error parser.

The error parser is used by the internal build tools to detect filename, error and line number information on an output string and make that line a hot link to the specified file and line number. For example, you can double-click an error line in the Output window that contains the error number, filename and line number where the error occurred, and jump directly to the referenced line in the correct source file.

The Find In Files dialog box also use the error parser. For instance, you can double-click any output line from a Find In Files operation and jump to the referenced file and line.

If the output to a tool you have installed and redirected to the output window has the correct error syntax, you can use it in the same way.

Example

For example, you could install Microsoft MASM on the Tools menu to compile assembly code and then jump to source code syntax errors directly from its error list in the Output window. The error syntax is as follows (+ denotes one or more; * denotes zero or more):

error_string	*::=*	*file_spec error_spec (STRING | file_spec STRING)*
file_spec	*::=*	*FILENAME '(' line_spec ')' ':'*
line_spec	*::=*	*NUMBER |* *NUMBER '-' NUMBER*
error_spec	*::=*	*ERRORKEYWORD ERRORNUMBER ':'*

where:

STRING	*::=*	Null terminated string
FILENAME	*::=*	Valid file specification & text file
NUMBER	*::=*	{1–9}{0–9}*
ERRORNUMBER	*::=*	{A–Z}+{0–9}{0–9}{0–9}{0–9}
ERRORKEYWORD	*::=*	"error"	"warning"	"fatal error"

Note Although the error number is part of this syntax, it is optional and not really useful to any tool except internal build tools. This error number is used internally to link to Help files.

Showing the Status Bar

The status bar at the bottom of the Visual C++ window displays information about the Visual C++ and about the portion of Visual C++ currently active. Its left-hand text field, for instance, describes the currently selected menu command or the action of the button currently under the mouse pointer when you press the mouse button.

It also displays progress information about the current operation. In a text editor window, it shows the line and column position of the insertion point, as well as the state of the NUM LOCK and CAPS LOCK keys, and whether the editor is in insertion mode or overstrike mode. Figure 17.8 depicts how the status bar might appear while you are debugging.

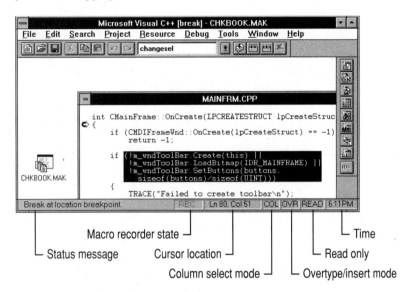

Figure 17.8   Status bar

The default choice is to show the status bar.

▶ **To show or hide the status bar**

1. From the Tools menu, choose Options.

   The Options dialog box appears.

2. On the Workspaces tab, select the Display Status Bar check box to show the status bar, or clear the Display Status Bar check box to hide the status bar.

Setting Directories

When Visual C++ is installed, the Setup program determines the correct directory paths for several file types and updates the Directories dialog box with these paths. The file types are:

- Build utilities (executable files)
- Include files
- Libraries

The Directories tab, accessed by choosing Options from the Tools menu, lets you edit the directory paths where Visual C++ looks for the file types.

The Show Directories For list box on Directories tab contains the following lists of directories:

File Type	Path Contents
Executable Files	Specifies where the build utilities, such as NMAKE, CL, LINK, and BSCMAKE, reside.
Include Files	Specifies where the compiler should look for include files surrounded by angle brackets (< and >) (for example, #include <stdio.h>).
Library Files	Specifies where the linker should look for libraries to resolve external references.

Directory information is stored in Windows NT registry entries.

▶ **To add a directory to a list**

1. From the Tools menu, choose Options.

   The Options dialog box appears.

2. Select the Directories tab.

3. If necessary, select the platform from the Platform drop-down list.

4. Select the category of directories from the Show Directories For drop-down list.

5. Choose the Add button.

   The Add Directory dialog box appears.

6. Type the directory name in the Directory text box.

   Alternatively, choose the Browse button and select the directory name from the Directory Name dialog box.

7. Choose OK.

8. Choose OK in the Options dialog box.

Visual C++ searches directories in the order in which they appear in the list. After adding a directory, you can move it up or down in the list by selecting it and choosing Move Up or Move Down.

▶ **To remove a directory from a list**

1. From the Tools menu, choose Options.

   The Options dialog box appears.

2. Select the Directories tab.

3. If necessary, select the platform from the Platform drop-down list.

4. Select the category of directories from the Show Directories For drop-down list.

5. Select the directory that you want to remove in the Directories list.

6. Choose Remove.

Specifying the Search Order for Help Files

You can choose which help files the help system searches, and the order in which it searches for them. Choosing specific help files allows you eliminate some help files in which you don't want to find information. Choosing the order allows you to specify the preferred help files to search.

When you are in a text editor, you can display help for a language keyword or for a function in one of the libraries included with Visual C++. After you move the cursor onto the keyword or function name, or you highlight it, you can get help in one of two ways:

- Press F1. The help system displays a list of all the instances found in its help files, and you can choose which to view. If it only finds one instance in all the help files, it displays that help topic directly. If it finds multiple instances in a single help file, it displays the Search dialog box, from which you can make a choice.

- Press CTRL+F1. The help system displays the first topic found in the list of help files that you have selected.

You might want to omit some help files from the search list if you are not using the features covered in those files. You might want to omit the OLE or ODBC references from the help file list, for instance, if you are not writing applications that use OLE or that access databases.

▶ **To select help files to search**

1. From the Tools menu, choose Options.

   The Options dialog box appears.

2. Select the Help tab.

3. In the Help Files list, select the check boxes for the help files that you want to search or clear the check boxes that you want to omit from the search.

4. Choose OK.

Now, when you request help on a language keyword or a function name, the Help system searches only in the files that are checked.

The Help system searches through the files in the order shown in the list, from top first to bottom last. As well as including or omitting a file from the order, you can specify the order for the list. You might be porting an application from one platform to another, and when you search for help on a function, you could specify the Porting Reference to be the first help file searched.

▶ **To specify the order for searching help files**

1. From the Tools menu, choose Options.

   The Options dialog box appears.

2. Select the Help tab.

3. In the Help Files list, select a help file to move.

4. Choose Move Up or Move Down repeatedly until the file reaches the place in the list where you want it.

5. Repeat steps 3 and 4 for any additional help files that you want to reorder in the list.

6. Choose OK.

Now, when you request help on a language keyword or a function name, the help system searches the files in the specified order, and it displays only the first topic found in the first file containing the language keyword or function name.

PART 2

Visual C++ Reference

C H A P T E R   1 8

Toolbar Reference

Visual C++ contains two types of toolbars. Some toolbars are available for use only when a view is active, such as the Dialog toolbar, which appears when the dialog editor is open. Other toolbars will always be available, regardless of the current view. You can create a custom toolbar made up of buttons from either type. For more information, see "Creating a Custom Toolbar" on page 254 in Chapter 17.

Visual C++ includes a number of default toolbars arranged around common functions such as editing, debugging, and browsing.

You can also customize toolbars by using the Customize command on the Tools menu. The Toolbars tab in the Customize dialog box displays the available buttons in functional categories that can be used to create custom toolbars.

Default Visual C++ Toolbars

There are nine default toolbars available in Visual C++:

- Standard
- Edit
- Resource
- Debug
- Browse
- Record
- Dialog
- Controls
- Graphics

Standard Toolbar

Button	Effect
	Creates a new source file.
	Opens an existing document.
	Saves the active document.
	Deletes the selection and puts it on the Clipboard.
	Copies the selection and puts it on the Clipboard.
	Inserts Clipboard contents at the insertion point.
	Undoes the last action.
	Redoes the previously undone action.
	Finds the next occurrence.
	Finds a string in files.
	Compiles the file.
	Builds an item and its children.
	Rebuilds the entire project, ignoring dependencies.
	Stops the build.
	Starts or continues the current program.
	Sets or clears a breakpoint.
	Edits application classes and connects resources to code.

Edit Toolbar

Button	Effect
	Toggles a bookmark for the current line.
	Moves to the next bookmark.
	Moves to the previous bookmark.
	Clears all bookmarks in the active window.
	Finds a string in files.
	Indents the selected text right one tab stop.
	Indents the selected text left one tab stop.
	Opens another window for the active document.
	Splits the active window into panes.
	Arranges windows so they overlap.
	Arranges windows as non-overlapping horizontal tiles.
	Arranges windows as non-overlapping vertical tiles.

Resource Toolbar

Button	Effect
	Creates a new dialog box resource.
	Creates a new menu resource.
	Creates a new cursor resource.
	Creates a new icon resource.
	Creates a new bitmap resource.
	Creates or opens the string table resource.
	Creates a new accelerator table resource.
	Creates a new version information resource.
	Browses and edits the symbols in the active file.

Debug Toolbar

Button	Effect
	Restarts the current program.
	Stops debugging the current program.
	Steps into the next statement.
	Steps over the next statement.
	Steps out of the current function.
	Runs the current program to the line containing the cursor.
	Shows variables and expressions quickly.
	Activates or deactivates the Watch window.
	Activates or deactivates the Locals window.
	Activates or deactivates the Registers window.
	Activates or deactivates the Memory window.
	Activates or deactivates the Call Stack window.
	Activates or deactivates the Disassembly window.

Browse Toolbar

Button	Effect
	Displays the definition of a symbol.
	Displays the reference to a symbol.
	Displays the next definition of or reference to a symbol.
	Displays the previous definition of or reference to a symbol.
	Returns to location preceding the last browse operation.
	Shows outline of the selected or current file.
	Shows the derived class graph of the selected or current class.
	Shows the base class graph of the selected or current class.

Record Toolbar

Button	Effect
	Stops keyboard macro recording.
	Pauses and unpauses keyboard macro recording or playback.

Dialog Toolbar

Button	Effect
	Aligns left edges of selected controls with the dominant control.
	Aligns right edges of selected controls with the dominant control.
	Aligns top edges of selected controls with the dominant control.
	Aligns bottom edges of selected controls with the dominant control.
	Centers controls vertically within the dialog box.
	Centers controls horizontally within the dialog box.
	Evenly spaces selected controls horizontally.
	Evenly spaces selected controls vertically.
	Resizes selected controls to have the same width as the dominant control.
	Resizes selected controls to have the same height as the dominant control.
	Resizes selected controls to have the same size as the dominant control.
	Toggles the grid on and off.

Controls Toolbar

Button	Effect
	Select controls.
	Creates a picture control.
	Creates a static text control.
	Creates a text box.
	Creates a group box.
	Creates a push button.
	Creates a check box.
	Creates a radio button.
	Creates a combo box.
	Creates a list box.
	Creates a horizontal scrollbar.
	Create a vertical scrollbar.
	Create a user-defined control.

Graphics Toolbar

Button	Effect
	Rectangular selection tool.
	Free-form selection tool.
	Color pickup tool.
	Eraser.
	Fill tool.
	Zoom tool.
	Pencil tool.
	Brush tool.
	Airbrush tool.
	Line tool.
	Curved-line tool.

Button	Effect
[A]	Text tool.
[▢]	Framed rectangle tool.
[▣]	Filled rectangle tool.
[▪]	Filled rectangle tool (borderless).
[▢]	Framed rounded rectangle tool.
[●]	Filled rounded rectangle tool.
[▪]	Filled rounded rectangle tool (borderless).
[○]	Framed ellipse tool.
[●]	Filled ellipse tool.
[●]	Filled ellipse tool (borderless).
[Z]	Framed free-form shape tool.
[◢]	Filled free-form shape tool.
[◣]	Filled free-form shape tool (borderless).

Toolbar Categories

The Toolbars tab in the Customize dialog box shows all the toolbar command buttons that are available in Visual C++. The buttons are categorized by function. You can drag a button from the Customize dialog box to an existing toolbar, or you can create a new toolbar and add to it. The categories are:

- File
- Edit
- Search
- Project
- Resource
- Layout
- Debug
- Tools
- Window
- Help

File Category

Button	Effect
	Creates a new document.
	Opens an existing document.
	Creates a new source file.
	Creates a new bitmap.
	Creates a new resource script.
	Saves the active document.
	Saves all open files.

Edit Category

Button	Effect
	Undoes the last action.
	Redoes the previously undone action.
	Deletes the selection and puts it on the Clipboard.
	Copies the selection and puts it on the Clipboard.
	Inserts the Clipboard contents at the insertion point.
	Erases the selection.
	Indents the selected text right one tab stop.
	Indents the selected text left one tab stop.
	Edits application classes and connects resources to code.

Search Category

Button	Effect
	Finds the specified text.
	Finds the next occurrence.
	Finds the previous occurrence.
	Finds a string in files.
	Toggles a bookmark for the current line.
	Moves to the next bookmark.
	Moves to the previous bookmark.
	Clears all bookmarks in the active window.
	Shows symbol references and definitions.

Button	Effect
	Shows an outline of the selected or current file.
	Shows the call graph of the selected or current function.
	Shows the derived class graph of the selected or current class.
	Shows the callers graph of the selected or current function.
	Shows the base class graph of the selected or current class.
	Displays the definition of a symbol.
	Displays the reference to a symbol.
	Displays the next definition of or reference to a symbol.
	Displays the previous definition of or reference to a symbol.
	Returns to location preceding the last browse operation.

Project Category

Button	Effect
	Compiles the file.
	Builds an item and its children.
	Rebuilds the entire project, ignoring dependencies.
	Stops the build.
	Moves to the line containing the next error tag.
	Moves to the line containing the previous error tag.

Resource Category

Button	Effect
	Browses and edits the symbols in the active file.
	Runs the current dialog box to test appearance and behavior.
	Creates a dialog box resource.
	Creates a cursor resource.
	Creates an icon resource.
	Creates a bitmap resource.
	Creates a menu resource.
	Creates or opens the string table resource.
	Creates an accelerator table resource.
	Creates a version information resource.

Layout Category

Button	Effect
	Toggles the grid on and off.
	Aligns left edges of selected controls with the dominant control.
	Aligns right edges of selected controls with the dominant control.
	Aligns top edges of selected controls with the dominant control.
	Aligns bottom edges of selected controls with the dominant control.
	Evenly spaces selected controls horizontally.
	Evenly spaces selected controls vertically.
	Centers controls vertically within the dialog box.
	Centers controls horizontally within the dialog box.
	Resizes selected controls to have the same width as the dominant control.
	Resizes selected controls to have the same height as the dominant control.
	Resizes selected controls to have the same size as the dominant control.

Debug Category

Button	Effect
	Runs the current dialog box to test appearance and behavior.
	Starts or continues the current program.
	Restarts the current program.
	Stops debugging the current program.
	Sets or clears a breakpoint.
	Steps into the next statement.
	Steps over the next statement.
	Steps out of the current function.
	Runs the current program to the line containing the cursor.
	Shows variables and expressions quickly.
	Clears all breakpoints.
	Sets or clears a breakpoint.
	Activates or deactivates the Output window.
	Activates or deactivates the Watch window.
	Activates or deactivates the Locals window.

Button	Effect
	Activates or deactivates the Registers window.
	Activates or deactivates the Memory window.
	Activates or deactivates the Call Stack window.
	Activates or deactivates the Disassembly window.

Tools Category

Button	Effect
	Starts and stops the keyboard macro recording.
	Stops keyboard macro recording.
	Plays the previously recorded keyboard macro.
	Pauses and unpauses keyboard macro recording or playback.

Window Category

Button	Effect
	Opens another window for the active document.
	Splits the active window into panes.
	Arranges windows so they overlap.
	Arranges windows as non-overlapping horizontal tiles.
	Arranges windows as non-overlapping vertical tiles.

Help Category

Button	Effect
	Displays program information, version number, and copyright.

CHAPTER 19

Keyboard Shortcuts

Keyboard shortcuts offer an alternative method of performing actions for users who prefer keyboard use over mouse use. If you have some preferences for shortcut keys other than the defaults, you can change any of the shortcut keys to your liking, add shortcut keys, set multiple shortcut keys for a command, and specify the windows in which any shortcut is active. The following categorical lists show the default Visual C++ shortcut keys.

Text editing	Window and dialog box management
File management	Building and compiling
Browsing	Debugging
Properties window	Contents browsing
Creating and editing resources	Editing graphics
Dialog editor	Menu editor
String editor	Binary data editor

Text Editing Keys

In the text editor, there are shortcut keys for:

- Moving the insertion point
- Selecting text
- Modifying text
- Deleting text
- Scrolling through text
- Searching

To move the insertion point	Press
One character left	LEFT ARROW
One character right	RIGHT ARROW
One word left	CTRL+LEFT ARROW
One word right	CTRL+RIGHT ARROW
One line up	UP ARROW
One line down	DOWN ARROW
To the first indentation of the current line	HOME
To the beginning of the current line	HOME, HOME
To the first indentation of the next line	CTRL+ENTER
To the end of the line	END
To the beginning of the file	CTRL+HOME
To the end of the file	CTRL+END

To select text	Press
Character to the left	SHIFT+LEFT ARROW
Character to the right	SHIFT+RIGHT ARROW
One word to the left	SHIFT+CTRL+LEFT ARROW
One word to the right	SHIFT+CTRL+RIGHT ARROW
Current line if insertion point is home	SHIFT+DOWN ARROW
Line above if insertion point is home	SHIFT+UP ARROW
To end of line	SHIFT+END
To beginning of line	SHIFT+HOME
One screen up	SHIFT+PAGE UP
One screen down	SHIFT+PAGE DOWN
To beginning of file	SHIFT+CTRL+HOME
To end of file	SHIFT+CTRL+END
To matching brace	SHIFT+CTRL+M
To enclosing **#ifdef**	SHIFT+CTRL+>
To enclosing **#endif, #else, #elif**	SHIFT+CTRL+<

To modify text	Press
Turn keyboard insert mode on or off	INS
Insert one blank line below	END, ENTER
Insert one blank line above	HOME, ENTER
Insert carriage return at insertion point and move cursor down one line	SHIFT+CTRL+N

To modify text	Press
Insert contents of the Clipboard	CTRL+V or SHIFT+INS
Copy selected text to Clipboard, keeping it	CTRL+C or CTRL+INS
Copy selected text to Clipboard, deleting it	CTRL+X or SHIFT+DEL
Copy current line to Clipboard, deleting it	CTRL+Y
Change selection to uppercase	CTRL+SHIFT+U
Change selection to lowercase	CTRL+U
Undo the last edit	CTRL+Z or ALT+BACKSPACE
Redo the last edit	CTRL+A
Insert a tab	TAB
Move all selected lines one tab stop right	TAB
Move all selected lines one tab stop left	SHIFT+TAB
Toggle display of tab symbols	CTRL+ALT+T

To delete	Press
One character to the left	BACKSPACE
One character to the right	DEL
Word to the left	CTRL+BACKSPACE
Selected text and copy it to the Clipboard	CTRL+X or SHIFT+DEL

To scroll	Press
Up one line at a time	CTRL+UP ARROW
Down one line at a time	CTRL+DOWN ARROW
Up one page at a time	PAGE UP
Down one page at a time	PAGE DOWN
Left one window width	CTRL+PAGE UP
Right one window width	CTRL+PAGE DOWN

Searching: To	Press
Look for context-sensitive help in all the files selected on the Help tab in the Options dialog box	F1
Look for context-sensitive help in help files with the file order set on the Help tab in the Options dialog box	CTRL+F1
Find the selected text (forwards)	CTRL+F3
Find the selected text (backwards)	SHIFT+CTRL+F3
Find next (forwards)	F3

Searching: To	Press
Find next (backwards)	SHIFT+F3
Open the Find dialog box	ALT+F3
Find the next error or Output window item	F4
Find the previous error or Output window item	SHIFT+F4
Find matching brace	CTRL+]
Find enclosing **#ifdef**	CTRL+<
Find **#endif**, **#else**, or **#elif**	CTRL+>
Find next bookmark	F2
Find previous bookmark	SHIFT+F2
Toggle bookmark	CTRL+F2

Window and Dialog Box Management Keys

To	Press
Activate next window	CTRL+F6 or CTRL+TAB
Activate previous window	CTRL+SHIFT+F6 or CTRL+SHIFT+TAB
Close current window	CTRL+F4
Activate the Properties window	ALT+ENTER
Scroll vertically	PAGE UP or PAGE DOWN
Scroll horizontally	CTRL+PAGE UP or CTRL+PAGE DOWN
Shift focus between panes in the browse window	TAB or SHIFT+TAB
In a tab dialog box:	
Activate next tab	CTRL+TAB
Activate previous tab	CTRL+SHIFT+TAB

File Management Keys

To	Press
Create a new file	CTRL+N
Open a file	CTRL+O
Save a file	CTRL+S

Build and Compile Keys

To	Press
Compile the active source file	CTRL+F8
Build the project using dependency rules	SHIFT+F8
Build the project from the start	ALT+F8
Stop the build	CTRL+BREAK
Execute the program	CTRL+F5

Browsing Keys

To	Press
Jump to the definition of a selected symbol	F11
Jump to the first reference of a selected symbol	SHIFT+F11
Open the Browse dialog box	CTRL+F11
Jump to the next reference in the browse window list	CTRL+NUMPAD PLUS SIGN
Jump to the previous reference in the browse window list	CTRL+NUMPAD MINUS SIGN
Pop context	CTRL+NUMPAD*
Expand active node one level	NUMPAD PLUS SIGN
Collapse active node one level	NUMPAD MINUS SIGN
Expand all nodes in the Project window	NUMPAD*

Debugging Keys

To	Press
Restart program execution from beginning	SHIFT+F5
Continue execution from current statement	F5
Stop debugging	ALT+F5
Execute program to location of insertion point	F7
Execute next statement, tracing into function calls	F8
Single-step, stepping over functions calls	F10
Execute program out of current function and stop on first line after function call	SHIFT+F7
Set next statement (move EIP or equivalent to current location of insertion point without executing intermediate statements)	CTRL+SHIFT+F7
Open the QuickWatch dialog box	SHIFT+F9
Open the Breakpoints dialog box	CTRL+B

To	Press
Open the Watch window	ALT+2
Open the Locals window	ALT+3
Open the Registers window	ALT+4
Open the Memory window	ALT+5
Open the Call Stack window	ALT+6
Open the Disassembly window	ALT+7
Toggle hexadecimal display	ALT+F9
Toggle a breakpoint	F9
Toggle mixed mode	CTRL+F7
In a Registers window:	
Move to the next register	TAB
Move to the previous register	SHIFT+TAB
Move to the first register of the line	HOME
Move to the last register of the line	END
Move to the first register	CTRL+HOME
Move to the last register	CTRL+END
In a Memory window:	
Display the next memory format	ALT+F7
Display previous memory format	ALT+SHIFT+F7
In the Disassembly window:	
Step into source	CTRL+F9
Step over source	CTRL+F10

Properties Window Keys

To	Press
Activate Properties window	ALT+ENTER
Select next tab	PAGE DOWN
Select previous tab	PAGE UP
Move to next option	TAB
Move to previous option	SHIFT+TAB
Open the Properties window and select the General properties page	CTRL+E
Open the Properties window and select the ID option	CTRL+Q
Switch focus from the Properties window to related object	ENTER or ESC

Contents Browsing Keys

To	Press
Select the first book	HOME
Select the last book	END
Select the next level down	DOWN ARROW
Select the next level up	UP ARROW
Page down the list of books	PAGE DOWN
Page up the list of books	PAGE UP
Expand the current level	RIGHT ARROW
Collapse the current level	LEFT ARROW
Use shortcut for double-click	ENTER

Creating and Editing Resources

To	Press
Create a resource	CTRL+R
Create a file	CTRL+N
Create a resource of type currently highlighted in the resource script window	INS
Create a dialog box	CTRL+1
Create a menu	CTRL+2
Create a cursor	CTRL+3
Create an icon	CTRL+4
Create a bitmap	CTRL+5
Create a string table, or open an existing string table	CTRL+6
Create an accelerator table	CTRL+7
Delete a resource in the resource script window	DEL
Open an existing resource selected in the resource browser window	ENTER
Open a resource's Properties window	ALT+ENTER
Connect user-interface objects to code (open ClassWizard)	CTRL+W
Test a dialog box	CTRL+T
Open the Properties window and select the General properties page	CTRL+E
Open the Properties window and select the ID control	CTRL+Q

Editing Graphics

To	Press
Increase the magnification factor	> (SHIFT+PERIOD)
Decrease the magnification factor	< (SHIFT+COMMA)
Use the framed-rectangle tool	R
Use the filled-rectangle tool	SHIFT+R
Use the framed rounded-rectangle tool	N
Use the filled rounded-rectangle tool	SHIFT+N
Use the framed-ellipse tool	E
Use the filled-ellipse tool	SHIFT+E
Use the pencil tool	P
Use the eraser tool	SHIFT+P
Use the brush tool	D
Use the selection tool	S
Use the fill tool	F
Use the line tool	L
Use the airbrush tool	A
Pick up a color	COMMA
Increase the brush size	PLUS SIGN or =
Decrease the brush size	MINUS SIGN
Use the single-pixel brush	PERIOD
Flip along horizontal axis	X
Flip along vertical axis	Y
Toggle background-color opacity	O
Outline custom brush with foreground color	SHIFT+O
Zoom under cursor	M
Move to the next pane	TAB or F6
Move to the previous pane	SHIFT+TAB or SHIFT+F6
Select the previous foreground color	[
Select the next foreground color	]
Select the previous background color	{
Select the next background color	}
Show or hide the pixel grid	G
Show or hide the tile grid	CTRL+G

Dialog Editor

To	Press
Move to the next control	TAB
Move to the previous control	SHIFT+TAB
Move control right one dialog unit (DLU)	RIGHT ARROW
Move control left one DLU	LEFT ARROW
Move control up one DLU	UP ARROW
Move control down one DLU	DOWN ARROW
Expand the selected control horizontally	SHIFT+RIGHT ARROW
Contract the selected control horizontally	SHIFT+LEFT ARROW
Expand the selected control vertically	SHIFT+DOWN ARROW
Contract the selected control vertically	SHIFT+UP ARROW
Align selected controls along left edge of the dialog box	CTRL+LEFT ARROW
Align selected controls along right edge of the dialog box	CTRL+RIGHT ARROW
Align selected controls along top edge of the dialog box	CTRL+UP ARROW
Align selected controls along bottom edge of the dialog box	CTRL+DOWN ARROW
Align selected controls horizontally on the centerline of the dialog box	F9
Align selected controls vertically on the centerline of the dialog box	SHIFT+F9
Center selected control vertically in dialog box	CTRL+F9
Center selected control horizontally in dialog box	CTRL+SHIFT+F9
Align buttons at right edge of dialog box	CTRL+B
Align buttons at bottom of dialog box	CTRL+SHIFT+B
Make selected controls the same width	CTRL+MINUS SIGN (not on the NUMPAD)
Make selected controls the same height	CTRL+BACKSLASH
Make selected controls the same height and width	CTRL+=
Size the control to its content	F7
Show or hide the alignment grid	CTRL+G
Set the tab order	CTRL+D

Menu Editor

To	Press
Insert empty menu at current location	INS
Delete selected menu item	DEL

String Editor

To	Press
Find text	ALT+F3 or CTRL+F or ALT+A
Find next occurrence of text	F3
Add a new string	INS
Delete current string	DEL

Binary Data Editor

To	Press
Move insertion point right	RIGHT ARROW
Move insertion point left	LEFT ARROW
Move insertion point up	UP ARROW
Move insertion point down	DOWN ARROW
Move between hexadecimal and ASCII listings	TAB

C H A P T E R   2 0

Setting Compiler Options

In Visual C++, you set compiler options on the C/C++ tab in the Project Settings dialog box. The settings you select control the Microsoft C and C++ compilers and linker. The compilers produce Common Object File Format (COFF) object files.

This chapter describes the Compiler option categories that are available from the C/C++ tab of the Project Settings dialog box.

- General
- Code Generation
- Precompiled Headers
- Optimizations
- C Language
- C++ Language
- Preprocessor
- Listing Files

The compiler options that are not available as controls within option categories in the C/C++ tab of the Project Settings dialog box are described in Appendix A, "CL Reference." Appendix A describes how to use the command-line compiler and linker driver, CL.EXE, from the command line.

General

These are the most commonly used options. All General options (see Figure 20.1), with the exception of the Debug Info option, are also available as settings in other option categories. Only the Debug Info option is described in this section. For information on the other General options, see the following pages: Warning Level, page 313; Warnings as Errors, page 314; Generate Browse Info, page 324; Optimizations, page 304; Preprocessor Definitions, page 322.

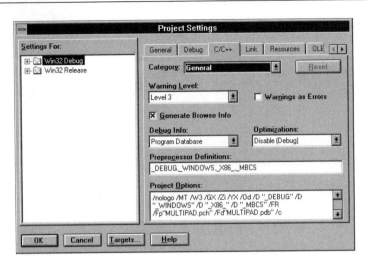

Figure 20.1   General Category on the C/C++ Tab

Debug Info   These options select the type of debugging information generated for your program and whether the debugging information is kept in object files or a program database.

None
>   Removes all debugging options from the command line. In this case, no debugging information is generated, and compilation is faster. No command-line equivalent.

Line Numbers Only
>   Produces an object file or executable file containing only global and external symbol and line-number information but not symbolic-debugging information. Use this option if you want to reduce the size of the executable file or if you don't want to use the expression evaluator. Command-line equivalent: /Zd

C7 Compatible
>   Produces an object file and an executable file containing line numbers and full symbolic-debugging information for use with the Visual C++ debugger. The symbolic information is a map of your source code and includes such things as the names and types of variables and functions. It also includes full symbol-table information and line numbers. Command-line equivalent: /Z7

>   If you use the Create .PCH File option, which is in the Precompiled Headers category, you can use the C7 Compatible option to eliminate duplicate type information. This method creates a significantly smaller library because type information resides in a single object file. In order to link to objects in the library and have access to the PCH type information, either the program being linked or the library objects must reference a public symbol in the object file that contains the type information.

Note This option has the same effect as /Zi in Microsoft C/C++ version 7.

Program Database

Produces a program database (PDB) that contains both types information as well as symbolic-debugging information for use with the Visual C++ debugger. The symbolic information is a map of your source code and includes such things as the names and types of variables and functions. It also includes full symbol-table information and line numbers. Command-line equivalent: /Zi

Object files contain references into the PDB for debugging information. This makes object files smaller. Using PDBs ensures that debugging information is up to date when using precompiled headers and helps speed build times.

The database with types information is named *project*.PDB. If you compile a file without a project, Visual C++ creates a database named VC20.PDB.

Object files created using this option contain the name of the associated .PDB file, which must be available at link time. The linker uses the embedded filename to find the file.

If you create a library from objects that were compiled using this option, the associated .PDB file must be available when the library is linked to a program. If you distribute the library, you must distribute the PDB. To create a library that contains debugging information without using PDBs, you must select the compiler's C7 Compatible (/Z7) option and clear the linker's Use Program Database (/PDB:NONE) option.

If you use the precompiled-headers options, debugging information for both the precompiled header and the rest of the source code is placed in the PDB. The /Yd option is ignored with the Program Database option.

Project, Source File, and Common Options This text box displays options that you've currently selected. The options are displayed using their command-line equivalents. You can type in this text box if a single project or a single source file is selected from the left pane of the Project Settings dialog box. With a project selected, the text box is named Project Options. With a source file selected, it is named Source File Options. With multiple projects or files selected, the text box is named Common Options and displays the options that are common to the selections. You cannot type in the text box when it is named Common Options.

When it is named Project Options or Source File Options, the text box accepts any option that is available from the C/C++ tab. It also accepts those compiler options that are otherwise available only from the command line.

You are responsible for the accuracy of any option you enter in the text box. If Visual C++ recognizes an option as one that can be set using a dialog-box control, it changes the dialog-box control to reflect the option. However, if the option is not recognized, it is left in the options string as is and passed to the compiler.

Reset   This button resets the project Settings of a target or a file back to the settings that existed when the target or file was created. It is enabled if both of the following conditions are met:

- A single target or a single file is selected in the left pane of the Project Settings dialog box.
- The settings of the selection have changed.

The Reset button is not enabled when multiple targets or files (including groups) are selected.

Code Generation

These options (see Figure 20.2) specify the CPU, run-time library, calling convention, and structure alignment.

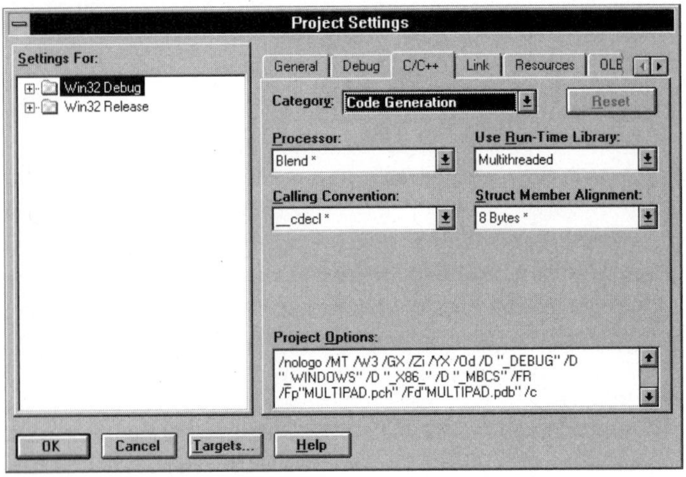

Figure 20.2   Code Generation Category on the C/C++ Tab

x86 Specific →

Processor   These options direct the compiler to optimize code generation to complement the 80386, 80486, and Pentium™ processors.

Blend

> Optimizes the code it generates to favor the 80486, but includes many Pentium optimizations that do not seriously impact performance on the 80386 or 80486. Both the 80386 and the 80486 options now map to the Blend option. Command-line equivalent: /GB

80386

Optimizes the code it generates in the same manner as does the new Blend option. The 80386 option is retained for compatibility with previous versions of Visual C++ and to force a value of 300 for the **_M_IX86** preprocessor macro. Command-line equivalent: /GB or /G3

80486

Optimizes the code it generates in the same manner as does the new Blend option. The 80486 option is retained for compatibility with previous versions of Visual C++. Command-line equivalent: /GB or /G4

Pentium

Optimizes the code it generates to favor the Pentium. Use this option for programs meant only for the Pentium. Code generated using Pentium does not perform as well on 80386- and 80486-based computers as code generated using Blend. Command-line equivalent: /G5

Note   Blocks of inline **_ _ asm** code cannot use 80x86 or Pentium mnemonics as labels.

The compiler generates a value for the **_M_IX86** preprocessor identifier that reflects the processor option specified as follows:

Option	Value
Blend	**_M_IX86 = 400** (Default. Future compilers will emit different values for Blend that reflect the dominant processor.)
80386	**_M_IX86 = 300**
80486	**_M_IX86 = 400**
Pentium	**_M_IX86 = 500**

END x86 Specific

Use Run-Time Library   These options let you select either single-threaded or multithreaded run-time routines, and to indicate that a multithreaded module is a DLL:

Single-threaded (libc.lib)

Causes the compiler to place the library name LIBC.LIB into the object file so that the linker will use LIBC.LIB to resolve external symbols. This is the compiler's default action. LIBC.LIB does not provide multithread support. Command-line equivalent: /ML

Multithreaded (libcmt.lib)

Defines _MT so that multithread-specific versions of the run-time routines are selected from the standard header files. It also causes the compiler to place the library name LIBCMT.LIB into the object file so that the linker will use

LIBCMT.LIB to resolve external symbols. Either /MT or /MD is required to create multithreaded programs. Command-line equivalent: /MT

Multithreaded using DLL (msvcrt.lib)

Defines _MT and _DLL so that both multithread- and DLL-specific versions of the run-time routines are selected from the standard header files. It also causes the compiler to place the library name MSVCRT.LIB into the object file. Command-line equivalent: /MD

Applications compiled with this option are statically linked to MSVCRT.LIB. This library provides a layer of code that allows the linker to resolve external references. The actual working code is contained in MSVCRT20.DLL, which must be available at run time to applications linked with MSVCRT.LIB.

Calling Convention The calling convention options determine the order in which arguments passed to functions are pushed on the stack; which function, calling or called, removes the arguments from the stack; and the name-decorating convention the compiler uses to identify individual functions.

_ _cdecl

Specifies the C calling convention for all functions that are not C++ member functions or are not marked as _ _**stdcall** or _ _**fastcall**. The called function's arguments are pushed onto the stack from right to left and the calling function pops these arguments from the stack when control returns to the calling function. This is the default. Command-line equivalent: /Gd

For C, the _ _**cdecl** naming convention uses the function name preceded by an underscore (_)—no case translation is done. Unless declared as **extern** "C", C++ methods use a different name-decorating scheme. For more information on decorated names, see Appendix J, "Decorated Names."

_ _fastcall

Specifies the fastcall calling convention for all functions that are not C++ member functions or are not marked as _ _**cdecl** or _ _**stdcall**. All fastcall functions must have prototypes. Command-line equivalent: /Gr

Some of a fastcall function's arguments are passed in registers **x86 Specific →** (ECX and EDX) **END x86 Specific** and the rest are pushed onto the stack from right to left. The called routine pops these arguments from the stack before it returns. Typically, /Gr decreases execution time.

Important Be careful when using the fastcall calling convention for any function written in inline assembly language. Your use of registers in assembly language could conflict with the compiler's use of registers for storing arguments.

For C, the fastcall naming convention uses the function name preceded by an at sign (@) and followed by an at sign. The second at sign is followed by the size of the function's arguments in bytes. No case translation is done. The compiler uses the following template for the naming convention:

```
@function_name@number
```

Note Microsoft does not guarantee the same implementation of the fastcall calling convention between compiler releases. For example, the implementation differs between the 16-bit and 32-bit x86 compilers.

When using the fastcall naming convention, use the standard include files. Otherwise, you get unresolved external references.

__stdcall

This option specifies the standard-call (__stdcall) calling convention for all prototyped C functions that do not take a variable number of arguments and are not marked as __cdecl or __fastcall. All __stdcall functions must have prototypes. Command-line equivalent: /Gz

A __stdcall function's arguments are pushed onto the stack from right to left, and the called function pops these arguments from the stack before it returns.

For C, the __stdcall convention uses the function name preceded by an underscore (_) and followed by an at sign (@) and the size of the function's arguments in bytes. No case translation is done. The compiler uses the following template for the naming convention:

```
_functionname@number
```

x86 Specific →
This option has no effect on the name decoration of C++ methods and functions. Unless declared as **extern** "C", C++ methods and functions use a different name-decorating scheme. For more information on decorated names, see Appendix J, "Decorated Names."
END x86 Specific

Note **x86 Specific →** By default, C++ member functions use a calling convention whereby the member function's **this** pointer is passed in the ECX register, all other arguments are pushed onto the stack from right to left, and the called routine pops the member function's arguments from the stack. **END x86 Specific** A member function that is explicitly marked as __cdecl, __fastcall, or __stdcall uses the specified calling convention. A member function that takes a variable number of arguments always uses the __cdecl calling convention.

Struct Member Byte Alignment   This option controls how the members of a structure are packed into memory and specifies the same packing for all structures in a module. When you specify this option, each structure member after the first is stored on the smaller of the size of the member type or *n*-byte boundaries, where *n* is either 1, 2, 4, 8, or 16.

You should not use this option unless you have specific alignment requirements.

List entry	Command-line equivalent	Result
1 Byte	/Zp1	Pack structures on 1-byte boundaries
2 Bytes	/Zp2	Pack structures on 2-byte boundaries
4 Bytes	/Zp4	Pack structures on 4-byte boundaries
8 Bytes	/Zp8	Pack structures on 8-byte boundaries
16 Bytes	/Zp16	Pack structures on 16-byte boundaries

You can also use the **pack** pragma to control structure packing. For information on the **pack** pragma, see Chapter 2 of the *Preprocessor Reference*.

Precompiled Headers

These options (see Figure 20.3) speed compile time. They also allow you to precompile any C or C++ code (including inline code).

Programming projects typically use code that is stable (such as WINDOWS.H and AFXWIN.H), and code that is still under development. You can speed up your build times by precompiling the stable code, saving the precompiled state in a precompiled header file (PCH) and then combining the PCH with uncompiled code in subsequent builds. This shortens the compile time for subsequent builds because the precompiled code is not recompiled, it is simply reused.

There are two different precompiled header systems:

- Per-File Use of Precompiled Headers
- Automatic Use of Precompiled Headers

The Per-File Use Of Precompiled Headers options manage a more efficient precompiled-header process than does the Automatic Use Of Precompiled Headers option (automatic). The Per-File Use Of Precompiled Headers system is used by default for projects that use the Microsoft Foundation Class Library. The Automatic Use Of Precompiled Headers is used by default for projects of any other type.

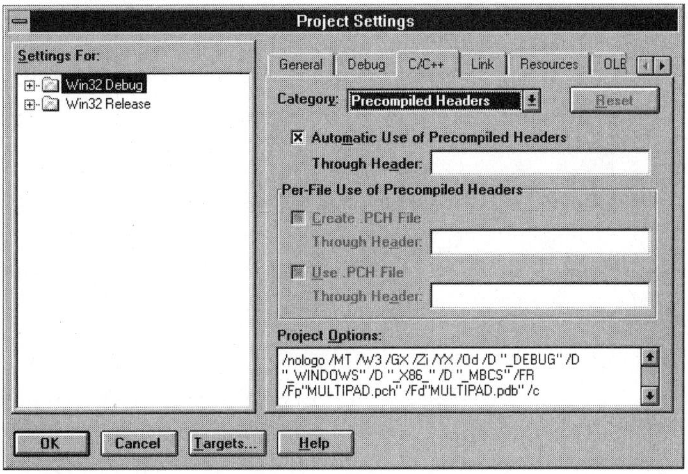

Figure 20.3   Precompiled Headers Category on the C/C++ Tab

Per-File Use of Precompiled Headers

For each project that uses the Microsoft Foundation Class Library, Visual C++ creates a file named STDAFX.H to act as a container for system and project header files that are used frequently and change infrequently. Visual C++ also creates a file named STDAFX.CPP to contain only a single include directive:

```
#include "stdafx.h"
```

In a Microsoft Foundation Class project, only STDAFX.CPP is compiled using the Create .PCH File option. This mechanism creates a file named STDAFX.PCH to contain stable precompiled code for use by all other C and C++ files in the project.

See "Consistency Rules for Per-File Use of Precompiled Headers" on page 302.

Create .PCH File   This option creates a precompiled header file (PCH). Only header files are precompiled into the PCH. The creation of the PCH stops after the compiler compiles the header file specified in the Through Header text box or when it encounters a **hdrstop** pragma. Command-line equivalent: /Yc

For more information on the **hdrstop** pragma, see Chapter 2 of the *Preprocessor Reference*.

Through Header   The compiler compiles all code up to and including the header file (.H) specified in this text box. Command-line equivalent: optional *filename* argument to /Yc. When used from the command-line, no space is allowed between /Yc and *filename*.

Use .PCH File   This option specifies using a precompiled header file (PCH) during builds. The PCH must have been created using the Create .PCH File option. Command-line equivalent: /Yu

Through Header Specify the name of a header file (.H) in this text box. The compiler assumes that all code occurring before the header file is precompiled. It skips to just beyond the **#include** directive associated with the header file, uses the code contained in the precompiled header file, and then compiles all code after *filename*. Command-line equivalent: optional *filename* argument to /Yu. When used from the command-line, no space is allowed between /Yu and *filename*.

Automatic Use of Precompiled Headers This option creates a file named *project*.PCH if it doesn't exist, and compiles only header files into this precompiled header file (PCH). If you have no project open, it creates a file named VC20.PCH. The inclusion of header files stops when the compiler encounters the first declaration, definition, **hdrstop** pragma, or **#line** directive in the source file being compiled with the option, or after the header file specified in the Through Header text box. In subsequent compilations, the precompiled header is used after the compiler makes its final consistency check. Command-line equivalent: /YX

See "Consistency Rules for Automatic Use of Precompiled Headers" on page 304. For more information on the **hdrstop** pragma, see Chapter 2 of the *Preprocessor Reference*.

Through Header When creating a precompiled header, the compiler compiles all code up to and including the header file (.H) specified in this text box. When using a precompiled header, the compiler assumes that all code occurring before the specified header file is precompiled. It skips to just beyond the **#include** directive associated with the header file, uses the code contained in the precompiled header file, and then compiles all code after *filename*. Command-line equivalent: optional *filename* argument to /YX. When used from the command-line, no space is allowed between /YX and *filename*.

Consistency Rules for Per-File Use of Precompiled Headers

When you use a precompiled header, the compiler assumes the same compilation environment—using consistent compiler options, pragmas, and so on—that was in effect when you created the precompiled header, unless you specify otherwise. If the compiler detects an inconsistency, it issues a warning and identifies the inconsistency where possible. Such warnings don't necessarily indicate a problem with the precompiled header; they simply warn of possible conflicts. The consistency requirements for precompiled headers are explained in the following list:

Compiler Option Consistency

The following compiler options can trigger an inconsistency warning when using a precompiled header:

- Macros created using the Preprocessor (/D) option must be the same between the compilation that created the precompiled header and the current compilation. The state of defined constants is not checked, but unpredictable results can occur if these change.

- Precompiled headers do not work with the /E and /EP options.

- Precompiled headers must be created using either the Generate Browse Info option (/FR) or the Exclude Local Variables (/Fr) option before subsequent compilations that use the precompiled header can use these options.

C7 Compatible (/Z7)

If this option is in effect when the precompiled header is created, subsequent compilations that use the precompiled header can use the debugging information.

If /Z7 is not in effect when the precompiled header is created, subsequent compilations that use the precompiled header and /Z7 option trigger a warning. The debugging information is placed in the current object file, and local symbols defined in the precompiled header are not available to the debugger.

Include Path Consistency

A precompiled header does not contain information about the include path that was in effect when it was created. When you use a precompiled header file, the compiler always uses the include path specified in the current compilation.

Source File Consistency

When you use a precompiled header (/Yu), the compiler ignores all preprocessor directives (including pragmas) that appear in the source code that will be precompiled. The compilation specified by such preprocessor directives must be the same as the compilation used to create the precompiled header (/Yc).

Pragma Consistency

Pragmas processed during the creation of a precompiled header normally affect the file with which the precompiled header is subsequently used. The **comment** and **message** pragmas do not affect the remainder of the compilation.

The following pragmas are retained as part of a precompiled header. They do affect the remainder of a compilation that uses the precompiled header.

alloc_text	**include_alias**	**pack**
auto_inline	**inline_depth**	**pointers_to_members**
check_stack	**inline_recursion**	**setlocale**
code_seg	**init_seg**	**vtordisp**
data_seg	**intrinsic**	**warning**
function	**optimize**	

Consistency Rules for Automatic Use of Precompiled Headers

If a precompiled header file exists, it is compared to the current compilation for consistency. The following requirements must be met; otherwise, a new precompiled header file is created, and the new file overwrites the old:

- The current compiler options must match those specified when the precompiled header was created. However, if a significant portion of the source code of the currently compiled module matches the module for which the precompiled header was created, the compiler can create a new precompiled header for the matching part. This subsetting action increases the number of modules for which a precompiled header can be used.

- The current working directory must match that specified when the precompiled header was created.

- The order and values of all **#include** and **#pragma** preprocessor directives must match those specified when the precompiled header was created. These, along with **#define** directives, are checked as they appear during subsequent compilations that use the precompiled header. The **#pragma** directives must be nearly identical—multiple spaces outside of strings are treated as a single space to allow for different programming styles.

- The values of **#define** directives must match. However, a group of **#define** directives in sequence need not occur in exactly the same order since there are no semantic order dependencies for **#define** directives.

- The value and order of include paths specified on the command line with /I options must match those specified when the precompiled header was created.

- The timestamps of all the header files (all files specified with **#include** directives) used to build the precompiled header must match those that existed when the precompiled header was created.

Tip The compiler provides increased information on its creation and use of precompiled header files with the use of Level 4 Warnings (/W4).

Optimizations

These options (see Figure 20.4) determine how the compiler fine-tunes the performance of your program. Four of the five optimization categories (Default, Disable, Maximize Speed, and Minimize Size) in the Optimizations drop-down box require no further optimization on your part. If you select the fifth optimization category, Customize, you can set specific optimizations using the selections in the list box in the Category Settings.

You can also use the **optimize** pragma to control optimization of your program. For more information on the **optimize** pragma, see Chapter 2 of the *Preprocessor Reference*.

Figure 20.4   Optimizations Category on the C/C++ Tab

Optimizations   You can select one of the following optimization categories:

Default
:   Removes all optimization options from the command line. In this case, the compiler favors generation of faster, but possibly larger, machine code. If there is a choice between multiple possible machine-code sequences for an expression, the code generator chooses the fastest sequence. Command-line equivalent: /Ot

Disable (Debug)
:   Turns off all optimizations in the program and speeds compilation. This option simplifies debugging because it suppresses code movement. Command-line equivalent: /Od

    From the command line, this option is the default.

Maximize Speed
:   Generates the fastest code in the majority of cases. Command-line equivalent: /O2

    The effect of using this option is the same as using the following options in the Options text box or on the command line:

    ```
    /Og /Oi /Ot /Oy /Ob1 /Gs /Gf /Gy
    ```

    x86 Specific →
    You can use other options to improve the speed of many applications. For example, this option doesn't use /G5 to produce code that is optimized for computers based on the Pentium processor.

    This option implies the Frame Pointer Omission option (/Oy). If your project requires EBP-based addressing, also specify the /Oy– option or use the **optimize** pragma with the "**y**" and **off** arguments to gain maximum optimization

with EBP-based addressing. The compiler detects most situations where EBP-based addressing is required (for instance, with the **_alloca** and **setjmp** functions and with structured exception handling).
END x86 Specific

Note   This is set by default for release builds.

Minimize Size
Generates the smallest code in the majority of cases. Command-line equivalent: /O1

The effect of using this option is the same as using the following options in the Options text box or on the command line:

`/Og /Os /Oy /Ob1 /Gs /Gf /Gy`

x86 Specific →
This option implies the Frame Pointer Omission option (/Oy). If your project requires EBP-based addressing, also specify the /Oy– option or use the **optimize** pragma with the "**y**" and **off** arguments to gain maximum optimization with EBP-based addressing. The compiler detects most situations where EBP-based addressing is required (for instance, with the **_alloca** and **setjmp** functions and with structured exception handling).
END x86 Specific

Customize
Enables a multiple-selection list box so that you can select a custom set of optimizations.

Customize   When selecting this option from the Optimizations category, you can select one or more of the following optimizations from the enabled list box. However, if you select this option from the General category, you must select the Optimizations category to choose any of the following optimizations:

Assume No Aliasing
Tells the compiler that your program does not use aliasing. An alias is a name that refers to a memory location that is already referred to by a different name. Using this option allows the compiler to apply optimizations it couldn't otherwise use, such as storing variables in registers and performing loop optimizations. Command-line equivalent: /Oa

The following rules must be followed for any variable not declared as **volatile** or else /Oa and /Ow are ignored. In these rules, a variable is referenced if it is on either side of an assignment or if a function uses it in an argument:

- No pointer references a variable that is used directly.

- No variable is used directly if a pointer to the variable is being used.

- No variable is used directly if the variable's address is taken within a function.

- No pointer is used to access a memory location if another pointer is used to modify the same memory location.

Aliasing bugs most frequently show up as corrupted data. If variables are assigned seemingly random values, compile the program with Disable (/Od). If the program works when compiled with /Od, do not use /Oa or /Ow.

You can disable optimizations around code that uses aliasing (for individual functions) by using the **optimize** pragma with the **a** or **w** option. For more information on the **optimize** pragma, see Chapter 2 of the *Preprocessor Reference*.

Assume Aliasing Across Function Calls

Tells the compiler that no aliasing occurs within function bodies but might occur across function calls. After each function call, pointer variables must be reloaded from memory. Command-line equivalent: /Ow

The following rules must be followed for any variable not declared as **volatile** or else /Oa and /Ow are ignored. In these rules, a variable is referenced if it is on either side of an assignment or if a function uses it in an argument:

- No pointer references a variable that is used directly.

- No variable is used directly if a pointer to the variable is being used.

- No variable is used directly if the variable's address is taken within a function.

- No pointer is used to access a memory location if another pointer is used to modify the same memory location.

Aliasing bugs most frequently show up as corrupted data. If variables are assigned seemingly random values, compile the program with Disable (/Od). If the program works when compiled with /Od, do not use /Oa or Ow.

You can disable optimizations around code that uses aliasing (for individual functions) by using the **optimize** pragma with the **a** or **w** option. For more information on the **optimize** pragma, see Chapter 2 of the *Preprocessor Reference*.

Global Optimization

Provides local and global optimizations, automatic-register allocation, and loop optimization. Command-line equivalent: /Og

Local and global common subexpression elimination

In this optimization, the value of a common subexpression is calculated once. In the following example, if the values of b and c do not change between the three expressions, the compiler can assign the calculation of b + c to a temporary variable, and substitute the variable for b + c:

```
a = b + c;
d = b + c;
e = b + c;
```

For local common subexpression optimization, the compiler examines short sections of code for common subexpressions. For global common subexpression optimization, the compiler searches entire functions for common subexpressions.

Automatic register allocation

This optimization allows the compiler to store frequently used variables and subexpressions in registers; the **register** keyword is ignored.

Loop optimization

This optimization removes invariant subexpressions from the body of a loop. An optimal loop contains only expressions whose values change through each execution of the loop. In the following example, the expression x + y does not change in the loop body:

```
i = -100;
while( i < 0 )
{
    i += x + y;
}
```

After optimization, x + y is calculated once rather than every time the loop is executed:

```
i = -100;
t = x + y;
while( i < 0 )
{
    i += t;
}
```

Loop optimization is much more effective when the compiler can assume no aliasing, which you set with /Oa or /Ow.

The following code fragment could have an aliasing problem:

```
i = -100;
while( i < 0 )
{
    i += x + y;
    *p = i;
}
```

Without /Oa or /Ow, the compiler must assume that x or y could be modified by the assignment to *p and cannot assume that x + y is constant for each loop iteration. If you specify /Oa or /Ow, the compiler assumes that modifying *p cannot affect either x or y and x + y can be removed from the loop.

You can enable or disable global optimization on a function-by-function basis using the **optimize** pragma with the **g** option. For more information on the **optimize** pragma, see Chapter 2 of the *Preprocessor Reference.*

Generate Intrinsic Functions

This option replaces some function calls with intrinsic or otherwise special forms of the function that help your application run faster. Programs that use intrinsic functions are faster because they do not have the overhead of function calls but may be larger due to the additional code generated. Command-line equivalent: /Oi

x86 Specific→

If you use Generate Intrinsic Functions, the following function calls are replaced with their intrinsic (inline) forms:

_disable	**_outp**	**abs**	**memset**
_enable	**_outpw**	**fabs**	**strcat**
_inp	**_rotl**	**labs**	**strcmp**
_inpw	**_rotr**	**memcmp**	**strcpy**
_lrotl	**_strset**	**memcpy**	**strlen**
_lrotr			

Note The **_alloca** and **setjmp** functions are always generated as intrinsics; this behavior is not affected by /Oi.

The floating-point functions listed below do not have true intrinsic forms. If you use Generate Intrinsic Functions, the listed functions are replaced with versions that pass arguments directly to the floating-point chip rather than pushing them onto the program stack.

acos	**cosh**	**pow**	**tanh**
asin	**fmod**	**sinh**	

The floating-point functions listed below have true intrinsic forms when you specify both /Oi and /Og (or any option that includes /Og: /Ox, /O1, and /O2):

atan	**exp**	**log10**	**sqrt**
atan2	**log**	**sin**	**tan**
cos			

The intrinsic floating-point functions do not perform any special checks on input values and so work in restricted ranges of input, and have different exception handling and boundary conditions than the library routines with the same name. Using the true intrinsic forms implies loss of IEEE exception handling, and loss of **_matherr**, and **errno** functionality; the latter implies loss of ANSI conformance. However, the intrinsic forms can considerably speed up floating-point intensive programs and for many programs the conformance issues are of little practical value.

You can use Improve Float Consistency (/Op) or Disable Language Extensions (/Za) to override generation of true intrinsic floating-point functions. In this case, the functions are generated as library routines that pass arguments directly to the floating-point chip instead of pushing them onto the program stack.

END x86 Specific

You also use the **intrinsic** pragma to generate intrinsic functions or the **function** pragma to explicitly force a function call. For more information on these pragmas, see Chapter 2 of the *Preprocessor Reference*.

Improve Float Consistency

Improves the consistency of floating-point tests for equality and inequality by disabling optimizations that could change the precision of floating-point calculations. Command-line equivalent: /Op

By default, the compiler uses the coprocessor's 80-bit registers to hold the intermediate results of floating-point calculations. This increases program speed and decreases program size. However, as the calculation involves floating-point data types that are represented in memory by less than 80 bits, carrying the extra bits of precision (80 bits minus the number of bits in a smaller floating-point type) through a lengthy calculation can produce inconsistent results.

With this option, the compiler loads data from memory prior to each floating-point operation and, if assignment occurs, writes the results back to memory upon completion. Loading the data prior to each operation guarantees that the data does not retain any significance greater than the capacity of its type.

A program compiled with this may be slower and larger than one compiled without it.

Note This option disables inline generation of floating-point functions. The standard run-time library routines are used instead.

If you select Disable Language Extensions (/Za) from the Customize group in order to compile for ANSI compatibility, use of Improve Float Consistency (/Op) is implied. The use of /Op improves the consistency of floating-point tests for equality and inequality. The nature of the improved consistency provides strict ANSI conformance and is the only situation under which /Op is selected by default. The /Op– option is provided to override the default selection of /Op with /Za. Use /Op– in the Options text box (or on the command line), after /Za to disable /Op.

Favor Small Code

Minimizes the size of executable files and DLLs by instructing the compiler to favor size over speed. The compiler can reduce many C and C++ constructs to functionally similar sequences of machine code. Occasionally these differences offer tradeoffs of size versus speed. If you do not select this option, code may be larger and may be faster. Command-line equivalent: /Os

Favor Fast Code

Maximizes the speed of executable files and DLLs by instructing the compiler to favor speed over size. The compiler can reduce many C and C++ constructs to functionally similar sequences of machine code. Occasionally these differences offer tradeoffs of size versus speed. Command-line equivalent: /Ot

x86 Specific →

The following example code demonstrates the difference between the Favor Small Code (/Os) option and the Favor Fast Code option:

```
/* differ.c
    This program implements a multiplication operator.
    Compile with /Os to implement multiply explicitly as multiply.
    Compile with /Ot to implement as a series of shift and LEA
    instructions.
 */
int differ(int x)
{
    return x * 71;
}
```

As shown in the fragment of machine code below, when DIFFER.C is compiled using Favor Small Code (/Os), the compiler implements the multiply expression in the return statement explicitly as a multiply to produce a short but slower sequence of code:

```
mov     eax, DWORD PTR _x$[ebp]
imul    eax, 71                 ; 00000047H
```

Alternatively, when DIFFER.C is compiled using Favor Fast Code (/Ot), the compiler implements the multiply expression in the return statement as a series of shift and LEA instructions to produce a fast but longer sequence of code:

```
mov     eax, DWORD PTR _x$[ebp]
mov     ecx, eax
shl     eax, 3
lea     eax, DWORD PTR [eax+eax*8]
sub     eax, ecx
```

END x86 Specific

Frame-Pointer Omission

Suppresses creation of frame pointers on the call stack. This option speeds function calls, since no frame pointers need to be set up and removed. It also frees one more register, **x86 Specific** → EBP, **END x86 Specific** for storing frequently used variables and subexpressions. Command-line equivalent: /Oy

The Full Optimization (/Ox), Minimize Size (/O1), and Maximize Speed (/O2) options imply Frame-Pointer Omission (/Oy). Placing /Oy– in the Options text box (or on the command line) after the /Ox, /O1, or /O2 option disables /Oy whether it is explicit or implied.

Full Optimization

Combines optimizing options to produce the fastest possible program. Command-line equivalent: /Ox

x86 Specific →

The effect of using this option is the same as using the following options in the Options text box or on the command line:

/Ob1 /Og /Oi /Ot /Oy /Gs

Note The use of Full Optimization implies /Oy. If your code requires EBP-based addressing, you can specify the /Oy– option after the /Ox option or use the **optimize** pragma with the "**y**" and **off** arguments to gain maximum optimization with EBP-based addressing. The compiler detects most situations where EBP-based addressing is required (for instance, with the **_alloca** and **setjmp** functions and with structured exception handling).

END x86 Specific

Inline-Function Expansion Controls which functions become expanded. Expanding a function inline makes the program faster because it does not incur the overhead of calling the function.

Disable

Disables inline expansion. This is the default. Command-line equivalent: /Ob0

Only __inline

Expands only functions marked as **inline** or **__inline** or, in a C++ member function, defined within a class declaration. Command-line equivalent: /Ob1

Any suitable

Expands functions marked as **inline** or **__inline**, as well as any other function that the compiler chooses. Command-line equivalent: /Ob2

The compiler treats the inline expansion options and keywords as suggestions. There is no guarantee that functions will be inlined, and there is no control over the inlining of individual functions.

You can also use the **auto_inline** pragma to exclude functions from being considered as candidates for inline expansion. For more information on the **auto_inline** pragma, see Chapter 2 of the *Preprocessor Reference*.

C Language

These options (see Figure 20.5) select the warning level, turn off Microsoft language extensions, enable function-level linking, enable string pooling, and suppress displaying the startup banner.

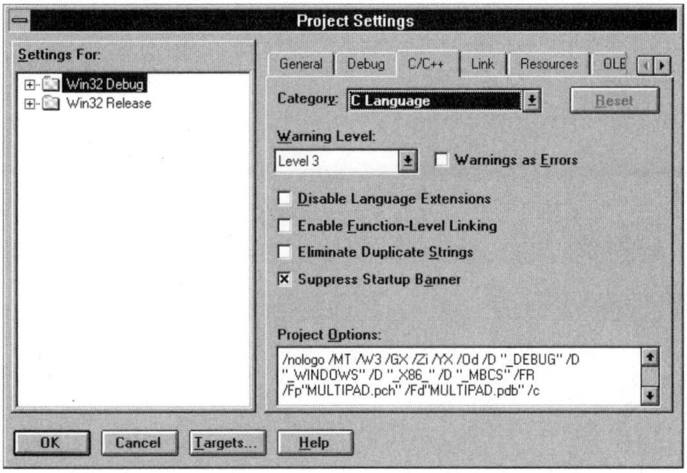

Figure 20.5   C Language Category on the C/C++ Tab

Warning Level   These options control the number of warning messages produced by the compiler. They affect only source files, not object files.

None
    Turns off all warning messages. Command-line equivalent: /W0 or /w

Level 1
    Displays only severe warnings. Command-line equivalent: /W1

Level 2
    Displays less severe warnings, such as the use of functions with no declared return type, failure to put return statements in functions that aren't void, and data conversions that would cause loss of data or precision. Command-line equivalent: /W2

Level 3
    Displays less severe warnings, such as warnings about function calls that precede their function prototypes. Command-line equivalent: /W3

Level 4

Displays least severe warnings, such as non-ANSI features and extended keywords. Command-line equivalent: /W4

Compiler warning messages begin with C4. Online help describes the warnings, indicates each warning's level, and indicates potential problems (rather than actual coding errors) with statements that may not compile as you intend.

You can also use the **warning** pragma to control the level of warning reported at compile time. For more information on the **warning** pragma, see Chapter 2 of the *Preprocessor Reference*.

Warning as Errors This option instructs the compiler to emit an error message rather than a warning. Command-line equivalent: /WX

Disable Language Extensions This option allows you to ensure that a C program uses ANSI C only.

Check box	Command-line equivalent	Result
Selected	/Za	ANSI C compatibility. Language constructs not compatible with ANSI C are flagged as errors.
Not selected	/Ze	Enables Microsoft extensions.

Note If you use Disable Language Extensions (/Za), Improve Float Consistency (/Op) is used to improve the consistency of floating-point tests for equality and inequality. This use of /Op with /Za is for strict ANSI conformance and is the only situation under which /Op is selected by default. The /Op– option is provided to override the default selection of /Op with /Za. Use /Op– in the Options text box (or on the command line), after /Za to disable /Op. For more information, see Generate Intrinsic Functions on page 309 and Improve Float Consistency on page 310.

Disable language extensions if you plan to port your program to other environments. The compiler treats extended keywords as simple identifiers, disables the other Microsoft extensions, and automatically defines the _ _**STDC**_ _ predefined macro for C programs. The following are Microsoft extensions:

Keywords

The following keywords are Microsoft specific: _ _**based**, _ _**cdecl**, _ _**except**, _ _**fastcall**, _ _**finally**, _ _**leave**, _ _**stdcall**, _ _**try**, and _ _**declspec**.

Casts

The Microsoft compiler supports the following two non-ANSI casts.

- Use of non-ANSI casts to produce l-values:

```
char *p;
(( int * ) p )++;
```

The preceding example could be rewritten to conform with the ANSI C standard as follows:

```
p = ( char * )(( int * )p + 1 );
```

- Non-ANSI casting of a function pointer to a data pointer:

```
int ( * pfunc ) ();
int *pdata;
pdata = ( int * ) pfunc;
```

To perform the same cast while maintaining ANSI compatibility, you must cast the function pointer to an **int** before casting it to a data pointer:

```
pdata = ( int * ) (int) pfunc;
```

Variable-Length Argument Lists

Use of a function declarator that specifies a variable number of arguments, followed by a function definition that provides a type instead:

```
void myfunc( int x, ... );

void myfunc( int x, char * c )
{ }
```

Single-Line Comments

The Microsoft C compiler supports single-line comments, which are introduced with two forward slash (//) characters:

```
// This is a single-line comment.
```

Scope

The Microsoft C compiler supports the following scope-related features:

- Redefinitions of **extern** items as **static**:

```
extern int clip();
static int clip()
{}
```

- Use of benign **typedef** redefinitions within the same scope:

```
typedef int INT;
typedef int INT;
```

- Scope of function declarators is file:

```
void func1()
{
    extern int func2( double );
}

void main( void )
{
    func2( 4 );        //  /Ze passes 4 as type double
}                      //  /Za passes 4 as type int
```

- Use of block-scope variables initialized with nonconstant expressions:

```
int clip( int );
int bar( int );

void main( void )
{
    int array[2] = { clip( 2 ), bar( 4 ) };
}

int clip( int x )
{
    return x;
}

int bar( int x )
{
    return x;
}
```

Data Declarations and Definitions

The Microsoft C compiler supports the following data declaration and definition features:

- Mixed character and string constants in an initializer:

```
char arr[5] = {'a', 'b', "cde"};
```

- Bit fields with base types other than **unsigned int** or **signed int**.

- Declarators without either a storage class or a type:

```
x;

void main( void )
{
    x = 1;
}
```

- Unsized arrays as the last field in structures and unions:

```
struct zero
{
    char *c;
    int zarray[];
};
```

- Unnamed (anonymous) structures:

```
struct
{
    int i;
    char *s;
};
```

- Unnamed (anonymous) unions:

```
union
{
    int i;
    float fl;
};
```

- Unnamed members:

```
struct s
{
    unsigned int flag : 1;
    unsigned int : 31;
}
```

Intrinsic Floating-Point Functions

The Microsoft compilers supports inline generation of the **x86 Specific** → **atan**, **atan2**, **cos**, **exp**, **log**, **log10**, **sin**, **sqrt**, and **tan** functions **END x86 Specific** when the Generate Intrinsic Functions (/Oi) option is specified. For C, ANSI conformance is lost when these intrinsics are used as they do not set the **errno** variable.

Enable Function-Level Linking   This option allows the compiler to package individual functions in the form of COMDATs. The linker requires that functions be packaged separately as COMDATs to exclude or order individual functions in a DLL or executable file. Command-line equivalent: /Gy

You can use the linker's /OPT:REF option to exclude unreferenced packaged functions from the executable file. For more information on /OPT:REF, see Appendix B, "LINK Reference." You can use the linker's /ORDER option to place packaged functions in a specified order in the executable file. For more information on /ORDER, see Appendix B, "LINK Reference."

Inline functions are always packaged if they are instantiated as calls (for example, if inlining is turned off or you take a functions address). Also, C++ member functions defined within the class declaration are automatically packaged; other functions are not, and selecting the Enable Function-Level Linking option is required to compile them as packaged functions.

Eliminate Duplicate Strings   This option enables the compiler to place a single copy of identical strings into the executable file. Because identical strings are copied into a single memory location, programs compiled with this option can be smaller than those compiled without it. This space optimization is also called "string pooling." Using this option ensures that string pooling occurs in most cases. Command-line equivalent: /Gf

When using Eliminate Duplicate Strings, your program must not write over pooled strings. Also, if you use identical strings to allocate string buffers, the Eliminate Duplicate Strings option pools the strings. Thus, what was intended as multiple pointers to multiple buffers ends up as multiple pointers to a single buffer. For example, with Eliminate Duplicate Strings the following code causes s and t to point to the same memory because they are initialized with the same string:

```
char *s = "This is a character buffer";
char *t = "This is a character buffer";
```

Suppress Startup Banner   This option suppresses display of the sign-on banner when the compiler starts up. Command-line equivalent: /nologo

C++ Language

These options (see Figure 20.6) specify an inheritance representation for the C++ pointers to class members in your application, control exception handling, and control the generation of hidden virtual constructor/destructor displacement fields in classes with virtual bases.

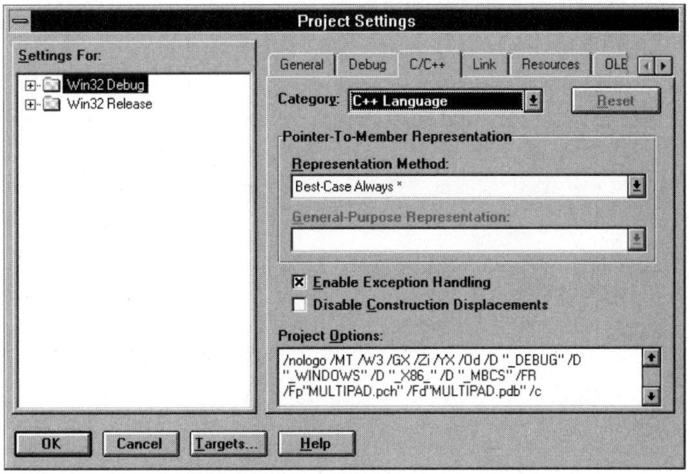

Figure 20.6   C++ Language Category on the C/C++ Tab

Pointer-To-Member Representation   Visual C++ supports pointers to members of any class. The number of bytes required to represent a pointer to a member of a class and the code required to interpret the representation vary considerably, depending upon whether the class is defined with no, single, multiple, or virtual inheritance (no inheritance being smallest and virtual inheritance largest).

Representation Method   These options select the method that the compiler uses to represent pointers to class members. You can also use the **pointers_to_members** pragma in your code to specify a pointer representation. For more information on the **pointers_to_members** pragma, see Chapter 2 of the *Preprocessor Reference*.

Best-Case Always

Use this option if you always define a class before you declare a pointer to a member of the class. Command-line equivalent: /vmb

If you define a class before declaring a pointer to a member of the class using Best-Case Always, the compiler knows the kind of inheritance used by the class when it encounters the declaration of the pointer. Thus, it can use the smallest possible representation of a pointer and generate the smallest amount of code required to operate on the pointer for each kind of inheritance.

With Best-Case Always, the compiler generates an error if it encounters the pointer declaration before the class definition. In this case, you must either reorganize your code or use the General-Purpose Always (/vmg) option. You can also use the **pointers_to_members** pragma or define the class using the __**single_inheritance**, __**multiple_inheritance**, or __**virtual_inheritance** keyword. These keywords allow control of the code generated on a per-class basis.

For information on the use of the __**single_inheritance**, __**multiple_inheritance**, and __**virtual_inheritance** keywords, see Chapter 7 of the *C++ Language Reference*.

For Best-Case Always, the corresponding argument to the **pointers_to_members** pragma is **best_case**.

General-Purpose Always

Use this option if you need to declare a pointer to a member of a class before defining the class. This need can arise if you define members in two different classes that reference each other. For such mutually referencing classes, one class must be referenced before it is defined. You must then choose an inheritance model from the General-Purpose Representation list box. Command-line equivalent: /vmg

For General-Purpose Always, the corresponding argument to the **pointers_to_members** pragma is **full_generality**.

General-Purpose Representation When the representation method is General-Purpose Always, you must also specify an option to indicate the inheritance model of the not-yet-encountered class definition. This can be one of following three options:

List entry	Command-line equivalent
Point to Single-Inheritance Classes	/vms
Point to Single- and Multiple-Inheritance Classes	/vmm
Point to Any Class	/vmv

When you specify one of these inheritance-model options, that model is used for all pointers to member classes, regardless of their inheritance type or whether the pointer is declared before or after the class. Therefore, if you always use single-inheritance classes, you can reduce code size by selecting Point to Single-Inheritance Classes; however, if you want to compile using the most general case (at the expense of the largest data representation), you can choose Point To Any Class, which allows pointers to classes of all inheritance types. Point To Any Class is the default.

Enable Exception Handling   This option controls whether destructors are called for automatic objects during a stack unwind that is caused by either a Windows NT-based structured exception or a C++ exception.

Select this option if you want the destructors of automatic objects called as the stack unwinds through the exception stack frames. Selecting this option produces slightly larger code than code generated without this option. Code compiled using the /GX option can rely on the **_CPPUNWIND** predefined macro being defined. Command-line equivalent: /GX

Clear this option if you do not want destructors called as the stack unwinds. Command-line equivalent: /GX–

Disable Construction Displacements   Select this option to suppress the vtordisp constructor/destructor displacement member, but only if you are certain that all class constructors and destructors call virtual functions virtually. Command-line equivalent: /vd0

Not selecting Disable Construction Displacements enables the generation of hidden vtordisp constructor/destructor displacement members. Command-line equivalent: /vd1

Visual C++ implements C++ construction displacement support in situations where virtual inheritance is used. Construction displacements solve the problem created when a virtual function, declared in a virtual base and overridden in a derived class, is called from a constructor during construction of a further derived class. The problem is that the virtual function may be passed an incorrect **this** pointer. This is caused by discrepancies between the displacements to virtual bases of a class and the displacements to its derived classes. The solution provides a single construction displacement adjustment, called a vtordisp field, for each virtual base of a class.

By default, vtordisp fields are introduced whenever the code both defines user-defined constructors and destructors and also overrides virtual functions of virtual bases.

These options affect entire source files. You can use the **vtordisp** pragma to suppress and then reenable vtordisp fields on a class-by-class basis. For more information on the **vtordisp** pragma, see Chapter 2 of the *Preprocessor Reference*.

Preprocessor

These options (see Figure 20.7) control symbols, macros, and include paths used by the C/C++ preprocessor.

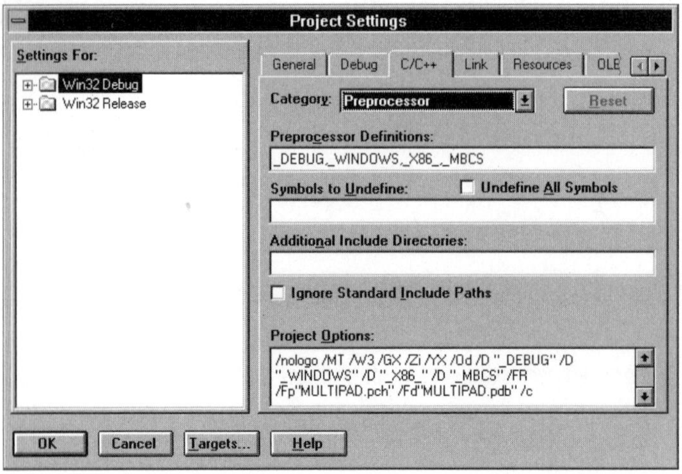

Figure 20.7   Preprocessor Category on the C/C++ Tab

Preprocessor Definitions Name one or more macros in this text box. You create these named macros for your own purposes. Macros entered in this text box are visible to only the preprocessor; you can use the **#if** or **#ifdef** preprocessor directives to test for their existence. The behavior of the Preprocessor Definitions text box differs from the behavior of the /D command-line option: you cannot use either an equal sign (=) or a pound sign (#) to assign a value to symbols entered in the text box.

Symbols to Undefine Enter the name of a previously defined macro to undefine it. To undefine additional macros, enter additional ones and use a space to separate each. This option cannot be used to undefine symbols created with a **#define** directive. Command-line equivalent: /U*macro*

When used from the command line, a space between /U and *macro* is optional. To undefine additional symbols, repeat /U*macro*.

Undefine All Symbols Select to undefine every previously defined macro. This option cannot be used to undefine macros created with a **#define** directive. Command-line equivalent: /u

Both the Symbols To Undefine and the Undefine All Symbols options turn off the following Microsoft-specific macros:

Macro	Function
_CHAR_UNSIGNED	Default **char** type is unsigned. Defined when /J is specified.
_DLL	Defined when Multithreaded using DLL (/MD) is specified.
_CPPUNWIND	Defined for code compiled with Enable Exception Handling (/GX).
_M_IX86	Defined as 400 for Blend (/GB), 300 for 80386 (/G3), 400 for 80486 (/G4), and 500 for Pentium (/G5).[1]
_MSC_VER	Defines the compiler version in the form ddd. Defined as 900 for Microsoft Visual C++ 2.0. Always defined.
_WIN32	Defined for applications for Win32. Always defined.[1]
_MT	Defined when Multithreaded using DLL (/MD) or Multithreaded (/MT) is specified.

[1] x86 Specific

Additional Include Directories   Add one or more directories to the list of directories searched for include files. Use a space to separate directories to be searched when entering more than one directory. Directories are searched only until the specified include file is found. You can use this option with the Ignore Standard Include Paths option. Command-line equivalent: /I*directory*

When used from the command line, a space between /I and *directory* is optional.

The compiler searches for directories in the following order:

1. Directories containing the source file.
2. Directories specified with /I, in the order that CL encounters them.
3. Directories specified in the INCLUDE environment variable.

Ignore Standard Include Paths   Prevents the compiler from searching for include files in directories specified in the PATH and INCLUDE environment variables. Command-line equivalent: /X

You can use this option with the Additional Include Directories option.

Listing Files

These options (see Figure 20.8) generate browse information files and code listing files.

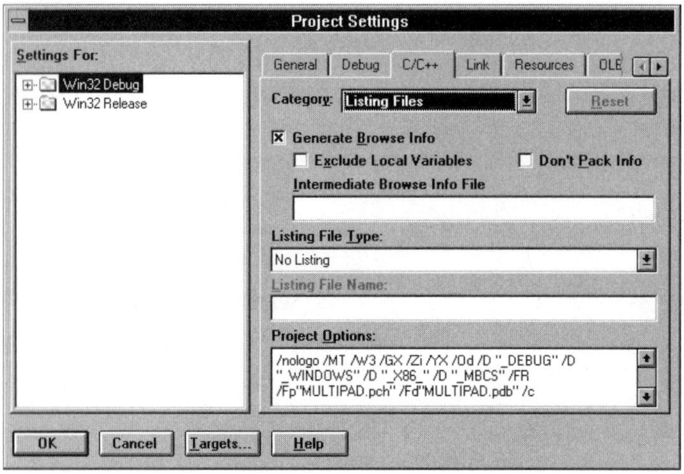

Figure 20.8   Listing Files Category on the C/C++ Tab

Generate Browse Info   This option generates .SBR files with complete symbolic information. Visual C++ runs the Microsoft Browse Information File Maintenance Utility (BSCMAKE) on the .SBR files to generate a browse information file (.BSC) that you can examine in browse windows. Command-line equivalent: /FR

For more information on browse windows, see Chapter 13, "Browsing Through Symbols."

Exclude Local Variables   This option generates .SBR files with complete symbolic information, excluding information about local variables. Visual C++ runs BSCMAKE on the .SBR files to generate a browse information file (.BSC) that you can examine in browse windows. Command-line equivalent: /Fr

For more information on browse windows, see Chapter 13, "Browsing Through Symbols."

Don't Pack Info   This option prevents packing information in the .SBR files that are generated when you use either the Generate Browse Info or the Exclude Local Variables option. This also keeps unreferenced symbol definitions in .SBR files. Command-line equivalent: /Zn

BSCMAKE uses the .SBR files to generate a .BSC file that you can examine in browse windows in Visual C++. Packing allows BSCMAKE to run faster and also saves disk space. However, BSCMAKE's /Iu option requires an unpacked .SBR file in order to include unreferenced symbols. Use /Zn only if you need to include unreferenced symbols or if compilation time is critical.

For more information on BSCMAKE, see Appendix E, "BSCMAKE Reference."

Intermediate Browse Info File Name   Use this text box to specify a directory and/or filename, DEBUG/ by default, for the .SBR and .BSC files generated by using Generate Browse Info. Command-line equivalent: the optional *filename* argument to /FR or /Fr. When used from the command line, no space is allowed before the *filename* argument.

Listing File Type   These options specify the type of listing files to be generated.

No listing
 Generates no listing file and is the default.

Assembly-only Listing
 Generates files with an assembly-language listing only. The default listing-file extension is .ASM. Command-line equivalent: /FA

Assembly, Machine Code, and Source
 Generates files containing source code, assembly code, and machine code. The default listing-file extension is .COD. Command-line equivalent: /FAcs

Assembly with Machine Code
 Generates files containing assembly code and machine code. The default listing-file extension is .COD. Command-line equivalent: /FAc

Assembly with Source Code
 Generates files containing assembly code and source code. The default listing-file extension is .ASM. Command-line equivalent: /FAs

Listing File Name   Use this option to specify a directory and/or filename for the listing file selected from the Listing File Type list box. Command-line equivalent: the optional *filename* argument of /Fa. When used from the command line, no space is allowed between /Fa and *filename*.

CHAPTER 21

Setting Linker Options

In Visual C++, you set linker options on the Link tab in the Project Settings dialog box. The settings you select control the Microsoft 32-Bit Incremental Linker (LINK.EXE).

This chapter describes the option categories that are available from the Link tab in the Project Settings dialog box:

- General Category
- Output Category
- Input Category
- Customize Category
- Debug Category

The linker options that are not available as controls within option categories on the Link tab are described in Appendix B, "LINK Reference." Appendix B describes how to use the linker from the command line. It also describes module-definition files.

General Category

This category summarizes the options that are most commonly used. Each General option, with the exception of Enable Profiling, is also available in another option category and is described in the section that discusses that category. Setting an option in the General category changes the same option in its other category, and vice versa.

The following options are in the General category (see Figure 21.1):

Option	Category
Output File Name	Customize
Object/Library Modules	Input
Generate Debug Info	Debug
Link Incrementally	Customize
Enable Profiling	General
Ignore All Default Libraries	Input
Generate Mapfile	Debug

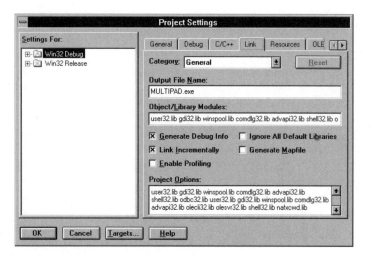

Figure 21.1 General Category on the Link Tab

Enable Profiling The Enable Profiling (/PROFILE) option creates an output file that can be used with the profiler. This option is found only in the General category on the Link tab. Command-line equivalent: /PROFILE

A profiler-ready program has a mapfile. If it contains debugging information, the information must be stored in the output file instead of a program database file (.PDB file) and must be in old-style format. It cannot be linked incrementally.

In Visual C++, setting Enable Profiling enables the Generate Mapfile option (described on page 338) in the General and Debug categories and disables the Link Incrementally option (described on page 335) in the General and Customize categories. If you set the Generate Debug option, be sure to choose Microsoft Format (described on page 339) in the Debug category.

On the command line, /PROFILE has the same effect as setting the /MAP option; if the /DEBUG option is specified, then /PROFILE also implies the options /DEBUGTYPE:CV and /PDB:NONE. In either case, /PROFILE implies /INCREMENTAL:NO.

Project Options, Common Options   This text box displays linker options that you've currently selected. The options are displayed using their command-line equivalents. You can type in this text box if a single project is selected from the left pane of the Project Settings dialog box. With a project selected, the text box is named Project Options. Otherwise, the text box is named Common Options. You cannot type in the text box when it is named Common Options.

The Project Options text box accepts any option that is available from the Link tab. It also accepts those linker options that are otherwise available only from the command line. For details on those options, see Appendix B, "LINK Reference."

You are responsible for the accuracy of any option you enter in the Project Options text box. If Visual C++ recognizes an option as one that can be set using a dialog-box control, it changes the dialog-box control to reflect the option. However, if the option is not recognized, it is left in the options string as is and passed to the linker.

Reset   This button resets the project settings of a target back to the settings that existed when the target was created. It is enabled if both of the following conditions are met:

- A single target is selected in the left pane of the Project Settings dialog box.
- The settings of the selection have changed.

The Reset button is not enabled when multiple targets are selected.

Output Category

These options (see Figure 21.2) control the linker when producing a Win32 target.

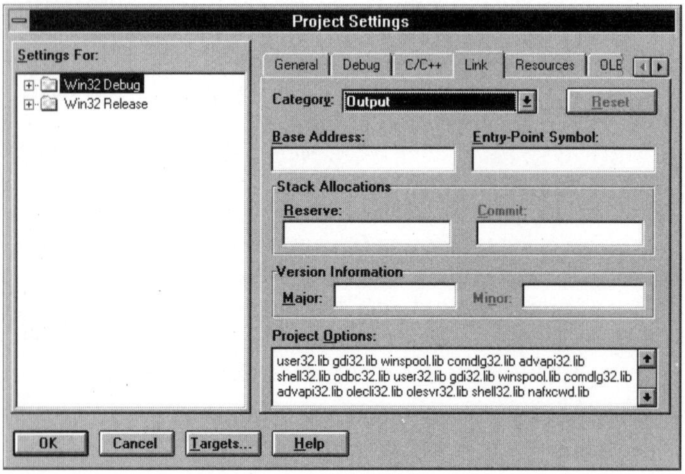

Figure 21.2   Output Category on the Link Tab

Base Address   This option sets a base address for the program, overriding the default location for an executable file (at 0x400000) or a DLL (at 0x10000000). The operating system first attempts to load a program at its specified or default base address. If sufficient space is not available there, the system relocates the program. To prevent relocation, use the /FIXED option. For details on /FIXED, see Appendix B, "LINK Reference." Command-line equivalent: /BASE:{*address* | @*filename,key*}

Specify the preferred base address in the text box (or in the *address* argument on the command line). The linker rounds the specified number up to the nearest multiple of 64K.

On the command line, another way to specify the base address is by using a *filename*, preceded by an at sign (@), and a *key* into the file. The *filename* is a text file that contains the locations and sizes of all DLLs your program will use. The linker looks for *filename* in either the specified path or, if no path is specified, in directories specified in the LIB environment variable. Each line in *filename* represents one DLL and has the following syntax:

key address size ;*comment*

The *key* is a string of alphanumeric characters and is not case sensitive. It is usually the name of a DLL but it need not be. The *key* is followed by a base *address* in C-notation hexadecimal or decimal and a maximum *size*. All three arguments are separated by spaces or tabs. The linker issues a warning if the specified *size* is less than the virtual address space required by the program. A *comment* is specified by a semicolon (;) and can be on the same or a separate line. The linker ignores all text from the semicolon to the end of the line. This example shows part of such a file:

```
main   0x00010000   0x08000000   ; for PROJECT.EXE
one    0x28000000   0x00100000   ; for DLLONE.DLL
two    0x28100000   0x00300000   ; for DLLTWO.DLL
```

If the file that contains these lines is called DLLS.TXT, the following example command applies this information:

```
link dlltwo.obj /dll /base:dlls.txt,two
```

You can reduce paging and improve performance of your program by assigning base addresses so that DLLs do not overlap in the address space.

An alternate way to set the base address is with the **BASE** argument in a **NAME** or **LIBRARY** statement. The /BASE and /DLL options together are equivalent to the **LIBRARY** statement. For details on /DLL, **NAME**, and **LIBRARY**, see Appendix B, "LINK Reference."

Entry-Point Symbol   This option sets the starting address for an executable file or DLL. Command-line equivalent: /ENTRY:*function*

Specify a function name in the text box (or in the *function* argument on the command line). The function must be defined with the __**stdcall** calling convention. The parameters and return value must be defined as documented in the Win32 API for **WinMain** (for an .EXE) or **DllEntryPoint** (for a DLL). It is recommended that you let the linker set the entry point so that the C run-time library is initialized correctly and C++ constructors for static objects are executed.

By default, the starting address is a function name from the C run-time library. The linker selects it according to the attributes of the program, as follows:

Function name	Default for
mainCRTStartup (or **wmainCRTStartup**)	An application using /SUBSYSTEM:CONSOLE; calls **main** (or **wmain**)
WinMainCRTStartup (or **wWinMainCRTStartup**)	An application using /SUBSYSTEM:WINDOWS; calls **WinMain** (or **wWinMain**), which must be defined with __**stdcall**
_DllMainCRTStartup	A DLL; calls **DllMain** (which must be defined with __**stdcall**) if it exists

If the /DLL or /SUBSYSTEM option is not specified, the linker selects a subsystem and entry point depending on whether **main** or **WinMain** is defined. For details on /DLL and /SUBSYSTEM, see Appendix B, "LINK Reference."

The functions **main**, **WinMain**, and **DllMain** are the three forms of the user-defined entry point.

Stack Allocations This option sets the size of the stack in bytes. Command-line equivalent: /STACK:*reserve*[[,*commit*]]

The Reserve text box (or the *reserve* argument on the command line) specifies the total stack allocation in virtual memory. The default stack size is 1MB. The linker rounds up the specified value to the nearest 4 bytes.

The optional Commit value (or the *commit* argument on the command line) is subject to interpretation by the operating system. In Windows NT, it specifies the amount of physical memory to allocate at a time. Committed virtual memory causes space to be reserved in the paging file. A higher Commit value saves time when the application needs more stack space but increases the memory requirements and possibly startup time.

Specify the Reserve and Commit values in decimal or C-language notation.

An alternate way to set the stack is with the **STACKSIZE** statement in a .DEF file. For details on **STACKSIZE**, see Appendix B, "LINK Reference." **STACKSIZE** overrides Stack Allocations (/STACK) if both are specified. You can change the stack after the executable file is built by using the EDITBIN.EXE tool. For details on EDITBIN, see Appendix G, "EDITBIN Reference."

Version Information This option tells the linker to put a version number in the header of the executable file or DLL. Command-line equivalent: /VERSION:*major*[[.*minor*]]

The *major* and *minor* arguments are decimal numbers in the range 0–65535. The default is version 0.0.

An alternate way to insert a version number is with the **VERSION** module-definition statement. For details on **VERSION**, see Appendix B, "LINK Reference."

Input Category

These options (see Figure 21.3) control how the linker uses libraries and stub files.

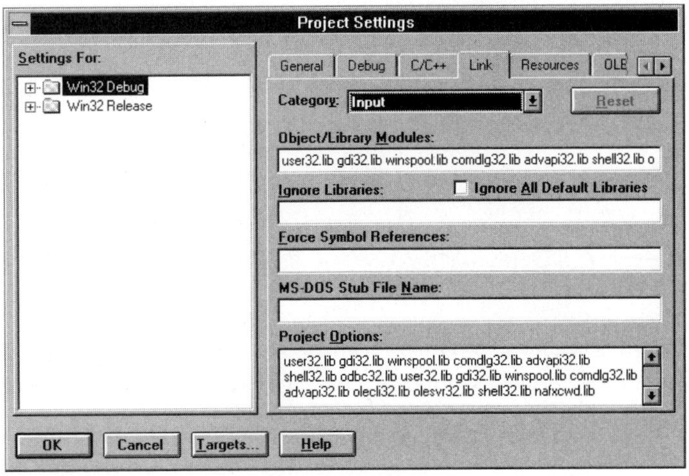

Figure 21.3   Input Category on the Link Tab

Object/Library Modules   This option passes an object file or standard library (either static or import) to the linker. Command-line equivalent: *filename* on command line

To pass a file to the linker, specify the filename in the text box. You can specify an absolute or relative path with the filename, and you can use wildcards in the filename. If you omit the dot (.) and filename extension, the linker assumes .OBJ for the purpose of finding the file. The linker does not use filename extensions or the lack of them to make assumptions about the contents of files; it determines the type of file by examining it and processes it accordingly.

Ignore Libraries   This option tells the linker to remove one or more default libraries from the list of libraries it searches when resolving external references. Command-line equivalent: /NODEFAULTLIB:*library*

The linker resolves references to external definitions by searching first in libraries specified in Object/Library Modules (or on the command line), then in default libraries specified with the /DEFAULTLIB option, then in default libraries named in object files.

To specify multiple *libraries*, type a comma (,) between the library names.

To suppress the search in all default libraries, use Ignore All Default Libraries (or specify /NODEFAULTLIB with no arguments).

Ignore Libraries (/NODEFAULTLIB:*library*) overrides /DEFAULTLIB:*library* when the same *library* name is specified in both.

Ignore All Default Libraries   This option tells the linker to remove all default libraries from the list of libraries it searches when resolving external references. Command-line equivalent: /NODEFAULTLIB

The linker resolves references to external definitions by searching first in libraries specified in Object/Library Modules (or on the command line), then in default libraries specified with the /DEFAULTLIB option, then in default libraries named in object files.

To suppress the search in a specific library, use Ignore Libraries (or specify a colon (:) and the library name).

Ignore All Default Libraries (/NODEFAULTLIB) overrides /DEFAULTLIB:*library*.

Force Symbol References   This option tells the linker to add a specified symbol to the symbol table. Command-line equivalent: /INCLUDE:*symbol*

Specify a *symbol* name in the text box. To specify multiple symbols, type a comma (,), a semicolon (;), or a space between the symbol names. On the command line, specify /INCLUDE:*symbol* once for each symbol.

The linker resolves *symbol* by adding the object that contains the symbol definition to the program. This is useful for including a library object that otherwise would not be linked to the program.

Specifying a symbol in Force Symbol References (/INCLUDE) overrides the removal of that symbol by /OPT:REF. For details on /OPT:REF, see Appendix B, "LINK Reference."

MS-DOS Stub File Name   This option attaches an MS-DOS stub program to a Win32 program. Command-line equivalent: /STUB:*filename*

A stub program is invoked if the file is executed in MS-DOS. Usually, it displays an appropriate message; however, any valid MS-DOS application can be a stub program.

Specify a *filename* for the stub program in the text box (or after a colon (:) on the command line). The linker checks *filename* to be sure that it is a valid MS-DOS executable file and issues an error if the file is not valid. The program must be an .EXE file; a .COM file is invalid for a stub program.

If MS-DOS Stub File Name (/STUB) is not used, the linker attaches a default stub program that generates the following message:

```
This program cannot be run in MS-DOS mode.
```

Customize Category

These options (see Figure 21.4) control the linking session and affect linker output.

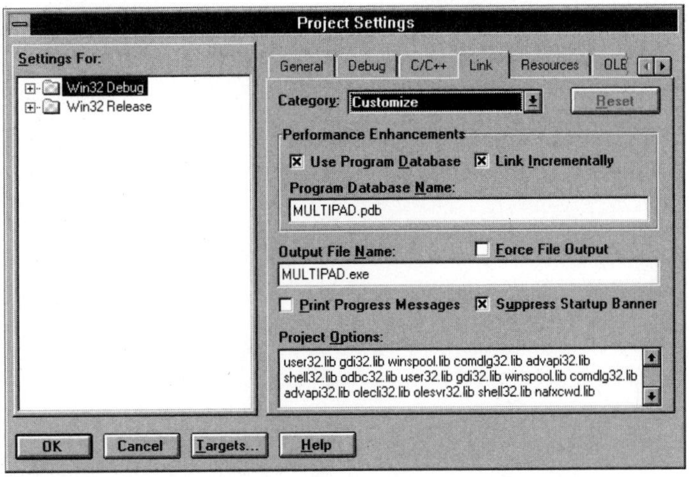

Figure 21.4   Customize Category on the Link Tab

Link Incrementally   This option controls how the linker handles incremental linking. Command-line equivalent: /INCREMENTAL:{YES|NO}

By default, the linker runs in nonincremental mode. However, the default mode is incremental if Generate Debug Info (/DEBUG) is specified. To override a default incremental build, turn off Link Incrementally (or specify /INCREMENTAL:NO on the command line).

To link incrementally regardless of the default, turn on Link Incrementally (or specify /INCREMENTAL:YES on the command line). When this option is specified, the linker issues a warning if it cannot link incrementally and then builds the program nonincrementally. Certain options and situations override Link Incrementally (/INCREMENTAL:YES).

For further details, see "Incremental Linking" on page 363 in Appendix B.

Use Program Database   This option controls how the linker produces debugging information. Command-line equivalent: /PDB:NONE

By default, when Generate Debug Info (/DEBUG) is specified, the linker creates a program database (PDB), which holds debugging information. If Generate Debug Info (/DEBUG) is not specified, Use Program Database (/PDB) is ignored.

If Use Program Database is turned off (or if /PDB:NONE is specified on the command line), the linker does not create a PDB, but instead puts old-style debugging information into the executable file or DLL. The linker then calls the CVPACK.EXE tool, which must be in the same directory as LINK.EXE or in a directory in the PATH environment variable.

Debugging information in a program database must be in Microsoft Format (/DEBUGTYPE:CV). If either COFF Format (/DEBUGTYPE:COFF) or Both Formats (/DEBUGTYPE:BOTH) is chosen, no PDB is created.

Incremental linking is suppressed if Use Program Database is turned off (or if /PDB:NONE is specified on the command line).

For information on overriding the default name of the PDB, see Program Database Name. For details about PDBs, see "Program Databases" on page 365 in Appendix B.

Program Database Name   This option sets the filename for the program database (PDB). Command-line equivalent: /PDB:*filename*

The linker creates a PDB when Generate Debug Info (/DEBUG) is specified. The default filename for the PDB has the base name of the program and the extension .PDB. To override the default name, specify a filename in the text box (or specify /PDB:*filename* on the command line).

Debugging information in a program database must be in Microsoft Format (/DEBUGTYPE:CV). If either COFF Format (/DEBUGTYPE:COFF) or Both Formats (/DEBUGTYPE:BOTH) is chosen, no PDB is created and Program Database Name (/PDB:*filename*) is ignored.

For information on controlling how the linker produces debugging information, see Use Program Database. For details about PDBs, see "Program Databases" on page 365 in Appendix B.

Output File Name   This option overrides the default name and location of the program that the linker creates. Command-line equivalent: /OUT:*filename*

By default, the linker forms the filename using the base name of the first object file specified and the appropriate extension (.EXE or .DLL).

The Output File Name option controls the default base name for a mapfile or import library. For details, see "Generate Mapfile" (/MAP) on page 338 and the description of the /IMPLIB option on page 378 in Appendix B.

Force File Output   This option tells the linker to create a valid executable file or DLL even if a symbol is referenced but not defined or is multiply defined. Command-line equivalent: /FORCE

On the command line, the /FORCE option can take an optional argument:

- Use /FORCE:MULTIPLE to create an output file whether or not LINK finds more than one definition for a symbol.

- Use /FORCE:UNDEFINED to create an output file whether or not LINK finds an undefined symbol.

A file created with this option may not run as expected.

Print Progress Messages This option displays details about the linking process. Command-line equivalent: /VERBOSE

The linker sends information about the progress of the linking session to the Output window. On the command line, the information is sent to standard output and can be redirected to a file.

The displayed information includes the library search process and lists each library and object name (with full path), the symbol being resolved from the library, and the list of objects that reference the symbol.

Suppress Startup Banner This option prevents display of the copyright message and version number. Command-line equivalent: /NOLOGO

This option also suppresses echoing of command files. For details, see "LINK Command Files" on page 369 in Appendix B.

By default, this information is sent by the linker to the Output window. On the command line, it is sent to standard output and can be redirected to a file.

Debug Category

These options (see Figure 21.5) control generation of debugging information and mapfile output.

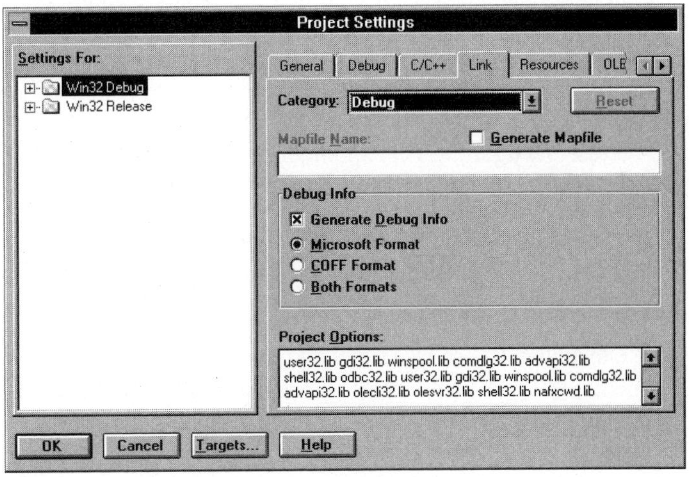

Figure 21.5 Debug Category on the Link Tab

Generate Mapfile   This option tells the linker to generate a mapfile. Command-line equivalent: /MAP

The linker names the mapfile with the base name of the program and the extension .MAP. To override the default name, use Mapfile Name.

A mapfile is a text file that contains the following information about the program being linked:

- The module name, which is the base name of the file
- The timestamp from the program file header (not from the file system)
- A list of groups in the program, with each group's start address (as *section:offset*), length, group name, and class
- A list of public symbols, with each address (as *section:offset*), symbol name, flat address, and object file where the symbol is defined
- The entry point (as *section:offset*)
- A list of fixups

Incremental linking is suppressed when Generate Mapfile is selected (or when /MAP is specified on the command line).

Mapfile Name   This option overrides the default name for a mapfile. Command-line equivalent: /MAP:*filename*

By default, when Generate Mapfile (/MAP) is specified, the linker names the mapfile with the base name of the program and the extension .MAP. To override the default name, specify a filename in the text box (or, on the command line, specify a colon (:) followed by *filename*).

Generate Debug Info   This option creates debugging information for the executable file or DLL. Command-line equivalent: /DEBUG

The linker puts the debugging information into a program database (PDB). It updates the PDB during subsequent builds of the program. For details about PDBs, see "Program Databases" on page 365 in Appendix B.

An executable file or DLL created for debugging contains the name and path of the corresponding PDB. Visual C++ reads the embedded name and uses the PDB when you debug the program. The linker uses the base name of the program and the extension .PDB to name the PDB, and embeds the path where it was created. To override this default, use Program Database Name (/PDB:*filename*).

The object files must contain debugging information. Use the compiler's Program Database (/Zi), Line Numbers Only (/Zd), or C7 Compatible (/Z7) option (described on pages 294 and 295 in Chapter 20). If an object (whether specified explicitly or supplied from a library) was compiled with Program Database, its debugging information is stored in a PDB for the object file, and the name and location of the .PDB file are embedded in the object. The linker looks for the object's PDB first in the absolute path written in the object file and then in the directory that contains the object file. You cannot specify a PDB's filename or location to the linker.

If Use Program Database is turned off (or if /PDB:NONE is specified on the command line), or if either COFF Format (/DEBUGTYPE:COFF) or Both Formats (/DEBUGTYPE:BOTH) is chosen, the linker does not create a PDB but instead puts the debugging information into the executable file or DLL.

The Generate Debug Info (/DEBUG) option changes the default for the /OPT option from REF to NOREF. For details on /OPT, see Appendix B, "LINK Reference."

Microsoft Format   This option generates Microsoft-style debugging information. Command-line equivalent: /DEBUGTYPE:CV

Visual C++ requires new-style Microsoft Symbolic Debugging Information in order to read a program for debugging. In Visual C++, choose Microsoft Format under Debug Info. If Generate Debug Info is not specified, this choice is disabled. On the command line, if /DEBUG is specified, the default type is /DEBUGTYPE:CV; if /DEBUG is not specified, /DEBUGTYPE is ignored.

COFF Format   This option generates COFF-style debugging information. Command-line equivalent: /DEBUGTYPE:COFF

Some debuggers require Common Object File Format (COFF) debugging information. In Visual C++, choose COFF Format under Debug Info. If Generate Debug Info is not specified, this choice is disabled. On the command line, specify /DEBUGTYPE:COFF; if /DEBUG is not specified, /DEBUGTYPE is ignored.

When this option is set, the linker does not create a PDB; in addition, incremental linking is disabled.

Both Formats   This option generates both COFF debugging information and old-style Microsoft debugging information. Command-line equivalent: /DEBUGTYPE:BOTH

To create a program with both old-style Microsoft Symbolic Debugging Information and Common Object File Format (COFF) debugging information, choose Both Formats under Debug Info. If Generate Debug Info is not specified, this choice is disabled. On the command line, specify /DEBUGTYPE:BOTH; if /DEBUG is not specified, /DEBUGTYPE is ignored.

When this option is set, the linker does not create a PDB; in addition, incremental linking is disabled. The linker must call the CVPACK.EXE tool to process the old-style Microsoft debugging information. CVPACK must be in the same directory as LINK or in a directory in the PATH environment variable.

PART 3

Appendixes

A P P E N D I X   A

CL Reference

This appendix describes the compiler-driver program CL.EXE (CL). It also describes compiler options not represented by options on the C/C++ tab in the Project Settings dialog box.

CL is a 32-bit tool that controls the Microsoft C and C++ compilers and linker. The compilers produce Common Object File Format (COFF) object files. The linker produces executable files or dynamic-link libraries (DLLs).

Most compiler options are available on the C/C++ tab in the Project Settings dialog box. Each of the options on the C/C++ tab is described in Chapter 20, "Setting Compiler Options." The description of each option includes the name of the equivalent command-line option.

An alphabetic reference to the CL options not available as options on the C/C++ tab in the Project Settings dialog box begins on page 348. Other topics covered in this appendix include:

- Description of CL syntax
- Using CL

Description of CL Syntax

The CL command line uses the following syntax:

CL [[*option*...]] *file*... [[*option* | *file*]]... [[*lib*...]] [[@*command-file*]] [[/link *link-opt*...]]

The following list describes input to the CL command:

Entry	Meaning
option	One or more CL options, see Chapter 20, "Setting Compiler Options," and "Reference to Command-line Only Options" on page 348 for more information.
	Note that all options apply to all specified source files.
file	The name of one or more source files, object files, or libraries. CL compiles source files and passes the names of the object files and libraries to the linker.
lib	One or more library names. CL passes these names to the linker.
command-file	A file that contains multiple options and filenames. See "CL Command Files" on page 345 for more information.
link-opt	One or more of the linker options described in Chapter 21, "Setting Linker Options," and Appendix B, "LINK Reference." CL passes these options to the linker.

You can specify any number of options, filenames, and library names, as long as the number of characters on the command line does not exceed 1,024, the limit dictated by the operating system.

Note The command-line input limit of 1,024 characters is not guaranteed to remain the same in future releases of Windows NT.

Filename Syntax

CL accepts files with names that follow FAT, HPFS, or NTFS naming conventions. Any filename can include a full or partial path. A full path includes a drive name and one or more directory names. CL accepts filenames separated either by backslashes (\) or forward slashes (/). A partial path omits the drive name, which CL assumes to be the current drive. If you don't specify a path, CL assumes the file is in the current directory.

The filename extension determines how files are processed. C and C++ files, which have the extension .C, .CXX, and .CPP, are compiled. Other files, including object files (.OBJ), libraries (.LIB), and module-definition files (.DEF), are passed to the linker without being processed.

Specifying CL Options

You can specify CL options on the command line, in command files, and in the CL environment variable. Options specified in the CL environment variable are used every time you invoke CL. If a command file is named in the CL environment variable or on the command line, the options specified in the command file are used. Unlike either the command line or the CL environment variable, a command file allows you to use multiple lines of options and filenames. See "CL Command Files" below and "CL Environment Variable" on page 346 for more information.

Options are specified by either a forward slash (/) or a dash (−). If an option takes an argument, the option's description documents whether a space is allowed between the option and the arguments. Option names (except for the /HELP option) are case sensitive.

Order of Options

Options can appear anywhere on the CL command line, except for the /link option, which must occur last. The compiler begins with options specified in the CL environment variable and then reads the command line from left to right— processing command files in the order it encounters them. Each option applies to all files on the command line. If CL encounters conflicting options, it uses the rightmost option.

CL Command Files

A command file is a text file that contains options and filenames you would otherwise type on the command line or specify using the CL environment variable. CL accepts a compiler command file as an argument in the CL environment variable or on the command line. Unlike either the command line or the CL environment variable, a command file allows you to use multiple lines of options and filenames.

Options and filenames in a command file are processed according to the location of a command filename within the CL environment variable or on the command line. However, if /link appears in the command file, all options on the rest of the line are passed to the linker. Options in subsequent lines in the command file and options on the command line after the command file invocation are still accepted as compiler options. For more information on how the order of options affects their interpretation, see "Order of Options" above.

A command file must not contain the CL command. Each option must begin and end on the same line; you cannot use the backslash (\) to combine an option across two lines.

A command file is specified by an at sign (@) followed by a filename; the filename can specify an absolute or relative path.

Example

If the following command is in a file named RESP:

```
/Og /link LIBC.LIB
```

and you specify the following CL command:

```
CL /Ob2 @RESP MYAPP.C
```

the command to CL is as follows:

```
CL /Ob2 /Og MYAPP.C /link LIBC.LIB
```

Note that the command line and the command-file commands are effectively combined.

CL Environment Variable

Use the CL environment variable to specify files and options without giving them on the command line. The environment variable has the following syntax:

SET CL=[[[[option]] ... [[file]] ...]] [[/link link-opt ...]]

The CL environment variable is useful if you often specify a large number of files and options when you compile. You can define the files and options you use most often with the CL variable and give only the files and options you need for specific purposes on the command line. The CL environment variable is currently limited to 1,024 characters—the command-line input limit in Windows NT.

You cannot use /D to define a symbol that uses an equal sign (=). You can substitute the number sign (#) for an equal sign. This allows you to use the CL environment variable to define preprocessor constants with explicit values (for example, /DDEBUG#1).

Example

The following example of a CL environment variable setting:

```
SET CL=/Zp2 /Ox /I\INCLUDE\MYINCLS \LIB\BINMODE.OBJ
```

is equivalent to the following CL command:

```
CL /Zp2 /Ox /I\INCLUDE\MYINCLS \LIB\BINMODE.OBJ INPUT.C
```

The following example causes CL to compile the source files FILE1.C and FILE2.C and then link the object files FILE1.OBJ, FILE2.OBJ, and FILE3.OBJ:

```
SET CL=FILE1.C FILE2.C
CL FILE3.OBJ
```

This has the same effect as the following command line:

```
CL FILE1.C FILE2.C FILE3.OBJ
```

Using CL

You can use CL to compile specified source files into COFF object files, or to compile and link source files, object files, and libraries into an executable file or a dynamic-link library (DLL). To compile without linking, use the /c option.

Fast Compilation

If you do not specify optimization options, CL uses the disable optimization option (/Od). This feature allows you to quickly compile code that is under development and postpone optimization until it is needed.

You can also use the precompiled header options and the **hdrstop** pragma to speed compilation. For more information on the precompiled header options, see "Precompiled Headers" on page 300 in Chapter 20. For more information on the **hdrstop** pragma, see Chapter 2 of the *Preprocessor Reference*.

Linking

CL automatically invokes the linker after compiling unless the /c option is used. CL passes to the linker the names of object files created during compiling and the names of any other files specified on the command line. The linker uses the options listed in the LINK environment variable. You can use /link to specify linker options on the CL command line. Options that follow /link override those in the LINK environment variable. The following options suppress linking:

Option	Description
/c	Compile without linking
/E, /EP, /P	Preprocess without compiling or linking
/Zg	Generate function prototypes
/Zs	Check syntax

For further details about linking, see Chapter 21, "Setting Linker Options," and Appendix B, "LINK Reference."

Example

Assume that you are compiling three C source files: MAIN.C, MOD1.C, and MOD2.C. Each file includes a call to a function defined in a different file:

- MAIN.C calls the function func1 in MOD1.C and the function func2 in MOD2.C.
- MOD1.C calls the standard library functions **printf** and **scanf**.
- MOD2.C calls graphics functions named myline and mycircle, which are defined in a library named MYGRAPH.LIB.

To build this program, compile with the following command line:

```
CL MAIN.C MOD1.C MOD2.C MYGRAPH.LIB
```

CL first compiles the C source files and creates the object files MAIN.OBJ, MOD1.OBJ, and MOD2.OBJ. The compiler places the name of the standard library in each object file. For more details, see "Use Run-Time Library" on page 297 in Chapter 20.

CL passes the names of the object files along with the name MYGRAPH.LIB to the linker. The linker resolves the external references as follows:

1. In MAIN.OBJ, the reference to func1 is resolved using the definition in MOD1.OBJ; the reference to func2 is resolved using the definition in MOD2.OBJ.

2. In MOD1.OBJ, the references to **printf** and **scanf** are resolved using the definitions in the library that the linker finds named within MOD1.OBJ.

3. In MOD2.OBJ, the references to myline and mycircle are resolved using the definitions in MYGRAPH.LIB.

Reference to Command-Line Only Options

The rest of this appendix is an alphabetic reference to the CL command-line options that are not available in the categories on the C/C++ tab of the Project Settings dialog box.

CL Options Set from the Command Line

The following CL options are set from the command line. If a command-line option can take one or more arguments, its syntax is shown under a Syntax heading before its description.

/C	/Fe	/Gs	/Tc
/c	/FI	/H	/Tp
/D	/Fm	/HELP	/V
/E	/Fo	/J	/Yd
/EP	/Fp	/LD	/Zg
/F	/Ge	/link	/Zl
/Fd	/Gh	/P	/Zs

CL Options Set from Visual C++

The following options are available in the categories on the C/C++ tab in the Project Settings dialog box. These options can also be used from the command line. For more information on these options see Chapter 20, "Setting Compiler Options."

/D	/Gz	/Os	/WX
/FA	/I	/Ot	/w
/Fa	/MD	/Ow	/X
/FR	/ML	/Ox	/Yc
/Fr	/MT	/Oy, /Oy–	/Yu
/G3	/nologo	/U	/YX
/G4	/O1	/u	/Z7
/G5	/O2	/vd$n$	/Za
/GB	/Oa	/vmb	/Zd
/Gd	/Obn	/vmg	/Ze
/Gf	/Od	/vmm	/Zi
/Gr	/Og	/vms	/Zn
/GX, /GX–	/Oi	/vmv	/Zp
/Gy	/Op, /Op–	/Wn	

/C

This option preserves comments during preprocessing when used with the /E, /P, or /EP option and is not valid if /E, /P, or /EP is not used. If you do not specify /C, the preprocessor does not pass source-file comments to its output file.

/c

This option suppresses linking; only object files are created. No executable file or DLL is produced.

Example

The following example creates the object file FIRST.OBJ and SECOND.OBJ. The file THIRD.OBJ is ignored.

```
CL /c FIRST.C SECOND.C THIRD.OBJ
```

/D

Syntax

/D*name*[[= | # [[{*string* | *number*}]]]]

This option defines symbols or constants for your source file.

The *name* is the name of the symbol or constant. It can be defined as a string or as a number. No space can separate /D and *name*. Enclose the *string* in double quotation marks if it includes spaces. If you omit both the equal sign and the *string* or *number*, the name is assumed to be defined, and its value is set to 1. Note that the *name* argument is case sensitive.

Defining symbols and constants with the /D option has the same effect as using a **#define** preprocessor directive at the beginning of your source file. The constant is defined until either an **#undef** directive in the source file removes the definition or the compiler reaches the end of the file.

You cannot set the CL environment variable to a string that contains an equal sign (=). To use /D with the CL environment variable, specify "#" instead of "=":

```
SET CL "/DTEST#0"
```

Note The action of /D differs from the Preprocessor Definitions option available in both the General category and the Preprocessor category. These categories are on the C/C++ tab of the Project Settings dialog box. The /D option allows you to define a symbol and use a "=" or a "#" to assign the symbol a value.

Use the constants created by the compiler and the /D option in combination with either the **#if** or **#ifdef** directive to compile source files conditionally.

You can redefine a keyword, identifier, or numeric constant that has been defined in a source file. If a constant defined in a /D option is also defined within the source file, CL uses the definition on the command line until it encounters a redefinition in the source file.

You can undefine a previous definition. To do so, use the /D option with a keyword, identifier, or numeric constant and append an equal sign followed by a space.

Examples

The following command removes all occurrences of the keyword **__far** in TEST.C:

```
CL /D__far=  TEST.C
```

The following command defines the symbol DEBUG in TEST.C:

```
CL /DDEBUG  TEST.C
```

/E

This option preprocesses C and C++ source files and copies the preprocessed file to the standard output device. The output is identical to the original source file except that all preprocessor directives are carried out, macro expansions are performed, and comments are removed. You can use /C with /E to preserve comments in the preprocessed output.

Unlike the /EP option, /E adds **#line** directives to the output. The **#line** directives are placed at the beginning and end of each included file and around lines removed by preprocessor directives that specify conditional compilation. Use /E when you want to resubmit the preprocessed listing for compilation. The **#line** directives renumber the lines of the preprocessed file so that errors generated during later stages of processing refer to the line numbers of the original source file rather than to the preprocessed file. You can use /EP to suppress **#line** directives.

The /E option suppresses compilation. It also suppresses the output files from the /FA, /Fa, and /Fm options.

Note You cannot use precompiled headers with the /E option.

The following list summarizes the actions of the /E, /EP, and /P options:

Options	Results
/E	Sends preprocessor output, including **#line** directives, to stdout.
/P	Sends preprocessor output, including **#line** directives, to a file (.I).
/EP	Sends preprocessor output, without **#line** directives, to stdout.
/E /EP	Sends preprocessor output, without **#line** directives, to stdout.
/P /EP	Sends preprocessor output, without **#line** directives, to a file (.I).

Example

The following command creates a preprocessed file from the source file ADD.C. It preserves comments and adds **#line** directives. The output is displayed.

```
CL /E /C ADD.C
```

/EP

The /EP option is similar to the /E option. It preprocesses C and C++ source files and copies the preprocessed file to the standard output device. The output is identical to the original source file except that all preprocessor directives are carried out, macro expansions are performed, and comments are removed. You can use the /C option with /EP to preserve comments in the preprocessed output. Unlike /E, however, /EP does not add **#line** directives to the output.

The /EP option suppresses compilation. It also suppresses the output files from the /FA, /Fa, and /Fm options.

The following list summarizes the actions of the /E, /EP, and /P options:

Options	Results
/E	Sends preprocessor output, including **#line** directives, to stdout.
/P	Sends preprocessor output, including **#line** directives, to a file (.I).
/EP	Sends preprocessor output, without **#line** directives, to stdout.
/E /EP	Sends preprocessor output, without **#line** directives, to stdout.
/P /EP	Sends preprocessor output, without **#line** directives, to a file (.I).

Example

The following command creates a preprocessed file from the source file ADD.C. It preserves comments but does not insert **#line** directives. The output is displayed.

```
CL /EP /C ADD.C
```

/F

Syntax

/F *number*

This option sets the program stack size to a specified number of bytes. If you don't specify this option, a stack size of 1 MB is used by default. The *number* argument can be in decimal or C notation. The argument can range from a lower limit of 1 to the maximum stack size accepted by your linker. A space is optional between /F and *number*.

You can also set stack size by using the linker's /STACK option or running EDITBIN on an executable file.

You may want to increase the stack size if your program gets stack-overflow diagnostic messages.

Output-File Options

These output-file options generate and/or rename output files. They affect all C or C++ source files specified in the CL environment variable, on the command line, or in any command file. They include:

- /Fd (Name the Program Database)
- /Fe (Name the Executable File)
- /Fm (Generate a Map File)
- /Fo (Name the Object File)
- /Fp (Name or Use a Precompiled Header File)

Other output-file options are available in the Listing Files category on the C/C++ tab of the Project Settings dialog box. They include:

- Generate Browse Info (/FR)
- Exclude Local Variables (/Fr)
- Intermediate Browse Info File Name (/FR[[*filename*]] or /Fr[[*filename*]])
- Listing File Type (/FA[[cls]])
- Listing File Name (/Fa[[*filename*]])

For more information on the Generate Browse Info, Exclude Local Variables, Intermediate Browse Info File Name, Listing File Type, and Listing File Name options, see "Listing Files" on page 324 in Chapter 20.

Drive, Path, and File Specifications

Each output-file option accepts a *filename* argument that allows you to specify a location and or name for the output file. The argument can include a drive name, a path specification, and/or a filename. No space is allowed between the option and the argument.

If *filename* is a path without a filename (that is, a directory), end the path with a backslash (\) to differentiate it from a filename. If a filename is specified without an extension, the output file is given a default extension. If no argument is specified, the output file is given the base name of the source file and an extension determined by the type of output file.

Device Names for Windows NT

You can append the device names AUX, CON, PRN, and NUL to the output-file options to direct the output file to the named device. No space is allowed between the option and the device name. Do not append a colon (:) to the device name. The device names and their behavior are as follows:

Device name	Result
AUX	Sends the listing file to an auxiliary device
CON	Sends the listing file to the console
PRN	Sends the listing file to a printer
NUL	No file is created

Example

In the following example, appending PRN to /Fm sends a map file to the printer:

```
CL /FmPRN HELLO.CPP
```

/Fd

Syntax   /Fd*filename*

This option specifies a filename for a program database (PDB) other than the default name, VC20.PDB, created by /Zi. No space is allowed between /Fd and *filename*. If you do not specify an extension to *filename*, the extension .PDB is used. If *filename* ends in a backslash (to specify the name of a directory), the default filename VC20.PDB used. For information on PDBs, see "Debug Info" on page 294 in Chapter 20.

Example

The following command creates a .PDB file called DPROG.PDB that contains debugging information.

```
CL /DDEBUG /Zi /FdDPROG.PDB PROG.CPP
```

/Fe

Syntax   /Fe*filename*

This option names an executable file or DLL and/or creates it in a different directory. No space is allowed between /Fe and *filename*. By default, CL names the executable file with the base name of the first file (source or object) on the command line plus the extension .EXE (or .DLL if you use the /LD option to create a dynamic-link library).

If you specify the /c option to suppress linking, /Fe has no effect.

Examples

The following example compiles and links all C source files in the current directory. The resulting executable file is named PROCESS.EXE and is created in the directory C: \BIN.

```
CL /FeC:\BIN\PROCESS *.C
```

The following example is similar to the first example except that the executable file is given the same base name as the first file compiled instead of being named PROCESS.EXE. The executable file is created in the directory C:\BIN.

```
CL /FeC:\BIN\ *.C
```

/Fm

Syntax

/Fm[[*filename*]]

This option instructs the linker to produce a mapfile. No space is allowed between /Fm and *filename*. The mapfile contains a list of segments in the order of their appearance within the corresponding executable file or DLL. By default, the mapfile is given the base name of the corresponding C or C++ source file with a .MAP extension. If you specify the /c option to suppress linking, /Fm has no effect.

Global symbols in a mapfile usually have one or more leading underscores because the compiler adds an underscore to the beginning of variable names. Many of the global symbols that appear in the mapfile are symbols used internally by the compiler and the standard libraries.

/Fo

Syntax

/Fo*filename*

This option names an object file and/or creates it in a different directory. No space is allowed between /Fo and *filename*. By default, CL names the object file with the base name of the source file plus the extension .OBJ. You can give any name and extension you want for *filename*. However, it is recommended that you use the conventional .OBJ extension.

Example

The following command line compiles the source file THIS.C and gives the resulting object file the name THIS.OBJ by default. The directory specification B:\OBJECT\ tells CL to create THIS.OBJ in an existing directory named \OBJECT on drive B.

```
CL /FoB:\OBJECT\ THIS.C
```

/Fp

/Fp*filename*

Use the /Fp option with the /YX, /Yc, and /Yu options to provide a name for a precompiled header file (and path) that is different from the default. You can also use /Fp to specify the use of a precompiled header file that is different from the *filename* argument to /Yc or the base name of the source file.

No space is allowed between /Fp and *filename*. If you do not specify an extension to *filename*, an extension of .PCH is assumed. If *filename* ends in a backslash (to specify the name of a directory), the default filename VC20.PCH is appended to *filename*. For more information, see the related options under "Precompiled Headers" on page 300 in Chapter 20.

Examples

The following command renames the default VC20.PCH file created and used by /YX:

```
CL /YX /FpMYPCH.PCH PROG.CPP
```

The following command creates a precompiled header file DPROG.PCH for a debugging version of a program:

```
CL /DDEBUG /Zi /Yc /FpDPROG.PCH PROG.CPP
```

The following command specifies the use of a precompiled header file named MYPCH.PCH. The compiler assumes that the source code in PROG.CPP has been precompiled through MYAPP.H and that the precompiled code resides in MYPCH.PCH. It uses the content of MYPCH.PCH and compiles the rest of PROG.CPP to create an object file. As none of these options suppresses the linker, the output of this example is a file named PROG.EXE.

```
CL /YuMYAPP.H /FpMYPCH.PCH PROG.CPP
```

/FI

/FI*filename*

The /FI option causes the preprocessor to process the header file specified by *filename*. Each *filename* is included as if it were specified with double quotation marks (" ") in an **#include** directive on line 0 of every C or C++ source file specified in the CL environment variable, on the command line, or in any command file. If multiple /FI options are used, the files are included in the order they are processed by CL. The space between /FI and *filename* is optional.

/Ge

This option (and the /Gs option with a *size* of 0) activates stack probes for every function call that requires storage for local variables. This mechanism is useful only if you rewrite the functionality of the stack probe. We recommend that you use the /Gh option rather than rewriting the stack probe.

/Gh

This option generates a call to _ _penter at the start of every method or function. The _ _penter function is not part of any library. This call is a hook for your use. Use assembly language to write the function.

Unless you plan to explicitly call _ _penter, you do not need to provide a prototype. The function must appear as if it had the following prototype and must push the content of all registers on entry and pop the unchanged content on exit:

```
void __cdecl __penter( void );
```

/Gs

Syntax

/Gssize

This option is an advanced feature that allows you to control stack probes. A stack probe is a sequence of code that the compiler inserts into every function call. When activated, a stack probe reaches benignly into memory by the amount of space required to store the associated function's local variables.

If a function requires more than *size* stack space for local variables, its stack probe is activated. The default value of *size* is the size of one page (4K for 80*x*86 processors). This value allows a carefully tuned interaction between an application for Win32 and the Windows NT virtual-memory manager to increase the amount of memory committed to the program stack at run time.

> **Warning** The default value of *size* is carefully chosen to allow the program stack of applications for Win32 to grow at run time. Do not change the default setting of /Gs unless you know exactly why you need to change it.

Some programs, such as virtual device drivers, do not require this default stack-growth mechanism. In such cases, the stack probes are not necessary. You can stop the compiler from generating stack probes by setting *size* to a value that is larger than any function will require for local variable storage. No space is allowed between /Gs and *size*.

The /Gs option with a *size* of 0 has the same action as the /Ge option.

You can turn stack probes on or off by using the **check_stack** pragma. Note that the /Gs option and the **check_stack** pragma have no effect on standard C library routines; they affect only the functions you compile. For more information on the **check_stack** pragma, see Chapter 2 of the *Preprocessor Reference*.

/H

/H*number*

This option restricts the length of external (public) names. The compiler ignores characters after the first *number* characters in external names. The program can contain external names longer than *number* characters, but the extra characters are ignored. A space between /H and *number* is optional. The compiler imposes no limit on the length of external identifiers.

The limit on length includes any compiler-generated leading underscore (_) or at sign (@). The compiler adds a leading underscore to names modified by the _ _**cdecl** (default) and _ _**stdcall** calling conventions and a leading at sign to names modified by the _ _**fastcall** calling convention. It appends argument size information to names modified by the _ _**fastcall** and _ _**stdcall** calling conventions and adds type information to C++ names.

You may find /H useful when creating mixed-language or portable programs or when using tools that impose limits on the length of external identifiers.

/HELP

/HELP
/help
/?

This option displays a listing of compiler options to standard output.

/J

This option changes the default **char** type from **signed char** to **unsigned char**, and the **char** type is zero-extended when widened to an **int** type. If a **char** value is explicitly declared **signed**, /J does not affect it, and the value is sign-extended when widened to **int** type.

The /J option defines **_CHAR_UNSIGNED**, which is used with **#ifndef** in the LIMITS.H file to define the range of the default **char** type.

Neither ANSI C nor C++ requires a specific implementation of the **char** type. This option is useful when you are working with character data that will eventually be translated into a language other than English.

/LD

This option creates a dynamic-link library (DLL). The option does the following:

- Passes the /DLL option to the linker. The linker looks for, but does not require, a **DllMain** function. If you do not write a **DllMain** function, the linker inserts a **DllMain** function that returns TRUE.

- Links the DLL startup code.

- Creates an import library, if an export file (.EXP) is not specified on the command line; you link the import library to applications that call your DLL.

- Interprets /Fe as naming a DLL rather than an executable file; the default program name becomes *basename*.DLL instead of *basename*.EXE. See page 354 for more information on /Fe.

- Changes default run-time library support to /MT if you have not explicitly specified one of /MD, /ML, or /MT. For more information on these options, see "Use Run-Time Library" on page 297 in Chapter 20.

Examples

The following command line:

```
CL /LD FILE1.CXX FILE2.CXX
```

tells the compiler to pass the following commands to the linker:

```
/OUT:FILE1.DLL
/DLL
/IMPLIB:FILE1.LIB
FILE1.OBJ FILE2.OBJ
```

The following command line creates both DLL\FILE1.DLL and DLL\FILE1.LIB:

```
CL /LD /FeDLL\ FILE1.C
```

If your source code contains no exported functions, the linker will not generate an import library (.LIB).

/link

Syntax /link [[*option*]]

This option passes one or more linker options to LINK. The /link option and its linker options must appear after any filenames and CL options. A space is required between /link and *option*. For more information on the linker, see Chapter 21, "Setting Linker Options," and Appendix B, "LINK Reference."

/P

This option writes preprocessor output to a file with the same base name as the source file but with the .I extension. It adds **#line** directives to the output file at the beginning and end of each included file and around lines removed by preprocessor directives that specify conditional compilation. The preprocessed listing file is identical to the original source file except that all preprocessor directives are carried out and macro expansions are performed.

This option suppresses compilation; CL does not produce an object file, even if the /Fo option is specified. The /P option also suppresses production of the alternate output files that the /FA, /Fa, or /Fm option generates.

The /P option is similar to the /E and /EP options, described on pages 351 through 352. Using /EP with /P suppresses placement of **#line** directives in the output file.

The following list summarizes the actions of the /E, /EP, and /P options:

Options	Results
/E	Sends preprocessor output, including **#line** directives, to stdout.
/P	Sends preprocessor output, including **#line** directives, to a file (.I).
/EP	Sends preprocessor output, without **#line** directives, to stdout.
/E /EP	Sends preprocessor output, without **#line** directives, to stdout.
/P /EP	Sends preprocessor output, without **#line** directives, to a file (.I).

/Tc, /Tp

Syntax

/Tc*filename*
/Tp*filename*

The /Tc option specifies that *filename* is a C source file, even if it doesn't have a .C extension. The /Tp option specifies that *filename* is a C++ source file, even if it doesn't have a .CPP or .CXX extension. Space between the option and *filename* is optional. Each option specifies one file; to specify additional files, repeat the option.

By default, CL assumes that files with the .C extension are C source files and files with the .CPP or the .CXX extension are C++ source files.

Example

The following CL command line specifies that MAIN.C, TEST.PRG, and COLLATE.PRG are all C source files. CL will not recognize PRINT.PRG.

```
CL MAIN.C /TcTEST.PRG /TcCOLLATE.PRG PRINT.PRG
```

/V

/V*string*

This option embeds a text string in the object file. This string can label an object file with a version number or a copyright notice. Any space or tab characters must be enclosed in double quotation marks (" ") if they are a part of the string. A backslash (\) must precede any double quotation marks if they are a part of the string. A space between /V and *string* is optional.

You can also use the **comment** pragma with the **compiler** comment-type argument to place the name and version number of the compiler in the object file. For more information on the **comment** pragma, see Chapter 2 of the *Preprocessor Reference*.

/Yd

This option, when used with the /Yc and /Z7 options, places complete debugging information in all object files created from a precompiled header (.PCH) file. Unless you need to distribute a library containing debugging information, use /Zi rather than /Z7 and /Yd. The /Yd option takes no argument. For more information on the debugging options, see "Debug Info" on page 294 in Chapter 20.

Storing complete debugging information in every object file is necessary only to distribute libraries that contain debugging information. It slows compilation and requires considerable disk space. When /Yc and /Z7 are used without /Yd, the compiler stores common debugging information in the first object file created from the .PCH file. The compiler does not insert this information into object files subsequently created from the .PCH file; it inserts cross-references to the information. No matter how many object files use the .PCH file, only one object file contains the common debugging information.

Although this default behavior results in faster build times and reduces disk-space demands, it is undesirable if a small change requires rebuilding the object file containing the common debugging information. In this case, the compiler must rebuild all object files containing cross-references to the original object file. Also, if a common .PCH file is used by different projects, reliance on cross-references to a single object file is difficult.

Note   The /Yd option is implied with use of the /YX option.

/Zg

This option generates a function prototype for each function defined in the source file but does not compile the source file.

The function prototype includes the function return type and an argument-type list. The argument-type list is created from the types of the formal parameters of the function. Any function prototypes already present in the source file are ignored.

The generated list of prototypes is written to standard output. You may find this list helpful to verify that actual arguments and formal parameters of a function are compatible. You can save the list by redirecting standard output to a file. Then you can use **#include** to make the list of function prototypes a part of your source file. Doing so causes the compiler to perform argument type checking.

If you use the /Zg option and your program contains formal parameters that have structure, enumeration, or union type (or pointers to such types), the prototype for each structure, enumeration, or union type must have a tag.

/Zl

This option omits the default-library name from the object file. By default, CL puts the name of the library in the object file to direct the linker to the correct library. For more information on the default library, see "Use Run-Time Library" on page 297 in Chapter 20.

You can use /Zl to compile object files you plan to put into a library. Although omitting the library name saves only a small amount of space for a single object file, the total space saved is significant in a library that contains many object modules.

/Zs

This option tells the compiler to check only the syntax of the source files on the command line. No output files are generated. Error messages are written to standard output. The /Zs option provides a quick way to find and correct syntax errors before you compile and link a source file.

A P P E N D I X   B

LINK Reference

This appendix describes the Microsoft 32-Bit Incremental Linker (LINK.EXE), version 2.50. LINK is a 32-bit tool that runs with Windows NT. It links Common Object File Format (COFF) object files and libraries to create a 32-bit executable file or dynamic-link library (DLL). LINK can be run incrementally, speeding up the build times for your program.

This appendix provides the following tables, which summarize LINK options:

- Alphabetic List of LINK Options
- Visual C++ LINK Options
- Compiler-Controlled LINK Options

The linker options available as controls within the Visual C++ development environment are described in Chapter 21, "Setting Linker Options."

New LINK Features

This version of the linker provides incremental linking and expands the use of program databases:

- Incremental linking decreases the time required to link your project.
- Program databases hold new-style debugging information in a file separate from the object file, library, executable file, or DLL.

Incremental Linking

You can run LINK incrementally to dramatically reduce your build times. In incremental mode, LINK processes only those files that have a timestamp that is more recent than the last link, and updates only those parts of the program that have changed.

The .ILK File

When LINK runs incrementally for the first time, it links fully and creates a state file. This file has the same base name as the executable file or DLL and the extension .ILK. During subsequent incremental builds, LINK updates the .ILK file. If the .ILK file is missing, LINK performs a full incremental build and creates a new .ILK file. If the .ILK file is unusable, LINK performs a nonincremental build. LINK is the only tool that uses the .ILK file.

The Incrementally Linked .EXE or .DLL

An incrementally linked program is functionally equivalent to a program that is linked nonincrementally, but it has some differences from a nonincremental program because it is prepared for subsequent incremental links. An incrementally linked executable file or DLL is larger due to padding of code and data. It may contain jump thunks to handle relocation of functions to new addresses.

It is recommended that a program be linked nonincrementally before it is released, to avoid padding and thunks. The default build is nonincremental when Generate Debug Info (/DEBUG) is not specified. If /DEBUG is specified, the default is an incremental link; you can turn off Link Incrementally (or specify /INCREMENTAL:NO) to perform a nonincremental debug build. To create a nonincremental debug build, choose the Debug configuration and then clear the Link Incrementally check box.

Restrictions on Incremental Linking

Most programs can be linked incrementally. However, some changes are too great to be linked incrementally, and some options are incompatible with incremental linking. LINK performs a full build if any of the following options are specified:

- Link Incrementally is turned off (/INCREMENTAL:NO)
- Generate Mapfile (/MAP)
- COFF Format (/DEBUGTYPE:COFF)
- Both Formats (/DEBUGTYPE:BOTH)
- /OPT:REF
- /ORDER
- Use Program Database is turned off (/PDB:NONE) when Generate Debug Info (/DEBUG) is specified

Additionally, LINK performs a full build if any of the following occur:

- Missing .ILK file. (LINK creates a new .ILK file in preparation for subsequent incremental linking.)
- Corrupt .ILK file. (LINK overwrites the .ILK file and links nonincrementally.)

- No write permission for the .ILK file. (LINK ignores the .ILK file and links nonincrementally.)

- Missing .EXE or .DLL output file.

- Changing the timestamp of the .ILK, .EXE, or .DLL.

- Changing a LINK option. Most LINK options, when changed between builds, cause a full link.

- Adding or omitting an object file.

- Adding, removing, or changing a library.

- In source code, adding called library functions.

- Changing an object that was compiled with /Yu /Z7.

Program Databases

A program database (PDB, or .PDB file) for an executable file or DLL stores debug symbol tables that Visual C++ requires to debug your program. This feature is new with Microsoft Visual C++ version 2.0.

In Microsoft Visual C++ version 1.0, the behavior of the CL /Zi option and the LINK /DEBUG option changed from previous versions. As of version 1.0, the compiler created a PDB for the object file when you specified /Zi. Then, when you linked using /DEBUG, LINK called CVPACK, which read the program databases for the object files. The resulting debugging information was stored in the executable file or DLL.

Now, in version 2.0, the debugging information is in a new format. When you use /DEBUG, LINK stores the debugging information in an output program database. During subsequent builds of the executable file or DLL, LINK updates the PDB, resulting in faster linking. LINK does not call CVPACK.

An executable file or DLL that uses a PDB is functionally identical to a nondebugging build of the same program. There are slight differences in the output to enable debugging. The program can be run in the absence of its PDB. However, Visual C++ requires the output PDB when you debug the program.

If you want LINK to create old-style Microsoft debugging information, which is stored in the executable file or DLL instead of in a PDB, either turn off Use Program Database (or specify /PDB:NONE) or use Both Formats (/DEBUGTYPE:BOTH). CVPACK is required for old-style Microsoft debugging information; be sure that this tool is in the same directory as LINK.EXE or in a directory specified on the PATH environment variable.

LINK Input Files

You provide the linker with files that contain objects, import and standard libraries, resources, module definitions, and command input. LINK does not use file extensions to make assumptions about the contents of a file. Instead, LINK examines each input file to determine what kind of file it is. LINK uses the following types of input files:

- Object modules (.OBJ files)
- Standard and import libraries (.LIB files)
- Export files (.EXP files)
- Module-definition files (.DEF files)
- Program databases (.PDB files)
- Resource files (.RES files)
- MS-DOS executable files (.EXE files)
- Various text files (.TXT files)
- Incremental status files (.ILK files)

.OBJ Files

LINK accepts object files that are either COFF (Common Object File Format) or 32-bit OMF (Object Module Format). The CL compiler provided with Visual C++ for Windows NT creates COFF object files. LINK automatically converts 32-bit OMF objects to COFF.

.LIB Files

LINK accepts standard COFF libraries and COFF import libraries, both of which usually have the extension .LIB. Standard libraries contain objects and are created by the LIB tool. Import libraries contain information about exports in other programs and are created either by LINK when it builds a program that contains exports or by the LIB tool. For information on using LIB to create standard or import libraries, see Appendix D, "LIB Reference." For details on using LINK to create an import library, see the /DLL option on page 376.

A library is specified to LINK as either a filename argument or a default library. LINK resolves external references by searching first in libraries specified on the command line, then in default libraries specified with the /DEFAULTLIB option, then in default libraries named in object files. If a path is specified with the library name, LINK looks for the library in that directory. If no path is specified, LINK looks first in the directory that LINK is running from, then in any directories specified in the LIB environment variable.

LINK cannot link a library of 32-bit OMF objects created by the 16-bit version of LIB. To use an OMF library, you must first use the 16-bit LIB (not provided in Visual C++ for Windows NT) to extract the objects. You can then either link the OMF objects or use the 32-bit LIB to convert them to COFF and put them in a library. You can also use the EDITBIN.EXE tool to convert an OMF object to COFF. For details on EDITBIN, see Appendix G.

.EXP Files

Export (.EXP) files contain information about exported functions and data items. When LIB creates an import library, it also creates an export (.EXP) file. You use the .EXP file when you link a program that both exports to and imports from another program, either directly or indirectly. If you link with an .EXP file, LINK does not produce an import library because it assumes that LIB already created one. For details about .EXP files and import libraries, see "Import Libraries and Exports Files" on page 406 in Appendix D.

.DEF Files

Module-definition (.DEF) files (described beginning on page 382) provide the linker with information about exports, attributes, and other information about the program to be linked. Use the /DEF option to specify the .DEF filename. Because LINK provides options and other features that can be used instead of module-definition statements, .DEF files are generally not necessary.

.PDB Files

Object files compiled using the /Zi option contain the name of a program database (PDB). You do not specify the object's PDB filename to the linker; LINK uses the embedded name to find the PDB if it is needed. This applies also to debuggable objects contained in a library; the PDB for a debuggable library must be available to the linker along with the library.

LINK also uses a PDB to hold debugging information for the executable file or .DLL. The program's PDB is both an output file and an input file, because LINK updates the PDB when it rebuilds the program.

For more information on how LINK uses PDBs, see "Generate Debug Info" on page 338 in Chapter 21.

.RES Files

You can specify a resource (.RES) file when linking a program. The .RES file is created by the Resource Compiler (RC). LINK automatically converts .RES files to COFF. The CVTRES.EXE tool must be in the same directory as LINK.EXE or in a directory specified on the PATH environment variable.

.EXE Files

The MS-DOS Stub File Name (/STUB) option specifies the name of an executable file that runs with MS-DOS. LINK examines the specified file to be sure that it is a valid MS-DOS program.

.TXT Files

LINK expects various text files as additional input. The command-file specifier (@) and the options Base Address (/BASE), /DEF, and /ORDER all specify text files. These files can have any extension, not just .TXT.

.ILK Files

When linking incrementally, LINK updates the .ILK status file that it created during the first incremental build. For details about .ILK files and incremental linking, see "Incremental Linking" on page 363 in this chapter and the Link Incrementally (/INCREMENTAL) option on page 335 in Chapter 21.

LINK Output

Link output includes executable files, DLLs, mapfiles, and messages.

Output Files

The default output file from LINK is an executable (.EXE) file. If the /DLL option is specified, LINK builds a dynamic-link library (.DLL file). You can control the output filename with the Output File Name (/OUT) option.

In incremental mode, LINK creates an .ILK file to hold status information for later incremental builds of the program. For details about .ILK files and incremental linking, see "Incremental Linking" on page 363 and the Link Incrementally (/INCREMENTAL) option on page 335 in Chapter 21.

When LINK creates a program that contains exports (usually a DLL), it also builds an import library (.LIB file), unless an .EXP file was used in the build. You can control the import library filename with the /IMPLIB option.

If Generate Mapfile (/MAP) is specified, LINK creates a mapfile.

If Generate Debug Info (/DEBUG) and Microsoft Format (/DEBUGTYPE:CV) are specified, LINK creates a PDB to contain debugging information for the program.

Other Output

When you type link without any other command-line input, LINK displays a usage statement that summarizes its options.

LINK displays a copyright and version message and echoes command-file input, unless Suppress Startup Banner (/NOLOGO) is used.

You can use Print Progress Messages (/VERBOSE) to display additional details about the build.

LINK issues error and warning messages in the form LNK*nnnn*. This error prefix and range of numbers is also used by LIB, DUMPBIN, and EDITBIN. Consult Help for documentation on these errors. You can control the display of warnings with the /WARN option.

Running LINK on the Command Line

When you run LINK at a command prompt, you can specify input in one or more ways:

- On the command line
- Using command files
- In environment variables

LINK Command Line

To run LINK, use the following command syntax:

LINK *arguments*

The *arguments* include options and filenames and can be specified in any order. Options are processed first, then files. Use one or more spaces or tabs to separate arguments.

To pass a file to the linker, specify the filename on the command line after the LINK command. You can specify an absolute or relative path with the filename, and you can use wildcards in the filename. If you omit the dot (.) and filename extension, LINK assumes .OBJ for the purpose of finding the file. LINK does not use filename extensions or the lack of them to make assumptions about the contents of files; it determines the type of file by examining it and processes it accordingly.

LINK Command Files

You can pass command-line arguments to LINK in the form of a command file. To specify a command file to the linker, use the following syntax:

LINK @*commandfile*

The *commandfile* is the name of a text file. No space or tab is allowed between the at sign (@) and the filename. There is no default extension; you must specify the full filename, including any extension. Wildcards cannot be used. You can specify an absolute or relative path with the filename. LINK does not use an environment variable to search for the file.

In the command file, arguments can be separated by spaces or tabs (as on the command line) and by newline characters. Use a semicolon (;) to mark a comment. LINK ignores all text from the semicolon to the end of the line.

You can specify all or part of the command line in a command file. You can use more than one command file in a LINK command. LINK accepts the command-file input as if it were specified in that location on the command line. Command files cannot be nested. LINK echoes the contents of command files, unless the /NOLOGO option is specified.

Example

The following command to build a DLL passes the names of object files and libraries in separate command files and uses a third command file for specifications of the /EXPORTS option:

```
link /dll @objlist.txt @liblist.txt @exports.txt
```

LINK Environment Variables

LINK uses environment variables as follows:

- If the LINK variable is defined, LINK processes arguments defined in the variable before it processes the command line. The LINK environment variable can contain any arguments to the linker.

- If the LIB variable is defined, LINK uses the LIB path when it searches for a file (such as an object or library) specified on the LINK command line or with the /BASE option, or for a PDB file named in an object. The LIB environment variable can contain one or more path specifications, separated by semicolons (;). You can set the LIB variable within the Visual C++ development environment by choosing Directories from the Options menu.

- If it needs to run CVPACK or CVTRES and cannot find it in the same directory as itself, LINK uses the PATH environment variable to look for the tool. CVPACK is required when creating old-style Microsoft debugging information. CVTRES is required when linking a .RES file.

- LINK uses the directory specified in the TMP environment variable when linking OMF or .RES files.

LINK Options

You can specify options to LINK either within the Visual C++ development environment or on the LINK command line. Chapter 21, "Setting Linker Options," describes the option categories that are available from the Link tab in the Project Settings dialog box. The LINK options that are not available as controls on the Link tab are described in this appendix.

An option consists of an option specifier, either a dash (−) or a forward slash (/), followed by the name of the option. Option names cannot be abbreviated. Some options take an argument, specified after a colon (:). No spaces or tabs are allowed within an option specification, except within a quoted string in the /COMMENT option. Specify numeric arguments in decimal or C-language notation. Option names and their keyword or filename arguments are not case sensitive, but identifiers as arguments are case sensitive.

LINK first processes options specified in the LINK environment variable. LINK next processes options in the order they are specified on the command line and in command files. If an option is repeated with different arguments, the last one processed takes precedence.

Options apply to the entire build; no options can be applied to specific input files.

Alphabetic List of LINK Options

Table B.1 lists the LINK options, along with the equivalent Visual C++ option if available. Options listed as command-line only are described in this appendix. Visual C++ options are described in Chapter 21, "Setting Linker Options." Options marked as specific to a target are described in the appropriate documentation for that target.

Table B.1   Alphabetic List of LINK Options

Command-line option	Visual C++ option
/ALIGN	Command-line only
/BASE	Output Category
/COMMENT	Command-line only
/DEBUG	Debug Category
/DEBUGTYPE	Debug Category
/DEF	Command-line only
/DEFAULTLIB	Command-line only
/DLL	Command-line only
/ENTRY	Output Category
/EXETYPE	Command-line only
/EXPORT	Command-line only
/FIXED	Command-line only
/FORCE	Customize Category
/GPSIZE	MIPS specific

Table B.1   Alphabetic List of LINK Options (*continued*)

Command-line option	Visual C++ option
/HEAP	Command-line only
/IMPLIB	Command-line only
/INCLUDE	Input Category
/INCREMENTAL	Customize Category
/MAC	68K specific
/MACDATA	68K specific
/MACHINE	Command-line only
/MACRES	68K specific
/MAP	Debug Category
/NODEFAULTLIB	Input Category
/NOENTRY	Command-line only
/NOLOGO	Customize Category
/OPT	Command-line only
/ORDER	Command-line only
/OUT	Customize Category
/PDB	Customize Category
/PROFILE	General Category
/RELEASE	Command-line only
/SECTION	Command-line only
/STACK	Output Category
/STUB	Input Category
/SUBSYSTEM	Command-line only
/VERBOSE	Customize Category
/VERSION	Output Category
/VXD	Command-line only
/WARN	Command-line only

Visual C++ LINK Options

You can set LINK options in Visual C++ by using the Link tab in the Project Settings dialog box. Table B.2 lists the options available in Visual C++, along with the equivalent command-line options.

Table B.2   Visual C++ LINK Options

Visual C++	Command-line equivalent
General Category	
Output File Name	/OUT:*filename*
Object/Library Modules	*filename* on command line
Generate Debug Info	/DEBUG
Ignore All Default Libraries	/NODEFAULTLIB
Link Incrementally	/INCREMENTAL:{YES|NO}
Generate Mapfile	/MAP
Enable Profiling	/PROFILE
Output Category	
Base Address	/BASE:*address*
Entry-Point Symbol	/ENTRY:*function*
Stack Allocations	/STACK:*reserve,commit*
Version Information	/VERSION:*major.minor*
Input Category	
Object/Library Modules	*filename* on command line
Ignore Libraries	/NODEFAULTLIB:*library*
Ignore All Default Libraries	/NODEFAULTLIB
Force Symbol References	/INCLUDE:*symbol*
MS-DOS Stub File Name	/STUB:*filename*
Customize Category	
Use Program Database	/PDB:*filename*
Link Incrementally	/INCREMENTAL:{YES|NO}
Program Database Name	/PDB:*filename*
Output File Name	/OUT:*filename*
Force File Output	/FORCE
Print Progress Messages	/VERBOSE
Suppress Startup Banner	/NOLOGO
Debug Category	
Mapfile Name	/MAP:*filename*
Generate Mapfile	/MAP
Generate Debug Info	/DEBUG
Microsoft Format	/DEBUGTYPE:CV
COFF Format	/DEBUGTYPE:COFF
Both Formats	/DEBUGTYPE:BOTH

Compiler-Controlled LINK Options

The CL compiler automatically calls LINK when you do not specify the /c option. CL provides some control over the linker through command-line options and arguments. Table B.3 summarizes the features in CL that affect linking.

Table B.3   Compiler-Controlled LINK Options

CL command-line specification	CL action that affects LINK
Any filename other than .C, .CXX, .CPP, or .DEF	Passes filename as input to LINK
filename.DEF	Passes /DEF:*filename*.DEF
/F*number*	Passes /STACK:*number*
/Fd *filename*	Passes /PDB:*filename*
/Fe *filename*	Passes /OUT:*filename*
/Fm *filename*	Passes /MAP:*filename*
/Gy	Creates packaged functions (COMDATs), enables function-level linking
/LD	Passes /DLL
/link	Passes remainder of command line to LINK
/MD, /ML, or /MT	Places a default library name in the object file
/nologo	Passes /NOLOGO
/Zd	Passes /DEBUG /DEBUGTYPE:COFF
/Zi or /Z7	Passes /DEBUG /DEBUGTYPE:CV
/Zl	Omits default library name from object file

For more information on CL, see Chapter 20, "Setting Compiler Options," and Appendix A, "CL Reference."

/ALIGN

Syntax

/ALIGN:*number*

This option specifies the alignment of each section within the linear address space of the program. The *number* argument is in bytes and must be a power of 2. The default is 4K. The linker generates a warning if the alignment produces an invalid image.

/COMMENT

/COMMENT:[["]]*comment*[["]]

This option inserts a comment string into the header of an executable file or DLL, after the array of section headers. The type of operating system determines whether the string is loaded into memory. This comment string, unlike the comment specified with the **DESCRIPTION** statement in a .DEF file, is not inserted into the data section. Comments are useful for embedding copyright and version information.

To specify a *comment* that contains spaces or tabs, enclose it in double quotation marks ("). LINK removes the quotation marks before inserting the string. If more than one /COMMENT option is specified, LINK concatenates the strings and places a null byte at the end of each string.

/DEF

/DEF:*filename*

This option passes a module-definition (.DEF) file to the linker. Only one .DEF file can be specified to LINK. For details about .DEF files, see "Module-Definition Files" on page 382.

When a .DEF file is used in a build, no matter whether the main output file is an executable file or a DLL, LINK creates an import library (.LIB) and an exports file (.EXP). These files are created regardless of whether the main output file contains exports.

Do not specify this option within the Visual C++ development environment; this option is for use only on the command line. To specify a .DEF file, add it to the project along with other files.

/DEFAULTLIB

/DEFAULTLIB:*libraries*...

This option adds one or more *libraries* to the list of libraries that LINK searches when resolving references. A library specified with /DEFAULTLIB is searched after libraries specified on the command line and before default libraries named in object files. To specify multiple libraries, type a comma (,) between library names.

Ignore All Default Libraries (/NODEFAULTLIB) overrides /DEFAULTLIB:*library*. Ignore Libraries (/NODEFAULTLIB:*library*) overrides /DEFAULTLIB:*library* when the same *library* name is specified in both.

/DLL

Syntax

/DLL

This option builds a DLL as the main output file. A DLL usually contains exports that can be used by another program. There are three methods for specifying exports, listed in recommended order of use:

- The __**declspec(dllexport)** keyword in the source code
- An /EXPORT specification in a LINK command
- An **EXPORTS** statement in a .DEF file

A program can use more than one method.

An alternate way to build a DLL is with the **LIBRARY** module-definition statement. The /BASE and /DLL options together are equivalent to the **LIBRARY** statement.

Do not specify this option within the Visual C++ development environment; this option is for use only on the command line. This option is set when you choose either MFC APPWizard (dll) or Dynamic-Link Library under Project Type in the New Project dialog box.

/EXETYPE

Syntax

/EXETYPE:{DEV386|DYNAMIC}

This option is used when building a virtual device driver (VXD). A VXD is linked using the /VXD option.

Specify DEV386 (the default) to create a VXD that is loaded by the operating system when it loads the program that uses it. Specify DYNAMIC to create a dynamically loaded VXD.

/EXPORT

Syntax

/EXPORT:*entryname*[[=*internalname*]][[,@*ordinal*[[,NONAME]]]][[,DATA]]

This option lets you export a function from your program to allow other programs to call the function. You can also export data. Exports are usually defined in a DLL.

The *entryname* is the name of the function or data item as it is to be used by the calling program. You can optionally specify the *internalname* as the function known in the defining program; by default, *internalname* is the same as *entryname*. The *ordinal* specifies an index into the exports table in the range 1–65535; if you do not specify *ordinal*, LINK assigns one. The NONAME keyword exports the function only as an ordinal, without an *entryname*.

The DATA keyword specifies that the exported item is a data item. The data item in the client program must be declared using **extern __declspec(dllimport)**.

There are three methods for exporting a definition, listed in recommended order of use:

- The **__declspec(dllexport)** keyword in the source code
- An /EXPORT specification in a LINK command
- An **EXPORTS** statement in a .DEF file

All three methods can be used in the same program. When LINK builds a program that contains exports, it also creates an import library, unless an .EXP file is used in the build.

LINK uses decorated forms of identifiers. The compiler decorates an identifier when it creates the object file. If *entryname* or *internalname* is specified to the linker in its undecorated form as it appears in the source code, LINK attempts to match the name. If it cannot find a unique match, LINK issues an error. Use the DUMPBIN tool (see Appendix F) to get the decorated form of an identifier when you need to specify it to the linker. Do not specify the decorated form of C identifiers that are declared **__cdecl** or **__stdcall**. For more information on decorated names, see Appendix J, "Decorated Names."

/FIXED

Syntax   /FIXED

This option tells the operating system to load the program only at its preferred base address. If the preferred base address is unavailable, the operating system will not load the file. For more information, see "Base Address" on page 330 in Chapter 21.

When /FIXED is specified, LINK does not generate a relocation section in the program. At run time, if the operating system is unable to load the program at that address, it issues an error and does not load the program.

Some Win32 operating systems, especially those that coexist with MS-DOS, frequently must relocate a program. A program created with /FIXED will not run on Win32s operating systems.

Do not use /FIXED when building device drivers for Windows NT.

/HEAP

Syntax   /HEAP:*reserve*[[,*commit*]]

This option sets the size of the heap in bytes.

The *reserve* argument specifies the total heap allocation in virtual memory. The default heap size is 1MB. The linker rounds up the specified value to the nearest 4 bytes.

The optional *commit* argument is subject to interpretation by the operating system. In Windows NT, it specifies the amount of physical memory to allocate at a time. Committed virtual memory causes space to be reserved in the paging file. A higher *commit* value saves time when the application needs more heap space but increases the memory requirements and possibly startup time.

Specify the *reserve* and *commit* values in decimal or C-language notation.

/IMPLIB

Syntax

/IMPLIB:*filename*

This option overrides the default name for the import library that LINK creates when it builds a program that contains exports. The default name is formed from the base name of the main output file and the extension .LIB. A program contains exports if one or more of the following are specified:

- The __**declspec(dllexport)** keyword in the source code
- An /EXPORT specification in a LINK command
- An **EXPORTS** statement in a .DEF file

LINK ignores /IMPLIB when an import library is not being created. If no exports are specified, LINK does not create an import library. If an export (.EXP) file is used in the build, LINK assumes an import library already exists and does not create one. For information on import libraries and export files, see Appendix D, "LIB Reference."

/MACHINE

Syntax

/MACHINE:{IX86|MIPS|M68K}

This option specifies the target platform for the program.

Usually, you do not need to specify /MACHINE. LINK infers the machine type from the object files. However, in some circumstances LINK cannot determine the machine type and issues an error. If such an error occurs, specify /MACHINE.

/NOENTRY

Syntax

/NOENTRY

This option is required for creating a resource-only DLL.

Use this option to prevent LINK from linking a reference to _main into the DLL.

/OPT

/OPT:{REF|NOREF}

This option controls the optimizations LINK performs during a build. Optimizations generally decrease the image size and increase the program speed, at a cost of increased link time.

By default, LINK removes unreferenced packaged functions (COMDATs). An object contains packaged functions if it has been compiled with the /Gy option. This optimization is called transitive COMDAT elimination. To override this default and keep unused packaged functions in the program, specify /OPT:NOREF. You can use the /INCLUDE option to override the removal of a specific symbol.

If the /DEBUG option is specified, the default for /OPT changes from REF to NOREF and all functions are preserved in the image. To override this default and optimize a debugging build, specify /OPT:REF. The /OPT:REF option disables incremental linking.

/ORDER

/ORDER:@*filename*

This option lets you perform optimization by telling LINK to place certain packaged functions into the image in a predetermined order. LINK places the functions in the specified order within each section in the image.

Specify the order in *filename*, which is a text file that lists the packaged functions in the order you want to link them. Each line in *filename* contains the name of one packaged function. An object contains packaged functions if it has been compiled with the /Gy option. Function names are case sensitive. A comment is specified by a semicolon (;) and can be on the same or a separate line. LINK ignores all text from the semicolon to the end of the line.

LINK uses decorated forms of identifiers. The compiler decorates an identifier when it creates the object file. If the name of the packaged function is specified to the linker in its undecorated form as it appears in the source code, LINK attempts to match the name. If it cannot find a unique match, LINK issues an error. Use the DUMPBIN tool (see Appendix F) to get the decorated form of an identifier when you need to specify it to the linker. Do not specify the decorated form of C identifiers that are declared _ _**cdecl** or _ _**stdcall**. For more information on decorated names, see Appendix J, "Decorated Names."

If more than one /ORDER specification is used, the last one specified takes effect.

Ordering allows you to optimize your program's paging behavior through swap tuning. Group a function with the functions it calls. You can also group frequently called functions together. These techniques increase the probability that a called function is in memory when it is needed and will not have to be paged from disk.

This option disables incremental linking.

/RELEASE

/RELEASE

This option sets the checksum in the header of an executable file.

The operating system requires the checksum for certain files such as device drivers. It is recommended that you set the checksum for release versions of your programs to ensure compatibility with future operating systems.

The /RELEASE option is set by default when the /SUBSYSTEM:NATIVE option is specified.

/SECTION

/SECTION:*name,attributes*

This option changes the attributes of a section, overriding the attributes set when the object file for the section was compiled.

Specify a colon (:) and a section *name*. The *name* is case sensitive.

Specify one or more *attributes* for the section. The attribute characters are E, R, W, and S and are not case sensitive. You must specify all attributes that you want the section to have; an omitted attribute character causes that attribute bit to be turned off. Attribute characters have the following meanings:

Character	Attribute	Meaning
E	execute	Allows code to be executed
R	read	Allows read operations on data
W	write	Allows write operations on data
S	shared	Shares the section among all processes that load the image

Note that Win32s operating systems load all DLL data sections as "shared" even if that attribute is not set.

A section that does not have E, R, or W set is probably invalid.

/SUBSYSTEM

/SUBSYSTEM:{CONSOLE|WINDOWS|NATIVE|POSIX}[[,*major*[[.*minor*]]]]

This option tells the operating system how to run the executable file. The subsystem is specified as follows:

- The CONSOLE subsystem is for a Win32 character-mode application. Console applications are given a console by the operating system. If **main** or **wmain** is defined, CONSOLE is the default.

- The WINDOWS subsystem applies to an application that does not require a console, probably because it creates its own windows for interaction with the user. Win32s operating systems can only run WINDOWS applications. If **WinMain** or **wWinMain** is defined, WINDOWS is the default.
- The NATIVE subsystem applies device drivers for Windows NT.
- The POSIX subsystem creates an application that runs under the POSIX subsystem in Windows NT.

The optional *major* and *minor* version numbers specify the minimum required version of the subsystem. The arguments are decimal numbers in the range 0–65535. The default is version 3.10 for CONSOLE and WINDOWS, 1.0 for NATIVE, and 19.90 for POSIX.

The choice of subsystem affects the default starting address for the program. For more information, see the Entry-Point Symbol option on page 331 in Chapter 21.

/VXD

Syntax

/VXD

This option creates a virtual device driver (VXD). When this option is specified, the default filename extension changes to .VXD. For details on VXDs, see the Microsoft Windows NT Device Driver Kit.

A .VXD file is not in Common Object File Format. It cannot be used with DUMPBIN or EDITBIN. It does not contain debugging information. However, you can create a mapfile when you link a .VXD file.

A .VXD file cannot be incrementally linked.

/WARN

Syntax

/WARN[[:*level*]]

This option lets you determine the output of LINK warnings. Specify the *level* as one of the following:

level	**Meaning**
0	Suppress all warnings.
1	Default if /WARN:*level* is not used; displays most warnings. Overrides a /WARN:*level* specified earlier on the LINK command line or in the LINK environment variable.
2	Default if /WARN is specified without *level*; displays additional warnings.

Module-Definition Files

A module-definition (.DEF) files is a text file that contains statements for defining an executable file or DLL. The following sections describes the statements in a .DEF file.

Because LINK provides equivalent command-line options for most module-definition statements, a typical program for Win32 does not usually require a .DEF file. The descriptions of the module-definition statements give the command-line equivalent for each statement.

Rules for Module-Definition Statements

The following syntax rules apply to all statements in a .DEF file. Other rules that apply to specific statements are described with each statement.

- Statements and attribute keywords are not case sensitive. User-specified identifiers are case sensitive.

- Use one or more spaces, tabs, or newline characters to separate a statement keyword from its arguments and to separate statements from each other. A colon (:) or equal sign (=) that designates an argument is surrounded by zero or more spaces, tabs, or newline characters.

- A **NAME** or **LIBRARY** statement, if used, must precede all other statements.

- Most statements appear at most once in the .DEF file and accept one specification of arguments. The specification follows the statement keyword on the same or subsequent line(s). If the statement is repeated with different arguments later in the file, the later statement overrides the earlier one.

- The **SECTIONS**, **EXPORTS**, and **IMPORTS** statements can appear more than once in the .DEF file. Each statement can take multiple specifications, which must be separated by one or more spaces, tabs, or newline characters. The statement keyword must appear once before the first specification and can be repeated before each additional specification.

- Many statements have an equivalent LINK command-line option. See the description of the LINK option for additional details.

- Comments in the .DEF file are designated by a semicolon (;) at the beginning of each comment line. A comment cannot share a line with a statement, but it can appear between specifications in a multiline statement. (**SECTIONS** and **EXPORTS** are multiline statements.)

- Numeric arguments are specified in decimal or in C-language notation.

- If a string argument matches a reserved word, it must be enclosed in double quotation marks (").

NAME

NAME [[*application*]][[BASE=*address*]]

This statement specifies a name for the main output file. An equivalent way to specify an output filename is with the /OUT option, and an equivalent way to set the base address is with the /BASE option. If both are specified, /OUT overrides **NAME**. See the Base Address (/BASE) and Output File Name (/OUT) options for details about output filenames and base addresses.

LIBRARY

LIBRARY [[*library*]][[BASE=*address*]]

This statement tells LINK to create a DLL. At the same time, LINK creates an import library, unless an .EXP file is used in the build.

The *library* argument specifies the internal name of the DLL. (Use the Output File Name (/OUT) option to specify the DLL's output name.)

The BASE=*address* argument sets the base address that the operating system uses to load the DLL. This argument overrides the default DLL location of 0x10000000. See the description of the Base Address (/BASE) option for details about base addresses.

An equivalent way to specify a DLL build is with the /DLL option, and an equivalent way to set the base address is with the /BASE option.

DESCRIPTION

DESCRIPTION "*text*"

This statement writes a string into an .rdata section. Enclose the specified *text* in single or double quotation marks (' or "). To use a literal quotation mark (either single or double) in the string, enclose the string with the other type of mark.

This feature differs from the comment specified with the /COMMENT option.

STACKSIZE

STACKSIZE *reserve*[[,*commit*]]

This statement sets the size of the stack in bytes. An equivalent way to set the stack is with the /STACK option. See the Stack Allocations option on page 376 in Chapter 21 for details about the *reserve* and *commit* arguments.

SECTIONS

SECTIONS *definitions*

This statement sets attributes for one or more sections in the image file. It can be used to override the default attributes for each type of section.

SECTIONS marks the beginning of a list of section *definitions*. Each definition must be on a separate line. The **SECTIONS** keyword can be on the same line as the first definition or on a preceding line. The .DEF file can contain one or more **SECTIONS** statements. The **SEGMENTS** keyword is supported as a synonym for **SECTIONS**.

The syntax for a section definition is:

section [[CLASS '*classname*']] *attributes*

The *section* name is case sensitive. The **CLASS** keyword is supported for compatibility but is ignored. The *attributes* are one or more of the following: **EXECUTE**, **READ**, **SHARED**, and **WRITE**.

An equivalent way to specify section attributes is with the /SECTION option.

EXPORTS

EXPORTS *definitions*

This statement makes one or more definitions available as exports to other programs.

EXPORTS marks the beginning of a list of export *definitions*. Each definition must be on a separate line. The **EXPORTS** keyword can be on the same line as the first definition or on a preceding line. The .DEF file can contain one or more **EXPORTS** statements.

The syntax for an export definition is:

entryname[[=*internalname*]] [[@*ordinal*[[NONAME]]]] [[DATA]]

For information on the *entryname*, *internalname*, *ordinal*, NONAME, and DATA arguments, see the /EXPORT option on page 376.

There are three methods for exporting a definition, listed in recommended order of use:

- The __**declspec(dllexport)** keyword in the source code
- An /EXPORT specification in a LINK command
- An **EXPORTS** statement in a .DEF file

All three methods can be used in the same program. When LINK builds a program that contains exports, it also creates an import library, unless an .EXP file is used in the build.

VERSION

VERSION *major*[[*.minor*]]

This statement tells LINK to put a number in the header of the executable file or DLL. The *major* and *minor* arguments are decimal numbers in the range 0–65535. The default is version 0.0.

An equivalent way to specify a version number is with the Version Information (/VERSION) option.

Reserved Words

The following words are reserved by the linker. These names can be used as arguments in module-definition statements only if the name is enclosed in double quotation marks (").

APPLOADER	INITINSTANCE	OLD
BASE	IOPL	PRELOAD
CODE	LIBRARY	PROTMODE
CONFORMING	LOADONCALL	PURE
DATA	LONGNAMES	READONLY
DESCRIPTION	MOVABLE	READWRITE
DEV386	MOVEABLE	REALMODE
DISCARDABLE	MULTIPLE	RESIDENT
DYNAMIC	NAME	RESIDENTNAME
EXECUTE-ONLY	NEWFILES	SECTIONS
EXECUTEONLY	NODATA	SEGMENTS
EXECUTEREAD	NOIOPL	SHARED
EXETYPE	NONAME	SINGLE
EXPORTS	NONCONFORMING	STACKSIZE
FIXED	NONDISCARDABLE	STUB
FUNCTIONS	NONE	VERSION
HEAPSIZE	NONSHARED	WINDOWAPI
IMPORTS	NOTWINDOWCOMPAT	WINDOWCOMPAT
IMPURE	OBJECTS	WINDOWS
INCLUDE		

A P P E N D I X   C

Profiler Reference

This appendix provides reference information for using the components of the profiler from the command line. The following topics are covered:

- Profiler batch processing
- Syntax and command-line options for PREP, PROFILE, and PLIST
- Exporting data from the profiler

Refer to Figure C.1 to see how the profiler components interact.

For information on running the profiler in the Visual C++ development environment, see Chapter 15, "Profiling Code."

Profiler Batch Processing

Profiling requires three separate programs: PREP, PROFILE, and PLIST. If you choose a standard option (other than Custom) from the Visual C++ Profile dialog box, Visual C++ executes these programs for you automatically, passing arguments to the PREP program.

If you want maximum profiling flexibility, including the ability to format your output and to specify function and line count profiling, you must write your own batch files that invoke PREP, PROFILE, and PLIST. You can run these batch files from either the Profile dialog box or from the command prompt in Windows NT. If you run the batch file from the dialog box, the PLIST output will, by default, be routed to a Visual C++ output window. Command-line batch output can be routed to a file.

To help you understand the profiler batch processing flow, refer to Figure C.1. This figure is a representation of the profiling process.

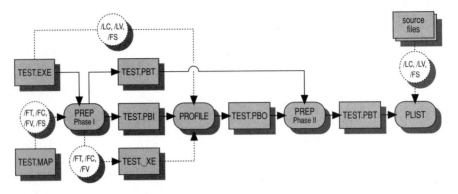

Figure C.1   Profiler Batch Processing Flow

Notice that the PREP program is called twice—once before the actual profiling and again afterward. The command-line arguments govern PREP's behavior.

The .PBI, .PBO, and .PBT files are intermediate files that are used to transfer information between profiling steps. The broken lines indicate connections that depend on the PREP (Phase I) command-line options.

A typical profiler batch file might look like this:

```
PREP /OM /FT /EXC nafxcwd.lib %1
if errorlevel == 1 goto done
PROFILE %1 %2 %3 %4 %5 %6 %7 %8 %9
if errorlevel == 1 goto done
PREP /M %1
if errorlevel == 1 goto done
PLIST /SC %1 >%1.1st
:done
```

Note When you run a profiler batch file from the Profile dialog box Custom option, the PLIST standard output is routed to the Profile tab in the Output window. In the preceding batch file, the PLIST output is redirected to a file, as it would normally be in a batch file run from the command line.

The command-line parameters for PREP, PROFILE, and PLIST are described in "Profiler Command-Line Options" on page 390. When the batch file is executed using the Custom option in the Profile dialog box, Visual C++ substitutes the project's program name for the %1 parameter. You can specify your program's command-line arguments on the Debug tab in the Project Settings dialog box.

If the preceding batch file was named FTIME.BAT, and you wanted to profile the program TEST from the Profile dialog box, you would select the Custom option, and then specify FTIME.BAT in the Custom Settings box. If you wanted to profile the TEST program from the command prompt, you would type:

```
FTIME \MSVC20\SAMPLES\WIN32\PROFILER\TEST.EXE
```

Note If you are running a profiler batch file from Visual C++, you can use Visual C++ to edit your batch file. Remember to save your batch files after editing, because Visual C++ will not save them automatically.

Profiler Batch Response Files

Like the linker, all three profiler programs accept response files. Thus the command line:

```
PREP /OM /FT /EXC nafxcwd.lib %1
```

can be replaced by the line:

```
PREP @opts.rsp %1
```

if you create a file OPTS.RSP that contains this text:

```
/OM /FT /EXC nafxcwd.lib    # this is a comment
```

The # character in a response file defines a comment that runs through the end of the line.

Standard Batch Files

Six standard batch files ship with the profiler:

Filename	Description
FTIME.BAT	Function timing
FCOUNT.BAT	Function counting
FCOVER.BAT	Function coverage
LCOUNT.BAT	Line counting
LCOVER.BAT	Line coverage

These batch files contain only the minimum parameters for PREP Phase I. Use them as prototypes for your own batch files, which should contain selection parameters. If you ran an unmodified LCOVER batch file for a Microsoft Foundation Class Library application, for example, the output report could be thousands of lines long.

Profiler Command-Line Options

The next three sections describe the command-line options for the three components of the profiler:

- PREP
- PROFILE
- PLIST

PREP

The PREP program runs twice during a normal profiling operation. In Phase I, it reads an .EXE file and then creates .PBI and .PBT files. In Phase II, it reads .PBT and .PBO files and then writes a new .PBT file for PLIST. An 'X' in the following Options table indicates that a PREP command-line option applies to a particular phase.

Syntax

PREP [[*options*]] [[*programname1*]] [[*programname2...programname8*]]

PREP reads the command line from left to right, so the rightmost options override contradictory options to the left. None of the options are case sensitive. You must prefix options with a forward slash (/) or a dash (–), and options must be separated by spaces.

Parameter	Description
options	See "Options."
programname1	Filename of primary program to profile (.DBG, .EXE, or .DLL). PROFILE adds the .EXE extension if no extension is given. This parameter must be specified for PREP Phase I and not for Phase II.
programname2 ... *programname8*	Additional programs to profile. These parameters can be specified for PREP Phase I only.

Options

Option	I	II	Description
/EXC	X		Excludes a specified module from the profile (see "Remarks").
/EXCALL	X		Excludes all modules from the profile (see "Remarks").
/FC	X		Selects function count profiling.
/FT	X		Selects function timing profiling. This option causes the profiler to generate count information as well.
/FV	X		Selects function coverage profiling.
/INC	X		Includes in profile (see "Remarks").
/H[[ELP]]	X	X	Provides a short summary of PREP options.

Option	I	II	Description
/IO *filename*		X	Merges an existing .PBO file. Up to eight .PBO files can be merged at a time. The default extension is .PBO.
/IT *filename*		X	Merges an existing .PBT file. Up to eight .PBT files can be merged at a time. You cannot merge .PBT files from different profiling methods. The default extension is .PBT.
/LC	X		Selects line count profiling.
/LV	X		Selects line coverage profiling.
/M *filename*		X	Substitutes for /IT, /IO, and /OT options.
/NOLOGO	X	X	Suppresses the PREP copyright message.
/OI *filename*	X		Creates a .PBI file. The default extension is .PBI. If /OI is not specified, the output .PBI file is *programname1*.PBI.
/OM	X		Creates a self-profiling file with _XE or _LL extension for function timing, function counting, and function coverage. Without this option, the executable code is stored in the .PBI file. This option speeds up profiling and is used by Visual C++.
/OT *filename*	X	X	Specifies the output .PBT file. The default extension is .PBT. If /OT is not specified, the output .PBT file is *programname1*.PBT.
/SF *function*	X		Starts profiling with *function*. The function name must correspond to an entry in the .MAP file.
/?	X	X	Provides a short summary of PREP options.

Environment Variable

PREP   Specifies default command-line options.

If a value for the PREP environment variable is not specified, the default options for PREP are:

```
/FT /OI filename /OT filename
```

where *filename* is set to the *programname1* parameter value.

Remarks

The /INC and /EXC options specify individual .LIB, .OBJ and .C (.CPP or .CXX) files. For line counting and line coverage, you can specify line numbers with source files as in:

```
/EXCALL /INC test.cpp(3-41,50-67)
```

This example includes only lines 3–41 and lines 50–67 from the source file TEST.CPP. Note the absence of spaces in the source specification.

To specify all source lines in a particular module, specify the .OBJ file like this:

```
/EXCALL /INC test.obj
```

or by using the source filename with zero line numbers like this:

```
/EXCALL /INC test.cpp(0-0)
```

The following statement profiles from line 50 to the end of the file:

```
/EXCALL /INC test.cpp(50-0)
```

PROFILE

PROFILE profiles an application and generates a .PBO file of the results. Use PROFILE after creating a .PBI file with PREP.

Syntax

PROFILE [[*options*]] *programname* [[*programargs*]]

PROFILE reads the command line from left to right, so the rightmost options override contradictory options to the left. None of the options are case sensitive. You must prefix options with a forward slash (/) or a dash (–), and options must be separated by spaces.

If you do not specify a .PBO filename on the command line, PROFILE uses the base name of the .PBI file with a .PBO extension. If you do not specify a .PBI or a .PBO file, PROFILE uses the base name of *programname* with the .PBI and .PBO extensions.

Parameter	Description
options	See "Options."
programname	Filename of program to profile. PROFILE adds the .EXE extension if no extension is given. See "Remarks."
programargs	Optional command-line arguments for *programname*. See "Remarks."

Options

Option	Description
/A	Appends any redirected error messages to an existing file. If the /E command-line option is used without /A, the file is overwritten. This option is valid only with the /E option.
/E *filename*	Sends profiler-generated error messages to *filename*.
/H[[ELP]]	Provides a short summary of PROFILE options.
/I *filename*	Specifies a .PBI file to be read. This file is generated by PREP.
/NOLOGO	Suppresses the PROFILE copyright message.
/O *filename*	Specifies a .PBO file to be generated. Use the PREP utility to merge with other .PBO files or to create a .PBT file for use with PLIST.
/X	Returns the exit code of the program being profiled.
/?	Provides a short summary of PROFILE options.

Remarks

You must specify the filename of the program to profile on the PROFILE command line. PROFILE assumes the .EXE extension, if no extension is given.

You can follow the program name with command-line arguments; these arguments are passed to the profiled program unchanged.

If you are profiling code in a .DLL file, give the name of an executable file that calls it. For example, if you want to profile SAMPLE.DLL, which is called by CALLER.EXE, you can type:

```
PROFILE CALLER.EXE
```

assuming that CALLER.PBI has `SAMPLE.DLL` selected for profiling. For more information, see "Profiling Dynamic-Link Libraries" in Chapter 11 of *Programming Techniques*.

Environment Variable

PROFILE   Specifies default command-line options.

If the PROFILE environment variable is not specified, there are no other defaults.

PLIST

PLIST converts results from a .PBT file into a formatted text file.

Syntax

PLIST [[*options*]] *inputfile*

PLIST reads the command line from left to right, so the rightmost options override contradictory options to the left. None of the options are case sensitive. You must prefix options with a forward slash (/) or a dash (–), and options must be separated by spaces.

PLIST results are sent to STDOUT by default. Use the greater-than (>) redirection character to send these results to a file or device.

PLIST must be run from the directory in which the profiled program was compiled.

Parameter	Description
options	See "Options."
inputfile	The .PBT file to be converted by PLIST.

Options

Option	Description
/C *count*	Specifies the minimum hit count to appear in the listing.
/D *directory*	Specifies an additional directory for PLIST to search for source files. Use multiple /D command-line options to specify multiple directories. Use this option when PLIST cannot find a source file.
/F	Lists full paths in tab-delimited report.
/H[[ELP]]	Provides a short summary of PLIST options.

Option	Description
/NOLOGO	Suppresses the PLIST copyright message.
/PL *length*	Sets page length (in lines) of output. The length must be 0 or 15–255. A length of 0 suppresses page breaks. The default length is 0.
/PW *width*	Sets page width (in characters) of output. The width must be 1–511. The default width is 511.
/SC	Sorts output by counts, highest first.
/SL	Sorts output in the order that the lines appear in the file. This is the default. This option is available only when profiling by line.
/SLS	Forces line count profile output to be printed in coverage format.
/SN	Sorts output in alphabetical order by function name. This option is available only when profiling by function.
/SNS	Displays function timing or function counting information in function coverage format. Sorts output in alphabetical order by function name.
/ST	Sorts output by time, highest first.
/T	Tab-separated output. Generates a tab-delimited database from the .PBT file for export to other applications. All other options, including sort specifications, are ignored when using this option. For more information, see "Exporting Data from the Profiler" below.
/?	Provides a summary of PLIST options.

Environment Variable

PLIST   Specifies default command-line options.

If the PLIST environment variable is not specified, the default options for PLIST depend on the profile type as shown:

Profile type	Sort option	Hit count option
Function timing	/ST	/C 1
Function counting	/SC	/C 1
Function coverage	/SN	/C 0
Line counting	/SL	/C 0
Line coverage	/SL	/C 0

Exporting Data from the Profiler

In addition to formatted reports, the PLIST report-generation utility can produce a tab-delimited report of profiler output. The following sections describe the data format of the report, steps for analyzing statistics in the report, and a Microsoft Excel macro that uses this report format.

The PLIST /T command-line option causes PLIST to dump the contents of a .PBT file into a tab-delimited format suitable for import into a spreadsheet or database. This format can also be used by user-written programs.

For example, to create a tab-delimited file called MYPROG.TXT from MYPROG.PBT, type:

```
PLIST /T MYPROG > MYPROG.TXT
```

Note The ASCII tab-delimited format was designed to be read by other programs; it was not intended for general reporting.

Tab-Delimited Record Format

Every piece of data stored by the profiler is available through the tab-delimited report. Because not all aspects of the database are recorded by every profiling method, unused fields within a record may be zero. For example, the total time of the program will be zero if the program was profiled for counts only. Also, all included functions will be listed for function counting and timing profiles, even if those functions were not executed.

The tab-delimited format is arranged with one record per line and two to eight fields per record. Figure C.2 shows how a database looks when loaded into Microsoft Excel. The database was produced using the PLIST /T command-line option.

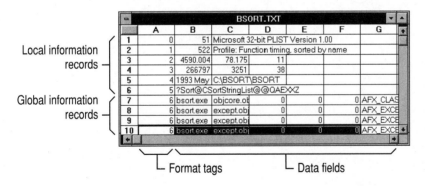

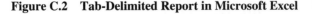

Figure C.2   Tab-Delimited Report in Microsoft Excel

The first item in each record is a format tag number. These tags range from 0 to 7 and indicate the kind of data given in the other fields of the record. The fields in each record are described in the next two sections:

- Global information records
- Local information records

Tab-delimited reports are generated with global information records first, organized in numerical order by format tag. The local information records, containing information about specific lines or functions, are generated last. Local information records are organized by line number.

If the .PBT file contains information from more than one .EXE or .DLL file, the global information will cover them all. Local information records include the EXE field, which specifies the name of the executable file that each record pertains to.

Global Information Records

The global information records contain information about the entire executable file. The format tag numbers for global information records are 0 through 5. The record formats are as follows:

Profiler Banner

0	Version	Banner

Field	Explanation
0	Format tag number
Version	PLIST version number
Banner	PLIST banner

Profiling Method

1	Method	Description

Field	Explanation
1	Format tag number
Method	Numeric value that indicates the profiling type (see Table C.1)
Description	ASCII description of the profiling type given by the method field

The profiling types are listed in Table C.1.

Table C.1   Profiling Types

Method	Description
321	Profile: Line counting, sorted by line
324	Profile: Line coverage, sorted by line
521	Profile: Function counting, sorted by function name
522	Profile: Function timing, sorted by function name
524	Profile: Function coverage, sorted by function name

Profiling Time and Depth

2	Total Time	Outside Time	Call Depth

Field	Explanation
2	Format tag number.
Total Time	Total amount of time used by the program being profiled. This field is zero for counting and coverage profiles.
Outside Time	Amount of time spent before the first profiled function (with function profiling) or line (with line profiling) was executed. This field is zero for counting and coverage profiles.
Call Depth	Maximum number of nested functions found while profiling. Only profiled functions are counted. This field is zero for line-level profiling.

Hit Counts

3	Total Hits	Lines/Funcs	Lines/Funcs Hit

Field	Explanation
3	Format tag number
Total Hits	Total number of times the profiler detected a profiled line or function being executed
Lines/Funcs	Total number of lines or functions marked for profiling
Lines/Funcs Hit	Number of marked lines or functions executed at least once while profiling

Date/Command Line

4	Date	Command Line

Field	Explanation
4	Format tag number
Date	The date/time the profile was run (ASCII format)
Command Line	The PLIST command-line arguments

Starting Function Name

5	Starting Function Name

Field	Explanation
5	Format tag number
Starting Function Name	The decorated name of the starting function identified by the PREP /SF parameter

Local Information Records

The local information records contain information about specific lines or functions that were profiled. The format tag numbers for local information records are 6 and 7. A report can have only one kind of local information record. The record formats are as follows:

Function Information

6	Exe	Source	Count	Time	Child	Func

Field	Explanation
6	Format tag number.
Exe	ASCII name of the executable file that contains this function.
Source	ASCII name of the object module (including the .OBJ extension) that contains this function.
Count	Number of times this function has been executed.
Time	Amount of time spent executing this function in milliseconds. This field is zero with profiling by counting or coverage.
Child	Amount of time spent executing the function and any child functions it calls. This field is zero with profiling by counting or coverage.
Func	ASCII name of the function.

Line Information

7	Exe	Source	Line	Count

Field	Explanation
7	Format tag number.
Exe	ASCII name of the executable file that contains this function.
Source	ASCII name of the source that contains the first line of this function.
Line	Line number of this line.
Count	Number of times this line has been executed. With coverage, this field is 1 if the line has been executed and 0 otherwise.

Steps to Analyze Profiler Statistics

The profiler tab-delimited report format can contain a great deal of information. You can use process this data in a spreadsheet, database, or user-written program.

▶ **To process the data in the tab-delimited report**

1. Collect the cumulative data from the global information records. These lines begin with the numbers 0 through 5. Each of these lines appears only once, and always in ascending order.

2. Determine the type of database by finding the value of the "Method" field. This field is the second field of record type 1.

   If the value in the "Method" field is greater than 400, the report comes from function profiling. If it is less than 400, the report comes from line profiling. The type of information in the local information records given later is directly related to this value.

   In any one report, the local information records are always of the same type, either line information or function information.

3. Process data from the local information records. For example, to calculate the percentage of hits on a given function, divide the value of the "Count" field in record type 6 by the total number of hits from the "Total Hits" field of record type 3.

   Remember that there can be only one type of local information record (either line or function information) in a report.

4. Send the results to a file or STDOUT.

Processing Profiler Output with Microsoft Excel

PROFILER.XLM is an example Microsoft Excel 4.0 macro that processes the tab-delimited report and graphs the results. The macro is in the \MSVC20\SAMPLES\WIN32\PROFILER directory.

Note The profiler sample code is installed when you set up Visual C++. If the Excel macro and other sample code are not on your disk, run Setup again to reinstall the Visual C++ sample code.

Using the PROFILER.XLM Macro

To run the macro, follow these steps from within Microsoft Excel:

1. Open PROFILER.XLM by choosing Open from the File menu.

2. Open the tab-delimited report that was created by PLIST by choosing Open from the File menu.

3. If you have several open worksheets, activate the one containing the profiler data by selecting it with the mouse or by choosing its title from the Windows menu.

4. Run the macro:

- Press CTRL+C for a chart based on hit counts.
- Press CTRL+T for a chart based on timing.

 You cannot get a timing chart if the report contains only counting or coverage information.

The macro typically takes only a few seconds to execute. When it is complete, Microsoft Excel displays a 3-D bar chart based on the results in the report (see Figure C.3). You can change the chart type by using the Gallery menu.

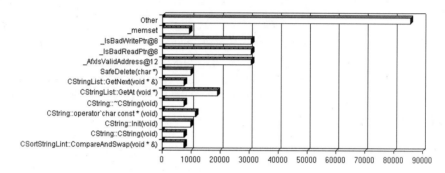

Figure C.3   Graph Created with CreateColumnChart Macro

Note This macro copies the data in the report to another worksheet before processing it. The original tab-delimited report is left untouched.

Changing the PROFILER.XLM Selection Criteria

The standard PROFILER.XLM macro displays hit counts greater than 0 (for CTRL+C) and times greater than .01 millisecond (for CTRL+T). If you need to narrow the selections without analyzing the macro, edit the formulas in cells C10 and D10.

A P P E N D I X   D

LIB Reference

This appendix describes the Microsoft 32-Bit Library Manager (LIB.EXE), version 2.50. LIB is a 32-bit tool that creates and manages a library of Common Object File Format (COFF) object files. LIB can also be used to create exports files and import libraries to reference exported definitions.

The following topics are covered in this appendix:

- Overview of LIB
- Running LIB
- Managing a library
- Extracting a library member
- Import libraries and exports files

Overview of LIB

LIB creates standard libraries, import libraries, and exports files that you can use with LINK when building a 32-bit program. (LINK is described in Chapter 21, "Setting Linker Options," and Appendix B, "LINK Reference.") LIB runs from a command prompt.

You can use LIB in the following modes:

- Building or modifying a COFF library (described on page 404)
- Extracting a member object to a file (described on page 406)
- Creating an exports file and an import library (described on page 406)

These modes are mutually exclusive; you can use LIB in only one mode at a time.

LIB Input Files

The input files expected by LIB depend on the mode in which it is used, as follows:

Mode	Input
Default (building or modifying a library)	COFF object (.OBJ) files, COFF libraries (.LIB), 32-bit OMF object (.OBJ) files
Extracting a member with /EXTRACT	COFF library (.LIB)
Building an exports file and import library with /DEF	Module-definition (.DEF) file, COFF object (.OBJ) files, COFF libraries (.LIB), 32-bit OMF object (.OBJ) files

Note   Object Model Format (OMF) libraries created by the 16-bit version of LIB cannot be used as input to the 32-bit LIB.

LIB Output Files

The output files produced by LIB depend on the usage mode as shown in the following table:

Mode	Output
Default (building or modifying a library)	COFF library (.LIB)
Extracting a member with /EXTRACT	Object (.OBJ) file
Building an exports file and import library with /DEF	Import library (.LIB) and exports (.EXP) file

Other LIB Output

In the default mode, you can use the /LIST option to display information about the resulting library. You can redirect this output to a file.

LIB displays a copyright and version message and echoes command files unless the /NOLOGO option is used.

When you type lib with no other input, LIB displays a usage statement that summarizes its options.

Error and warning messages issued by LIB have the form LNK*nnnn*. The LINK, DUMPBIN, and EDITBIN tools also use this range of errors. Documentation on these errors is available in Help.

Structure of a Library

A library contains COFF objects. Objects in a library contain functions and data that can be referenced externally by other objects in a program. An object in a library is sometimes referred to as a library member.

You can get additional information about the contents of a library by running the DUMPBIN tool with the /LINKERMEMBER option. For more information, see Appendix F, "DUMPBIN Reference."

Running LIB

This section presents information on running LIB in any mode. It describes the LIB command line, discusses the use of command files, and gives general rules for using options. For details about running LIB in a specific mode, see the appropriate section.

LIB Command Line

To run LIB, type the command lib followed by the options and filenames for the task you are using LIB to perform. LIB also accepts command-line input in command files, which are described below. LIB does not use an environment variable.

Note If you are accustomed to the LINK32.EXE and LIB32.EXE tools provided with the Microsoft Win32 Software Development Kit for Windows NT, you may have been using either the command link32 -lib or the command lib32 for managing libraries and creating import libraries. Be sure to change your makefiles and batch files to use the lib command instead.

LIB Command Files

You can pass command-line arguments to LIB in a command file by using the following syntax:

LIB @*commandfile*

The *commandfile* is the name of a text file. No space or tab is allowed between the at sign (@) and the filename. There is no default extension; you must specify the full filename, including any extension. Wildcards cannot be used. You can specify an absolute or relative path with the filename.

In the command file, arguments can be separated by spaces or tabs as they can on the command line, and they can also be separated by newline characters. Use a semicolon (;) to mark a comment. LIB ignores all text from the semicolon to the end of the line.

You can specify either all or part of the command line in a command file, and you can use more than one command file in a LIB command. LIB accepts the command-file input as if it were specified in that location on the command line. Command files cannot be nested. LIB echoes the contents of command files unless the /NOLOGO option is used.

Using LIB Options

An option consists of an option specifier, which is either a dash (−) or a forward slash (/), followed by the name of the option. Option names cannot be abbreviated. Some options take an argument, specified after a colon (:). No spaces or tabs are allowed within an option specification. Use one or more spaces or tabs to separate option specifications on the command line. Option names and their keyword or filename arguments are not case sensitive, but identifiers used as arguments are case sensitive. LIB processes options in the order specified on the command line and in command files. If an option is repeated with different arguments, the last one to be processed takes precedence.

The following options apply to all modes of LIB:

/MACHINE:{IX86|MIPS|M68K}

Specifies the target platform for the program. Usually, you do not need to specify /MACHINE. LIB infers the machine type from the object files. However, in some circumstances it cannot determine the machine type and issues an error. If such an error occurs, specify /MACHINE. In /EXTRACT mode, this option is for verification only.

/NOLOGO

Suppresses display of the LIB copyright message and version number and prevents echoing of command files.

/VERBOSE

Displays details about the progress of the session. The information is sent to standard output and can be redirected to a file.

Other options apply only to specific modes of LIB. These options are discussed in the sections describing each mode.

Managing a Library

The default mode for LIB is to build or modify a library of COFF objects. LIB runs in this mode when you do not specify /EXTRACT (to copy an object to a file) or /DEF (to build an import library).

To build a library from objects and/or libraries, use the following syntax:

LIB [[*options*...]] *files*...

This command creates a library from one or more input *files*. The *files* can be COFF object files, 32-bit OMF object files, and existing COFF libraries. LIB creates one library that contains all objects in the specified files. If an input file is a 32-bit OMF object file, LIB converts it to COFF before building the library. LIB cannot accept a 32-bit OMF object that is in a library created by the 16-bit version of LIB. You must first use the 16-bit LIB to extract the object, then you can use the extracted object file as input to the 32-bit LIB. The 16-bit version of LIB is not provided with the Visual C++ development system for Windows NT.

By default, LIB names the output file using the base name of the first object or library file and the extension .LIB. If a file already exists with the same name, the output file overwrites the existing file. To preserve an existing library, use the /OUT option to specify a name for the output file.

The following options apply to building and modifying a library:

/LIST
>   Displays information about the output library to standard output. The output can be redirected to a file. You can use /LIST to determine the contents of an existing library without modifying it.

/OUT:*filename*
>   Overrides the default output filename. By default, the output library has the base name of the first library or object on the command line and the extension .LIB.

/REMOVE:*object*
>   Omits the specified *object* from the output library. LIB creates an output library by first combining all objects (whether in object files or libraries), then deleting any objects specified with /REMOVE.

/SUBSYSTEM
>   Tells the operating system how to run a program created by linking to the output library. For more information, see the description of the LINK /SUBSYSTEM option in Appendix B.

You can use LIB to perform the following library-management tasks:

- To add objects to a library, specify the filename for the existing library and the filenames for the new objects.

- To combine libraries, specify the library filenames. You can add objects and combine libraries in a single LIB command.

- To replace a library member with a new object, specify the library containing the member object to be replaced and the filename for the new object (or the library that contains it). When an object that has the same name exists in more than one input file, LIB puts the last object specified in the LIB command into the output library. When you replace a library member, be sure to specify the new object or library after the library that contains the old object.

- To delete a member from a library, use the /REMOVE option. LIB processes any specifications of /REMOVE after combining all input objects, regardless of command-line order.

Note You cannot both delete a member and extract it to a file in the same step. You must first extract the member object using /EXTRACT, then run LIB again using /REMOVE. This behavior differs from that of the 16-bit LIB (for OMF libraries) provided in other Microsoft products.

Extracting a Library Member

You can use LIB to create an object (.OBJ) file that contains a copy of a member of an existing library. To extract a copy of a member, use the following syntax:

LIB *library* /EXTRACT:*member* /OUT:*objectfile*

This command creates an .OBJ file called *objectfile* that contains a copy of a *member* of a *library*. The *member* name is case sensitive. You can extract only one member in a single command. The /OUT option is required; there is no default output name. If a file called *objectfile* already exists in the specified directory (or current directory, if no directory is specified with *objectfile*), the extracted *objectfile* overwrites the existing file.

Import Libraries and Exports Files

You can use LIB with the /DEF option to create an import library and an exports file. LINK uses the exports file to build a program that contains exports (usually a DLL), and it uses the import library to resolve references to those exports in other programs.

In most situations, you do not need to use LIB to create your import library. When you link a program (either an executable file or a DLL) that contains exports, LINK automatically creates an import library that describes the exports. Later, when you link a program that references those exports, you specify the import library.

However, when a DLL exports to a program that it also imports from, whether directly or indirectly, you must use LIB to create one of the import libraries. When LIB creates an import library, it also creates an exports file. You must use the exports file when linking one of the DLLs.

Building an Import Library and Exports File

To build an import library and exports file, use the following syntax:

LIB /DEF[[:*deffile*]] [[*options*]] [[*objfiles*]] [[*libraries*]]

When /DEF is specified, LIB creates the output files from export specifications that are passed in the LIB command. There are three methods for specifying exports, listed in recommended order of use:

- A **__declspec(dllexport)** definition in one of the *objfiles* or *libraries*
- A specification of /EXPORT:*name* on the LIB command line
- A definition in an EXPORTS statement in a *deffile*

These are the same methods you use to specify exports when linking an exporting program. A program can use more than one method. You can specify parts of the LIB command (such as multiple *objfiles* or /EXPORT specifications) in a command file in the LIB command, just as you can in a LINK command.

The following options apply to building an import library and exports file:

/DEBUGTYPE:{CV|COFF|BOTH}
Sets the format of debugging information. Specify CV for new-style Microsoft Symbolic Debugging Information, required by Visual C++. Specify COFF for Common Object File Format (COFF) debugging information. Specify BOTH for both COFF debugging information and old-style Microsoft debugging information.

/OUT:*import*
Overrides the default output filename for the *import* library being created. When /OUT is not specified, the default name is the base name of the first object file or library in the LIB command and the extension .LIB. The exports file is given the same base name as the import library and the extension .EXP.

/EXPORT:*entryname*[[=*internalname*]][[,@*ordinal*[[,NONAME]]]][[,DATA]]
Exports a function from your program to allow other programs to call the function. You can also export data. Exports are usually defined in a DLL.

The *entryname* is the name of the function or data item as it is to be used by the calling program. You can optionally specify the *internalname* as the function known in the defining program; by default, *internalname* is the same as *entryname*. The *ordinal* specifies an index into the exports table in the range 1–65535; if you do not specify *ordinal*, LIB assigns one. The NONAME keyword exports the function only as an ordinal, without an *entryname*.

/INCLUDE:*symbol*
Adds the specified symbol to the symbol table. This is useful for forcing the use of a library object that otherwise would not be included.

Using an Import Library and Exports File

When a program (either an executable file or a DLL) exports to another program that it also imports from, or if more than two programs both export to and import from each other, the commands to link these programs must accommodate the circular exports.

In a situation without circular exports, when you link a program that uses exports from another program, you must specify the import library for the exporting program. The import library for the exporting program is created when you link that exporting program. This requires that you link the exporting program before the importing program. For example, if TWO.DLL imports from ONE.DLL, you must first link ONE.DLL and get the import library ONE.LIB. You then specify ONE.LIB when you link TWO.DLL. When the linker creates TWO.DLL, it also creates its import library, TWO.LIB. You use TWO.LIB when linking programs that import from TWO.DLL.

However, in a circular export situation, it is not possible to link all of the interdependent programs using import libraries from the other programs. In the example discussed earlier, if TWO.DLL also exports to ONE.DLL, the import library for TWO.DLL won't exist yet when ONE.DLL is linked. When circular exports exist, you must use LIB to create an import library and exports file for one of the programs.

To begin, choose one of the programs on which to run LIB. In the LIB command, list all objects and libraries for the program and specify /DEF. If the program uses a .DEF file or /EXPORT specifications, specify these as well.

After you create the import library (.LIB) and the export file (.EXP) for the program, you then use the import library when linking the other program or programs. LINK creates an import library for each exporting program it builds. For example, if you ran LIB on the objects and exports for ONE.DLL, you created ONE.LIB and ONE.EXP. You can now use ONE.LIB when linking TWO.DLL; this step also creates the import library TWO.LIB.

Finally, link the program you began with. In the LINK command, specify the objects and libraries for the program, the .EXP file that LIB created for the program, and the import library or libraries for the exports used by the program. In the continuing example, the LINK command for ONE.DLL contains ONE.EXP and TWO.LIB, as well as the objects and libraries that go into ONE.DLL. Do not specify the .DEF file and /EXPORT specifications in the LINK command; these are not needed, because the exports definitions are contained in the .EXP file. When you link using an .EXP file, LINK does not create an import library, because it assumes that one was created when the .EXP file was created.

APPENDIX E

BSCMAKE Reference

This appendix describes the Microsoft Browse Information Maintenance Utility (BSCMAKE.EXE), version 2.60. BSCMAKE builds a browse information file (.BSC) from .SBR files created during compilation. You view a browse information file in a browse window in Visual C++. For information about browse windows, see Chapter 13, "Browsing Through Symbols."

When you build your program in Visual C++, you can tell Visual C++ to create a browse information file for your program automatically. Visual C++ calls BSCMAKE to build the file. You do not need to know how to run BSCMAKE if you create your browse information file in Visual C++. However, you may want to read this appendix to understand the choices available in Visual C++.

If you build your program outside of Visual C++, you can still create a custom browse information file that you can examine in Visual C++. Run BSCMAKE on the .SBR files that you created during compilation.

The following topics are covered in this appendix:

- Building a .BSC file
- BSCMAKE command line
- BSCMAKE command file
- BSCMAKE options
- BSCMAKE exit codes

Building a .BSC File

BSCMAKE can build a new browse information file from newly created .SBR files. It can also maintain an existing .BSC file using .SBR files for object files that have changed since the last build.

The following sections describe:

- How to create an .SBR file
- How BSCMAKE builds a .BSC file
- How to increase BSCMAKE efficiency

Creating an .SBR File

The input files for BSCMAKE are .SBR files. The compiler creates an .SBR file for each .OBJ file it compiles. When you build or update your browse information file, all .SBR files for your project must be available on disk.

To create an .SBR file with all possible information, specify Generate Browse Info in Visual C++ (or specify /FR) when compiling).

To create an .SBR file that doesn't contain local symbols, specify Generate Browse Information and then check Exclude Local Variables (or specify /Fr on the compiler command line). If the .SBR files contain local symbols, you can still omit them from the .BSC file by using BSCMAKE's /El option, described on page 413.

You can create an .SBR file without performing a full compile. For example, you can specify the /Zs option to the compiler to perform a syntax check and still generate an .SBR file if you specify /FR or /Fr.

The build process can be more efficient if the .SBR files are first packed to remove unreferenced definitions. The compiler automatically packs .SBR files. An unpacked .SBR file is required if you want to use the /Iu option with BSCMAKE to include unreferenced symbols in the browse information file. If you want to prevent packing, specify Don't Pack Information in Visual C++ (or specify /Zn on the compiler command line).

How BSCMAKE Builds a .BSC File

BSCMAKE builds or rebuilds a .BSC file in the most efficient way it can. To avoid potential problems, it is important to understand the build process.

When BSCMAKE builds a browse information file, it truncates the .SBR files to zero length. During a subsequent build of the same file, a zero-length (or empty) .SBR file tells BSCMAKE that the .SBR file has no new contribution to make. It lets BSCMAKE know that an update of that part of the file is not required and an incremental build will be sufficient. During every build (unless the /n option is specified), BSCMAKE first attempts to update the file incrementally by using only those .SBR files that have changed.

BSCMAKE looks for a .BSC file that has the name specified with the /o option. If /o is not specified, BSCMAKE looks for a file that has the base name of the first .SBR file and a .BSC extension. If the file exists, BSCMAKE performs an incremental build of the browse information file using only the contributing .SBR files. If the file does not exist, BSCMAKE performs a full build using all .SBR files. The rules for builds are as follows:

- For a full build to succeed, all specified .SBR files must exist and must not be truncated. If an .SBR file is truncated, you must rebuild it (by recompiling or assembling) before running BSCMAKE.

- For an incremental build to succeed, the .BSC file must exist. All contributing .SBR files, even empty files, must exist and must be specified on the BSCMAKE command line. If you omit an .SBR file from the command line, BSCMAKE removes its contribution from the file.

Increasing Efficiency with BSCMAKE

The building process can require large amounts of time, memory, and disk space. However, you can reduce these requirements by creating a smaller browse information file and by avoiding unreferenced definitions.

Making a Smaller Browse Information File

Smaller browse information files take less time to build, use less disk space, reduce the risk of BSCMAKE running out of memory, and run faster in the browse window. You can use one or more of the following methods to create a smaller file:

- Use BSCMAKE options to exclude information from the browse information file. These options are described on page 413.

- Omit local symbols in one or more .SBR files when compiling or assembling.

- If an object file does not contain information that you need for your current stage of debugging, omit its .SBR file from the BSCMAKE command when rebuilding the browse information file.

Saving Build Time and Disk Space

Unreferenced definitions cause .SBR files to take up more disk space and cause BSCMAKE to run less efficiently. The compiler automatically packs .SBR files to remove unreferenced definitions. The /Zn (Don't Pack Info) option prevents this packing. You can increase efficiency of disk space and BSCMAKE speed by not using /Zn and allowing the compiler to pack the .SBR files.

BSCMAKE Command Line

To run BSCMAKE, use the following command line:

BSCMAKE [[*options*]] *sbrfiles*

Options can appear only in the *options* field on the command line.

The *sbrfiles* field specifies one or more .SBR files created by a compiler or assembler. Separate the names of .SBR files with spaces or tabs. You must specify the extension; there is no default. You can specify a path with the filename, and you can use operating-system wildcards (* and ?).

During an incremental build, you can specify new .SBR files that were not part of the original build. If you want all contributions to remain in the browse information file, you must specify all .SBR files (including truncated files) that were originally used to create the .BSC file. If you omit an .SBR file, that file's contribution to the browse information file is removed.

Do not specify a truncated .SBR file for a full build. A full build requires contributions from all specified .SBR files. Before you perform a full build, recompile the project and create a new .SBR file for each empty file.

The following command runs BSCMAKE to build a file called MAIN.BSC from three .SBR files:

```
BSCMAKE main.sbr file1.sbr file2.sbr
```

BSCMAKE Command File

You can provide part or all of the command-line input in a command file. Specify the command file using the following syntax:

BSCMAKE @*filename*

Only one command file is allowed. You can specify a path with *filename*. Precede *filename* with an at sign (@). BSCMAKE does not assume an extension. You can specify additional *sbrfiles* on the command line after *filename*. The command file is a text file that contains the input to BSCMAKE in the same order as you would specify it on the command line. Separate the command-line arguments with one or more spaces, tabs, or newline characters.

The following command calls BSCMAKE using a command file:

```
BSCMAKE @prog1.txt
```

The following is a sample command file:

```
/n /v /o main.bsc /E1
/S (
toolbox.h
verdate.h c:\src\inc\screen.h
)
file1.sbr file2.sbr file3.sbr file4.sbr
```

BSCMAKE Options

This section describes the options available for controlling BSCMAKE. Several options control the content of the browse information file by excluding or including certain information. The exclusion options can allow BSCMAKE to run faster and may result in a smaller .BSC file. Option names are case sensitive (except for /HELP and /NOLOGO).

/Ei (*filename...*)

Excludes the contents of the specified include files from the browse information file. To specify multiple files, separate the names with spaces and enclose the list in parentheses. Parentheses are not necessary if you specify only one *filename*. Use /Ei along with the /Es option to exclude files not excluded by /Es.

/El

Excludes local symbols. The default is to include local symbols. For more information about local symbols, see "Creating an .SBR File" on page 410.

/Em

Excludes symbols in the body of macros. Use /Em to include only the names of macros in the browse information file. The default is to include both the macro names and the result of the macro expansions.

/Er (*symbol...*)

Excludes the specified symbols from the browse information file. To specify multiple symbol names, separate the names with spaces and enclose the list in parentheses. Parentheses are not necessary if you specify only one *symbol*.

/Es

Excludes from the browse information file every include file specified with an absolute path or found in an absolute path specified in the INCLUDE environment variable. (Usually, these are the system include files, which contain a lot of information that you may not need in your browse information file.) This option does not exclude files specified without a path or with relative paths or found in a relative path in INCLUDE. You can use the /Ei option along with /Es to exclude files that /Es does not exclude. If you want to exclude only some of the files that /Es excludes, use /Ei instead of /Es and list the files you want to exclude.

/HELP

Displays a summary of the BSCMAKE command-line syntax.

/Iu

Includes unreferenced symbols. By default, BSCMAKE does not record any symbols that are defined but not referenced. If an .SBR file has been packed, this option has no effect for that input file because the compiler has already removed the unreferenced symbols.

/n

Forces a nonincremental build. Use /n to force a full build of the browse information file whether or not a .BSC file exists and to prevent .SBR files from being truncated. See "How BSCMAKE Builds a .BSC File" on page 410.

/NOLOGO

Suppresses the BSCMAKE copyright message.

/o *filename*

Specifies a name for the browse information file. By default, BSCMAKE assumes that the browse information file has the base name of the first .SBR file and a .BSC extension.

/S (*filename*...)

Tells BSCMAKE to process the specified include file the first time it is encountered and to exclude it otherwise. Use this option to save processing time when a file (such as a header, or .H, file for a .C or .CPP source file) is included in several source files but is unchanged by preprocessing directives each time. You may also want to use this option if a file is changed in ways that are unimportant for the browse information file you are creating. To specify multiple files, separate the names with spaces and enclose the list in parentheses. Parentheses are not necessary if you specify only one *filename*. If you want to exclude the file every time it is included, use the /Ei or /Es option.

/v

Provides verbose output, which includes the name of each .SBR file being processed and information about the complete BSCMAKE run.

/?

Displays a brief summary of BSCMAKE command-line syntax.

The following command line tells BSCMAKE to do a full build of MAIN.BSC from three .SBR files. It also tells BSCMAKE to exclude duplicate instances of TOOLBOX.H:

```
BSCMAKE /n /S toolbox.h /o main.bsc file1.sbr file2.sbr file3.sbr
```

BSCMAKE Exit Codes

BSCMAKE returns an exit code (also called return code or error code) to the operating system or the calling program. You can use the exit code to control the operation of batch files or makefiles.

Code	Meaning
0	No error
1	Command-line error
4	Fatal error during build

A P P E N D I X   F

DUMPBIN Reference

This appendix describes the Microsoft COFF Binary File Dumper (DUMPBIN.EXE), version 2.50. DUMPBIN displays information about 32-bit Common Object File Format (COFF) binary files. You can use DUMPBIN to examine COFF object files, standard libraries of COFF objects, executable files, and dynamic-link libraries (DLLs).

DUMPBIN is a 32-bit tool that runs only from a command prompt. Visual C++ does not provide controls for DUMPBIN.

This following topics are covered in this appendix:

- DUMPBIN command line
- DUMPBIN options

DUMPBIN Command Line

To run DUMPBIN, use the following syntax:

DUMPBIN [[*options*]] *files*...

Specify one or more binary files, along with any options required to control the information. DUMPBIN displays the information to standard output. You can either redirect it to a file or use the /OUT option to specify a filename for the output.

When you run DUMPBIN on a file without specifying an option, DUMPBIN displays the /SUMMARY output.

When you type the command dumpbin without any other command-line input, DUMPBIN displays a usage statement that summarizes its options.

DUMPBIN Options

An option consists of an option specifier, which is either a dash (−) or a forward slash (/), followed by the name of the option. Option names cannot be abbreviated. Some options take arguments, specified after a colon (:). No spaces or tabs are allowed within an option specification. Use one or more spaces or tabs to separate option specifications on the command line. Option names and their keyword or filename arguments are not case sensitive. Most options apply to all binary files; a few apply only to certain types of files.

DUMPBIN has the following options:

/ALL

Displays all available information except code disassembly. Use /DISASM to display disassembly. You can use /RAWDATA:NONE with /ALL to omit the raw binary details of the file.

/ARCHIVEMEMBERS

Displays minimal information about member objects in a library.

/DISASM

Displays disassembly of code sections, using symbols if present in the file.

/EXPORTS

Displays all definitions exported from an executable file or DLL.

/FPO

Displays Frame Pointer Optimization (FPO) records.

/HEADERS

Displays the file header and the header for each section. When used with a library, it displays the header for each member object.

/IMPORTS

Displays all definitions imported to an executable file or DLL.

/LINENUMBERS

Displays COFF line numbers. Line numbers exist in an object file if it was compiled with Program Database (/Zi), C7 Compatible (/Z7), or Line Numbers Only (/Zd). An executable file or DLL contains COFF line numbers if it was linked with Generate Debug Info (/DEBUG) and COFF Format (/DEBUGTYPE:COFF).

/LINKERMEMBER[[:{1|2}]]

Displays public symbols defined in a library. Specify the 1 argument to display symbols in object order, along with their offsets. Specify the 2 argument to display offsets and index numbers of objects, then list the symbols in alphabetical order along with the object index for each. To get both outputs, specify /LINKERMEMBER without the number argument.

/OUT:*filename*

Specifies a *filename* for the output. By default, DUMPBIN displays the information to standard output.

/RAWDATA[[:{BYTES|SHORTS|LONGS|NONE}[[,*number*]]]]

Displays the raw contents of each section in the file. The arguments control the format of the display, as follows:

Argument	Result
BYTES	The default. Contents are displayed in hexadecimal bytes, and also as ASCII if they have a printed representation.
SHORTS	Contents are displayed in hexadecimal words.
LONGS	Contents are displayed in hexadecimal longwords.
NONE	Raw data is suppressed. This is useful to control the output of /ALL.
number	Displayed lines are set to a width that holds *number* values per line.

/RELOCATIONS

Displays any relocations in the object or image.

/SECTION:*section*

Restricts the output to information on the specified *section*.

/SUMMARY

Displays minimal information about sections, including total size. This option is the default if no other option is specified.

/SYMBOLS

Displays the COFF symbol table. Symbol tables exist in all object files. A COFF symbol table appears in an image file only if it is linked with the Generate Debug Info and COFF Format options under Debug Info on the Debug category for the linker (or the /DEBUG and /DEBUGTYPE:COFF options on the command line).

A P P E N D I X   G

EDITBIN Reference

This appendix describes the Microsoft COFF Binary File Editor (EDITBIN.EXE), version 2.50. EDITBIN modifies 32-bit Common Object File Format (COFF) binary files. You can use EDITBIN to modify object files, executable files, and dynamic-link libraries (DLLs).

EDITBIN is a 32-bit tool that runs only from a command prompt. Visual C++ does not provide controls for EDITBIN.

EDITBIN converts the format of an Object Module Format (OMF) input file to COFF before making other changes to the file. You can use EDITBIN to convert the format of a file to COFF by running EDITBIN with no options.

The following topics are covered in this appendix:

- EDITBIN command line
- EDITBIN options

EDITBIN Command Line

To run EDITBIN, use the following syntax:

EDITBIN [[*options*]] *files*...

Specify one or more files for the objects or images to be changed, and one or more *options* for changing the files.

When you type the command editbin without any other command-line input, EDITBIN displays a usage statement that summarizes its options.

EDITBIN Options

An option consists of an option specifier, which is either a dash (−) or a forward slash (/), followed by the name of the option. Option names cannot be abbreviated. Some options take arguments, specified after a colon (:). No spaces or tabs are allowed within an option specification. Use one or more spaces or tabs to separate option specifications on the command line. Option names and their keyword or filename arguments are not case sensitive.

/BIND

This option sets the addresses of the entry points in the import address table for an executable file or DLL. Use this option to reduce load time of a program.

/BIND:[[PATH=*path*]]

Specify the program's executable file and DLLs in the *files* argument on the EDITBIN command line. The optional *path* argument to /BIND specifies the location of the DLLs used by the specified files. Separate multiple directories with semicolons (;). If *path* is not specified, EDITBIN searches the directories specified in the PATH environment variable. If *path* is specified, EDITBIN ignores the PATH variable.

By default, the NT loader sets the addresses of entry points when it loads a program. The amount of time this takes varies depending on the number of DLLs and the number of entry points referenced in the program. If a program has been modified with /BIND, and if the base addresses for the executable file and its DLLs do not conflict with DLLs that are already loaded, the operating system does not need to set these addresses. In a situation where the files are incorrectly based, the operating system will relocate the program's DLLs and recalculate the entry-point addresses; this adds to the program's load time.

/HEAP

This option sets the size of the heap in bytes.

/HEAP:*reserve*[[,*commit*]]

The *reserve* argument specifies the total heap allocation in virtual memory. The default heap size is 1MB. The linker rounds up the specified value to the nearest 4 bytes.

The optional *commit* argument is subject to interpretation by the operating system. In Windows NT, it specifies the amount of physical memory to allocate at a time. Committed virtual memory causes space to be reserved in the paging file. A higher *commit* value saves time when the application needs more heap space but increases the memory requirements and possibly startup time.

Specify the *reserve* and *commit* values in decimal or C-language notation.

/NOLOGO

This option suppresses display of the EDITBIN copyright message and version number.

/NOLOGO

/REBASE

This option sets the base addresses for the specified files. EDITBIN assigns new base addresses in a contiguous address space according to the size of each file rounded up to the nearest 64K. For details about base addresses, see "Base Address" on page 330 in Chapter 21.

/REBASE[[:*modifiers*]]

Specify the program's executable files and DLLs in the *files* argument on the EDITBIN command line in the order in which they are to be based. You can optionally specify one or more *modifiers*, each separated by a comma (,):

Modifier	Action
BASE=*address*	Provides a beginning address for reassigning base addresses to the files. Specify *address* in decimal or C-language notation. If BASE is not specified, the default starting base address is 0x400000. If DOWN is used, BASE must be specified, and *address* sets the end of the range of base addresses.
BASEFILE	Creates a file named COFFBASE.TXT, which is a text file in the format expected by LINK's /BASE option.
DOWN	Tells EDITBIN to reassign base addresses downward from an ending address. The files are reassigned in the order specified, with the first file located in the highest possible address below the end of the address range. BASE must be used with DOWN to ensure sufficient address space for basing the files. To determine the address space needed by the specified files, run EDITBIN with /REBASE on the files and add 64K to the displayed total size.

/RELEASE

This option sets the checksum in the header of an executable file.

/RELEASE

The operating system requires the checksum for certain files such as device drivers. It is recommended that you set the checksum for release versions of your programs to ensure compatibility with future operating systems.

/SECTION

This option changes the attributes of a section, overriding the attributes that were set when the object file for the section was compiled or linked.

/SECTION:*name*[[=*newname*]][[,*attributes*]][[,*alignment*]]

After the colon (:), specify the *name* of the section. To change the section name, follow *name* with an equal sign (=) and a *newname* for the section.

To set or change the section's *attributes*, specify a comma (,) followed by one or more attributes characters. To negate an attribute, precede its character with an exclamation point (!). The following characters specify memory attributes:

Attribute	Setting
c	code
d	discardable
e	executable
i	initialized data
k	cached virtual memory
m	link remove
o	link info
p	paged virtual memory
r	read
s	shared
u	uninitialized data
w	write

To control *alignment*, specify the character a followed by a character to set the size of alignment in bytes, as follows:

Character	Alignment size in bytes
1	1
2	2
4	4
8	8
p	16
t	32
s	64
x	no alignment

Specify the *attributes* and *alignment* characters as a string with no white space. The characters are not case sensitive.

/STACK

This option sets the size of the stack in bytes and takes arguments in decimal or C-language notation. The /STACK option applies only to an executable file.

/STACK:*reserve*[[,*commit*]]

The *reserve* argument specifies the total stack allocation in virtual memory. EDITBIN rounds up the specified value to the nearest 4 bytes.

The optional *commit* argument is subject to interpretation by the operating system. In Windows NT, *commit* specifies the amount of physical memory to allocate at a time. Committed virtual memory causes space to be reserved in the paging file. A higher *commit* value saves time when the application needs more stack space but increases the memory requirements and possibly startup time.

APPENDIX H

NMAKE Reference

The Microsoft Program Maintenance Utility (NMAKE.EXE), version 1.50, is a 32-bit tool that runs in Windows NT. This appendix discusses the following topics:

- Running NMAKE
- Contents of a makefile
- Description blocks
- Commands in a makefile
- Macros
- Inference rules
- Dot directives
- Makefile preprocessing

Running NMAKE

The syntax for NMAKE is:

NMAKE [[*option...*]] [[*macros...*]] [[*targets...*]] [[@*commandfile...*]]

NMAKE builds only specified *targets* or, if none is specified, the first target in the makefile. The first makefile target can be a pseudotarget that builds other targets. NMAKE uses makefiles specified with /F; if /F is not specified, it uses the MAKEFILE file in the current directory. If no makefile is specified, it uses inference rules to build command-line *targets*.

The *commandfile* text file contains command-line input. Other input can precede or follow @*commandfile*. A path is permitted. In *commandfile*, line breaks are treated as spaces. Enclose macro definitions in quotation marks if they contain spaces.

NMAKE Options

NMAKE options are described in the following table. Options are preceded by either a slash (/) or a dash (−) and are not case sensitive. Use **!CMDSWITCHES** to change option settings in a makefile or in TOOLS.INI.

Option	Action
/A	Forces build of all evaluated targets, even if not out-of-date with respect to dependents. Does not force build of unrelated targets.
/B	Forces build even if timestamps are equal. Recommended for very fast systems (resolution of two seconds or less).
/C	Suppresses default output, including nonfatal NMAKE errors or warnings, timestamps, and NMAKE copyright message. Suppresses warnings issued by /K.
/D	Displays timestamps of each evaluated target and dependent and a message when a target does not exist. Useful with /P for debugging a makefile. Use **!CMDSWITCHES** to set or clear /D for part of a makefile.
/E	Causes environment variables to override makefile macro definitions.
/F *filename*	Specifies *filename* as a makefile. Spaces or tabs can precede *filename*. Specify /F once for each makefile. To supply a makefile from standard input, specify − (dash) for *filename*; end keyboard input with either F6 or CTRL+Z.
/HELP, /?	Displays a brief summary of NMAKE command-line syntax.
/I	Ignores exit codes from all commands. To set or clear /I for part of a makefile, use **!CMDSWITCHES**. To ignore exit codes for part of a makefile, use a dash (−) command modifier or **.IGNORE**. Overrides /K if both are specified.
/K	Continues building unrelated dependencies, if a command returns an error; also issues a warning and returns an exit code of 1. By default, NMAKE halts if any command returns a nonzero exit code. Warnings from /K are suppressed by /C; /I overrides /K if both are specified.
/N	Displays but does not execute commands; preprocessing commands are executed. Does not display commands in recursive NMAKE calls. Useful for debugging makefiles and checking timestamps. To set or clear /N for part of a makefile, use **!CMDSWITCHES**.
/NOLOGO	Suppresses the NMAKE copyright message.
/P	Displays information (macro definitions, inference rules, targets, **.SUFFIXES** list) to standard output, then runs the build. If no makefile or command-line target exists, it displays information only. Use with /D to debug a makefile.
/Q	Checks timestamps of targets; does not run the build. Returns a zero exit code if all are up-to-date and a nonzero exit code if any target is not. Preprocessing commands are executed. Useful when running NMAKE from a batch file.

Option	Action
/R	Clears the **.SUFFIXES** list and ignores inference rules and macros that are defined in the TOOLS.INI file or that are predefined.
/S	Suppresses display of executed commands. To suppress display in part of a makefile, use @ command modifier or **.SILENT**. To set or clear /S for part of a makefile, use **!CMDSWITCHES**.
/T	Updates timestamps of command-line targets (or first makefile target) and executes preprocessing commands but does not run the build.
/X *filename*	Sends NMAKE error output to *filename* instead of standard error. Spaces or tabs can precede *filename*. To send error output to standard output, specify a dash (–) for *filename*. Does not affect output from commands to standard error.

TOOLS.INI and NMAKE

NMAKE reads TOOLS.INI before it reads makefiles, unless /R is used. It looks for TOOLS.INI first in the current directory and then in the directory specified by the INIT environment variable. The section for NMAKE settings in the initialization file begins with [NMAKE] and can contain any makefile information. Specify a comment on a separate line beginning with a semicolon (;) or a number sign (#).

Exit Codes from NMAKE

Code	Meaning
0	No error (possibly a warning)
1	Incomplete build (issued only when /K is used)
2	Program error, possibly due to one of the following:
	■ A syntax error in the makefile
	■ An error or exit code from a command
	■ An interruption by the user
4	System error—out of memory
255	Target is not up-to-date (issued only when /Q is used)

Contents of a Makefile

A makefile contains:

- Description blocks
- Commands
- Macros
- Inference rules
- Dot directives
- Preprocessing directives

Other features of a makefile include wildcards, long filenames, comments, and special characters.

Wildcards and NMAKE

NMAKE expands filename wildcards (* and ?) in dependency lines. A wildcard specified in a command is passed to the command; NMAKE does not expand it.

Long Filenames in a Makefile

Enclose long filenames in double quotation marks, as follows:

```
all : "VeryLongFileName.exe"
```

Comments in a Makefile

Precede a comment with a number sign (#). NMAKE ignores text from the number sign to the next newline character. The following are examples of comments:

```
# Comment on line by itself
OPTIONS = /MAP  # Comment on macro definition line

all.exe : one.obj two.obj  # Comment on dependency line
    link one.obj two.obj
# Comment in commands block
#   copy *.obj \objects  # Command turned into comment
    copy one.exe \release

.obj.exe:  # Comment on inference rule line
    link $<

my.exe : my.obj ; link my.obj  # Error: cannot comment this
 # Error: # must be the first character
.obj.exe: ; link $<  # Error: cannot comment this
```

To specify a literal number sign, precede it with a caret (^), as follows:

```
DEF = ^#define  #Macro representing a C preprocessing directive
```

Special Characters in a Makefile

To use an NMAKE special character as a literal character, place a caret (^) in front of it. NMAKE ignores carets that precede other characters. The special characters are:

```
:   ;   #   (   )   $   ^   \   {   }   !   @   —
```

A caret within a quoted string is treated as a literal caret character. A caret at the end of a line inserts a literal newline character in a string or macro.

In macros, a backslash followed by a newline character is replaced by a space.

In commands, a percent symbol (%) is a file specifier. To represent % literally in a command, specify a double percent sign (%%) in place of a single one. In other situations, NMAKE interprets a single % literally, but it always interprets a double %% as a single %. Therefore, to represent a literal %%, specify either three percent signs, %%%, or four percent signs, %%%%.

To use the dollar sign ($) as a literal character in a command, specify two dollar signs ($$); this method can also be used in other situations where ^$ also works.

Description Blocks

A description block is a dependency line optionally followed by a commands block:

```
targets... : dependents...
    commands...
```

A dependency line specifies one or more targets and zero or more dependents. A target must be at the start of the line. Separate targets from dependents by a colon (:); spaces or tabs are allowed. To split the line, use a backslash (\ ) after a target or dependent. If a target does not exist, has an earlier timestamp than a dependent, or is a pseudotarget, NMAKE executes the commands. If a dependent is a target elsewhere and does not exist or is out-of-date with respect to its own dependents, NMAKE updates the dependent before updating the current dependency.

Targets

In a dependency line, specify one or more targets, using any valid filename or pseudotarget. Separate multiple targets with one or more spaces or tabs. Targets are not case sensitive. Paths are permitted with filenames. A target cannot exceed 256 characters. If the target preceding the colon is a single character, use a separating space; otherwise, NMAKE interprets the letter-colon combination as a drive specifier.

Pseudotargets

A pseudotarget is a label used in place of a filename in a dependency line. It is interpreted as a file that does not exist and so is out-of-date. NMAKE assumes a pseudotarget's timestamp is the most recent of all its dependents; if it has no dependents, the current time is assumed. If a pseudotarget is used as a target, its commands are always executed. A pseudotarget used as a dependent must also appear as a target in another dependency; however, that dependency does not need to have a commands block.

Pseudotarget names follow the filename syntax rules for targets. However, if the name does not have an extension (that is, does not contain a period), it can exceed the 8-character limit for filenames and can be up to 256 characters long.

Multiple Targets

NMAKE evaluates multiple targets in a single dependency as if each were specified in a separate description block.

This...	...is evaluated as this
| ```
bounce.exe leap.exe : jump.obj
    echo Building...
``` | ```
bounce.exe : jump.obj
    echo Building...
leap.exe : jump.obj
    echo Building...
``` |

Cumulative Dependencies

Dependencies are cumulative in a description block if a target is repeated.

This...	...is evaluated as this
| ```
bounce.exe : jump.obj
bounce.exe : up.obj
    echo Building bounce.exe...
``` | ```
bounce.exe : jump.obj up.obj
    echo Building bounce.exe...
``` |

Multiple targets in multiple dependency lines in a single description block are evaluated as if each were specified in a separate description block, but targets that are not in the last dependency line do not use the commands block.

This...	...is evaluated as this
| ```
bounce.exe leap.exe : jump.obj
bounce.exe climb.exe : up.obj
    echo Building...
``` | ```
bounce.exe : jump.obj up.obj
    echo Building bounce.exe...
climb.exe : up.obj
    echo Building climb.exe...
leap.exe : jump.obj
# invokes an inference rule
``` |

Targets in Multiple Description Blocks

To update a target in more than one description block using different commands, specify two consecutive colons (::) between targets and dependents.

```
target.lib :: one.asm two.asm three.asm
    ml one.asm two.asm three.asm
    lib target one.obj two.obj three.obj
target.lib :: four.c five.c
    cl /c four.c five.c
    lib target four.obj five.obj
```

A Side Effect

If a target is specified with a colon (:) in two dependency lines in different locations, and if commands appear after only one of the lines, NMAKE interprets the dependencies as if adjacent or combined. It does not invoke an inference rule for the dependency that has no commands, but instead assumes that the dependencies belong to one description block and executes the commands specified with the other dependency.

This...	...is evaluated as this
| ```
bounce.exe : jump.obj
    echo Building bounce.exe...

bounce.exe : up.obj
``` | ```
bounce.exe : jump.obj up.obj
    echo Building bounce.exe...
``` |

This effect does not occur if **::** is used.

This...	...is evaluated as this
| ```
bounce.exe :: jump.obj
    echo Building bounce.exe...

bounce.exe :: up.obj
``` | ```
bounce.exe : jump.obj
    echo Building bounce.exe...

bounce.exe : up.obj
# invokes an inference rule
``` |

Dependents

In a dependency line, specify zero or more dependents after the **:** or **::**, using any valid filename or pseudotarget. Separate multiple dependents with one or more spaces or tabs. Dependents are not case sensitive. Paths are permitted with filenames.

Inferred Dependents

An inferred dependent is derived from an inference rule and is evaluated before explicit dependents. If an inferred dependent is out-of-date with respect to its target, NMAKE invokes the commands block for the dependency. If an inferred dependent does not exist or is out-of-date with respect to its own dependents, NMAKE first updates the inferred dependent. For more information, see "Inference Rules" on page 438.

Search Paths for Dependents

Each dependent has an optional search path, specified as follows:

{*directory*[[;*directory*...]]}*dependent*

NMAKE looks for a dependent first in the current directory, and then in directories in the order specified. A macro can specify part or all of a search path. Enclose directory names in braces ({ }); separate multiple directories with a semicolon (;). No spaces or tabs are allowed.

Commands in a Makefile

A description block or inference rule specifies a block of commands to run if the dependency is out-of-date. NMAKE displays each command before running it, unless /S, **.SILENT**, **!CMDSWITCHES**, or @ is used. NMAKE looks for a matching inference rule if a description block is not followed by a commands block.

A commands block contains one or more commands, each on its own line. No blank line can appear between the dependency or rule and the commands block. However, a line containing only spaces or tabs can appear; this line is interpreted as a null command, and no error occurs. Blank lines are permitted between command lines.

A command line begins with one or more spaces or tabs. A backslash (\) followed by a newline character is interpreted as a space in the command; use a backslash at the end of a line to continue a command onto the next line. NMAKE interprets the backslash literally if any other character, including a space or tab, follows the backslash.

A command preceded by a semicolon (;) can appear on a dependency line or inference rule, whether or not a commands block follows:

```
project.obj : project.c project.h ; cl /c project.c
```

Command Modifiers

You can specify one or more command modifiers preceding a command, optionally separated by spaces or tabs. As with commands, modifiers must be indented.

Modifier	Action
@command	Prevents display of the command. Display by commands is not suppressed. By default, NMAKE echoes all executed commands. Use /S to suppress display for the entire makefile; use **.SILENT** to suppress display for part of the makefile.
–[[number]]command	Turns off error checking for command. By default, NMAKE halts when a command returns a nonzero exit code. If –number is used, NMAKE stops if the exit code exceeds number. Spaces or tabs cannot appear between the dash and number; at least one space or tab must appear between number and command. Use /I to turn off error checking for the entire makefile; use **.IGNORE** to turn off error checking for part of the makefile.
!command	Executes command for each dependent file if command uses $** (all dependent files in the dependency) or $? (all dependent files in the dependency with a later timestamp than the target).

Filename-Parts Syntax

Filename-parts syntax in commands represents components of the first dependent filename (which may be an implied dependent). Filename components are the file's drive, path, base name, and extension as specified, not as it exists on disk. Use **%s** to represent the complete filename. Use **%|[[*parts*]]F** to represent parts of the filename, where *parts* can be zero or more of the following letters, in any order.

Letter	Description
No letter	Complete name
d	Drive
p	Path
f	File base name
e	File extension

Inline Files in a Makefile

An inline file contains text you specify in the makefile. Its name can be used in commands as input (for example, a LINK command file), or it can pass commands to the operating system. The file is created on disk when a command that creates the file is run.

Specifying an Inline File

The syntax for specifying an inline file in a command is:

    <<[[*filename*]]

Specify two angle brackets (<<) in the command where the filename is to appear. The angle brackets cannot be a macro expansion. When the command is run, the angle brackets are replaced by *filename*, if specified, or by a unique NMAKE-generated name. If specified, *filename* must follow angle brackets without a space or tab. A path is permitted. No extension is required or assumed. If *filename* is specified, the file is created in the current or specified directory, overwriting any existing file by that name; else, it is created in the TMP directory (or the current directory, if the TMP environment variable is not defined). If a previous *filename* is reused, NMAKE overwrites the previous file.

Creating Inline File Text

The syntax to create the content of an inline file is:

inlinetext
    .
    .
    .
<<[[**KEEP** | **NOKEEP**]]

Specify *inlinetext* on the first line after the command. Mark the end with double brackets at the beginning of a separate line. The file contains all *inlinetext* before the delimiting brackets. The *inlinetext* can have macro expansions and substitutions, but not directives or makefile comments. Spaces, tabs, and newline characters are treated literally.

Inline files are temporary or permanent. A temporary file exists for the duration of the session and can be reused by other commands. Specify **KEEP** after the closing angle brackets to retain the file after the NMAKE session; an unnamed file is preserved on disk with the generated filename. Specify **NOKEEP** or nothing for a temporary file. **KEEP** and **NOKEEP** are not case sensitive.

Reusing Inline Files

To reuse an inline file, specify <<*filename* where the file is defined and first used, then reuse *filename* without << later in the same or another command. The command to create the inline file must run before all commands that use the file.

Multiple Inline Files

A command can create more than one inline file. The syntax to do this is:

> *command* << <<
> *inlinetext*
> <<[[**KEEP** | **NOKEEP**]]
> *inlinetext*
> <<[[**KEEP** | **NOKEEP**]]

For each file, specify one or more lines of inline text followed by a closing line containing the delimiter. Begin the second file's text on the line following the delimiting line for the first file.

Macros and NMAKE

Macros replace a particular string in the makefile with another string. Using macros, you can create a makefile that can build different projects, specify options for commands, or set environment variables. You can define your own macros or use NMAKE's predefined macros.

Defining an NMAKE Macro

Use the following syntax to define a macro:

macroname=string

The *macroname* is a combination of letters, digits, and underscores (_) up to 1024 characters, and is case sensitive. The *macroname* can contain an invoked macro. If *macroname* consists entirely of an invoked macro, the macro being invoked cannot be null or undefined.

The *string* can be any sequence of zero or more characters. A null string contains zero characters or only spaces or tabs. The *string* can contain a macro invocation.

Special Characters in Macros

A number sign (#) after a definition specifies a comment. To specify a literal number sign in a macro, use a caret (^), as in ^#.

A dollar sign ($) specifies a macro invocation. To specify a literal $, use $$.

To extend a definition to a new line, end the line with a backslash (\ ). When the macro is invoked, the backslash plus newline character is replaced with a space. To specify a literal backslash at the end of the line, precede it with a caret (^), or follow it with a comment specifier (#).

To specify a literal newline character, end the line with a caret (^), as in:

```
CMDS = cls^
dir
```

Null and Undefined Macros

Both null and undefined macros expand to null strings, but a macro defined as a null string is considered defined in preprocessing expressions. To define a macro as a null string, specify no characters except spaces or tabs after the equal sign (=) in a command line or command file, enclosed the null string or definition in double quotation marks (" "). To undefine a macro, use **!UNDEF.**

Where to Define Macros

Define macros in a command line, command file, makefile, or TOOLS.INI.

In a makefile or TOOLS.INI, each macro definition must appear on a separate line and cannot start with a space or tab. Spaces or tabs around the equal sign are ignored. All *string* characters are literal, including surrounding quotation marks and embedded spaces.

In a command line or command file, spaces and tabs delimit arguments and cannot surround the equal sign. If *string* has embedded spaces or tabs, enclose either the string itself or the entire macro in double quotation marks (" ").

Precedence in Macro Definitions

If a macro is multiply defined, NMAKE uses the highest-precedence definition:

1. A macro defined on the command line
2. A macro defined in a makefile or include file
3. An inherited environment-variable macro
4. A macro defined in the TOOLS.INI file
5. A predefined macro, such as **CC** and **AS**

Use /E to cause macros inherited from environment variables to override makefile macros with the same name. Use **!UNDEF** to override a command line.

Using an NMAKE Macro

To use a macro, enclose its name in parentheses preceded by a dollar sign (**$**):

$(*macroname***)**

No spaces are allowed. The parentheses are optional if *macroname* is a single character. The definition string replaces **$(***macroname***)**; an undefined macro is replaced by a null string.

Macro Substitution

To substitute text within a macro, use the following syntax:

$(*macroname***:***string1***=***string2***)**

When *macroname* is invoked, each occurrence of *string1* in its definition string is replaced by *string2*. Macro substitution is case sensitive and is literal; *string1* and *string2* cannot invoke macros. Substitution does not modify the original definition. You can substitute text in any predefined macro except **$$@**.

No spaces or tabs precede the colon; any after the colon are interpreted as literal. If *string2* is null, all occurrences of *string1* are deleted from the macro's definition string.

Special NMAKE Macros

NMAKE provides several special macros to represent various filenames and commands. One use for some of these macros is in the predefined inference rules. Like all macros, the macros provided by NMAKE are case sensitive.

- Filename macros
- Recursion macros
- Command macros and options macros
- Environment-variable macros

Filename Macros

Filename macros are predefined as filenames specified in the dependency (not full filename specifications on disk). These macros do not need to be enclosed in parentheses when invoked; specify only a $ as shown.

Macro	Meaning
$@	Current target's full name (path, base name, extension), as currently specified.
$$@	Current target's full name (path, base name, extension), as currently specified. Valid only as a dependent in a dependency.
$*	Current target's path and base name minus file extension.
$**	All dependents of the current target.
$?	All dependents with a later timestamp than the current target.
$<	Dependent file with a later timestamp than the current target. Valid only in commands in inference rules.

To specify part of a predefined filename macro, append a macro modifier and enclose the modified macro in parentheses.

Modifier	Resulting filename part
D	Drive plus directory
B	Base name
F	Base name plus extension
R	Drive plus directory plus base name

Recursion Macros

Use recursion macros to call NMAKE recursively. Recursive sessions inherit command-line and environment-variable macros and TOOLS.INI information. They do not inherit makefile-defined inference rules or **.SUFFIXES** and **.PRECIOUS** specifications. To pass macros to a recursive NMAKE session, either set an environment variable with SET before the recursive call, or define a macro in the command for the recursive call, or define a macro in TOOLS.INI.

Macro	Definition
MAKE	Command used originally to invoke NMAKE.
MAKEDIR	Current directory when NMAKE was invoked.
MAKEFLAGS	Options currently in effect. Use as /$(MAKEFLAGS).

Command Macros, Options Macros

Command macros are predefined for Microsoft products. Options macros represent options to these products and are undefined by default. Both are used in predefined inference rules and can be used in description blocks or user-defined inference rules. Command macros can be redefined to represent part or all of a command line, including options. Options macros generate a null string if left undefined.

Microsoft product	Command macro	Defined as	Options macro
Macro Assembler	AS	ml	AFLAGS
Basic Compiler	BC	bc	BFLAGS
C Compiler	CC	cl	CFLAGS
COBOL Compiler	COBOL	cobol	COBFLAGS
C++ Compiler	CPP	cl	CPPFLAGS
C++ Compiler	CXX	cl	CXXFLAGS
FORTRAN Compiler	FOR	fl	FFLAGS
Pascal Compiler	PASCAL	pl	PFLAGS
Resource Compiler	RC	rc	RFLAGS

Environment-Variable Macros

NMAKE inherits macro definitions for environment variables that exist before the start of the session. If a variable was set in the operating-system environment, it is available as an NMAKE macro. The inherited names are converted to uppercase. Inheritance occurs before preprocessing. Use /E to cause macros inherited from environment variables to override any macros with the same name in the makefile.

Environment-variable macros can be redefined in the session, but this does not change the corresponding environment variable; to change the variable, use a SET command. Using the SET command to change an environment variable in a session does not change the corresponding macro.

If an environment variable is defined as a string that would be syntactically incorrect in a makefile, no macro is created and no warning is generated. If a variable's value contains a dollar sign ($), NMAKE interprets it as the beginning of a macro invocation; using the macro can cause unexpected behavior.

Inference Rules

Inference rules supply commands to update targets and to infer dependents for targets. Extensions in an inference rule match a single target and dependent that have the same base name. Inference rules are user-defined or predefined; predefined rules can be redefined.

If an out-of-date dependency has no commands and if **.SUFFIXES** contains the dependent's extension, NMAKE uses a rule whose extensions match the target and an existing file in the current or specified directory. If more than one rule matches existing files, the **.SUFFIXES** list determines which to use; list priority descends from left to right. If a dependent file doesn't exist and is not listed as a target in another description block, an inference rule can create the missing dependent from another file with the same base name. If a description block's target has no dependents or commands, an inference rule can update the target. Inference rules can build a command-line target even if no description block exists. NMAKE may invoke a rule for an inferred dependent even if an explicit dependent is specified.

Defining a Rule

To define an inference rule, use the following syntax:

.fromext.toext:
    commands

The *fromext* represents the extension of a dependent file, and *toext* represents the extension of a target file. Extensions are not case sensitive. Macros can be invoked to represent *fromext* and *toext*; the macros are expanded during preprocessing. The period (**.**) preceding *fromext* must appear at the beginning of the line. The colon (**:**) is preceded by zero or more spaces or tabs; it can be followed only by spaces or tabs, a semicolon (**;**) to specify a command, a number sign (**#**) to specify a comment, or a newline character. No other spaces are allowed. Commands are specified as in description blocks.

Search Paths in Rules

An inference rule that specifies paths has the following syntax:

{*frompath*}.*fromext*{*topath*}.*toext*:
    commands

An inference rule applies to a dependency only if paths specified in the dependency exactly match the inference-rule paths. Specify the dependent's directory in *frompath* and the target's directory in *topath*; no spaces are allowed. Specify only one path for each extension. A path on one extension requires a path on the other. To specify the current directory, use either a period (**.**) or empty braces (**{ }**). Macros can represent *frompath* and *topath*; they are invoked during preprocessing.

Predefined Rules

Predefined inference rules use NMAKE-supplied command and option macros.

Rule	Command	Default action
.asm.exe	$(AS) $(AFLAGS) $*.asm	ml $*.asm
.asm.obj	$(AS) $(AFLAGS) /c $*.asm	ml /c $*.asm
.c.exe	$(CC) $(CFLAGS) $*.c	cl $*.c
.c.obj	$(CC) $(CFLAGS) /c $*.c	cl /c $*.c
.cpp.exe	$(CPP) $(CPPFLAGS) $*.cpp	cl $*.cpp
.cpp.obj	$(CPP) $(CPPFLAGS) /c $*.cpp	cl /c $*.cpp
.cxx.exe	$(CXX) $(CXXFLAGS) $*.cxx	cl $*.cxx
.cxx.obj	$(CXX) $(CXXFLAGS) /c $*.cxx	cl /c $*.cxx
.bas.obj	$(BC) $(BFLAGS) $*.bas;	bc $*.bas;
.cbl.exe	$(COBOL) $(COBFLAGS) $*.cbl, $*.exe;	cobol $*.cbl, $*.exe;
.cbl.obj	$(COBOL) $(COBFLAGS) $*.cbl;	cobol $*.cbl;
.for.exe	$(FOR) $(FFLAGS) $*.for	fl $*.for
.for.obj	$(FOR) /c $(FFLAGS) $*.for	fl /c $*.for
.pas.exe	$(PASCAL) $(PFLAGS) $*.pas	pl $*.pas
.pas.obj	$(PASCAL) /c $(PFLAGS) $*.pas	pl /c $*.pas
.rc.res	$(RC) $(RFLAGS) /r $*	rc /r $*

Inferred Dependents and Rules

NMAKE assumes an inferred dependent for a target if an applicable inference rule exists. A rule applies if:

- *toext* matches the target's extension.
- *fromext* matches the extension of a file that has the target's base name and that exists in the current or specified directory.
- *fromext* is in **.SUFFIXES**; no other *fromext* in a matching rule has a higher **.SUFFIXES** priority.
- No explicit dependent has a higher **.SUFFIXES** priority.

Inferred dependents can cause unexpected side effects. If the target's description block contains commands, NMAKE executes those commands and not the commands in the rule.

Precedence in Inference Rules

If an inference rule is multiply defined, the highest-precedence rule applies:

1. An inference rule defined in a makefile; later definitions have precedence.
2. An inference rule defined in TOOLS.INI; later definitions have precedence.
3. A predefined inference rule.

Dot Directives

Specify dot directives outside a description block, at the start of a line. Dot directives begin with a period (**.**) and are followed by a colon (**:**). Spaces and tabs are allowed. Dot directive names are case sensitive and are uppercase.

Directive	Action
.IGNORE :	Ignores nonzero exit codes returned by commands, from the place it is specified to the end of the makefile. By default, NMAKE halts if a command returns a nonzero exit code. To restore error checking, use **!CMDSWITCHES**. To ignore the exit code for a single command, use the dash modifier. To ignore exit codes for an entire file, use /I.
.PRECIOUS : *targets*	Preserves *targets* on disk if the commands to update them are halted; has no effect if a command handles an interrupt by deleting the file. Separate the target names with one or more spaces or tabs. By default, NMAKE deletes a target if a build is interrupted by CTRL+C or CTRL+BREAK. Each use of **.PRECIOUS** applies to the entire makefile; multiple specifications are cumulative.
.SILENT :	Suppresses display of executed commands, from the place it is specified to the end of the makefile. By default, NMAKE displays the commands it invokes. To restore echoing, use **!CMDSWITCHES**. To suppress echoing of a single command, use the @ modifier. To suppress echoing for an entire file, use /S.
.SUFFIXES : *list*	Lists extensions for inference-rule matching; predefined as: .exe .obj .asm .c .cpp .cxx .bas .cbl .for .pas .res .rc

To change the **.SUFFIXES** list order or to specify a new list, clear the list and specify a new setting. To clear the list, specify no extensions after the colon:

```
.SUFFIXES :
```

To add additional suffixes to the end of the list, specify

```
.SUFFIXES : suffixlist
```

where *suffixlist* is a list of the additional suffixes, separated by one or more spaces or tabs. To see the current setting of **.SUFFIXES**, run NMAKE with /P.

Makefile Preprocessing

You can control the NMAKE session by using preprocessing directives and expressions. Preprocessing instructions can be placed in the makefile or in TOOLS.INI. Using directives, you can conditionally process your makefile, display error messages, include other makefiles, undefine a macro, and turn certain options on or off.

Makefile Preprocessing Directives

Preprocessing directives are not case sensitive. The initial exclamation point (**!**) must appear at the beginning of the line. Zero or more spaces or tabs can appear after the exclamation point, for indentation.

!CMDSWITCHES {+| –}*option...*
Turns each *option* listed on or off. Spaces or tabs must appear before the + or – operator; none can appear between the operator and the option letters. Letters are not case sensitive and are specified without a slash (**/**). To turn some options on and others off, use separate specifications of **!CMDSWITCHES**.

Only D, I, N, and S can be used in a makefile. In TOOLS.INI, all options are allowed except F, HELP, NOLOGO, X, and ?. Changes specified in a description block do not take effect until the next description block. This directive updates **MAKEFLAGS**; changes are inherited during recursion if **MAKEFLAGS** is specified.

!ERROR *text*
Displays *text* in error U1050, then halts NMAKE, even if /K, /I, **.IGNORE**, **!CMDSWITCHES**, or the dash (–) command modifier is used. Spaces or tabs before *text* are ignored.

!MESSAGE *text*
Displays *text* to standard output. Spaces or tabs before *text* are ignored.

!INCLUDE [[<]]*filename*[[>]]
Reads *filename* as a makefile, then continues with the current makefile. NMAKE searches for *filename* first in the specified or current directory, then recursively through directories of any parent makefiles, then, if *filename* is enclosed by angle brackets (< >), in directories specified by the **INCLUDE** macro, which is initially set to the INCLUDE environment variable. Useful to pass **.SUFFIXES** settings, **.PRECIOUS**, and inference rules to recursive makefiles.

!IF *constantexpression*
Processes statements between **!IF** and the next **!ELSE** or **!ENDIF** if *constantexpression* evaluates to a nonzero value.

!IFDEF *macroname*
Processes statements between **!IFDEF** and the next **!ELSE** or **!ENDIF** if *macroname* is defined. A null macro is considered to be defined.

!IFNDEF *macroname*

Processes statements between **!IFNDEF** and the next **!ELSE** or **!ENDIF** if *macroname* is not defined.

!ELSE[[IF *constantexpression*| **IFDEF** *macroname*|**IFNDEF** *macroname*]]

Processes statements between **!ELSE** and the next **!ENDIF** if the prior **!IF**, **!IFDEF**, or **!IFNDEF** statement evaluated to zero. The optional keywords give further control of preprocessing.

!ELSEIF

Synonym for **!ELSE IF**.

!ELSEIFDEF

Synonym for **!ELSE IFDEF**.

!ELSEIFNDEF

Synonym for **!ELSE IFNDEF**.

!ENDIF

Marks the end of an **!IF**, **!IFDEF**, or **!IFNDEF** block. Any text after **!ENDIF** on the same line is ignored.

!UNDEF *macroname*

Undefines *macroname*.

Expressions in Makefile Preprocessing

The **!IF** or **!ELSE IF** *constantexpression* consists of integer constants (in decimal or C-language notation), string constants, or commands. Use parentheses to group expressions. Expressions use C-style signed long integer arithmetic; numbers are in 32-bit two's-complement form in the range -2147483648 to 2147483647.

Expressions can use operators that act on constant values, exit codes from commands, strings, macros, and file-system paths.

Makefile Preprocessing Operators

The **DEFINED** operator is a logical operator that acts on a macro name. The expression **DEFINED** (*macroname*) is true if *macroname* is defined. **DEFINED** in combination with **!IF** or **!ELSE IF** is equivalent to **!IFDEF** or **!ELSE IFDEF**. However, unlike these directives, **DEFINED** can be used in complex expressions using binary logical operators.

The **EXIST** operator is a logical operator that acts on a file-system path. **EXIST** (*path*) is true if *path* exists. The result from **EXIST** can be used in binary expressions. If *path* contains spaces, enclose it in double quotation marks.

Integer constants can use the unary operators for numerical negation ($-$), one's complement ($\sim$), and logical negation (**!**).

Constant expressions can use the following binary operators:

Operator	Description	Operator	Description
+	Addition	||	Logical OR
–	Subtraction	<<	Left shift
*	Multiplication	>>	Right shift
/	Division	==	Equality
%	Modulus	!=	Inequality
&	Bitwise AND	<	Less than
|	Bitwise OR	>	Greater than
^	Bitwise XOR	<=	Less than or equal to
&&	Logical AND	>=	Greater than or equal to

To compare two strings, use the equality (==) operator and the inequality (!=) operator. Enclose strings in double quotation marks.

Executing a Program in Preprocessing

To use a command's exit code during preprocessing, specify the command, with any arguments, within brackets ([ ]). Any macros are expanded before the command is executed. NMAKE replaces the command specification with the command's exit code, which can be used in an expression to control preprocessing.

A P P E N D I X   I

Resource Compiler

This appendix describes the preprocessing directives and statements that make up a resource-definition (script) file and how to use RC.EXE (a command-line tool) to compile your application's resources and add them to an application's executable file.

You need to read this appendix only if you need information on the internal structure of scripts.

If you use the Microsoft Foundation Class Library when you begin a project, the Visual C++ resource editors and the Visual C++ development environment offer easy, time-saving alternatives to the traditional hand-coded scripts. These new visual tools create and manage your project's script—you no longer need to hand-code scripts. For more information on the Visual C++ resource editors, see Chapters 4 through 11.

The following topics are covered in this appendix:

- Including resources in an application
- Creating a resource definition file
- The RC command line

Including Resources in an Application

▶ **To include resources in your application**

1. Use the Visual C++ resource editors to create individual resources for cursors, icons, bitmaps, menus, and dialog boxes. See Chapters 4 through 11 for more information on how to do this.

2. Create a resource-definition file (also called a script) that describes all resources used by the application. Unless your project uses the Microsoft Foundation Class Library, you'll have to use a text editor to hand-code the script.

3. Compile the script into a resource (.RES) file with RC.EXE (RC).

4. Link the compiled resource files into the application's executable file.

You do not use RC to include compiled resources into the executable file or to mark the file as an application for Windows. The linker recognizes the compiled resource files and links them to the executable file.

Creating a Resource-Definition File

After creating individual resource files for your application's icon, cursor, font, bitmap, and dialog-box resources, you create a resource-definition file, or script. A script is a text file with the extension .RC.

The script lists every resource in your application and describes some types of resources in great detail. For a resource that exists in a separate file, such as an icon or cursor, the script names the resource and the file that contains it. For some resources, such as a menu, the entire definition of the resource exists within the script.

A script file can contain the following information:

- Preprocessing directives, which instruct RC to perform actions on the script before compiling. Directives can also assign values to names.
- Statements, which name and describe resources.

Preprocessing Directives

The directives listed in the following table can be used in the script to instruct RC to perform actions or assign values to names. The syntax and semantics for the RC preprocessor are the same as for the C compiler.

Directive	Description
#define	Defines a specified name by assigning it a given value.
#elif	Marks an optional clause of a conditional-compilation block.
#else	Marks the last optional clause of a conditional-compilation block.
#endif	Marks the end of a conditional-compilation block.
#if	Conditionally compiles the script if a specified expression is true.
#ifdef	Conditionally compiles the script if a specified name is defined.
#ifndef	Conditionally compiles the script if a specified name is not defined.
#include	Copies the contents of a file into the resource-definition file.
#undef	Removes the definition of the specified name.

Single-Line Statements

A single-line statement can begin with any of the following keywords:

Keyword	Description
BITMAP	Defines a bitmap by naming it and specifying the name of the file that contains it. (To use a particular bitmap, the application requests it by name.)
CURSOR	Defines a cursor by naming it and specifying the name of the file that contains it. (To use a particular cursor, the application requests it by name.)
FONT	Specifies the name of a file that contains a font.
ICON	Defines an icon by naming it and specifying the name of the file that contains it. (To use a particular icon, the application requests it by name.)
LANGUAGE	Sets the language for all resources up to the next **LANGUAGE** statement or to the end of the file. When the **LANGUAGE** statement appears before the **BEGIN** in an **ACCELERATORS**, **DIALOG**, **MENU**, **RCDATA**, or **STRINGTABLE** resource definition, the specified language applies only to that resource.
MESSAGETABLE	Defines a message table by naming it and specifying the name of the file that contains it. The file is a binary resource file generated by the Message Compiler (MC). (The Message Compiler is documented in Help.)

Multiline Statements

A multiline statement can begin with any of the following keywords:

Keyword	Description
ACCELERATORS	Defines menu accelerator keys.
DIALOG	Defines a template that an application can use to create dialog boxes.
MENU	Defines the appearance and function of a menu.
RCDATA	Defines data resources. Data resources let you include binary data in the executable file.
STRINGTABLE	Defines string resources. String resources are Unicode strings that can be loaded from the executable file.

Each of these multiline statements allows you to specify zero or more optional statements before the **BEGIN ... END** block that defines the resource. You can specify the following statements:

Statement	Description
CHARACTERISTICS *dword*	User-defined information about the resource that can be used by tools that read and write resource files. The value appears in the compiled resource file; it is not stored in the executable file and is not used by Windows.
LANGUAGE *language, sublanguage*	Specifies the language for the resource. The arguments are constants from WINNLS.H.
VERSION *dword*	User-defined version number for the resource that can be used by tools that read and write resource files. The value appears in the compiled resource file; it is not stored in the executable file and is not used by Windows.

Sample Script File

The following example shows a script file that defines the resources for an application named Shapes:

```
#include "SHAPES.H"

ShapesCursor   CURSOR   SHAPES.CUR
ShapesIcon     ICON     SHAPES.ICO

ShapesMenu     MENU
    BEGIN
        POPUP "&Shape"
            BEGIN
                MENUITEM "&Clear", ID_CLEAR
                MENUITEM "&Rectangle", ID_RECT
                MENUITEM "&Triangle", ID_TRIANGLE
                MENUITEM "&Star", ID_STAR
                MENUITEM "&Ellipse", ID_ELLIPSE
            END
    END
```

The **CURSOR** statement names the application's cursor resource ShapesCursor and specifies the cursor file SHAPES.CUR, which contains the image for that cursor.

The **ICON** statement names the application's icon resource ShapesIcon and specifies the icon file SHAPES.ICO, which contains the image for that icon.

The **MENU** statement defines an application menu named ShapesMenu, a pop-up menu with five menu items.

The menu definition, enclosed by the **BEGIN** and **END** keywords, specifies each menu item and the menu identifier that is returned when the user selects that item. For example, the first item on the menu, Clear, returns the menu identifier ID_CLEAR when the user selects it. The menu identifiers are defined in the application header file, SHAPES.H.

RC Command Line

To start RC, use the following command-line syntax:

RC [[*options*]] *script-file*

The *options* argument can include one or more of the following options:

/?

Displays a list of RC command-line options.

/d

Defines a symbol for the preprocessor that you can test with the **#ifdef** directive.

/fo *resname*

Uses *resname* for the name of the .RES file.

/h

Displays a list of RC command-line options.

/i *directory*

Causes RC to search the specified directory before searching the directories specified by the INCLUDE environment variable.

/r

Ignored. Provided for compatibility with existing makefiles.

/v

Causes a display of messages that report on the progress of the compiler.

/x

Prevents RC from checking the INCLUDE environment variable when searching for header files or resource files.

Options are not case sensitive, and a dash (−) can be used in place of a forward slash (/). You can combine single-letter options if they do not require additional arguments. For example, the following commands are equivalent:

```
RC /V /X SAMPLE.RC
rc -vx sample.rc
```

The *script-file* argument specifies the name of the resource-definition script that contains the names, types, filenames, and descriptions of the resources to be compiled.

Defining Names for the Preprocessor

You can use the /d option to specify conditional compilation in a script, based on whether a name is defined on the RC command line. You can also use the **#define** directive to specify conditional compilation in the file or an include file.

For example, suppose your application has a pop-up menu, the Debug menu, that should appear only with debugging versions of the application. When you compile the application for normal use, the Debug menu is not included. The following example shows the statements that can be added to the resource-definition file to define the Debug menu:

```
MainMenu MENU
BEGIN
    . . .
#ifdef DEBUG
        POPUP "&Debug"
        BEGIN
                MENUITEM "&Memory usage", ID_MEMORY
                MENUITEM "&Walk data heap", ID_WALK_HEAP
        END
#endif
END
```

When compiling resources for a debugging version of the application, you could include the Debug menu by using the following RC command:

```
rc -d DEBUG myapp.rc
```

To compile resources for a normal version of the application—one that does not include the Debug menu—you could use the following RC command:

```
rc myapp.rc
```

Naming the Compiled Resource File

By default, when compiling resources, RC names the compiled resource (.RES) file with the base name of the .RC file and places it in the same directory as the .RC file. The following example compiles MYAPP.RC and creates a compiled resource file named MYAPP.RES in the same directory as MYAPP.RC:

```
rc myapp.rc
```

The /fo option lets you give the resulting .RES file a name that differs from the name of the corresponding .RC file. For example, to name the resulting .RES file NEWFILE.RES, you would use the following command:

```
rc -fo newfile.res myapp.rc
```

The /fo option can also place the .RES file in a different directory. For example, the following command places the compiled resource file MYAPP.RES in the directory C:\SOURCE\RESOURCE:

```
rc -fo c:\source\resource\myapp.res myapp.rc
```

Searching for Files

By default, RC searches for header files and resource files (such as icon and cursor files) first in the current directory and then in the directories specified by the INCLUDE environment variable. (The PATH environment variable has no effect on which directories RC searches.)

Adding a Directory to Search

You can use the /i option to add a directory to the list of directories RC searches. The compiler then searches the directories in the following order:

1. The current directory
2. The directory or directories you specify by using the /i option, in the order in which they appear on the RC command line
3. The list of directories specified by the INCLUDE environment variable, in the order in which the variable lists them, unless you specify the /x option

The following example compiles the resource-definition file MYAPP.RC:

```
rc /i c:\source\stuff /i d:\resources myapp.rc
```

When compiling the script MYAPP.RC, RC searches for header files and resource files first in the current directory, then in C:\SOURCE\STUFF and D:\RESOURCES, and then in the directories specified by the INCLUDE environment variable.

Suppressing the INCLUDE Environment Variable

You can prevent RC from using the INCLUDE environment variable when determining the directories to search. To do so, use the /x option. The compiler then searches for files only in the current directory and in any directories you specify by using the /i option.

The following example compiles the script file MYAPP.RC:

```
rc /x /i c:\source\stuff myapp.rc
```

When compiling the script MYAPP.RC, RC searches for header files and resource files first in the current directory and then in C:\SOURCE\STUFF. It does not search the directories specified by the INCLUDE environment variable.

Displaying Progress Messages

You can use the /v option to specify that RC is to display progress messages. The following example causes RC to display progress messages as it compiles the resource-definition script SAMPLE.RC and creates the compiled resource file SAMPLE.RES:

```
rc /v sample.rc
```

Common Statement Arguments

The following sections list arguments in common among the resource or control statements. Occasionally, a certain statement will use an argument differently, or may ignore an argument.

- Common control arguments
- Common resource attributes
- Memory attributes

Common Control Arguments

The syntax for a control definition is as follows:

control [[*text*,]] *id*, *x*, *y*, *width*, *height* [[, *style* [[, *extended-style*]]]]

Horizontal dialog units are 1/4 of the dialog base width unit. Vertical units are 1/8 of the dialog base height unit. The current dialog base units are computed from the height and width of the current system font. The **GetDialogBaseUnits** function returns the dialog base units in pixels. The coordinates are relative to the origin of the dialog box.

The arguments are as follows:

control
> Specifies the keyword that indicates the type of control being defined, such as **PUSHBUTTON** or **CHECKBOX**.

text
> Specifies text that is displayed with the control. The text is positioned within the control's specified dimensions, or adjacent to the control.

> The *text* argument must contain zero or more characters enclosed in double quotation marks. Strings are automatically null-terminated and converted to Unicode in the resulting resource file, except for strings specified in *raw-data*

statements (*raw-data* can be specified in **RCDATA** and user-defined resources). To specify a Unicode string in *raw-data,* explicitly qualify the string as a wide-character string by using the **L** prefix.

By default, the characters listed between the double quotation marks are ANSI characters and escape sequences are interpreted as byte escape sequences. If the string is preceded by the **L** prefix, the string is a wide-character string and escape sequences are interpreted as two-byte escape sequences that specify Unicode characters. If a double quotation mark is required in the text, you must include the double quotation mark twice or use the \" escape sequence.

An ampersand (&) character in the text indicates that the following character is used as a mnemonic character for the control. When the control is displayed, the ampersand is not shown, but the mnemonic character is underlined. The user can choose the control by pressing the key corresponding to the underlined mnemonic character. To use the ampersand as a character in a string, insert two ampersands (&&).

id

Specifies the control identifier. This value must be a 16-bit unsigned integer in the range 0 to 65,535 or a simple arithmetic expression that evaluates to a value in that range.

x

Specifies the x-coordinate of the left side of the control relative to the left side of the dialog box. This value must be a 16-bit unsigned integer in the range 0 to 65,535. The coordinate is in dialog units and is relative to the origin of the dialog box, window, or control containing the specified control.

y

Specifies the y-coordinate of the top side of the control relative to the top of the dialog box. This value must be a 16-bit unsigned integer in the range 0 to 65,535. The coordinate is in dialog units relative to the origin of the dialog box, window, or control containing the specified control.

width

Specifies the width of the control. This value must be a 16-bit unsigned integer in the range 1 to 65,535. The width is in 1/4-character units.

height

Specifies the height of the control. This value must be a 16-bit unsigned integer in the range 1 to 65,535. The height is in 1/8-character units.

style

Specifies the control styles. Use the bitwise OR (|) operator to combine styles.

extended-style

Specifies extended (WS_EX_*xxx*) styles. You must specify a *style* to specify an *extended-style.*

Common Resource Attributes

All resource-definition statements include a *load-mem* option that specifies the loading and memory characteristics of the resource. These options include load attributes and memory attributes. The only attribute used by Win32 is the **DISCARDABLE** attribute. The remaining attribute specifiers are allowed in the script for compatibility with existing scripts, but are ignored.

Load Attributes

The load attributes specify when the resource is to be loaded. The load argument must be one of the following:

- **PRELOAD**

  Ignored. In 16-bit Windows, the resource is loaded with the executable file.

- **LOADONCALL**

  Ignored. In 16-bit Windows, the resource is loaded when called.

Memory Attributes

The memory attributes specify whether the resource is fixed or movable, whether it is discardable, and whether it is pure. The memory argument can be one or more of the following:

- **FIXED**

  Ignored. In 16-bit Windows, the resource remains at a fixed memory location.

- **MOVEABLE**

  Ignored. In 16-bit Windows, the resource can be moved if necessary in order to compact memory.

- **DISCARDABLE**

  Resource can be discarded if no longer needed.

- **PURE**

  Ignored. Accepted for compatibility with existing resource scripts.

- **IMPURE**

  Ignored. Accepted for compatibility with existing resource scripts.

The default is **DISCARDABLE** for cursor, icon, and font resources.

APPENDIX J

Decorated Names

This appendix discusses compiler-generated decorated names for functions in C and C++ programs. A decorated name is sometimes required when you specify a function name to LINK or other tools. For details about the situations that require decorated names, consult the documentation for the tool you are using.

This appendix discusses the following topics:

- Using Decorated Names
- Viewing Decorated Names

Using Decorated Names

Functions in C and C++ programs are known internally by their decorated names. A decorated name is a string created by the compiler during compilation of the function definition or prototype.

In most circumstances, you do not need to know the decorated name of a function. LINK and other tools can usually handle the name in its undecorated form.

However, certain situations require that you specify the name in its decorated form. You must specify the decorated name of C++ functions that are overloaded and special member functions such as constructor and destructor functions in order for LINK and other tools to be able to match the name. You must also use decorated names in assembly source files that reference a C or C++ function name.

Warning If you change the function name, class, calling convention, any parameter, or the return type, the old decorated name is no longer valid. You must get the new version of the function name and use it everywhere the decorated name is specified.

Format of a C++ Decorated Name

A decorated name for a C++ function contains the following information:

- The function name.
- The class that the function is a member of, if it is a member function. This may include the class that encloses the function's class, and so on.
- The types of the function's parameters.
- The calling convention.
- The return type of the function.

The function and class names are expressed literally in the string. The rest of the string is a code that has internal meaning only for the compiler and linker. The following are examples of undecorated and decorated C++ names:

Undecorated Name	Decorated Name
`int a(char){int i=3;return i;};`	`?a@@YAHD@Z`
`void __stdcall b::c(float){};`	`?c@b@@QAGXM@Z`

Format of a C Decorated Name

The form of decoration for a C function depends on the calling convention used in its declaration:

Calling Convention	Decoration
__cdecl (the default)	Leading underscore (_)
__stdcall	Leading underscore (_) and a trailing at sign (@) followed by a number representing the number of bytes in the parameter list
__fastcall	Same as __stdcall, but prepended by an at sign instead of an underscore

Viewing Decorated Names

You can get the decorated form of a function name after you compile the source file that contains the function definition or prototype. To examine decorated names in your program, you can do one of the following:

- Use a listing.
- Use the DUMPBIN tool.

Using a Listing to View Decorated Names

To get the decorated form of a function using a compiler listing, do the following:

1. Generate a listing by compiling the source file that contains the function definition or prototype with the Listing File Type (/FA[[c|s]]) compiler option set to one of the following: Assembly with Machine Code; Assembly with Source Code; Assembly, Machine Code, and Source.

2. Find the undecorated function definition in the resulting listing.

3. Examine the previous line. The label for the PROC NEAR command is the decorated form of the function name.

Using DUMPBIN to View Decorated Names

To get the decorated form of a function using DUMPBIN, run DUMPBIN on the .OBJ or .LIB file using the /SYMBOLS option. Find the undecorated function definition in the output. The undecorated name is followed by the decorated name, each enclosed in parentheses.

Index

O

P

Z